MEANINGS IN THE MOUNTAINS

by Dr. Jeff Strickler

sweetgrassbooks
an imprint of Farcountry Press

ISBN 978-1-59152-307-9

Design by Steph Lehmann

For more information or to order extra copies of this book call Farcountry Press toll free at (800) 821-3874 or visit www.farcountrypress.com

Cover photos courtesy of Rick Graetz.
Front cover photo: South Face of Granite Peak.
Back top cover photo: Morning comes to the Crazies.
Back bottom cover photo: Lonesome Peak.

Produced by Sweetgrass Books
PO Box 5630, Helena, MT, 59604; (800) 821-3874; www.sweetgrassbooks.com

 Produced and printed in the United States of America

26 25 24 23 22   1 2 3 4 5

TABLE OF CONTENTS

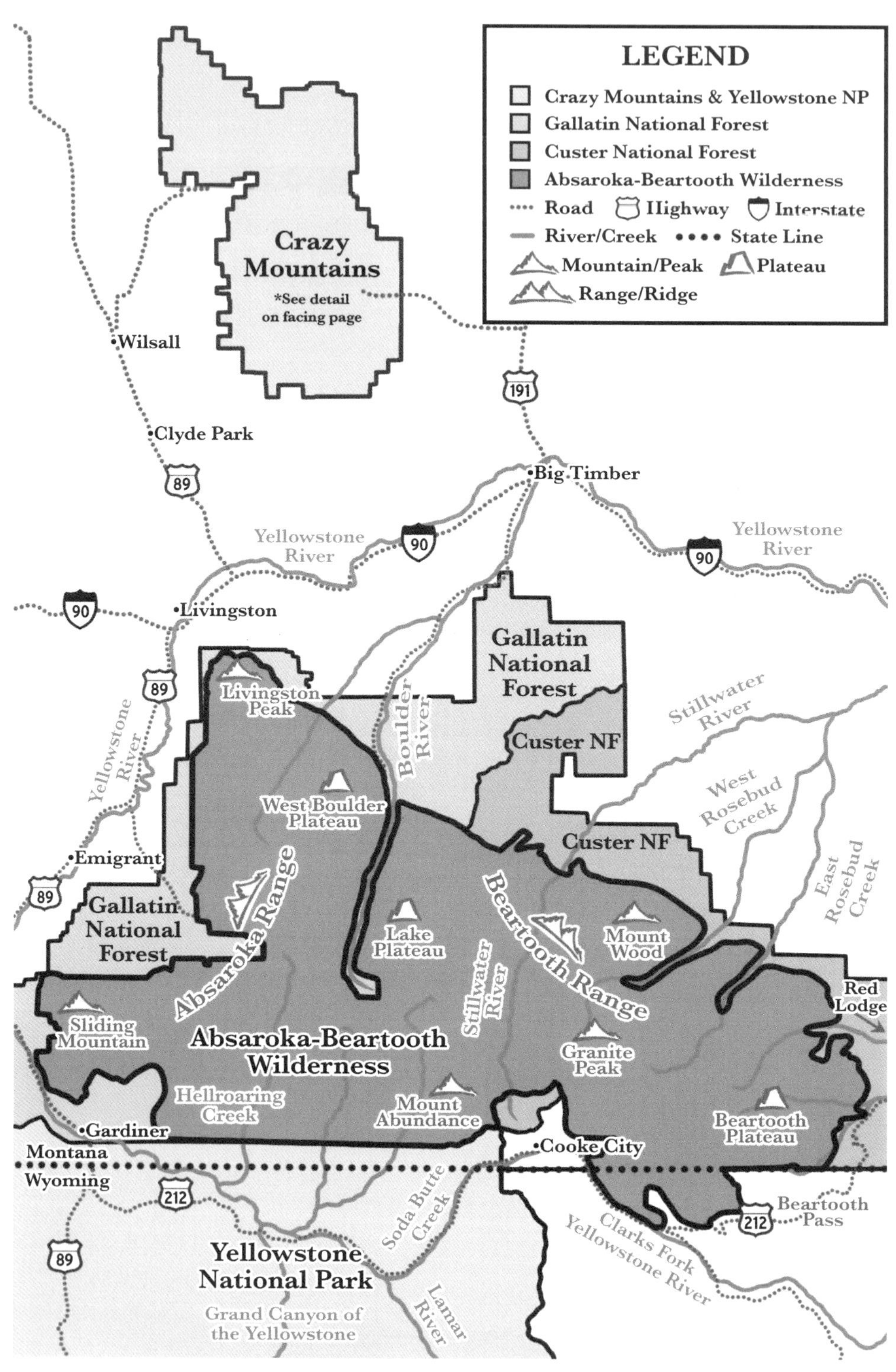

ABSAROKA-BEARTOOTH WILDERNESS

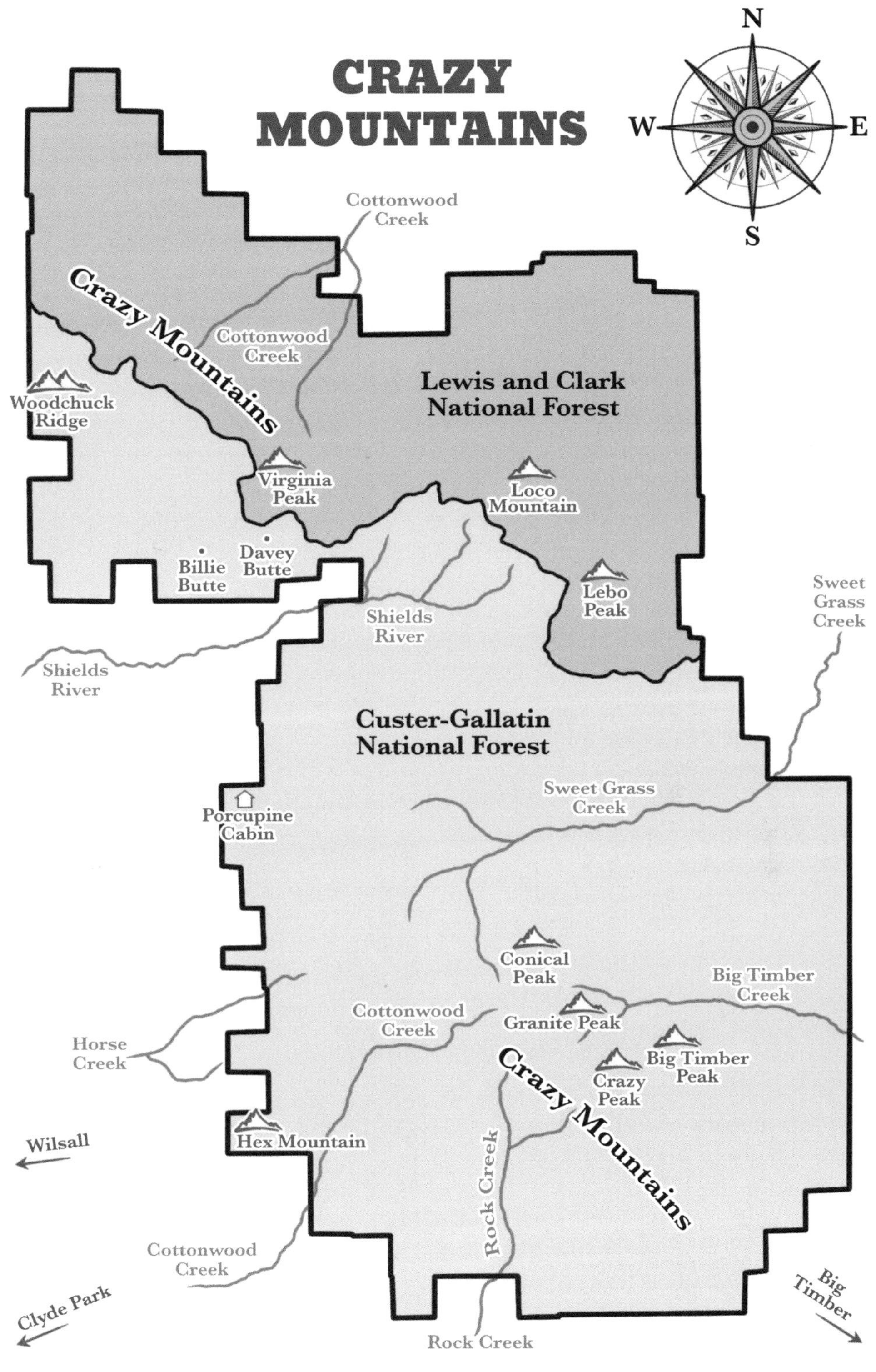
CRAZY MOUNTAINS
N
W
E
S
Cottonwood Creek
Crazy Mountains
Cottonwood Creek
Lewis and Clark National Forest
Woodchuck Ridge
Virginia Peak
Loco Mountain
Billie Butte
Davey Butte
Lebo Peak
Sweet Grass Creek
Shields River
Shields River
Custer-Gallatin National Forest
Porcupine Cabin
Sweet Grass Creek
Conical Peak
Big Timber Creek
Cottonwood Creek
Granite Peak
Big Timber Peak
Horse Creek
Crazy Peak
Crazy Mountains
Wilsall
Hex Mountain
Rock Creek
Cottonwood Creek
Clyde Park
Big Timber
Rock Creek

INTRODUCTION

Names, the ultimate nouns, swirl about us. In *Meanings in the Mountains* they crowd the USGS topos and the hiking maps of the Absaroka, Beartooth, and Crazy Mountains. With a brief glance you may think that they are simple place markers that tell you where you are, what mountain looms ahead, or what lake or stream you've been fishing. But behind the names on our maps, one can also delve deeply into the history and the ecology of the land.

Here one finds examples of the fish and fowl, the trees and plants, the animals and even the bugs that inhabit these forests and mountains. We have Arnold Hague, an early leader of the U.S. survey crews, to thank for the names that started the promotion of the natural history of this country. In 1887, he directed "that the necessary new names to designate the unnamed mountains, valleys, and streams should mainly be selected from the beasts, birds, fishes, trees, flowers, and minerals found within the park or adjacent country." Forest Service and fisheries personnel have continued this plan, and we now have an almost complete description of the ecosystem as described in the names on our mountains, lakes, and streams.

Even more fascinating are the stories behind the names of many of the people that preceded us. The European culture in America has a penchant for putting names on everything, so we find that D. Boone killed a bear by that tree, and W. Clark's name can still be seen scratched into the rock on Pompey's Pillar. As a result of this habit, our maps have become filled with the names of people, some famous and some not. There are trappers and miners, explorers and surveyors, ranchers and homesteaders, and some of the local characters that haunted this land. You will find some truth in the 2004 comment in the *Bozeman Chronicle* where its editorial board said that "naming landmarks has served as a kind of Oscars ceremony for historic

Adam "Horn" Miller flanked by John Curl and "Uncle" Joe Brown. ELIZABETH RENNER STUDIO, YELLOWSTONE GATEWAY MUSEUM, 2006.044.0833.

figures." Lewis and Clark were the first to do this, and they populated the Missouri and Yellowstone Rivers and their tributaries with their own names as well as those of contemporary public figures, expedition members, and even girlfriends back home. Other explorers were also not shy. The survey expeditions of Ferdinand V. Hayden in the Greater Yellowstone from 1871 to 1878, Arnold Hague, who continued that work for several years from 1883, and James P. Kimball's expedition of 1898 created many of the names familiar to us all. Honoring famous people makes sense: people such as President Theodore Roosevelt for his leadership in the conservation effort; Ernest Hemingway, who did much of his best writing during his summers on the Clarks Fork; or Senator Lee Metcalf of Montana for his work in getting the Wilderness Act of 1964 through Congress. However, the maps are also cluttered with the names of early pioneers, local characters, or someone's wife or sweetheart, so you find Joe and Molly Stands in Stands Basin and Tom Hawley's cabin on Hawley Creek, "Skookum Joe" Anderson and "Happy Jack" Aldrich have their gulches, and Daisy Dean her creek. This is not to mention the murder and mayhem that involved such miscreants as Kid Royal, Barney Hanlon, Jim Smith, and Bud Hart, whose stories are also etched on the maps. There are unfortunately few references to the Native Americans who first inhabited these lands, but there are Arapooash and Little Face Lakes, and a few Indian stories and artifacts appear here and there.

Certainly, there are also poetic or just commonplace names. When the national forests were started in the early part of the twentieth century, the rangers of the Forest Service added many names that were needed to locate specific features in their territory. With the 1920s came the development of tourism and the dude ranches like Dick Randall's OTO, John Branger's TO Bar, Al Croonquist's Camp Senia, and Larry Nordquist's L bar T. Those ranchers put names on the local features so that they could tell their guests where they were going and what they were seeing. Fishing also flourished at that time, so many names were added that related to the sport as well as the names of the people who packed the fingerlings into the backcountry. In the 1960s the fisheries departments from Montana and Wyoming began organized stocking of the lakes in the Absaroka-Beartooths. They surveyed and studied all 942 of them and had to add a large number of names to identify the lakes where they were working. Some of these are descriptive, like Marsh and Storm; some scientific, think Varve and Aufwuchs; some are just humorous, like Mutt and Jeff Lakes and the dental Molar, Incisor, and Cavity Lakes. But who was the demented biologist wandering around the wilderness who named Planaria, Copepod, and Cladocera Lakes? Was he, as suspected, a fisheries biologist, or just a graduate student trying to impress the professor? Did Spider and Fly Lakes get named for an invasion of the camp by bugs, or was this an allusion to the 1828 poem "The Spider to the Fly?" How about the ancient references to Favonius and the Cimmerians? Who were they? Read and find out.

The first book in this series on the Custer-Gallatin National Forest was called *Bozeman's Backyard*, and came out in 2019. It dealt with the Bridger, Gallatin, and Madison Ranges. This book continues that search by investigating the sources of the names within the Absaroka, Beartooth, and Crazy Mountains; places that constitute Billings' backyard. These names are all those that are official and certified by the United States Board on Geographic Names in their Geographic Names Information Service website (GNIS)—the names that you will find on the United States Geological Survey (USGS) topo maps. However, officially uncertified names are also included as they are found on many commercial maps and publications and are used by both the U.S. Forest Service (USFS) and Montana Fish, Wildlife and Parks.

It was also important to set geographic limits. Unless one has borders, one could chase names all the way to Ekalaka. In general, the Custer-Gallatin National Forest maps as published in 2012 set the limits. However, in order to include all of the Absaroka-Beartooth Wilderness and the northern part of the Crazy Mountains, those contiguous parts of the Shoshone National Forest and the Lewis and Clark National Forest have been included. I have also taken the liberty to add the curious and interesting features that lie just south of the Absaroka Beartooths and north of the Yellowstone and Lamar Rivers in the park. Since the northern border of Yellowstone National Park is just an arbitrary administrative line through the southern Absaroka massif I decided, for interest's sake, that one doesn't always have to color within the lines.

It has been an amusing and interesting experience digging up all the sources of these names. With the whimsical names, one must wonder whether the content of the flask in the backpack had some influence? There has to be a story behind Tomato Can Creek, but what was it? Did someone actually see a Yeti near Big Foot Lake? Certainly, the hiker responsible for the humorous names would have been a better companion than the one who named Dreary, Trouble, Vengence, Nightmare, Desolation, and the other lakes of grim emotion.

Finally, wherever possible, archival photographs from our museums have been used to try to put a person, flower, or critter's face on the names in our mountains. The end result is a kaleidoscopic collection that reveals much of the human and natural history of this land that will hopefully amuse and enlighten you. Whether you use the book as an accompaniment to your hiking book, as a companion to your topo maps searches, or just open it for your interest or amusement, have a wander through the names in *Meanings in the Mountains*. Use it to gain some history, learn some ecology, get the answers to the mystery questions, and, I hope, find a bit of pleasure.

Enjoy!

Dr. Jeff Strickler
January 2022

ABSAROKA-BEARTOOTHS

What amazing country! The highest mountain range in Montana has 166 summits over 10,000 feet, the most of any range in the state, and it contains the only ones over 12,000 feet—29 in all. A land of stark and rocky plateaus, its eastern side is formed by some of the oldest rocks on the planet: Precambrian granites, gneisses, and schists that are 3.3 to 3.9 billion years old. The sedimentary caps remain on the western section, and these limestones of 340 million years ago are filled with fossils from that time. Although the more western Absarokas are

The Bear's Tooth. PHOTO BY WILLIAM KELLER, NATIONAL PARK SERVICE.

not as vertical nor as high as the granitic Beartooths, they still retain many high, beautiful peaks and have been, and still are, a source of great mining riches.

Rugged, hostile, beautiful, pristine—the Absaroka-Beartooth area has been called many things, not just with adjectives, but with names as well. It is these that this chapter will explore.

This whole collection of mountains was originally called the "Snowy Range" or "Snowy Mountains" by Ferdinand Hayden in his report of his visit during his survey of 1871. That name was probably adopted from the miners of Cooke City, who were impressed by the deep snow and slides they found. It also fits with William Clark, who was the first Anglo-European to describe them in the summer of 1806 as "rocky rugid [*sic*] and on them are great quantities of snow." That Snowy Mountain name still persists in the Snowy Mountain Ranch that currently sits on the East Fork of Mill Creek, but the name of the mountains themselves has morphed many times. In 1872 Hayden changed the name in his writings to the "Yellowstone Range," after the plateau and future park to the south, and this name continued to be used until 1885. There were other names that were used as well. Capt. W.A. Jones crossed the mountains in 1873 and insisted that they be called the Sierra Shoshone Mountains. However, he must not have been of a high enough rank or fame to have his suggestion adopted, and, except for a few monographs, this name was forgotten. In 1885 Arnold Hague, surveying for the USGS, gave the name Absaroka to all of the mountains in the range, from the Paradise Valley of the Yellowstone to the Bighorns. This was apparently on the instructions from his superior, Grand Canyon explorer John Wesley Powell, then the director of the USGS. Absaroka means "Children of the Large Beaked Bird" in the Hidatsa language, and refers to the Crow Indians, so the name was placed to honor this tribe. Ironically, even at the time that the name Absaroka was applied, the western section, those mountains east of the Boulder River, what we now call the Absarokas in Montana, had already been ceded away from the reservation. Today, after successive treaties, the reservation border has shrunk even further to its current location east of the mountains around Crow Agency and the Bighorn River. None of the Absaroka-Beartooth area remains Crow land.

As mentioned, the entire massif was initially the Absarokas, but in 1908 when the Absaroka and Beartooth National Forests were carved from the Yellowstone National Forest Reserves, the northeast section of high mountains and plateaus became officially referred to as "the Beartooths." This separated the Montana Absarokas from the Absarokas in Wyoming, which run from the Beartooths south to the Wind Rivers and form the eastern border of Yellowstone Park. Of course, the Wyoming Absarokas contain the North Absaroka Wilderness, which is south of the Montana Absarokas, to which they are no longer connected. Since few of the mountains in Wyoming are a focus of this book, I will let you ponder this by yourselves.

The northeast section of this huge range of mountains is called the Beartooths, a name that comes from a sharp spire on Beartooth Mountain that the Crow called *Daxpitcheeihte*, translated as "Bear's Tooth." (see image on page 1) The word Beartooths was first noted in negotiations with the Crow in the 1850s and was first documented on a map in 1891. Not to be too straightforward, but the use of the word Beartooths has since led to some naming gymnastics and a bit of a confusing jumble. The resident miners of Cooke City called the range to the northeast the "Granite Mountains," which was used on some maps until 1943 when the USGS ruled that the name should properly be the Beartooths. Official government rules notwithstanding, the descendants of those original settlers and many people living near Cooke City still refer to the mountains as The Granites. Adding to the confusion, the people from Billings to Red Lodge insisted on keeping the name of Beartooths for the high granitic plateaus and peaks, but there was no definitive separation between this area and the Absarokas to the west. Voluminous USGS notes from the early decades of the twentieth century express differing opinions as to how to define Beartooth and Absaroka. The separation was variously identified as the Stillwater River, the Boulder River, or the Stillwater-Boulder Divide. Of course, neither of these tributaries of the Yellowstone River approach Yellowstone Park or the Clarks Fork River, so the southern border is fuzzy with no definitive divide. Then in 1932, the Beartooth National Forest was absorbed into the Custer National Forest, further removing official boundaries. Naturally, there is the problem of the Beartooth Plateau itself. It contains Beartooth Mountain and the Bear's Tooth, giving name to the whole area, but is, itself, only one plateau of the many that make up the "Beartooths." And did I mention that Beartooth Butte, Creek, and Lake are to the south in Wyoming and separated from the Beartooth Plateau?

Does this make everything entirely clear? I thought not. The federal government, which is often criticized for many of its decisions, in this case, solved the confusing dispute with a simple hyphen. On March 27, 1978, President Jimmy Carter signed the Absaroka-Beartooth Wilderness bill and the two names became officially one. So now you can call it what you will. It is massive, high, beautiful, and the focus of this chapter.

But the names go beyond the mountain range itself, so you will also find in this chapter the names that celebrate American pioneers or their activities. The history of these people has become a part of our maps, and as you read the various entries, you will learn about the miners, ranchers, homesteaders, and just plain characters that put their names on this land. Then there are all of the references to the birds, animals, trees, and flowers that inhabit this beautiful part of nature. These snippets, taken together, should give you bit of enjoyment and a feeling for the ecology of the Absaroka-Beartooths. Absorb the bits and pieces, because, put together, you will get a better understanding of this beautiful land.

Abandoned Lake

This lake is located on Lonesome Mountain, just north of the Beartooth Highway, and is one of the mournful names found in this high, remote country. It is just upstream from Lonesome Lake with no trail to it, so it appears "abandoned."

Abiathar Peak

Distinctive Abiathar Peak is just south of the Northeast Entrance of Yellowstone Park and the Beartooth Highway. Although actually in the Park and a bit south of our national forest boundaries, the historical prominence of the man prompted its inclusion.

The mountain was named by the U.S. Geological Survey under Arnold Hague in 1885 for Charles Abiathar White (1826–1910), who worked for the USGS until 1892. After 1895 he was an associate in paleontology at the National Museum in Washington, D.C., and a member of the National Academy of Sciences. He collected fossils from areas around Yellowstone Park and wrote numerous scientific reports on the western United States.

Charles Abiathar White, ca. 1848.

Lake Abundance/Creek

The Lake Abundance and Daisy Pass Road from Cooke City leads to this lake, which is found just inside the boundary of the Absaroka-Beartooth Wilderness. The road formerly went all the way to the lake, but with the establishment of the wilderness, it stops a bit short, with the last little mile an easy hiking trail.

In the early twentieth century, Ranger L.P. McKnight said that it was named for the abundance of fish found in the lake. Since it is one of the few lakes in the Beartooths that contain an indigenous population of trout, this descriptive name was felt to be in order.

It is also the site of one of the area's many Wild West stories. Bud Hart, a local miner and stonemason, had a gold mine above the lake, and in 1931 he shot and killed Walter McCall and Clarence Leitner. Apparently these two broke into his cabin at Willow Park, and the jury in Butte took only an hour to find Hart innocent because of "self defense and claim jumping." (see Willow Park)

Mount Abundance

Mount Abundance sits on the Absaroka-Beartooth Wilderness boundary just south of the lake that gave it its name. (see Lake Abundance/Creek) On its east slope are the headwaters of the Stillwater River.

An older and now extinct name for this mountain was Mount Pease, named for Maj. Fellows D. Pease (1835–1920). He came west in 1861 after his three brothers were killed in the Civil War, and, originally a fur trader, built Fort Pease at the mouth of the Bighorn River. This was burned to the ground by the Sioux during the Plains Wars and that ended that venture. In 1869 he became an Indian agent under Gen. Sully in Blackfeet country and then in 1870 succeeded E.M. Camp as agent at the First Crow Agency at Fort Parker near modern-day Livingston, Montana, where he served until 1873. He married Magretta Wallace of the Crow Tribe and is buried in the Rosebud Cemetery at Absarokee, site of the Second Crow Agency.

Fellows D. Pease. JIM ANNIN COLLECTION, MUSEUM OF THE BEARTOOTHS.

Aero Lake/Upper & Lower

Upper Aero Lake is the largest lake in the Clarks Fork drainage, with Lower Areo second. In the entire Absaroka-Beartooths, only Mystic Lake is bigger, and that was enlarged with a dam. Upper Aero Lake is also among the deeper lakes and drops to a 100-foot depth within five feet of the shoreline.

Aero is a Greek prefix relating to flight or air. At 10,000 feet and above tree line, these lakes definitely give you the impression that you are up high.

Agate Springs

Agates are ornamental stones that are formed from chalcedony, a microcrystalline form of quartz, and typically appear banded. They have been found in this spring that is located on the East Fork of Mill Creek, on the trail up from the Snowy Range Ranch, which is at the end of the road out of Pray.

Albino Lake

The exact source of the name of this lake near Lonesome Mountain on the Wyoming border is not recorded. It is thought that it is probably for the albino trout that may have once been planted here. They have since died out and the lake is now regularly stocked with cutthroats. Since there are plenty of Trout and Rainbow Lakes, the Albino name remains

Albino trout, *Oncorhynchus mykiss* Walbaum, is not a true albino, but rather a lighter variant of the rainbow trout. It is regularly stocked in Utah and has been raised in the Jocko Fish Hatchery in Arlee, Montana. Because its bright yellow color stands out, it is easily seen by predators so does not survive well in the wild.

Alp Lake

Alp is an old Indo-European word that in Celtic meant "mountain," and in Europe it currently refers to a high mountain pasture used for grazing. The European mountain range is the Alps (plural), where there are many of these pastures—think Switzerland, cows, and giant cowbells. Because the Alps are so vertical and rocky, the word *alp* has begun to swing back to reference high mountains, especially in snowcapped country.

The lake is well above tree line at 9,642 feet in the Sierra Creek drainage of the Beartooth Plateau. The name is clearly a reference to its alpine location.

Alp Rock

This rocky point is due north of Cooke City near the wilderness boundary. It must have reminded someone of a prominence in the Swiss Alps.

Alpine Lake/Alpine (Community)

Alpine is the name of the little community on East Rosebud Lake.

Settlement began in 1894 when Maj. Henry Armstrong got permission from the federal government to purchase 105 acres on what had been reservation land. A former U.S. Army officer, he was the agent to the Crow Tribe from 1882 to 1885, and the lake was originally called Armstrong Lake after him. He had a small ranch but sold his holdings in 1905 after a big fire. In 1908 a road was blazed, and in 1911 the Billings developers formed the East Rosebud Lake Association to maintain a pleasure resort for the vacation homeowners. John and Rosina Branger built their homestead nearby in 1913 and operated the TO Bar dude ranch until 1932. A native of Switzerland, John named the hamlet Alpine because it reminded him of his home.

Alpine had its own post office from 1915 to 1953, and from 1913 to 1921 a normal school for girls operated during the summer where the girls lived in tents and studied to qualify for a Montana teaching certificate. Alpine is now a quiet little collection of summer homes and cabins.

Alpine Lake is quite separate and sits on a little bench near the head of Three Creeks in the West Boulder River drainage on the Mount Cowen quad. It is a descriptive name for the location of this widening of the creek.

Amphitheater Lake

(see Wand Lake)

Anchor Lake

This lake was named in the early part of the twentieth century because its outline is in the shape of an anchor. It sits on the south slope of Snowbank Mountain in the high Beartooths.

Anderson Ridge/Creek

There are two Anderson Ridges.

One **Anderson Ridge** overlooks the Slough Creek country to its east and was named for "Hellroaring" Jim Anderson who managed the Silver Tip Ranch. The trail up to the ridge starts at the ranch on Slough Creek and has beautiful views of the area just north of Yellowstone National Park. (see Silver Tip Ranch)

The other **Anderson Ridge** is named for nearby **Anderson Creek** and is the rise that is found between The Pyramid and Knowles Peak, which separates the East Fork and the main branch of Mill Creek. The USFS Anderson Ridge Trail #54 starts off the East Fork of Mill Creek Trail near Agate Springs and follows the ridge up 1,000 feet and 11 miles to Jomaha Creek and a trailhead on the Mill Creek road.

Anderson Creek flows down the valley southeast of Anderson Ridge and joins Mill Creek two miles east of Snowbank Campground on the road from Pray.

Although local residents and miners have no recollection of this Anderson, he was probably the J.R. Anderson who filed a claim on the Snow Slide Copper Lode in 1885. Gool Counts (see Counts Creek) had an active copper mine here for many years. His tunnels into the sidehill can still be found.

Anderson Springs

John Anderson was one of the early characters of the Boulder River country. Originally from Canada, he proved up on a desert claim where Big Timber is now located and platted the town. Later, in 1892, he became superintendent of the Independence Mine near the head of the Main Boulder River where he is said to have found a 16-inch vein of gold.

In 1894, he filed a homestead claim at this spring on the East Boulder River, located on the northern edge of the forest some 35 miles by road south of Big Timber. He started with a lime kiln, but, taking advantage of the mineral spring, he built a hotel, bathhouse, and pool and called it Anderson Lithia Spring. Lithia, an older name for lithium oxide, is a form of soda, and the drinking of and soaking in the spring water gained a reputation for curing arthritis and other complaints. Cabins and tents were added later, and it became a popular place in the summer months.

Anderson died in 1915, and ownership changed several times after that as use dwindled.

Anvil Lake

There are two Anvil Lakes in the Beartooths. One is on the Cooke City quad, and the other on the Castle Mountain map just north of the Montana/Wyoming border. Both were named for their shape. One might think that there should be a Hammer Lake nearby, but there isn't.

Aquarius Lake

You might think that this lake was named by some New Age hippie for the Age of Aquarius. This is our current astrological "age," and was supposed to have arrived in the twentieth century when the vernal equinox moved into the constellation of the water carrier. You would be as wrong as the astrologers who predict this to be a time of mental enlightenment.

It might bug you, but the source is a bit more prosaic. This lake in the Sedge Creek drainage on the Fossil Lake quad was named for insects of the genus *Aquarius*, a group of large North American water striders.

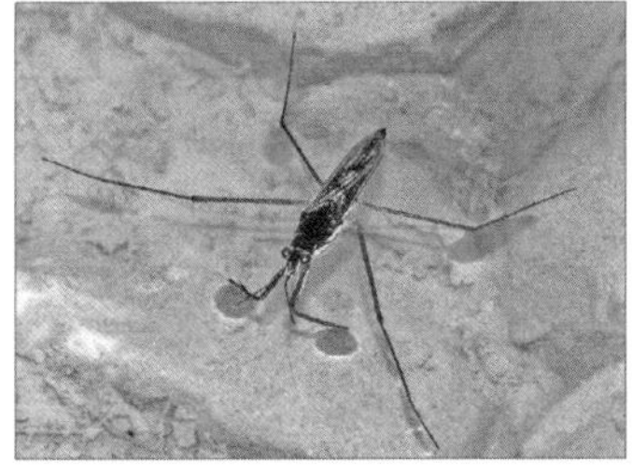

Aquarius najas. WIKI CREATIVE COMMONS.

Arapooash Lake

The lake, located above Mystic Lake in the West Rosebud drainage, is among several little lakes that were unnamed until the later twentieth century when outdoorsmen from Stillwater County used them to honor certain locals. Earl Nott (see Knott Lake) called it JerBob Lake for Bob and Jerry Svee of Columbus, but that name never made the official maps. Pat Marcuson of Montana Fish, Wildlife and Parks changed it to Arapoosh to recognize the Crow leader and as a better fit with the other Indian-named lakes in the areas. (see Little Face, Weeluna, and Nemidgi Lakes)

Arapooash (also spelled Arapooish or Arapoosh) is *Eelapuash* in modern Crow and can be translated as "Sore Belly." He was a famous River Crow war chief who lived from about 1795 to 1834 and was known as a fierce warrior who received his shield after a vision quest. It was said to have the powers of prophecy, gave him spiritual protection, and aided him during battle.

In 1834 the River Crow besieged Fort McKenzie on the Missouri, but they were repelled by the Blackfeet. During this encounter, Arapooash saw that his shield predicted his death and, indeed, he was killed by the Blackfeet.

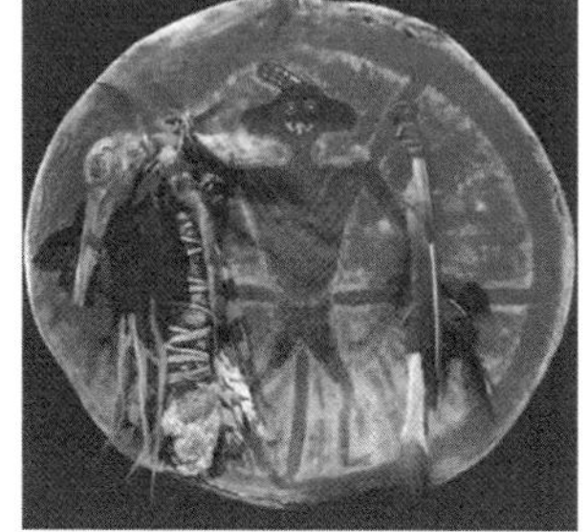

Arapoosh's shield. SMITHSONIAN MUSEUM OF THE AMERICAN INDIAN.

The shield was used long after his death and into the reservation period and was eventually purchased by a Chicago museum. It is now in the National Museum of the American Indian in Washington, D.C.

Arapooash is quoted in Mark Brown's *The Plainsmen of the Yellowstone* as saying, "The Crow country is exactly in the right place. It has snowy mountains and sunny plains, all kinds of climates, and good things for every season. When the summer heat scorches the prairies, you can draw up under the mountains, where the air is sweet and cool, the grass fresh, and the bright streams come tumbling out of the snowbanks. There you can hunt the elk, the deer, and the antelope, when their skins are fit for dressing; there you will find plenty of white bears and mountain sheep. In the autumn when your horses are fat and strong from mountain pastures, you can go down to the plains to hunt the buffalo or trap beavers on the stream." Is this still not a wonderful description of the Absaroka-Beartooths?

Arch Rock/Creek, Little Arch Lake, Lower Arch Lake, Arch Lake

The more famous **Arch Rock** is on **Arch Creek**, a tributary of the East Rosebud Creek on the Alpine USGS quad. This 15-foot-high rock arch was first found in 1914 by John Branger of the TO Bar dude ranch at Alpine when he and a party hiked up the creek and discovered it in the canyon above the creek. It is now best approached via the Derby Mountain Trail that starts at the West Bridger rental cabin, then passes around the east side of Derby Mountain to end at the arch. The three **Arch Lakes** are the creek's headwaters and are situated in a basin below Phantom Glacier.

There is a second **Arch Rock,** without an Arch Creek, on the Sliderock Mountain quad. It is on a ridge of Hicks Mountain at the head of Blind Bridger Creek.

Arctic Lake

This small lake near Lonesome Lake and the Wyoming line appears in a 1970 fishing guide. It is now officially unnamed but probably corresponds to Gus Lake. With the temperatures at its nearly 10,000-foot location, it deserves the name. (see Gus Lake)

Lake Aries

Aries is a constellation of the zodiac, and it is the Latin word for a ram. It came to represent the ram whose fleece became the Golden Fleece of Greek mythology, but this particular constellation has been known as a ram since Babylonian times. Lake Aries is located in the Sourdough Basin north of Cooke City near the headwaters of the Stillwater River. It is near Sheep Mountain, Sheep Creek, and Ovis Lake. Any attempt at punning this would leave the author feeling a bit sheepish.

Armour Pond

The pond, actually a glacial pot hole along the Boulder River, was named in 1999 for Keith L. Armour (1958–1981). Keith was a Forest Service employee who worked on projects involving forest regeneration along the Boulder River watershed. On September 15, 1981, after a day of collecting Douglas-fir cones for the regeneration project, he and another Forest Service employee, Chuck Barone, were involved in a head-on collision with a semi-trailer truck east of Big Timber. Chuck survived with minor injuries, but Keith died shortly after the accident. The pond, a Watchable Wildlife site, was named in his honor.

The variant names of Moose Pond and Beaver Pond are no longer active.

Armstrong Creek

This creek flows into East Rosebud Lake near the hamlet of Alpine. The creek's name comes from the lake, which was once called Armstrong Lake for Maj. Henry Armstrong. He had been the Indian agent for the Crow Tribe at the Second Crow Agency near Absarokee, Montana, from 1882 to 1885, and obtained a patent for the land and built a cabin by the lake in 1895. (see Alpine)

Arrastra Creek/Lake

Arrastra is a Spanish word for a primitive drag mill that was used for crushing ore. The flat-bottomed drag stones were pulled by an animal around a circular pit paved with other flat stones, which pulverized the ore.

Floyd Counts located a mining claim near this creek and lake up Mill Creek near Emigrant. (see Counts Creek) An old burro-worked gold quartz mill, an arrastra, was reported to have been used here.

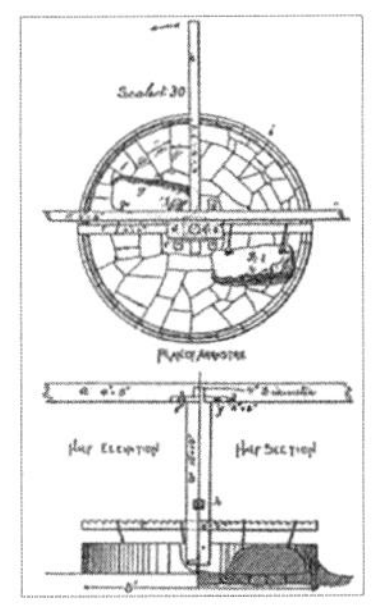

Arrastra, Mining and Scientific Press, 1886.

Arrow Peak

This was Crow Indian country when the first "emigrants" arrived in the Paradise Valley in search of gold. The 9,000-foot peak is near the mines along Mill Creek but is neither sharp nor arrow shaped, so one must assume that arrows and other Indian artifacts were found on it.

Arrowhead Lake

The shape of this lake is pointed like an arrowhead, and thus the name. It is located just north of the Montana/Wyoming line and just northwest of Lonesome Mountain in the Sierra Creek drainage.

Ash Mountain

Located in the USGS quad of the same name, this mountain near Jardine, Montana, has the color and appearance of ash. It is a well-known landmark and the name, long in local use, was recorded by Ranger L.P. McKnight in the early part of the twentieth century.

A prior name of Sunset Peak was established in 1893 and used intermittently. It was formally changed to Ash Mountain by a Board on Geographic Names decision in 1957.

Asp Gulch

The name of this gulch, found a bit south of Big Timber, refers to the aspen tree, *Populus tremuloides*, not the poisonous snake that was fatal to Cleopatra. A clipping from the Bozeman *Avant Courier* of 1891 tells of the editor, E.C. Alderson, finding the skull and head of a mountain sheep embedded in "a Quaking Asp" tree. Another newspaper report of a death in Yellowstone in 1892 reported that the body was found in "a small clump of quaking asp willows." Clearly *asp* is a proper, but archaic, term for the aspen tree.

Aspen USFS Campground

The campground is close to Big Beaver Campground on the Main Boulder River just north of Chippy Park. It gets its name from the many aspen groves that are found above it on the slope of Chrome Mountain.

The aspen tree, *Populus tremuloides*, is also called the quaking aspen. The fluttering of the leaves is due to a flattened, flexible leaf petiole, and the action is responsible for the freely translated Indian name for this tree—"woman's tongue."

Along with its close cousin, the cottonwood, aspen is the most common deciduous tree in our forests. Whereas the cottonwood prefers wet riverbanks, aspen groves are found on the drier and higher slopes. These groves are actually clones of the same plant that have sprung from the parent's roots. This cloning explains why all the trees in an aspen grove will leaf out at the same time in the spring and turn their golden yellow together in the fall.

Asteroid Lake

The clear skies in the high country enhance the wonder of the stars, so there are several lakes in the Beartooths that have an astronomical reference. This lake, named in the latter part of the twentieth century, is near Comet Lake in the Flood Creek chain.

Astral Lake

"Astral" means connected with or resembling the stars. It comes from the Latin word *astrum* meaning "star."

This pretty lake is located north of Cooke City on that quad and is drained by Star Creek with Star Lake nearby—clearly a heavenly location.

Aufwuchs Lake

Aufwuchs is a German noun that means "surface growth" or "overgrowth." It has been adopted by biologists to refer to complex communities of algae, small plants, and animals such as crustaceans, insect larvae, rotifers, and protozoans that form an interconnected mat attached to open surfaces on the lake bottom. Such a mat can be found in this lake.

Avalanche Lake/Mountain

The **lake** sits below Granite Peak in the Huckleberry Creek drainage where a small glacier regularly avalanches down into it.

Avalanche Mountain is an unofficial name given by climbers to a 12,010-foot point above Jasper Lake and to the east of Spirit Mountain. Its name comes from evidence of a huge avalanche on one side of the mountain.

B-47 Ridge

In 1962 an Air Force B-47 bomber on a training mission from Texas crashed into the Absaroka Mountains, and debris from the plane is still to be found on this ridge on Emigrant Peak. The crew of Capt. Bill Faulconer, Lt. Fred Hixenbaugh, Lt. David Sutton, and Lt. Lloyd Sawyers were all killed in the crash.

B-47E in flight. UNITED STATES AIR FORCE.

In 2016 a commemorative plaque was placed in the Chico cemetery, and in 2018, a bill to name the site B-47 Ridge was introduced by the Montana delegation and passed by Congress. Just prior to the publication of this book, Governor Gianforte led relatives of the fallen airmen and Montana leaders on a commemorative hike to the crash site where they placed a granite plaque.

Baboon Mountain

John Allen and Barney Hughes were the first to discover gold on this mountain back in 1864. Because it was on the Crow Reservation at that time, actual mining had to be postponed until the reservation boundary was moved in 1882. Located just north of the ghost town of Independence, it was part of what was called the Boulder Mining District. (see Independence)

The name comes from one of the mines that was located on its slopes.

Bad Canyon/Creek

The name of this creek and canyon comes from the abundance of locoweed that is poisonous to livestock. Because of this, local stockmen avoided this as range land and kept their stock out of it in the summer. (see Loco Mountain in the Crazy Mountains section)

It is just east of the Meyers Creek Ranger Station and a bit north of Nye.

Baker Mountain/Draw

George Baker. CRAZY MOUNTAIN MUSEUM.

Baker Mountain is just east of Natural Bridge State Park at the end of the paving on the Boulder River Road. The draw is on the mountain and both were named for George W. Baker, one of the pioneer settlers and ranchers in the Boulder River valley.

George was born in Essex County, Vermont, in 1840, and at age 19 he caught "gold fever" and headed to California. He was in Nevada in 1866 and came to Sweet Grass County in 1881 where he prospected a bit and had a farm of 450 irrigated acres that he used for alfalfa hay for his cattle and Norman horses. He married Emma Cowles in 1876, and his children continued ranching on the Boulder into the early part of the twentieth century.

The Lionhead formation that is described on the interpretive signs at Natural Bridges State Park is exposed limestone on Baker Mountain. The figure of the lion's head is more apparent when seen from the south as you drive north on the Main Boulder Road.

Bald Knob

There are two Bald Knobs in the Absaroka-Beartooths.

One is on the USGS topo map of that name. It is open alpine country with talus slopes along the north side that give it a barren ridge that is above tree line. As one of the locals noted, "Nothing could grow there and the wind never stops." The other Bald Knob is immediately south of Fossil Lake on the quad of that lake's name. Packing guides like Dennis Dodge liked to leave the horses between Ouzel and Skull Lakes at the base of this knob before hiking into Fossil Lake. It is bald as it is over 10,000 feet and well above tree line.

Bald Mountain

Bald Mountain is a long, barren ridge that is located north of the Yellowstone Park boundary, two miles south of Jardine, Montana, and Mineral Hill. Many of the "bald" features in the Custer-Gallatin National Forest became so as a result of forest fires. Others are above tree line. This one is bald because the rock base is not conducive to tree growth.

Baldy Peak/East and West Baldy Basin

Baldy is a variant name for Chico Peak, which rises east of the Chico Hot Springs Resort. It was named Baldy by the miners in the gold rush era of the late 1800s because of its distinctive bald summit that was a result of logging for timber for the town and mines. The trees on the summit have regrown and it is no longer "bald."

For unknown reasons, maps began to appear with this mountain called Chico Peak, and that became the commonly used name. There was a move to call a smaller peak to the south Chico Peak and rename this Baldy. However, in 1990, the Board on Geographic Names ruled that this would be too confusing, so the small peak remains unnamed and this peak is officially Chico Peak with Baldy an antiquated variant name.

Baldy is also a variant name for Livingston Peak, which rises south of the Yellowstone River and overlooks that town. It was called Baldy in the early days because a huge forest fire denuded the top. However, seen from I-90 today, the top is quite fuzzy with trees as they regrew some time ago. The Baldy name persists with the **two basins** on Livingston Peak's east and west slopes. (see Livingston Peak)

Balm of Gilead Creek

Balm of Gilead is an ancient biblical term for a rare perfume that was extracted from cedars, a relative of the juniper. It got its name from the region of Gilead in the Holy Lands where it was produced, and the 1611 King James Bible used the term figuratively to signify a universal cure. This creek, near Emigrant, gets its name from the scent of the local juniper trees found there.

The creek also carries a variant name of Mama Gaylord Creek, and it was called Mother Gilliam's Creek as well. Local sources have no idea who this woman was or if she existed, and there are no deed or homestead records in these names.

In 1920 Billy Carr started his Hy-Grade Mine on this creek. It was productive for some years, not only in ore, but as an investment scheme. (see White City)

Bare Mountain

This is a slightly different word than "Bald," but the reason is the same since the top 300 feet are treeless.

The rumor of streaking campers from nearby Camp Senia has not been confirmed.

Barney Creek

Barney Creek on the Dexter Point quad near Emigrant was named for an early settler. It appears on an 1888 map, but nothing further is known about him.

The variant name of Barnes Creek is reported by the USGS as a misspelling.

Barrier Lake

Although this looks like a solitary lake, it is actually a widening in the North Fork of Wounded Man Creek. It is a "slide" lake, where a huge rockfall created a barrier, or dam, that formed the lake. The long, steep-walled lake actually has no visible outlet as the creek flows underground through the rocks of the slide for about a mile, popping out as a spring where the North Fork of Wounded Man Creek resumes.

Barronette Peak

Barronette Peak in the northeast corner of Yellowstone Park was named in 1878 by Ferdinand Hayden's Geological Survey team for Collins John H. "Yellowstone Jack" Barronette (1829–1901). Jack apparently spelled his name Barronnette, but there have been many official spellings of this peak—Baronet, Baronett, and Baronette—which is not unusual for late nineteenth-century orthography. The current spelling is Barronette and is considered official, if incorrect.

Jack Baronette. YELLOWSTONE HERITAGE AND RESEARCH CENTER, YEL 40423

Jack was born in Glencoe, Scotland, and came to the Yellowstone country in 1864 to prospect for gold. He was a scout for both Lt. Col. George Armstrong Custer in 1868, and Gen. Phil Sheridan on several trips, and was the only member of the civilian police to be retained when the U.S. Army took over policing the Park in 1884. With the discovery of gold near Cooke City, he recognized that there would be a need to cross the Yellowstone River, so in 1871 he built a toll bridge at the confluence of the Lamar and Yellowstone Rivers. He also gained some fame when he and George Pritchard found Truman Everts and nursed him back to health. Everts had been with the Washburn Expedition in 1870 when they explored what was to become Yellowstone Park. He became lost and separated from the group, wandering 37 days alone, on foot, and nearly starving before being rescued. (see Druid Peak)

Barronette Peak is prominent along the north side of Yellowstone Park's Northeast Entrance road, with the beautiful Barronette ski trail running along Soda Butte Creek at its base.

Basin Creek/Falls/Lake, Basin Creek Lakes

Geologically, a basin is a circumscribed area within which the rock strata dip toward the center. It looks a bit like the old-fashioned, oval washbasin, and there are several in the Absaroka-Beartooths.

The most historic **Basin Creek** is in the big gold mining country of the Boulder River. It sits between Baboon and Independence Mountains and runs through the ghost town of Independence. The creek was first noted by the Ferdinand Hayden Survey party when they found gold color in this creek in 1872. Seven years later, William Langford, Seth Porter, and Albert Schmidt found gold and silver quartz there, but could not file claims as it was on the Crow Reservation. In 1882, when the reservation borders had been moved east, Elias "Joe" Keeney staked his claims to the "Big Spirit" and "Little Spirit" at a site on Basin Creek that he called "The Independence." Later that year, there were 500 miners working from the little town of Independence on Basin Creek, and productive mining continued until 1905. (see Independence) The name of the creek, a tributary of the Main Boulder River, comes because its headwaters start in a large, open, grassy basin.

There is a second **Basin Creek** that is a tributary of the West Boulder River on the Mount Rae quad. It starts in a basin, too, but does not have such a rich, historical background.

The third **Basin Creek** drains the Basin Creek Lakes on the Silver Run Plateau and joins the West Fork of Rock Creek in the flats near the old Camp Senia in Red Lodge country. The Upper and Lower **Basin Creek Lakes** are served by a beautiful National Recreation Trail that starts at the Basin Campground on the Rock Creek Road. Although not noted on the USGS map, the impressive **Basin Creek Falls** can be seen about half a mile up this trail.

Finally, there is another **Basin Lake** on the Fossil Lake quad that sits in a high, rocky mountain basin in the Sodalite to Broadwater drainage. Officially Basin Lake, it is also called Picasso Lake because the outline of its shore and island bear a strange resemblance to one of Pablo Picasso's more unusual profile portraits. (see map at Picasso Lake)

Bassett Creek

There were several Bassetts who were associated with this creek, a tributary of Bear Creek north of Gardiner.

Fred and William Bassett were brothers who lived near each other and squatted on upper Bassett Creek not far from Corwin Springs. William married one of "Frisky" John Mulherin's daughters, and Ranger L.P.

Fred and Florence Bassett. YELLOWSTONE GATEWAY MUSEUM, 2006.044.1961.

McKnight said that the creek was named for this brother who was at one time the owner of Corwin Hot Springs. However, he traded his land for two saddle horses and left the area. Fred remained, but moved across the Yellowstone River to the Cinnabar Basin where he proved up on a homestead in 1895. There was also a Harvey C. Bassett who was named as an early homesteader on this stream. Phillip Bassett, another relative who also lived at Cinnabar, made the news in 1884 when he killed himself with an unspecified poison.

Bear Creek/Gulch

There are lots of bears in our Montana forests, and consequently many bear creeks. Dillon, Helena, Drummond, and Missoula all have one, and most are associated with mining.

The most famous **Bear Creek** in the Absarokas is just east of Gardiner. It was first found in 1866 by the Austin party who were retreating up the Yellowstone River after Indians had run off their horses. They discovered fair placer gold where the creek enters the river, as well as a burned and hairless bear cub. Hence the name Bear Creek/Gulch that became one of the biggest gold strikes in Montana. "Uncle" Joe Brown, who will appear throughout this book, was with that party and steadily worked the area as a placer site. In 1870, he and James Graham were prospecting and struck gold-bearing quartz on nearby Mineral Hill. Development was slowed by the fact that the land was on the Crow Reservation, but the cession of the Crow land in 1882 and the completion of the Northern Pacific Railroad to Livingston at about the same time spurred hydraulic placer and hardrock mining. The Bear Gulch Placer Company was incorporated in 1884 and a stamp mill was constructed.

In 1898 a natural landslide on Mineral Hill revealed one of the richest lodes ever found in Montana and things really boomed. In 1897 the little hamlet of **Bear Gulch** had four log cabins, but after the lode was found and the Bear Gulch Mining Company was formed, the town was renamed Jardine for the company's treasurer. (see Jardine) By 1900 there were 130 commercial and residential buildings, a 200-pupil school, telephones, electric lights, and a water and sewer system. There were three stamp mills, and the Revenue mill had 40 1,000-pound stamps capable of crushing five tons of ore a day. These mines produced gold and silver ore, as well as arsenic trioxide, continuously until 1947 when they were closed. A brief resurgence of gold mining by TMX Mineral Hill Inc. started in 1989 but closed again for good in 1996.

There are two other **Bear Creeks** in the Absaroka-Beartooths. One is on the Ross Canyon quad just to the south of Big Timber, and the other is on the Sliderock Mountain quad in Deer Creek country. Both may be the haunt of many bears, but don't have the gold found at Jardine's Bear Gulch.

These are not to be confused with the Bear Creek north of Red Lodge that is the site of the town of Bearcreek and the former huge coal mines. It is nearby, but outside of the national forest boundaries covered in this book.

Bear Draw, Little Bear Draw

These valleys are on the Livingston Mountain quad and enter Mission Creek directly across from one another.

Little Bear Lake and Creek

More bears, but Goldilocks is sadly missing! This lake and its creek are located next to the Beartooth Highway in Wyoming and are near Beartooth and Island Lakes.

Grizzly bear family. NATIONAL PARK SERVICE.

Bear Pen Creek

This tributary of Picket Pin Creek on the Meyer Mountain quad was named for a bear pen that was probably placed in the area by Jonas Hedges, an early trapper. Bear pens were traps with one-way doors that were the safest way to capture and easily kill bears. The meat was often sold to miners as "poor man's pork."

Beartooth Mountain/Plateau/Glacier/Creek/Falls/Lake/Butte/Ranch/Highway

The Crow called the sharp 500- to 700-foot-tall promontory on the side of **Beartooth Mountain,** *Daxpitcheeihte*, translated as the "bear's tooth." (see image on page 1)

This name was used to refer to the whole area in nineteenth-century dealings with this tribe and was used locally to refer to the mountainous area. It came into official use in 1908 with the formation of the Beartooth National Forest and now is used for the entire northeastern section of this massif and the Absaroka-Beartooth Wilderness.

Beartooth Mountain anchors the eastern side of the **Beartooth Plateau,** which is actually just one of the several high plateaus that are found in the Beartooth Mountains. The **Beartooth Glacier** is on the north slope of the mountain.

Beartooth Lake and the **Creek** that drains into it are on the Wyoming side of the Beartooth Highway and are separated from the Beartooth Mountains and Plateau. **Beartooth Creek** flows south along the eastern side of the Butte, and **Beartooth Falls** can be found just before the creek enters the lake. Beartooth Lake was once the site of a popular resort. Jim Redfern built the first cabin at the lake in 1912, and in 1913, Roy Hickock built the Beartooth Lodge and housed guests in tents. Herb Flett obtained the lease in 1940 and added 16 cabins and the Top of the World Store. In 1966 the permit was terminated by the USFS and the buildings and gas station were removed to Cooke Pass (now known as Colter Pass, see citation). The lake now sits with a new beautiful, unspoiled vista.

Beartooth Butte with its white limestone cliffs rises right above the lake. It is located just to the south of the Beartooth Plateau, but the names are only coincidentally related. Local lore says that the name comes from the cliffs and a promontory on the butte where the ridges look like the many teeth of a bear.

Beartooth Butte and Lake. PHOTO BY THE AUTHOR.

Most of the sedimentary rock has been eroded completely off of the Beartooths, but on this butte and neighboring Clay Butte, the remaining limestone cap has been preserved. It is not only a beautiful formation, but within the limestone are thousands of varied fossils, from the bony, plated Devonian fish called an Ostracoderm to many primitive terrestrial plants, among the oldest found in North America. (see Clay Butte)

The **Beartooth Highway,** U.S. 212, was completed in 1936 and goes from Red Lodge, Montana, up over the 10,947-foot **Beartooth Pass,** and on through Wyoming, to Cooke City and the Northeast Entrance to Yellowstone Park. The late broadcaster, Charles Kuralt, called this road "the most beautiful drive in America."

The **Beartooth Ranch** is farther north on the Stillwater River near Nye. It was homesteaded in 1892 by Byron Wood, whose Woodbine Creek enters the river at the ranch. Ed Ickerman bought it in 1921 and gave it the name of Beartooth Ranch. He originally used it as a physical training center for boys, and later expanded it to guide outfitting and pack trips. It still exists at the end of the Nye Road. (see Woodbine Creek and Cairn Lake/Mountain)

Beartrap Draw

This draw is off Trout Creek in the extreme northeast corner of the Custer-Gallatin National Forest.

(see Bear Pen Creek for a description of these pens and traps)

Beauty Lake

It's beautiful country, so it is only fitting that there are more than one if these.

The first can be found on the Cooke City quad just to the east of the headwaters of the Stillwater River. The other is on the Beartooth Plateau just to the north of U.S. Highway 212, Beartooth Lake, and Beartooth Butte.

Beaver Creek/Meadows/Campground

The beaver, *Castor canadensis*, brought the mountain men to Montana, trapping them for their pelts. Knowing this, one would expect, and will find, many references to them in our mountains.

American beaver. NATIONAL PARK SERVICE.

One **Beaver Creek** flows north off Livingston Peak toward the Yellowstone River. Michael and Rosa Graham emigrated from Scotland and were among the early homesteaders on this creek. Their descendants still live in Park County.

There is another **Beaver Creek** on Hummingbird Peak just to the north of Yellowstone Park. It is a tributary of Hellroaring Creek and joins with Elk Creek in a swampy area that is typical beaver habitat.

Beaver Meadows is a flat swampy area on the West Boulder River. Their dam building created ponds for their lodges, and these subsequently silted in to become meadows.

Big Beaver USFS Campground is on the Main Boulder River between Graham and Blakely Creeks. It is just upstream from some ponds and willows that are a good demonstration of the effects of beaver activity.

Although the trapping activities of the mountain men and the Indians who traded their pelts severely impacted the beaver population, they were still present in large numbers in the early twentieth century. Plentiful numbers of beaver were reported in the northern Yellowstone Slough and Hellroaring drainages until 1910, but by the 1950s they had nearly disappeared from Yellowstone Park and the Absaroka-Beartooths. Hunting and trapping was not a factor, and their aquatic habitat protected them from most predators, so the decline was thought to be food related. Since willows are the beaver's primary food and dam construction material, it is now felt that the huge explosion of elk numbers and destruction of the willows by overgrazing the stream banks led to the population drop. In the 1980s a beaver reintroduction program was started, but it was the wolf reintroduction that really helped the beaver. Elk numbers in the northern range of Yellowstone fell 70 percent from 1995 to 2011, and stream bank willows have increased in height and density. Although not back to 1910 numbers, the beaver are returning.

Becker Lake

Becker Lake sits just to the south of the Wyoming border on the Beartooth Plateau. Although there is no citation that provides a definitive source for the name, it is likely that it was named for a Maj. E.H. Becker who was the Crow Indian agent in 1902. He was removed from his position for probable graft, a common problem.

The punishment suggests that it was significant malfeasance... but not enough to take his name off the lake. (see Mount Delano)

Beckwourth Lake

James P. Beckwourth, ca. 1856. FROM *THE LIFE AND ADVENTURES OF JAMES P.BECKWOURTH* BY T. D. BONNER, 1856.

James P. Beckwourth (ca. 1798–1867) was a mountain man, fur trapper, and explorer. Born into slavery in Fredericksburg, Virginia, he was freed by his father/master and apprenticed to a blacksmith. He moved to Missouri and in 1825 joined Gen. W. Ashley's trapping brigade to the Rocky Mountains, where he later worked as a free trapper with Jedediah Smith. In 1829 he moved in with the Crow Nation and lived with them for many years. He served as a scout and an interpreter and is credited with finding Beckwourth Pass through the Sierra Nevada, where his Beckwourth Trail from Reno, Nevada, to Portola, California, was used by thousands of settlers during the California gold rush. *The Life and Adventures of James P. Beckwourth: Mountaineer, Scout and Pioneer, and Chief of the Crow Nations of Indians,* was narrated to Thomas D. Bonner. Published in 1856, it helped preserve his fame.

Because of his reputation and association with the Crow Nation, it was felt appropriate to honor him with this lake in the West Rosebud, upstream from Mystic Lake.

Benbow Mine

T.C. "Chalky" and Ida Benbow. JIM ANNIN COLLECTION, MUSEUM OF THE BEARTOOTHS, #23.

T.C. "Chalky" Benbow (1864–1932) discovered the chromite deposits near Nye in 1882.

The Benbow Mine sits to the east of Nye on Black Butte on the divide between the Stillwater and Fishtail drainages. Financial and Crow Reservation issues delayed mining until 1904 but thereafter it continued actively until failing during the Great Depression of 1929. Chalky died in 1932 and the mine remained dormant until World War II, when the mines geared back up and produced huge amounts of ore when Germany cut off supplies from Africa and Russia. Chrome was an essential material for armor coating for tanks and planes, and the Benbow Mine was reported to have treated 500 tons of ore per day. The Benbow Mine is now part of the modern Stillwater Mining Complex at Old Nye.

Other mines were developed in the same vein as the Benbow Mine. The Gish Mine was started by the brother of actresses Lillian and Dorothy Gish in 1915. The Mouat Mine was named for William M. Mouat, a geologist and nephew of the president of the Minneapolis Mining and Smelting Co. This Mouat Mine, renamed the American when it geared up for the Korean conflict, extracted 900,000 short tons of concentrate between 1952 and 1960. In the 1980s platinum and palladium were discovered at the Mouat Mine in the igneous band of the Stillwater Complex. Currently very active, its big plant on the Stillwater River near the site of Old Nye is the only producer of these metals in the United States.

William M. Mouat. JIM ANNIN COLLECTION #2036, MUSEUM OF THE BEARTOOTHS .

Chalky himself was the classic Western character. He was originally from Iowa, went west to Colorado, then in 1882 to Montana and lived at first at Hilo's stock ranch near Absarokee, where he had a bar in town. He homesteaded in the Stillwater Valley in 1892 and lived many years on what was then known as Benbow Creek near Old Nye on the Stillwater River. His mining activity was mentioned, but he was also quite the inventor, with patents for an automatic train coupler, a train brake, a spring wheel for automobiles, and, most famously, for an airship (dirigible), which he displayed and demonstrated at the 1904 St. Louis World's Fair.

Bergschrund Lake

Bergschrund is a word adopted from German, which means a "mountain cleft." In English, it means a crevasse that forms where moving glacial ice separates from the stagnant ice, or firn above. It generally extends to the bedrock and can have a depth of several hundred feet.

This lake is tucked in a high-walled cirque between Sundance and Summit Mountains at 10,000 feet. Were the glacier still there, the bergschrund would be along the cirque wall behind the lake.

It has been called Boot Lake by some for its shape, but Bergschrund is official for both the USGS and the Forest Service.

Big Foot Lake

This is a humorous name for a lake that is found just a bit west of Little Face Lake above Alpine in the East Rosebud. The lake's name ties Little Face Lake with an amusing allusion to the Sasquatch or Yeti. However, Little Face was a real person, a Crow Indian, who served as a scout for the U.S. Army toward the end of the Plains Wars. His oral histories serve as an important resource of tribal history and cosmology. (see Little Face Lake)

According to the Bigfoot Field Researchers Association, Montana has had 47 Bigfoot sightings (out of 5,251), but there have been only two in the Beartooths. The author tried to get a picture of one for inclusion here, but it ducked out of sight just as the shutter clicked...

Big Moose Lake

(see Moose Lake)

Big Mountain

Big Mountain is located just south of Little Park Mountain on the quad of that name. At 11,350 feet it is higher than any other peak in Montana outside of the Beartooths. It thus qualifies as one big hill. Perhaps we should consider the 29 over 12,000 feet as the "Really Big" mountains.

Big Park/Lake

(see citation under Park)

Bill Lake

Bill Lake is the first lake that is found when ascending Flood Creek from the Stillwater River.

It had an earlier, unofficial name as Grant Lake, but no citation could be found to identify who either Grant or Bill were. With all of the mysterious women who have had their names placed on the maps of the Custer-Gallatin National Forest, it would seem appropriate that we have at least one mystery man as well.

Black Butte

There are four of these dark-colored, flat-topped hills in the Absaroka-Beartooths, the result of lava, granite, and the eroding away of the light-colored limestone cap.

The one in the northwest portion of Yellowstone National Park was named as early as 1910 for its dark-colored lava.

There is another on the Mackay Ranch quad where the Rosebud Cattle Company had one of its headquarters. The former East Rosebud Ranger Station was located at the base of this Black Butte in the early part of the twentieth century.

The Black Butte near West Fishtail Creek near the head of Nye Creek is the site of the Benbow Mine. (see Benbow Mine and Chrome Lake)

A final one can be found on the Ross Canyon quad.

Black Canyon/Lake

Named for the dark color, an unnamed creek flows northward from **Black Canyon** to the West Rosebud.

Black Canyon Lake is quite separate and lies in a steep-walled valley farther south between Mount Rearguard and Thunder Mountain on the Silver Run Peak quad. It was named around 1915

Black Canyon Lake. COURTESY RICK GRAETZ

by M.E. Martin, a Red Lodge prospector active from the 1880s to the 1930s. He was impressed by the dark dikes exposed here, and the dark water, which is due to the steep walls and 185-foot depth of the lake. The cliff walls around this lake are a good habitat for the mountain goat, which are commonly seen here.

Black Mountain

Volcanic activity caused many of the Black Mountains throughout southwestern Montana. They are found in the Tom Miner Basin in the Paradise Valley, near Campfire Lake in the Crazies, and here, overlooking the South Fork of Pine Creek near Emigrant.

The name was suggested in 1923 due to the dark and rugged appearance of this mountain, and first appears on a 1925 Absaroka National Forest map.

The interesting George Lake Marble can be found at several outcroppings near the top of this mountain. The marble formation is a result of the hot lava that came in contact with the basal granite metamorphosing it. (see George Lake)

Black Pyramid Mountain

The shape and color obviously gives name to this mountain on the quad of the same name.

Black Stone Lake

Would you believe that there are black stones of volcanic origin in this lake? It sits just south of and is visible from the Beartooth Pass.

Blacktail Creek/Lake

The black-tailed deer, *Odocoileus hemionus columbianus*, is a subspecies of the mule deer, and was once found as far east as Wyoming. It is now restricted to the Pacific coastal areas from Alaska to northern California.

They must have been plentiful 100 to 150 years ago as there are four creeks and a lake named Blacktail that are spread throughout the Absaroka-Beartooths. The lake is in a deep cirque on Livingston Peak with one of the Blacktail Creeks flowing out of it. Of the other three creeks, one flows north off Picket Pin Mountain, another is a tributary of Emigrant Creek, and the third comes into the West Fork of Rock Creek near Camp Senia.

Blakely Creek

Charles Blakeley (note extra e) had a deed for a lot in Big Timber in 1881 and was reported in ranger notes to be "a pioneer settler in the Boulder Valley" around 1888. In 1916 he filed a deed on this creek where it comes off Contact Mountain to join the Main Boulder.

There is still private mining inholding in the national forest at that location.

Blind Bridger Creek

The creek was not named for a blind person, but for the fact that there is a lack of visibility as it wends its way around tall rock walls to join the main Bridger Creek.

Blind Sheep Spring/Creek

This creek, and the spring that heads it, can be found near Nye. It descends to Sheep Creek along a steep-walled canyon that blocks the view up to the creek.

Blue Lake

The reflection of the sky and a bit of glacial flour creates the deep blue color that gives this lake its name. It sits beneath Haystack Peak near the Independence mines at the headwaters of the Boulder River.

Bob Lake

Bob and Dick Lakes are found a half mile apart north of Cooke City along the Goose Lake jeep trail at the head of Lady of the Lakes Creek. The names do not have a citation for actual people as they are another humorous pair of names that Montana Fish, Wildlife and Parks used as a reference for their fish stocking program. They are just to the east of Mutt and Jeff Lakes, which like Dick and Bob are commonly seen as a funny pair of guys in both film and literature.

Bohee Creek

This creek near Big Timber is a tributary of the Boulder River, and the name is most certainly a misspelling of Bovee. William Corker, who was murdered in 1892, had his cabin on this creek, which news and court reports at the time called Bovee Creek. (see Corker Canyon) There are no specifics or homestead records, but a man named Bovee must have been a squatter on this creek in the latter nineteenth century.

Boone Mountain

Boone Mountain at 8,963 feet can be found south of Big Timber and directly above Skookum Joe Canyon between the heads of East and West Sheep Creeks. There are no federal homestead or county deed records that identify any Boones in Sweet Grass County, and the Board on Geographic Names has no citation as to why this particular Boone was so honored. Local sources feel that he must have been a person who was in the area prior to 1900, but they have no recollection of him.

Bott Sotts Camp/Lake

The camp and lake were named by Al Croonquist in 1917, and the name was apparently derived from the Crow Indian expression *Baesaetse,* which he said meant "heap good."

The camp was near the current trailhead at the end of the road up the West Fork of Rock Creek just past Croonquist's Camp Senia. It was shown on a 1937 map, but no structures now remain, and the camp and lake are not currently shown by the USGS.

Boulder Creek/River/Mountain/Pass/Lakes/Meadows/Ranger Station

Because of the important mines in this river valley, and because the river provides 50 miles of access deep into the Absaroka-Beartooths, the Boulder name fills our maps and our history.

The **Boulder River** was first mentioned in 1806 by William Clark, who referred to it as the Stinking Cabin Creek, a name that he got from Mandan or Hidatsa sources. He called the place where it enters the Yellowstone River "Rivers Across" as Big Timber Creek enters the Yellowstone directly across from it. The Crow called the river *Me-had-at-se-pa*, the Sinking or Diving River, in reference to the cataract at Natural Bridge where the river drops into a cavern underground to re-appear several hundred yards downstream. (see Natural Bridge) It was first noted as the Big Boulder by Lt. J.H. Bradley in 1862, who said that "it derives its name from the profusion of large round stones with which its channel is filled." When DeLacy did his 1865 map for the Montana Territorial Legislature, he called it the Big Boulder Creek, and it became the Boulder River on USGS maps in 1924. As one drives the Main Boulder River Road near McLeod, the name is reinforced by the huge medicine ball–sized boulders that are scattered around the pasture land.

The **Boulder River Mining District** is located along the Boulder River valley in the area of Contact Mountain where much of the mining activity in the district occurred. (see Contact Mountain)

The **East Boulder River** was also a significant mining area. Ansel Hubble first developed the placer gold mines there in 1893 up by Iron Creek and Hubble Gulch. It now is the site of the big underground East Boulder Mine that produces large amounts of platinum and palladium.

The **West Boulder River** just below McLeod has a beautiful flat area along its course that is now the site of luxury homes and ranches that provide an escape to Montana for some wealthy members of the more populous parts of the country. The West Boulder road is a scenic drive worth taking. It ends at a campground and a six-person ranger cabin that can be rented December to May.

West Boulder Meadows is found after a short, roadless hike two to four miles south of the campground. It is in the Absaroka-Beartooth Wilderness and is a lovely area that is well worth the effort to see. Thank the beavers.

Boulder Mountain is at the head of the West Boulder River, and the name was certified by the Board on Geographic Names in 1922. It forms the divide between the West Boulder River and Mill Creek on the Paradise Valley side, and it can plainly be seen from almost all points in the West Boulder Valley. This also was a big mining district, and Calamity Jane, who frequented many Montana mining camps, is rumored to have had a saloon on this mountain in 1882. Evidence of mining is further noted by the presence of Prospect and Speculator Lakes on its flanks, and Silver Lake to the south.

West Boulder Lake is on the east side of Boulder Mountain and is the head-waters of the West Boulder River. There are some other Boulder Lakes to the south on the Fossil Lake quad. They are just to the east of Broadwater Lake in the Sodalite drainage. Although they are unrelated to the Boulder River country, they are also named for the large boulders found in and around the lakes. Must be that there are a fair number of big rocks in this high country.

Boulder Pass is on the trail from the Buffalo Fork drainage north of the Park to the Boulder River.

The **Main Boulder Ranger Station** is of great historical interest. It was built in 1905 by Harry Kaufman when he was assigned to be the first guard ranger for the Absaroka Division of the Yellowstone Forest Reserve, and represents what is perhaps the oldest facility in the Forest Service system. He and his wife, Coral, lived there for over 30 years and managed it as the Boulder District Headquarters. In 1945, when the Absaroka National Forest was consolidated into the Custer and Gallatin National Forests, the office was moved to Big Timber and the cabin became a museum. It is still in use and open to visitors some 30 miles up the road from Big Timber and just two miles past the end of the paving at Natural Bridge State Park.

Boundary Creek

Ranger L.P. McKnight said that this creek was named because it is near the Yellowstone National Park boundary. It is mentioned in Gallatin National Forest ranger notes from 1936-42 but cannot be found on modern maps or in current USGS or Forest Service notes.

Boundary Draw/Spring

This draw, on the north side of Bad Canyon Creek near Nye, gets its name because it parallels the national forest boundary for about a mile. Boundary Draw Spring is at the head of the draw.

Bowback Mountain/Lake

The back rest of a bowback chair is formed by a single length of wood that is bent into a horseshoe, which is then attached to the seat and arms and filled with slats or spindles. This mountain was obviously named for that shape.

There is also a story that goes with this mountain. Al Croonquist of Red Lodge and Camp Senia first climbed it in 1921. He left a check for $25 on top, wrapped in tin foil. The following year, David Kjell, "the Galloping Swede," climbed it and found the check along with a note: "Some view from here, Eh, Boy!?"

Box Canyon

A box canyon, well known from Zane Gray and other Western writers, is a canyon that has a flat floor and a single entrance with the other three sides enclosed by steep walls—like an open box.

There are two such canyons of this name in our national forest. One is on the Sliderock Mountain quad between Evergreen and Iron Mountains. The other is on the north end of the national forest near Big Timber on the Ross Canyon quad. This latter canyon has a ranger station that is still in use as an administrative center.

Bramble Creek/Lakes

Brambles are thorny fruit-bearing shrubs of the species *Rubus fruticosus*. The term generally refers to the blackberry but can include raspberries as well. This little creek is just upstream from Raspberry Creek on the west side of the Boulder River. A tasty place.

Although unofficial, the four tiny lakes at the head of this creek are known in the fishing guides as **Bramble Lakes.**

Breakneck Mountain/Plateau

Just north of Mount Douglas on the quad of that name is this mountain with a very abrupt geological formation. Ranger Harry Kaufman tells the story that it was named by an early sheepman who had a stampede of his pack outfit and one of the horses fell and broke its neck.

Brent Lake

Brent Lake is high up on the Froze-to-Death Plateau next to Turgulse Lake. It can be used as the site of a base camp for climbing both Spirit Mountain and Granite Peak. The origin of the names of both of these lakes is unknown.

Bridge Creek/Lake

The lake sits in a beautiful cirque of volcanic rock at the head of Bridge Creek, which flows off Crow Mountain to join the Boulder River. In the early twentieth century a wooden wagon bridge crossed the river just below this juncture and gave the creek its name. It is now a modern bridge on Forest Service Road 6639.

Bridger Creek

Jim Bridger, the famous scout, fur trader, and guide, is honored by having his name on this creek. Although there is a more famous Bridger Creek and Canyon in the Bridger Range north of Bozeman, this one also commemorates his presence. It is located in the north end of the Absarokas and flows into the Yellowstone River near the town of Greycliff.

Jim Bridger blazed a route from the Oregon Trail to the Montana goldfields that, since it went to the west of the Bighorn Mountains and avoided the Sioux hunting lands, was thought to be safer than the Bozeman Trail. It passed along the south side of the Yellowstone River and would have crossed this creek. It was, however, used only briefly in 1864 and by only five wagon trains. Thereafter, the U.S. Army closed all northward travel because of the Indian victories in Red Cloud's War.

Jim Bridger, ca. 1860. KANSAS HISTORICAL SOCIETY.

Broadwater River/Lake

The river that is the proper head of the Clarks Fork River takes its name from the wide character of its lower course.

There are two Broadwater Lakes. One, on the Fossil Lake quad, is a widening of the Broadwater River. This had its original trout population stocked when Al Croonquist and A.J. Salo packed the fish up in milk cans in 1919. It has become a popular destination for anglers, so, although less Western cowboy-romantic, Montana Fish, Wildlife and Parks now stocks it regularly with air drops.

The second Broadwater Lake, farther east on the Black Pyramid quad, is a widening of Lake Fork Creek.

Brogan's Landing

Brogan's Landing is a fishing access site on the Yellowstone River north of Gardiner. It is on land that was once owned by the Brogan who had the nearby ranch where he raised elk for the Chinese antler market. He changed his herd to bison after a dispute with Montana Fish, Wildlife and Parks and their fear that chronic wasting disease could get to wild herds if any of his elk escaped.

Brown Lake

Brown Lake is just north of Granite Peak and above the Mystic, Island, and Silver Lakes chain.

It is among those small lakes that locals used in the latter part of the twentieth century to honor prominent Stillwater County notables. It was named for a Gene Brown who died in 1982. Gene was a past sheriff of Stillwater County, a Montana highway patrolman, and the local baseball coach.

Brown or Joe Brown Creek

The creek, on the east side of the Yellowstone River across from Yankee Jim's place, was named for Joe Brown.

"Uncle Joe" was one of the original prospectors at Bear Gulch/Jardine and is credited with the discovery of gold there. In 1866 he is said to have found $1,800 worth of gold at his placer mine at the mouth of the creek. He put in the first arrastra there in 1877 and the first quartz mill in 1885. Along with James Graham, he also discovered the rich lode on Mineral Mountain near Jardine. Joe lived his entire adult life working in Bear Gulch and on Joe Brown Creek until his death in 1913. (see other image in Introduction page vi)

Joe Brown, 1864. YELLOWSTONE GATEWAY MUSEUM, 2006.044.1892.

Brownlee Creek

In 1925 Robert Brownlee bought "Happy Jack" Aldrich's ranch on this creek that is 11 miles south of Big Timber. (see Happy Jack Gulch) He was born in Scotland, but his family emigrated to Canada in 1864 when he was six years old. Robert first came to Montana in 1886 where he started a large sheep ranch north of Melville. He was elected to the Montana State Legislature from Sweet Grass County as a representative in 1900, and moved up to the Senate in 1912, where he served one term.

Records show that family members were still living on the Main Boulder in 1955.

Robert Brownlee. CRAZY MOUNTAIN MUSEUM.

Brundage Creek

Al Brundage was a trapper who lived by this creek up the Hellroaring drainage. He also worked as a stage driver in Yellowstone Park in the 1890s and died in Jardine in 1900.

Buffalo Butte/Plateau

Famed prospector A. Bart Henderson recorded in his diary in 1870, "[We] came to a beautiful flat, which we gave the name Buffalo Flat as we found thousands of buffalo quietly grazing." His fellow prospector, James Gourley, called it the "Buffalo Tables," but this was ultimately changed to **Buffalo Plateau,** and is located between the Buffalo River and Coyote Creek. The Buffalo Plateau Ranger Station can be found on its eastern side.

Buffalo Butte, on the north end of the plateau, was at one time embarrassingly called "Niggerhead Butte." The slur was appropriately removed and is now not even considered a USGS variant name.

Buffalo Fork/Creek/River

The early exploring and prospecting party of Ansel Hubble, Lou Anderson, George Reese, and two others came here in 1867. (see Slough Creek) They called this stream just to the north of the park Buffalo Fork, for the many bison that were common in the area. That name was confirmed in 1883.

The Buffalo Fork Ranger Station was built in 1913 and still stands. It is now used for administrative purposes.

Buffalo Jump

Native Americans used a "pishkun" or buffalo jump to drive a bison herd over a cliff as a hunting method. The term *pishkun* is from the Blackfoot language and is freely translated as "deep blood kettle." Where the animals fell and were injured they could easily be killed and butchered.

This steep bluff over the Stillwater River just west of Nye and Old Nye was called by the Crow *Ahr-nah-puma-ta*, "Where the Buffalo Jumped Off."

The Montana FWP Buffalo Jump fishing access site on the Stillwater River is about a mile north and downstream of the actual pishkun.

Buffalo Mountain

The mountain rises in the buffalo country immediately north of Yellowstone National Park and the Black Canyon of the Yellowstone River, not far east of Gardiner.

In 1899, geologist James P. Kimball wrote that "it constitutes the true southern termination of the Snowy Range."

Bull Creek/Mountain

Bull Creek is a tributary of Slough Creek, north of the Park, and drains the rise to the east of Buffalo Creek. It was named in 1883, again for the bison that were plentiful in this area.

Bull Mountain sits across the Montana/Yellowstone Park boundary overlooking Hellroaring and Coyote Creeks, and it has the same ore body that is found around Jardine.

Bull of the Woods Pass

Bull of the Woods Pass is a historical term that recognizes the male woods bison. It is a low point on a ridge in the rich Cooke City mining country, south of Daisy Pass and Crown Butte. The road or trail that previously went over the pass is no longer noted on maps.

Yellowstone bison bull. PHOTO BY THE AUTHOR.

Bulldozer Creek

This creek can be found just east of Chico Peak in the Emigrant mining country. It must be assumed that a piece of equipment went for an unscheduled wash.

Burnt Bacon Creek/Lake

These features are located in a cluster of lakes near Granite Lake in Carbon County just north of the Montana/Wyoming border. It is a beautiful area that is in prime early season elk hunting country. Apparently the scenery must have distracted one of the elk hunters from his cooking chores and his inattention has been burned into history.

Burnt Gulch/Lake/Creek/Fork/Mountain

All of these "burnt" names refer to the results of forest fires that are common and natural in the forest.

The **Gulch** contains an unnamed creek that flows into the East Boulder River.

In that same area, which was burned long ago, one can find **Burnt Lake**. It is on the north shoulder of Columbine Peak in a basin between two forks of Rainbow Creek where one can see beautifully shaped fire-scarred snags.

There are two **Burnt Creeks,** one near Nye, and another a tributary of Mill Creek near Pray. Kester Counts had a mining claim on this latter one that he called the Galena Queen. (see Counts Creek)

Burnt Mountain is next to the East Fork of Red Lodge Creek and had a bald summit. **Burnt Fork Creek** comes off this mountain.

Burrls Flat

This is certainly a misspelling of the name Burris with the "i" miscopied as an "l." Ed Burris was an old railroad man, a freight conductor on the Northern Pacific, who ran sheep on the West Boulder up on this flat. As part of the sheep and wool boom of the late nineteenth century, the *Livingston Enterprise* noted that the firm of Burris and Muncaster had 3,000 sheep in 1890 with plans to go to 6,000. In 1900, they reported that Mitchell E. "Ed" Burris patented his homestead on this flat. He unfortunately died in 1902 after being struck by lightning.

Butcher Creek/Mountain

The Second Crow Agency was located near **Butcher Creek** from 1875–1883, and the government maintained a slaughterhouse nearby. It all fell to ruin after the agency moved east, but the name and memory persists.

In the 1890s this was an oil development area because of the asphalt seeps noted. The wells were a project of Helena millionaire Thomas Cruse, whose Butcher Creek Oil Company was the first to use an oil rig and standard drill in Montana. Unfortunately, all nine holes that were drilled came up dry and were abandoned.

    Butcher Mountain is on the Red Lodge Creek Plateau at the headwaters of Butcher Creek.

Big Butte Lake

This lake is south of Snowbank Mountain on the eastern Beartooth Plateau. The unnamed butte between Big Butte and Desolation Lakes gave rise to the name.

Cache Creek

Cache Creek is a bit out of the boundaries of this book as it is in the Lamar Valley of Yellowstone Park. It is included here because of its historical interest and because of its association with the early miners in the Absaroka-Beartooths.

    The word "cache" comes from the French verb meaning "to hide" and was used in 1864 to name this creek for an event that happened the previous year. That spring a party of about 40 prospectors that included "Horn" Miller and James Henderson had their horses stolen by Indians. They were forced to cache, or hide, their gear near this creek, and most of them walked the 100 miles back to the Yellowstone Valley. When they were able to return the next season, they recovered the equipment and wandered on to discover the fabulous gold strike at Bear Creek/Gulch (Jardine).

    The name was well established when it first appeared on Ferdinand Hayden's 1878 map.

Cairn Lake/Mountain

A cairn is a mound of stones purpose built as a memorial, landmark, or trail marker. This lake and mountain are found just south of Granite Peak in that high, rocky country where the peak, a pile of stone blocks, looks rather like a giant cairn.

    There was a move to have this 12,214-foot mountain called Ickerman Mountain in honor of Ed Ickerman. Ed spent his whole life in the Beartooths where he ran the Beartooth Ranch on the Stillwater River, built trails, stocked lakes with fish, and led packing and hunting parties. That name has not been accepted by the Board on Geographic Names, so Cairn it is. (see Favonius Lake, Beartooth Ranch)

Calamity Falls

Calamity Jane comes to mind since she has been claimed by most of the towns around southern Montana—but only after she achieved some posthumous fame in Western lore. She had been located for a time in Red Lodge, Bridger (when it was Stringtown), Gardiner, Horr, Cooke City, Bozeman, and may even have had a tavern on Boulder Mountain.

    However, these falls on the West Fork of Rock Creek have a less historic origin. Al Croonquist and a crew from Camp Senia were cutting a trail in 1917 when one of the crew members lost a valuable camera in the falls. Al said that it was "quite a calamity," and that is where the name of this falls comes from.

Cameron Creek/Lake

Cameron Creek flows off Mineral Mountain into the West Fork of Mill Creek. It was named for William Cameron, one of the old-time prospectors and residents of Emigrant Gulch and Chico. He had a molybdenum mine on the gulch that he worked for many years, but it was never very successful.

The small lake at the head of the creek is called **Cameron Lake,** but this name is unofficial and is used only by locals and as a reference by Montana Fish, Wildlife and Parks.

William Cameron at his molybdenum mine. YELLOWSTONE GATEWAY MUSEUM, 2006.044.1692.

Camp Lake

This lake is at the head of the Canyon Creek on Contact Mountain in the East Boulder River drainage. It is, however, best reached from the Main Boulder River by going up the Graham Creek trail. It was apparently a good place to camp.

Canyon Creek

During his 1898 survey, James P. Kimball named the **Canyon Creek** on Mount Dewey. There is a sizable glacier at the head of the creek, and the stream drops an impressive 2,700 feet into a deep canyon on the north side of the mountain where it ends in a lake, which he called **Canyon Lake.** This lake is erroneously labeled Crazy Lake on some maps.

Another **Canyon Creek** can be found in the East Boulder drainage named for a similar gorge. (see Camp Lake above)

Carbella

Carbella is a small community, bridge, and camping access site on the Yellowstone River just north of Yankee Jim Canyon. It was named in the early 1900s by Alex Stewart. Alex was a Scotsman who, along with his wife, Belle, homesteaded on the west side of the river where he was able to work at the mines at Aldrich. Alex combined his wife's name, Belle, with that of her good friend Cary

Belle and Ale Stewart. YELLOWSTONE GATEWAY MUSEUM, 2006.044.0553.

D'Wart of the nearby Dome Mountain Ranch to create Carbella. There was also a railroad siding, but that closed when the line from Livingston to Gardiner was abandoned in 1981.

The Carbella Bridge was built in 1918, shortly after Yellowstone Park allowed automobiles to tour the Park. It became part of the Yellowstone Trail from Minneapolis/St. Paul to the Park and was posted to the National Register of Historic Places in 2020. It now provides access to second homes and ranches on the road to Tom Miner Basin.

Carbon County

Carbon County is the easternmost Montana county that contains some of the Absaroka-Beartooths. It was formed in 1895 from parts of Yellowstone and Park Counties, and from land of the Crow Indian Reservation. Red Lodge is the county seat.

The name comes from the abundant coal found beneath Red Lodge and Bearcreek. The Smith Mine disaster of 1943 and drop in the use of coal after 1950 caused a decrease in mining, and the last of the coal mines closed in the early 1970s. Tourism and agriculture are now the principal industries.

Carbonate Mountain

A carbonate is any salt of carbonic acid. The minerals, sodium carbonate, soda or natron, and potassium carbonate, or potash, have been known since antiquity. They are widely used in industry in iron smelting, glass manufacture, and as an ingredient in Portland cement. Calcium carbonate is the main ingredient in the shells of sea invertebrates and is the chief constituent of limestone.

This mountain, overlooking the Main Boulder River, was named for the presence of this mineral via its limestone formations.

Carpenter Lake

Ranger notes from the 1930s state that this lake was named "in honor of Mr. Carpenter, now deceased." It is up the Hellroaring Creek that flows into Yellowstone Park so has also been called Hell Roaring Lake.

Further information on the deceased Mr. Carpenter is lacking, but there are a couple of local Carpenters who might be the culprit. The most likely is a Lewis Carpenter who, in 1905, filed for 100 inches of water from Lake Creek in Park County, presumably to power a hydraulic sluice for mining up the Hellroaring. Lake Creek no longer exists on any maps, but is probably the currently unnamed stream that flows out of Carpenter Lake to Grizzly Creek. If so, then Lewis is the man.

Cascade Creek/Falls

A cascade is a series of small waterfalls down a steep, rocky slope.

There are two Cascade Creeks in our forest. One is a tributary of the West Fork of Rock Creek, and the other, with an actual waterfall on it, is near Dexter Point on the east side of the Paradise Valley.

Casey Lake

It is not certain, but it is presumed that the lake was named for L.R. Casey who, in 1887, was the vice president of the Yellowstone Park Association that ran the Park concessions. The company was based in Gardiner, and this swampy lake is on the south slope of Parker Point near that town.

Castle Butte/Creek/Glacier/Lake/Mountain/Rock/Spire

The many references to Castles stem from eroded rock, primarily limestone, that has the appearance of a medieval castle.

Castle Butte is near the Boulder River south of Big Timber in the Deer Creek country. A **Castle Creek** flows west off this, getting its name from the butte. This is not to be confused with the other **Castle Creek** that has no relationship to a butte or mountain. It flows east off Picket Pin Mountain to join Limestone Creek and the Stillwater River near Nye. It is named for a huge rock that resembles a ruined medieval castle that is near the confluence of this creek and the Stillwater River.

There are two **Castle Lakes.** One is in view of Castle Mountain in the cluster of lakes just north of the Montana/Wyoming border. For unknown reasons that might pique your curiosity, it carries an alternate name of Queer Lake. The other is essentially a wide-water lake on a tributary of the East Fork of Bear Creek above Jardine. This latter Castle Lake was initially called Knox Lake by Dick Randall of the famous OTO Ranch. (see Knox Lake) For unstated reasons, the Board on Geographic Names changed the name of this lake to Castle in 1957. It is still referred to as Knox Lake on Montana Fish, Wildlife and Parks documents, and the National Geographic hiking map of 2013 calls it Knox Lake as well. The trail that goes by it is labeled the Knox Lake Trail on the USGS map, so the history is still preserved, if somewhat bypassed for this common name.

Castle Mountain is the third-highest peak in Montana at 12,625 feet. With 2,000-foot walls on three side that give the "castle" appearance, the name becomes clear, especially when approached from Sundance Pass. It is on a ridge on the Castle Mountain quad along with **Castle Rock Spire, Castle Rock Mountain,** Snowbank Mountain, and Summit Mountain. This is important because these names are like shuffled cards. Castle Rock Spire is over 12,400 feet, and its narrow, spire-like shape and location between Castle and Castle Rock Mountains gives it the name. Not to be too comfortable, the Spire is on the flat plateau that has been called Rainbow Peak by some. That name is not recognized by the USGS, which has the entire summit as Castle Rock Spire. Today's Castle Mountain was first named Sundance Mountain, which is now the next mountain to the northeast. This explains why Sundance Glacier is on the northwest slope of Castle Mountain and quite some distance from Sundance Mountain. Confused? How about if we add that Castle Rock Mountain was once named Summit Mountain, and Summit was Castle Rock Mountain, although the current Summit Mountain is well west of Castle Rock Spire on the other side of Snowbank Mountain. Anyway, look at your topo map. What you see today are the official names.

Castle Rock Glacier sits, appropriately, on the south slope of that mountain. Unlike the peaks, it has not changed position, but it was once caller Hopper Glacier for the locusts embedded in it.

The two **Castle Rocks** are somewhere else entirely. One is on Arrow Peak, overlooking Mill Creek near Chico Hot Springs. There is also a Castle Rock with a campground and primitive launch on the Stillwater River near Beehive. This is just outside of the national forest, and the name comes from a large square cliff that looks like a medieval castle looming over the river.

Cat Creek

There are three members of the feline family in our forest, the lynx, *Lynx canadensis*, the mountain lion, *Puma concolor*, and the bobcat, *Lynx rufus*. It is not stated which cat frequented this creek in the Telephone Basin/ Buffalo Creek area, but since the bobcat is the mascot of Montana State University in nearby Bozeman, that is who will be given the credit and whose image you see here.

Bobcat, Grand Teton. NATIONAL PARK SERVICE.

Cataract Lake

This lake is actually a widening in Falls Creek. Which Falls Creek, you might ask; there are five of them. Well, it is the Falls Creek that flows northeast off Twin Peaks to the Stillwater River. This lake was once called Falls Creek Lake, of which there also have been several, so the name change to the more unique Cataract seems an appropriate synonym.

Cathedral Creek/Mountain/Point

The Point rises some 600 feet off the southeast ridge of **Cathedral Mountain** where Flood Creek enters the Stillwater River. The tall, vertical granite looks remarkably like the towers and flying buttresses of the great cathedrals of Europe.

Cathedral Creek flows off the north slope of the mountain to the West Fork of the Stillwater.

Cavity Lake

This little round hole is a bit of the dental humor found on several other lakes' names. It is close to Incisor Lake and is found near Little Goose Lake on the Little Park Mountain quad.

Cedar Creek

The only true cedar found in Montana is the western red cedar, *Thuja plicata*. This is a huge tree that requires wet soil and is only found in any numbers in the northwestern part of the state. The Trail of the Cedars near Apgar on the west side of Glacier National Park has excellent examples. What is incorrectly, but commonly, called a "cedar" in this part of Montana is the Rocky Mountain juniper, *Juniperus scopulorum*. Generally a shrub, it can grow to 35 feet and is found on dry, rocky, open sites throughout Montana. The overlapping scaly leaves and the oily scent resemble that of the true cedar.

The creek is found just to the south of Yankee Jim Canyon, with Dick Randall Point overlooking it. Rangers' notes from the 1930s state that the name came from "the abundance of Cedar Growth in the early days."

The name is quite obvious, but the creek holds an important place in Montana and dude ranching history. Around 1890 James N. "Pretty Dick" Randall started wintering his Yellowstone Park horses on this creek where Al Joliff and Ben Blakeslee had their mountain valley claim. In the spring of 1898, Dick and his wife, Dora, bought out their squatters' rights, as well as some homesteads and railroad land for a total of 5,000 acres, which he used to create the OTO Ranch. Originally a hunting camp, by 1910 it evolved into what Randall claimed was the first true dude ranch in the country. He had a hydroelectric plant on Cedar Creek, a large main lodge, 12 cabins, a post office, and a general store. Seriously affected by the Great Depression, it was sold in 1934 to Chan Libby, a former guest, but dude ranching ceased in 1939. After a period as a cattle operation, it was acquired by the Rocky Mountain Elk Foundation in a land swap after the Fires of 1988, and they donated it to the Gallatin National Forest. Falling into disrepair, the ranch buildings have recently been restored by volunteers and achieved its listing on the National Register of Historic Places in 1998. By 2004 it had reopened for public visits. (see Dick Randall Point)

Chain Creek/Lakes

Chain Creek is on the Montana/Wyoming border south of Red Lodge and drains a chain, or series, of lakes in Wyoming.

The **Chain Lakes** are also in Wyoming, but quite separate from the creek as they are farther west. This chain is another series of lakes along Canyon Creek as it flows south of the Beartooth Highway from Long Lake.

Chalice Peak/Lakes

The name was applied in 1940 to this peak on the Tumble Mountain quad because, as the forest supervisor wrote to the USGS, "The east side of this peak is hollowed out forming a huge bowl... awesome in proportion. The two small lakes at the head of Rabbit Gulch lie within this bowl." Since a chalice is a large cup or goblet, typically used for drinking wine, the peak's bowl-like shape was thought to look like one—built for giants.

Charlie Falls

In 1962 the Forest Service decided to extend the East Rosebud Trail past Duggan Lake and on up to Fossil Lake. The problem was Impasse Falls, whose steep granite walls blocked the route and required a three-year job blasting the trail. A construction camp was assembled at the base of these nearby falls, which were named for Forest Service employee Charlie Martin, who led the first crew.

Charlie White Lake

Charlie was a "half-breed" Indian trapper and was a noted character in Gardiner around 1900. References to him appear on a mining claim at the Homestake Lode in the New World Mining District near Cooke City in 1889 as well as communications in the Yellowstone National Park archives when he served as a scout in 1897–1898. This lake in the Buffalo Creek drainage at the head of the North Fork of Horse Creek near Jardine was named for him.

Cherry Creek

The creek on the Ross Canyon quad south of Big Timber was named for the chokecherry, *Prunus virginiana*. This streamside shrub is found throughout the northern Rocky Mountains and was the most important fruit in many Native American tribes' diets. It is still collected to make jams, jellies, or syrup. However, the bitter flavor of the fruit requires a great deal of sugar to sweeten the preserves for modern tastes.

Chokecherry blossom on the Stillwater. PHOTO BY THE AUTHOR.

Black-capped chickadee, Algonquin Provincial Park. WIKI CREATIVE COMMONS.

Chickadee Lake

This little lake is located on the Lake Plateau in the same basin as Mirror Lake.

It is currently unnamed by the USGS but is found on older hiking maps and is mentioned in the Montana Fish, Wildlife and Parks 2016 *Mountain Lakes Guide.*

The chickadee, *Poecile tricapillus*, is a common North American bird in the tit family that lives in forest environments. These small birds are comfortable around humans, and those that are particularly bold can be induced to eat seeds right from your hand. Their name reputedly comes from the fact that their calls make a distinctive "chick-a-dee-dee-dee."

Chicken Creek

This tributary of the West Rosebud was named for the grouse that are so common in our mountains. Grouse are of the Order *Galliformis*, the same as the barnyard chicken, which they resemble. (see Grouse Creek)

Chico Hot Springs/Peak

The peak overlooking Chico Hot Springs was originally called Baldy, and that name and Chico Peak continued to be used off and on for some years. (see Baldy citation) The Baldy name came from the miners of the late 1800s because of the distinctive summit whose trees had been felled for timber for the town and mines. In 1990 the Board on Geographic Names settled on Chico Peak, which is probably appropriate as the trees on the summit have regrown and it is no longer bald.

The original mining settlement, Yellowstone City, now Old Chico, was abandoned around 1867 as it was unsafe due to Indian troubles. The settlement was moved out to the area around the hot springs and needed a name. Coincidentally a prospecting party came by that had a young Mexican in it. His pleasant personality and good humor made him well liked by the miners, so they named the town Chico after him.

There was a post office at Chico from 1874 to 1919, and a school that was started in 1877 but abandoned in 1955 when the mining had died out and the town's population dropped. The hot springs opened to the public in 1883 and became the focus of the area in 1902 with a hotel and plunge pools, and in 1910 Dr. George Townsend transformed the hotel into a 24-bed hospital where he performed surgery and treated polio victims. It became a dude ranch in the 1950s and is now a popular spa, hotel, and dining facility.

Chimney Rock

This spire on Henderson Mountain near Daisy Pass resembles a chimney. It does not draw very well, however.

Chippy Creek

The flat area on the Boulder River in the Boulder Mining District became known as Chippy Park in the late 1800s when brothels sprang up to service the thousand or so miners that swarmed the area. The prostitutes were known as "Chippys," which was derived from the chips paid as tender by some of the mining companies.

Chippy Park now is the site of a USFS campground of that name. It is a nice location along the Main Boulder River, and one can imagine where the brothels stood in the late 1800s, but no sign of the mining camp structures remains.

In the 1940s the U.S. Forest Service tried to rename East and West Chippy Creeks with the more polite names of Bobcat and Weasel. Locals would have none of that and those names didn't catch on. The Board on Geographic Names confirmed East and West Chippy Creek in 1980.

Chrome Mountain/Creek/Lake

The mountain overlooks the Boulder River and was named for the vast amount of chromite ore, an oxide of chromium, found there. The chromite vein is a mile wide and 30 miles long and extends all the way over to the Stillwater and Black Butte where T.C. "Chalky" Benbow originally discovered the ore in 1883. (See the Benbow Mine) The find was extensive but extraction was delayed because of financial and Crow Reservation issues. Full-scale mining at the Benbow was started in 1905, and the works on Chrome Mountain began in earnest with the need for that metal during World War I.

During peace time, things went dormant as chromite was available more cheaply from foreign, particularly African, sources.

Chrome Lake and its creek are located on Black Butte below the Benbow Mine. During World War II a large camp called Lake Camp was built here. It housed over 900 workers and their families in 100 homes and 8 dormitories, and boasted a school, mess hall, and a recreation center with a bowling alley. The ore was stockpiled for the war effort, as it was needed to reinforce steel for armor coating for tanks and planes. Everything was shut down after the war and all of the buildings were removed.

Cimmerian Lake

The Cimmerians are mentioned in Homer's *Odyssey* in the eighth century BC. The actual people were probably of Pontic origins from north of the Black Sea and were noted to be at war with the Assyrians from 714 to 619 BC. However, the Homeric Kimmerioi were said to be living beyond Oceanus near the entrance to Hades in a land of fog and darkness at the edge of the world.

The forest supervisor's note to the USGS in 1940 says, "This lake lies at the bottom of the Flood Creek gorge, it is bounded on all sides by high rock walls and peaks, due to this fact it gives the appearance of being black and gloomy. This is further added to by the presence of tall dark spruce around its margins. It has the appearance of being the abode of unnatural beings."

Cirque Lake

In geologic terms, a cirque is a half-open steep-sided hollow at the head of a valley or on a mountainside. It is formed by glacial erosion.

This lake is at the head of the Middle Fork of Wounded Man Creek, and, with mountain walls on three sides, it is clearly in a cirque.

Cladocera Lake

The fisheries biologists had a heyday up in this basin in the Sierra Creek drainage south of Castle Rock Mountain. Copepod Lake is just to the east of this lake, and Fish, Shrimp, and Snail Lakes are nearby.

Cladocera is an Order of small crustaceans that are commonly called water fleas. There are over 600 recognized species that are ubiquitous in inland freshwater habitats. The tiny critters, a type of plankton, are little specks, with most ranging from 0.2 to 6.0 mm. They are an important food source for fish.

Leptodora kindii, Cladocera. PHOTO BY A. MILNES MARSHALL, WIKI CREATIVE COMMONSS.

Clam Lake

Another of the lakes named for the creatures within, this is at the head of the Flood Creek drainage in the Stillwater country.

Clarks Creek

Clarks Creek flows from the north slope of Wolf Mountain and drains Wolf Glacier and Wolf Voice Lake before joining the Stillwater River at its upper end.

There is no report of a miner or homesteader on this creek, either by first or last name. One possibility is a James W. Clark who was known to be mining out of Cooke City from 1888 to 1994 and at Crevasse in 1896. The road from Cooke City to Goose Lake comes close to the mines at Wolf Mountain (see Wolf Mountain and Lake Vernon), so if his prospecting took him a bit north, this stream could easily have been named for him.

However, lacking a person, it is also possible that this stream was named for Clark's nutcracker, *Nucifraga columbiana*. In any case, this ambiguity gives a good reason to introduce this cousin to the crow that is common to the high alpine forests. Like other members of the Corvid family, it spends its summers gathering and hiding food. Because its primary food is the pine nut, this bird has developed a mutual relationship with the whitebark pine. The cones of the whitebark do not open spontaneously, and the tree depends on birds and animals, like grizzlies and nutcrackers, to spread its seeds.

Clarks Nutcracker. DRAWING BY ALEXANDER WILSON CA. 1810.

It is estimated that this bird, whose beak is designed to open the cones, will gather and bury between 30,000 and 100,000 seeds each summer. It remembers where most of them are hidden, and these are used for winter food and for feeding their chicks in the spring. Those that were forgotten will germinate and help the pines spread.

Clarks Fork

In 1806, during their return trip from the Pacific, Lewis and Clark split up before reuniting where the Missouri and Yellowstone Rivers converge. Lewis went north up the Missouri looking for a possible easier route to the Columbia River, while Clark's group explored the Yellowstone River. On July 24, William Clark's party passed by this southern fork of the Yellowstone where they saw "a large council lodge... where all danc, [*sic*]" and he named it for himself.

William Clark, 1810. PORTRAIT BY CHARLES WILSON PEALE.

Probably reflecting their activities at this location, the Crow Indians called it Lodge River or Rotten Sun Dance River.

It originates on the east side of Colter Pass near Cooke City in the Absaroka-Beartooth Wilderness then enters the rugged canyon country of Wyoming where it is further protected by Wild and Scenic River status. Swinging around the mountains, it finally turns north and returns to Montana near Belfry and joins the Yellowstone near the present city of Laurel.

Although there was much gold prospecting in the area surrounding the Clarks Fork, there was little along this river itself, because the placer gold is so fine that it makes recovery very difficult.

Claw Lake

Claw Lake, which looks like a hand in profile held in a claw position, sits between Echo and Grayling Lakes north of Beartooth Butte. It is the recommended camping stop on the loop trail that starts at Beartooth Lake and goes from the Beauty Lake Trail to the Beartooth Creek Trail. Claw Lake has an entire chapter in Bill Schneider's book, *Hiking the Beartooth Wilderness,* but the name is not recognized by the USGS or mentioned on any other maps.

Clay Butte

Clay Butte is in Wyoming, just outside of the Absaroka-Beartooth Wilderness. It is near the Beartooth Highway and next to Beartooth Butte. Its "clay" is derived from erosion of the same fossil-filled limestone that is found on that butte.

In 1942 the CCC built a lookout on top of the butte that served as a fire watchtower until the 1960s when aircraft assumed that chore. The lookout is now a visitor information center with a "grandiose" view and is just a short dirt road drive off the Beartooth Highway.

Clear Creek

This creek on the Mount Douglas quad was, not surprisingly, noted by the rangers in the 1930s to have its name because of the clearness of the water. It is a tributary of the Main Boulder.

Cliff Lake

Cliff Lake is near Washtub Lake in a basin north of the Broadwater River in the Sky Top drainage. Where the name comes from is a mystery as the basin is not particularly steep walled. Pat Marcuson, a Montana fisheries biologist says, "If Cliff Lake is supposed to be a reflection of the area's geology, then it's poorly named. The shoreline has numerous islands but no cliffs."

Clover Creek/Basin

There is a **Clover Creek** with an attendant **Clover Basin** at the headwaters of the North Fork of Hellroaring Creek north of Yellowstone Park. Another Clover Creek can be found in the northernmost part of the Custer-Gallatin National Forest south of Elk Mountain on the Enos Mountain quad.

Clover, of the genus *Trifolium,* are plants of the pea family that have a worldwide distribution. Native clovers such as deer clover, *Trifolium nanum* and longstalked clover, *Trifolium longipes,* can be found throughout the West. However, most of the clover that is seen, red clover, *Trifolium pratense*, white clover, *Trifolium repens*, yellow clover, *Melilotus officinalis*, and alfalfa, *Meticago sativa,* are foreign plants that were introduced as crops for fodder. They arrive in our mountains after the hay is processed through the intestines of horses.

Cloverleaf Lakes

Clover is of the genus *Trifolium*, meaning "three leaf" in Latin, and these three similar-sized lakes on the Beartooth Plateau look like a clover leaf on the map.

Apparently unsympathetic to anglers, the proposal to call them No Luck Lakes was denied by the Board on Geographic Names in 1975.

Coffee Pot Creek

This is a common name for creeks in western Montana and refers to the boiling sound made as the water bubbles over the rocks. It is a tributary of the West Fork of Mill Creek.

Cold Creek/Lake

Cold Creek flows north into the West Rosebud. **Cold Lake** is above Mystic Lake and is also in the West Rosebud country. Appropriate to its name, the lake is near Froze-to-Death Plateau and the Snowball Lakes and is not recommended for swimming.

Cole Creek

The *Red Lodge Picket* reported that gold prospectors were active on Cole Creek in the 1880s. The name comes from a John W. Cole who came a bit later. He patented his homestead on this creek near Red Lodge in 1895 and ran a sheep operation.

Colley Creek/Lake

Colley Creek can be found up along Mill Creek at the end of Snowbank Road near the former spa at Montanapolis. The lake is close by but is said to have not been generally known prior to 1930.

It was named for J.A. "Josh" Colley, who was an early settler in what was then big sheep grazing country. He was first listed as a "claimant" in this locality by the U.S. Forest Service in 1909. In addition to sheep, Colley supplemented his ranching efforts by working for Billy Carr at his Hy-Grade Mine on nearby Balm of Gilead Creek in the Mill Creek Mining District. (see White City and Balm of Gilead Creek)

Colter Pass

John Colter, 1915. WATERCOLOR BY EDGAR PAXSON.

John Colter (ca. 1770–1813) was one of the great mountain men. He first came west with the Lewis and Clark Corps of Discovery in 1804–1806 but left that group just before they got back to St. Joseph, Missouri, returning upriver to trap. He is probably best known for his exploration of 1807–1808 of the region around Yellowstone Park. His tales of hot pools and geysers were discounted as "tall tales" and gave rise to the nickname of the area as "Colter's Hell." There is no confirmation, but it is thought that his route from Jackson Hole in the Tetons went north up the west shore of Yellowstone Lake to the Lamar Valley and Soda Butte Creek. From there he was supposed to have gone over this pass to the Clarks Fork and on to the Crow camp in Sunlight Basin.

In 1951, W.K. Cadman, a petroleum geologist, backed by the residents of Cooke City, proposed that this pass on the Beartooth Highway just east of town, formerly known as Cooke Pass, be named for Colter. Since this mountain man was only commemorated by Colter Peak, an inaccessible mountain south of the Park's southeast corner, the suggestion was accepted by the Board on Geographic Names.

Columbine Peak/Pass/Lake/Creek

Columbine. PHOTO BY JULIE G. TEST, NATIONAL PARK SERVICE.

All of these features were named by the district forester in 1923 because of the profusion of columbine flowers found in the area. Columbine Peak, Lake and Creek are east of Independence and Baboon Mountain in the drainage of the East Fork of the Boulder River. The trail over the pass heads east to Wounded Man Creek and the Stillwater.

Columbine, *Aquilegia*, is a genus common in our mountains and is known for the spurred petals on the flower. The term *Aquilegia* is derived from the Latin name for "eagle" because the flower petals are said to resemble an eagle's claw. On a more peaceful note, the word columbine dervives from the Latin word for "dove," as the inverted flower is said to resemble five doves clustered together. I guess the true derivation depends on the day and how feisty you feel.

Comet Lake

Neither Comet Lake nor nearby Asteroid Lake in the Flood Creek chain in Stillwater County was named on the 1943 USGS Mount Douglas quad map. The astronomy buff who is responsible for these names must have been a more recent visitor.

Companion Lake

The "companion" of this lake is not specified, but the easy access and many campsites by the lake make it a good place for you and your companion. It can be found north of Cooke City along the Goose Lake jeep trail where it is a neighbor of Long Lake.

Conant Creek

This creek that joins the Boulder River was named for the Conant family. They came to Montana in 1877 and settled here along the river in 1885. References to the family in the *Big Timber Pioneer* continue until 1914.

Conlin Gulch

John "Jack" Conlin (1873–1964) operated a sawmill and herded sheep in this gulch near Emigrant, so it was named for him. He came to Chico in 1899 to soak in the hot springs to treat his rheumatoid arthritis. Initially boarding with Percie Keough, he married Maude Keough, but that marriage ended in divorce after she switched her affection to his best friend, a Mr. McAllister. In 1904, Jack married Annie Lorne DeVoe and they had eight children. Although he had originally homesteaded up this gulch, when the sawmill business failed they moved and built the largest building in Old Chico, the Conlin Saloon and Boarding House. His children, Arthur and Ruth, ran the ranch until 1981.

Contact Creek/Mountain/Town

Contact Creek runs east from Mount Rae to enter the Main Boulder between the ghost town of Contact and the historic Main Boulder Ranger Station. **Contact Mountain** is the long ridge immediately to the east of the town on the east side of the Main Boulder River.

The name Contact comes from the fact that two mineral deposits, one of quartz and the other of limestone, meet at the mountain.

The mining **town of Contact** sprang up along the Main Boulder in 1887. Among the many miners were Antonio Drago and Hector McRae, who in 1893 developed their Minnie Mine in a vein of quartz "fairly glistening with native gold." The town not only served the local miners but was a stage stop midway between Big Timber and the mines and town of Independence farther south up the river. Contact had a school in 1887 and a post office in A.B. Gould's Halfway House hotel. There was also a livery and Joe Keeney's Bucket of Blood Saloon. (see Basin Creek and Independence) Keeney purchased a ranch from Sam Cowen in 1896 that became "Gould's Resort," a dude ranch that opened in 1900. Later called Ol' Kaintuck, it was sold to Walter Aller in 1918, who changed the name again to the more Montana-sounding Boulder River Ranch, which is still in operation. The post office closed in 1935, and all that can be found of the town today is the remains of a root cellar and a barn for the Minnie Mine.

Contact appears as an area on the USGS maps, and they still list the school (Historic). However, as one drives the Main Boulder River Road, the only buildings seen now are modern homes and ranch buildings. The town's former location can easily be observed from the road in a flat hayfield between the river and the road, but it is all private land with no trespassing signs. There is no evidence now of the mining town and its wild hotel and saloon.

Cooke City

Cooke City was located at the southern edge of the New World Mining District and is now at the western end of the Beartooth Highway and serves as the gateway city to the Northeast Entrance to Yellowstone National Park.

Mining started in 1870, and the place was variously called Miner's Camp, Clark Fork City, Edelweiss, and Shoo-Fly (after a nearby mine). However, the high cost of transporting coal and processed ore to and from its Republic Smelter limited profits, so local townsfolk looked to get a railroad connection. Jay Cooke Jr., son of the financier of the Northern Pacific Railway, visited the town on a trip to the Park and pledged $5,000 for the development. The town was then named for the Cooke family in further hopes of getting the railroad. The pledge was never delivered, and the failure of Jay Cooke and Co. and the loss of the railroad to Henry

Jay Cooke. WIKI CREATIVE COMMONS.

Villard put an end to that. Furthermore, opposition in Congress prohibited the proposed rail line up the Lamar Valley in Yellowstone National Park, the only reasonably buildable route, so the bonanza dwindled.

In 1885 Cooke City was recorded as having 135 log cabins, two smelters, three general stores, two sawmills, two livery stables, a meat market, two hotels, and 15 saloons. The population never exceeded 2,000 people and is now primarily a winter and summer recreation destination with a population around 200.

Copeland Lake/Mountain

Copeland Lake is immediately north of the Montana/Wyoming border between Granite and Widewater Lakes.

Frederick Kirk Copeland. EMILY COPELAND FAMILY PHOTOGRAPH.

It was named by Lawrence Nordquist of the L bar T Ranch for Frederick Kirk Copeland, a Chicago businessman. In the early 1920s Copeland and his friend, William Sidley, came to Cody, Wyoming, for a summer pack trip. The outfitter failed to show up, and a bartender referred them to the young Nordquist who was just starting in the business. A lifelong friendship developed, and in 1924 Copeland and Sidley helped him buy the L bar T Ranch, on the Clarks Fork just into Wyoming. In thanks, Nordquist gave them each 15 deeded acres and a cabin, and named this lake, which is on the route of one of his pack trips, after Copeland. The cabins remain in the Copeland family five generations later. (see Lake Elaine and Gilbert Creek)

There is also a **Copeland Mountain,** a 9,200-foot rise south of the old L bar T Ranch between Blacktail and Squaw Creeks. A brass plaque was placed near the summit in August 1929 that reads, "In memory of Frederick Kent Copeland who loved and understood this country. 1855–1928." The mountain's name is not recognized by the USGS but looms prominent for the local residents.

Copepod Lake

Our fisheries biologist has been at it again! (see Cladocera Lake) This is another of those aquatic critter lakes in the Sierra Creek drainage on the Castle Mountain quad. It was named officially in 1991.

Harpaticoid copepod. PHOTO BY H. LIMIN, WIKI CREATIVE COMMONS.

Copepod means "oar feet" and describes a group of tiny crustaceans that look like wee shrimp. Found in the oceans and in almost every freshwater habitat, they are typically only 1 to 2 mm in size. You may be drinking them without knowing it—they are harmless, and delicious to the trout.

Copper Creek

Copper Creek was originally named for the mineral found in this watershed. It is a tributary of the Boulder River and was used in the 1930s as a stock driveway for sheep en route to the Hell Roaring country.

Cora Creek

This small, currently unnamed stream on Mount Wood runs from Wood Lake to Lake Wildness where it joins Woodbine Creek to flow to the Beartooth Ranch and the Stillwater River. However, it has been called Cora Creek by the locals in the Nye area for more than a century. Wood Lake, where it begins, was named for Byron Wood, who started his ranch in the 1890s and ran until 1921. Cora was Byron's wife. Her creek certainly deserves to formally carry her name. (see Woodbine Creek and Beartooth Ranch)

Corker Canyon

William Corker was murdered in 1892 near his home on Bovee Creek, which is next to this canyon. He was more than a bit of trouble with his cabin illegally on the Crow Reservation, and he first came to the attention of the news when he ran off with a Miss Kimberline. Her mother swore out a warrant for his arrest for "abduction," but they were able to get married before getting caught. He had been in jail in Livingston for horse stealing shortly before his murder and had long had the attention of Sheriff Oliver P. Templeton, who had once said that "you are going to find that fellow shot full of holes some day."

On the day of the murder, Corker went out after some horses. When he didn't return, his wife went looking for him and found the body with five bullet holes. The mail carrier, "Happy Jack" Aldrich, located the ambush site and an unusual horseshoe print that implicated the Kearns brothers. They were caught and tried but were acquitted, probably on the basis of Corker's reputation. (see Bohee Creek)

Corkscrew Lake/Creek, Upper Corkscrew Lake

Corkscrew Creek, just to the west of Little Park Mountain, makes a twisting descent from the lakes to the Stillwater River.

Corner Lake

This triangular-shaped lake is located along the Goose Lake jeep trail north of Cooke City. It is in a shapely area as it sits near Round and Long Lakes.

Corral Creek

The land around the Absaroka-Beartooths is stockman's country, so finding corrals to hold cattle and horses is no surprise. There are two Corral Creeks. One is in Sweet Grass County in the north. The other is near Red Lodge and Mount Maurice to the east.

Corwin Springs

Dr. F.E. Fred Corwin was the resident physician employed at Chico Hot Springs starting in 1902. In 1909 he, along with a consortium of others, acquired the rights to the hot water from the recently closed LaDuke Spring south of Chico and built a 72-room Mission-style hotel and spa. It had all of the latest accoutrements like steam heat, hot and cold running water, electric lights, and a telephone in every room. A bridge across the Yellowstone River made it accessible to Northern Pacific Railway passengers, and it had a brief period of success. However, Dr. Corwin left for Hunter's Hot Springs near Springdale, Montana, in 1912 and the building burned down in 1916.

Railroad magnate J.J. Hill's son Walter bought the property in the 1920s and rebuilt the pool and bathhouse and added cabins, a dance hall, a restaurant, and a 9-hole golf course and renamed it the Eagle's Nest Dude Ranch. This closed in the 1940s and the buildings were razed by the new owners in 1981.

In 2018 the pool was reconstructed and reopened to the public in March of 2019 as Yellowstone Hot Springs. It still uses the hot water piped over from LaDuke Spring. (see LaDuke Spring)

Cottonwood Draw, Upper and Lower Cottonwood Spring/Creek

The cottonwood, *Populus trichocarpa*, is one of the primary deciduous trees in Montana. It is a close cousin to the quaking aspen, which prefers dry slopes, while the cottonwood is found close to water. Because it is so common and is found streamside, the name is ubiquitous on streams throughout Montana.

Cottonwood Draw and **Springs** are found near Nye. **Cottonwood** and **Little Cottonwood Creeks** flow south into Yellowstone National Park on the Specimen Creek quad. (see Cottonwood Creek in the Crazies section)

Counts Creek

This creek by Mill Creek was named for Floyd Counts. He first came to Emigrant in 1890 where he filed his first mining claim in the Mill Creek District and also mined Emigrant Gulch. He established his ranch on Mill Creek and had a mine at the head of Arrastra Creek.

The Counts name has been associated with Emigrant since its earliest days, with numerous Counts in the area. The first was John J., a Confederate veteran who was wounded at the Second Manassas (Bull Run). He came west in 1865 and settled at Yellowstone City (Old Chico), and filed claims in Emigrant Gulch in 1874 and 1881. John later moved to a ranch on the Yellowstone River south of Chico. Many other Counts followed him, and all were from the same area around Stratton, Virginia. Floyd was mentioned above, and Abraham Kester "Kes" Counts settled on the East Fork of Mill Creek. Dewey did placer mining in Emigrant Gulch and worked at the Maxey Mine. Garland worked for the Northern Pacific Railroad on the Emigrant section along the Yellowstone. Gool came out

Kester Counts. YELLOWSTONE GATEWAY MUSEUM, 2011.021.0025.

from Virginia as well, and Lundy Counts arrived in Old Chico in 1939, but it was Floyd for whom the creek was named.

Courthouse Mountain/Lake

Like many other mountains thought to look like a giant's building, the shape of this one near Cooke City is said to resemble a courthouse. The lake is in a long basin below the southeast wall of the mountain.

Mount Cowen

Mount Cowen is south of Livingston Peak at the head of the West Boulder River. According to forest ranger Harry Kaufman, it was named by Ferdinand Hayden for the assistant secretary of the interior, Gen. Benjamin Rush Cowen (1831–1908), who served under Secretary Columbus Delano and President U.S. Grant from 1871 to 1876. He was particularly instrumental in helping to establish Yellowstone as the first national park.

Benjamin Rush Cowen, ca. 1898. *HISTORY OF THE REPUBLICAN PARTY IN OHIO.*

There are several erroneous historical reports, even those in government publications, that say that this mountain was named for one of the pioneer families of the Upper Yellowstone Valley or for a George Cowen, an attorney from Radersburg, Montana. The latter was a Yellowstone tourist in 1877 who was shot and nearly killed by the Nez Perce in their flight across the Park. The name, however, appears on Hayden's 1871 map, well before the Nez Perce trek. The pioneer Cowen family didn't appear in the Paradise Valley until even later, about 1888.

On a more amusing note, climber Conrad Anker of Bozeman calls the set of spires on the north end of Mount Cowen, Eenie, Meenie, Miney, and Moe, as they look like a giant's toes.

Coyote Creek

There are two creeks of this name. One flows into Yellowstone National Park on the Specimen Creek quad. The other, on the Needles quad east of Mill Creek and the Paradise Valley, was said by Ranger L.P. McKnight to be a favorite haunt of the coyote.

The coyote, *Canis latrans,* is a common carnivore that has adapted well to humans. Smaller than a wolf, it loses in direct competition with its larger cousin. Wolves and coyotes were both seen as pests by the early white settlers and were shot, trapped, and poisoned. Wolves became extinct in Montana by the

Coyote along the Madison. PHOTO BY JACOB W. FRANK, NATIONAL PARK SERVICE.

mid-twentieth century, but coyotes have expanded their range and are thought to be much more numerous than they were when Lewis and Clark came through. Coyotes live in family units or loosely knit packs, and being carnivores generally feed on smaller prey such as rabbits and rodents. Like its cousin the wolf, it also has a characteristic howl.

Cradle Lake

It is said that this deep, cold lake is "cradled in a small alpine valley" in the Red Rock drainage between Lake of the Clouds and Lake of the Winds.

Crandall Creek

Jack Crandall was one of the early prospectors along the northern border of what is now Yellowstone National Park. He brought the first news of gold to Bozeman in 1869 and was probably the one who inspired Adam "Horn" Miller to prospect in the Cooke City area in what became the productive New World Mining District.

He was first at Crevice Creek in 1867, and in 1869, not doing as well as he had hoped, organized a party to prospect the northern Yellowstone area. Crandall and a man called Daugherty stayed over in the Lamar area when the others returned to the Upper Yellowstone to resupply. A party of about 20 men including "Horn" Miller and Frederick Bottler were supposed to meet them back on the upper river. When Crandall and Daugherty did not show up, Bottler began a search and found them near this creek southeast of Cooke City, killed by Indians. Their heads were stuck on the points of their picks and their tin cups were placed in front of them, apparently indicating they were surprised while eating. The headless bodies were nearby, eaten by coyotes. Crandall and Daugherty's graves are by this creek and behind the Kaple family's cabin. Their murders were later used as an excuse to remove all of the Sheepeater Shoshoni Indians from the Park.

When traversing the Park in 1877 en route to find the Crow and to avoid the U.S. Army, the Nez Perce disappeared for 10 days. It is thought by historians trying to reconstruct their route that they went out of the Park by way of Crandall Creek.

Crane Lake

The sandhill crane, *Antigone canadensis*, is so named for its habit of stopping during its migration in the Sand Hills of Nebraska. These large birds can be up to 4½ feet tall with a 7½-foot wingspan. They commonly nest in Montana in late spring, and are quite distinctive with their loud clacking call, and in flying with their long necks stretched ahead, their legs trailing behind. It is the bird's long neck that gives us the term "to crane your neck."

Lesser sandhill crane.

Crane Lake is near Beauty Lake on the Beartooth Plateau in Wyoming and just north of Beartooth Butte.

Crazy Mountain/Lakes/Creek

These features all get their names from the **creek,** which has a wild descent from the lakes into the Clarks Fork in Wyoming. Although some locals report that it was once named Crazy Woman Creek for a "weird" woman who lived nearby, its particularly crazy fall as it passes the Beartooth Highway, U.S. 212, attests to the official reason for the name. **Crazy Lake** itself is a widening of the creek that sits just south of the Montana/Wyoming border in the Absaroka-Beartooth Wilderness. The other Crazy Lakes in the chain are the Fox, Widewater, Big Moose, and Ivy, which are found just to the west of **Crazy Mountain.**

The section of the stream that is in Montana is now known as Farley Creek but was once called the East Fork of Crazy Creek. (see Farley Lake/Creek for these name changes)

Crescent Creek/Lake

Crescent Lake is tucked up against a crescent-shaped cliff along with the other Hellroaring Lakes. Its drainage is via an unnamed stream into Hellroaring Creek, in the Rock Creek drainage.

Crescent Creek is on the Stillwater. It joins that river after a wide crescent-shaped course near Iron Mountain and Creek.

Crevice Mountain/Creek/Lake

The 1867 prospecting party that contained Ansel Hubble, Lou Anderson, George W. Reese, William Simms, and a Caldwell found gold in a rock crevice at the mouth of this stream, the first major creek on the Yellowstone River above Bear Gulch. Hubble named it Crevice Gulch, but Ferdinand Hayden's 1871 map made it **Crevice Creek** and that is now official. It has been commonly misspelled Crevasse, and, although Crevice is proper according to the USGS, Crevasse is still used by some Montana state agencies. The Gardiner theater is called "The Crevasse Players," and Yellowstone National Park used Crevasse for the ranger station it situated on the creek to deter mining in the Park. One must wonder why they used Crevasse, because it was named for a crevice in the rock and not a gap in glacial ice.

That Crevasse Ranger Station was important to deter prospecting because mining this rich stream within the Park boundary was a problem. The creek originates in the mountains north of the Park, so the miners naturally followed the placer gold south into the Park. Tom Miner, whose basin is on the west side of the Paradise Valley, had a mine here. He left Montana in disgust when the army kicked him out of the Park and closed his mine. Zackwell "Red" Sowash, one of the early prospectors on this creek, also mined in the Park. He later built a saloon near Cooke City but that, too, was found to be in the Park and, along with Red, was "removed."

Crevice Lake is close to the Yellowstone River, a bit east of the creek. It was once known as Knowles Lake for a John S. Knowles. (see Knowles Falls) He came in 1876 to mine Emigrant Gulch but moved to a cabin on Crevice Creek. There he was said to have made a strike worth $40,000, but he also was evicted by the army. Rangers began calling the lake Crevice Lake in the 1920s and that is now official.

Crevice Mountain is in Montana north of the Park and was named for the creek and gulch that it overlooks. The gulch was worked as a placer strike, but Crevice Mountain's gold quartz lodes were discovered in 1879 and were worked as hardrock mines simultaneously with those in nearby Bear Gulch and Mineral Hill.

Crow Mountain/Lake

Crow Mountain is at the head of Mill Creek on the Mill Creek/Boulder River divide. It was named by Montana officials in the 1920s or 30s to honor the Crow Tribe, even though after 1883 it was no longer a part of their reservation. The name first appears on USGS maps in 1943.

The Crow were a branch of the Hidatsa, but with the coming of the horse between 1700 and 1725, they left their farming relatives on the northern plains and migrated to their present homeland that stretched from the Bighorn Basin to the Absaroka Mountains. The Hidatsa word for these people was *Apsa'alooke* (also spelled Apsaalooka or Absaroka) and is freely translated as "Children of the large-beaked bird" or Crow.

There is another **Crow Mountain,** with a **Crow Lake** to its southeast, that is found on the East Rosebud Plateau. Crow Mountain and Butcher Mountain form the basin that holds the headwaters of the northern Hellroaring Creek. Since Butcher Creek was the site of the Second Crow Agency prior to 1892, this mountain also carries the memories of that tribe.

Crown Butte

Named for the shape of the limestone cap, this butte is north of Cooke City between Daisy Pass and Chimney Rock. It was big mining country, and "Horn" Miller's cabin was located below Crown Butte.

The butte itself received an unwarranted ill name when in the 1990s the Noranda Mining Corporation called their new project the Crown Butte Mining Corporation. The plan, which received initial government approval, was to reopen the McLaren Mine on Henderson Mountain with a huge open pit operation. Public outcry against the possibility of further contamination of Soda Butte Creek and Yellowstone Park led to the 1996 settlement that ended the project. (see Soda Butte and Margaret Lake)

Crystal Creek/Lakes

These features were so named for the clarity of the water.

Crystal Creek goes into Davis Creek and on to the West Boulder.

One of the **Crystal Lakes** is found in the Sierra Creek drainage just north of the Montana/Wyoming border. The other is near Mill Creek and Emigrant.

Curl Lake

Curl Lake is a widening of the Broadwater River east of Cooke City. It was named for one of the early miners and businessmen of that town.

John F. "Johnny" Curl (1847–1924) was born in Pennsylvania and came to Montana in 1883. He was a mining partner and friend of one of the original prospectors, "Horn" Miller (see Miller Mountain), and was willed the Josephine Mine upon Horn's death. John and Zona owned the Curl House, a hotel and boardinghouse in Cooke City, and the A.O. Saloon next door. When the Top-of-the-World Road, the current Beartooth Highway, from Red Lodge, was completed in June of 1936, he opened the first gas station along the route.

When the Yellowstone fires of 1988 swept through this area, they burned the entire shoreline of this lake, leaving a lot of deadfall. Like much of that burn, the 30+ years since has greatly aided the forest's recovery.

John Curl. ELIZABETH RENNER STUDIO PORTRAIT, YELLOWSTONE GATEWAY MUSEUM, 2006.044.0833.

Cutoff Mountain/Creek

Cutoff Mountain is on the northern border of Yellowstone Park to the west of Cooke City. Its creek flows south and west into the Park to join Slough Creek.

The Montana side of the mountain has an abrupt broken or cut-off appearance with a sheer 2,200-foot drop, thus the name.

Cyclone Creek

According to O.J. Salo's report, there was a terrific windstorm around 1900 that blew through the area south of Red Lodge and Mount Maurice. It was so strong that it carried rocks and debris that killed a man at his cabin door. The area was named for this "cyclone."

Dailey Basin/Lake

The lake, the basin it sits in, and the maintenance station for the Northern Pacific Yellowstone Branch line south of Emigrant were named for the Dailey family who lived and ranched near the lake.

Ebeneezer and Katharine Dailey brought their family over the Bozeman Trail to the Paradise Valley in 1866. They stayed at Yellowstone City at the entrance to Emigrant Gulch for two years then moved on to Oregon. Returning in 1872, Ebeneezer established the Lake Ranch on what was then Duck Lake. Their sons Andrew and Samuel also proved up homesteads near Dailey Lake. Noted to be the first tourists to take wagons to see Yellowstone National Park in 1878, the family ranched at the lake until Andrew's death in 1928.

There is now a Montana state fishing access site and campground at the lake.

Andrew and Agnes Dailey, ca. 1910. YELLOW-STONE GATEWAY MUSEUM.

Daisy Pass

Daisy Pass is north of Cooke City on the shoulder of Henderson Mountain on the road to the Daisy Mine. Henry Sommerland reports that Daisy was the wife of one of the original discoverers of minerals at Cooke City, and the mine, founded in 1888, was named for her. Along with the Independence and Hidden Treasure, the Daisy was one of the main producers of gold, copper, silver, and lead in the area. The financial Panic of 1893 caused a drop in the price of silver and the Daisy, along with many other mines in the West, ceased production.

With a steady demand for a product that was perhaps more reliably profitable than mining, the little hamlet of Daisy was also noted for its several stills. Ed Sorenson continued his operation there until it was closed by Prohibition in the 1920s.

Dale Creek/Bridge

The word dale means, particularly in England, a valley, especially a broad one. This creek flows through a dale-like valley as it comes out of the hills and goes through the rolling grasslands east of Nye before joining the Stillwater River. There are no homestead or county records of a person named Dale, so the name comes from the location.

The Dale Creek bridge crosses that creek on the Nye Cemetery Road just east of the town.

Daly Lake

This lake can be found among the cluster of Hellroaring Lakes in the Rock Creek drainage west of Red Lodge.

It was probably named for either or both of the Daly brothers, William and Marcus, who were noted to be living in Red Lodge between 1900 and 1910.

East Dam Creek

East Dam Creek is a tributary of Mill Creek north of Emigrant and can be found just upstream from the former spa of Montanapolis.

After the gold in the gulches around Emigrant was exhausted by panning and ordinary rocker boxes, hydraulic sluicing was used to power-wash the gravel down to bedrock. Water was obtained from a source upstream so that gravity could deliver high pressure to the sluicing hoses. The purpose of the dam on this creek was to provide the water for those hoses.

Daphnia Lake

Another of the lakes named by the fish biologists can be found south of the Beartooth Highway and is visible from the top of the pass.

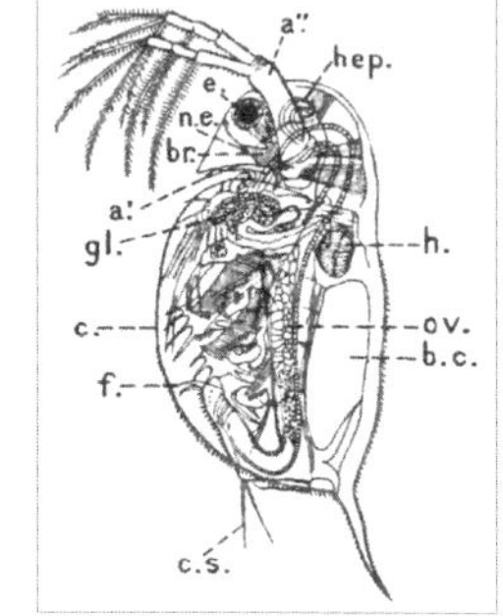

Daphnia. E. RAY LANKESTER, *TREATISE ON ZOOLOGY* 1909.

Daphnia are a genus of small planktonic crustaceans about 0.2–0.5 mm in size that form an important base of the food chain in freshwater lakes. In fact, they are even sold commercially as a live food for feeding tropical aquarium fish. They are filter feeders so cannot bite, and are often called "water fleas" because their swimming style resembles the movements of fleas. They are members of the Order Cladocera. (see Lake Cladocera)

Mount Darlene

The peak on the ridge between Castle Rock and Snowbank Mountains is not named on the USGS maps. At 12,160 feet it is the 17th-highest point in Montana, so it does appear on climbers' and peakbaggers' lists and on commercial maps of the Beartooths, some of which now call it Mount Salo. (see Spirit Mountain)

Harrison Fagg, who climbed all of the peaks over 12,000 feet, did one of the series of climbers' maps prior to the wilderness designation in 1978. Wanting to name a mountain for his wife, who had put up with all his time in the Beartooths, he chose this point. Perhaps her name will appear on future maps.

Darroch Creek

John Malcolm Darroch (1850–1932) moved to Park County from Indiana in 1893 and began ranching on Trail Creek south of Livingston. He ran up to 3,400 head of sheep and had grazing permits in the early 1890s up Big Creek on the west side of the Paradise Valley and also along this creek near Jardine. Although he only served as a senator for Park County in the Montana Legislature for one term, from 1913 to 1915, he was always called "Senator."

Senator John Darroch. YELLOWSTONE GATEWAY MUSEUM, 2006.044.1941.

Davis Creek/Gulch/Lake

Davis is a rather common name, and there were a lot of them living in the Absaroka-Beartooth country in the late nineteenth and early twentieth centuries.

One **Davis Creek** to mention is on Mill Creek near Emigrant. The first recorded settler on it was a Bill Moore, but the name of the creek comes from the Davis ranch and sawmill located there. Nothing is recorded about this Davis, but the property was purchased in the late 1880s by a James H. Lyons from Cooke City and further reference to this Davis disappears from history.

There is another **Davis Creek,** which is the right fork of Eagle Creek by Gardiner. It was named for Winifred Davis, who had a homestead there and maintained one of the early hunting lodges near Jardine.

Mount McKnight hosts a **Davis Creek** on its southeast slope. This was named for a Davis who arrived in about 1880 as the first settler in the West Boulder Canyon. **Davis Lake** sits in a beautiful setting at the head of this stream. The name of the lake is not official and is only used for reference by Montana Fish, Wildlife and Parks.

Finally, there is a **Davis Gulch,** a tributary of Deer Creek in Stillwater County near Nye. That one was named for a George Davis who homesteaded at Nye in 1910.

The Black Eyed Kid (left) and Winifred Davis (right). L.A. HUFFINGTON STUDIO, MILES CITY, MT, YELLOWSTONE GATEWAY MUSEUM, 2006.044.2599.

Dayton Cabin/Falls

Dayton Farmer was a trapper, prospector, and packer who had a cabin on the southern, or upstream, end of Sioux Charley Lake on the Stillwater River. Built in the mid-1920s on a public land lease from the forest, it was abandoned in the early 1980s, and disappeared from the maps when the structure was removed from the wilderness in 2002. He is said to have been responsible, along with his friend Ed Ickerman, for cutting many of the trails in the Absaroka-Beartooths. (see Beartooth Ranch)

An impressive waterfall a half mile up nearby Flood Creek is known by many as **Dayton Falls,** but this also is not recognized by the Board on Geographic Names and appears on no maps. Although it is only a short distance from the lake, there is no trail but requires a steep and difficult bushwhack to view it.

Like Sioux Charley Lake on whose shore the cabin sat, it is unfortunate that the USGS has removed any reference to these historical figures from the early days of the forest.

Dead Indian Creek/Hill/Spring

Dead Indian Spring is at the head of **Dead Indian Creek** and just south of the hill that carries that local name. It is in the northeast section of the Custer-Gallatin National Forest and just to the north of the Meyers Creek Ranger Station.

Although sometimes confused with Dead Indian Peak in Wyoming, which refers to an Indian fight, in fact this spring and stream were named for a humbler, if still tragic, event. Sometime in the late 1800s, a group of five Indians were chasing a small herd of elk. The elk triggered an avalanche that buried them and killed three of the party. Further confirmation of this story is seen by the fact that the lower stream to the south was called Squaw Creek. It is now Meyers Creek (see that citation) but carried the earlier name because it was the place where, for years, the women relatives of those killed would come to pray and honor them.

Deckard Flats

These flats, just east of Gardiner, were formerly called Buffalo Flats and were a place of much killing.

The area was named for Alexander Deckard, or Decker, who lived there and drove freight teams from Cooke City to the railroad at Cinnabar. Around 1900 he was thrown from a wagon full of ore and crushed to death under the wheels. His son Frank Deckard committed suicide at his cabin on the flats in 1930, apparently depressed by the government's use of eminent domain when it took his land for inclusion in the Cinnabar Triangle in Yellowstone Park.

It was also a very unhealthy place for elk. During the fall migration from the Park to the winter feeding grounds in the Paradise Valley, huge numbers were shot and killed at Deckard Flats on what was known as "the firing line."

South Fork Deep Creek

The number of Deep Creeks in Montana have not been counted, but it is huge. This one starts on Mount McKnight and flows north toward Livingston and the Yellowstone River.

Deer Creek

The mule deer, *Odocoileus hemionus*, is a bit larger than that other Montana deer, the whitetail, and prefers the higher mountain environment to the river bottoms and meadows favored by its cousin.

This country on the northern end of the Custer-Gallatin National Forest, just east of the Boulder River, must have had good hunting. There is an Upper Deer Creek, Lower Deer Creek, an East Fork, a West Fork, and a Middle Fork of

Mule deer. PHOTO BY JIM PEACO, YELLOWSTONE NATIONAL PARK, #19760.

Upper Deer Creek, not to mention Elk Mountain, Elk Creek, and East and West Sheep Creeks.

A ranger station was located on Deer Creek in the 1920s, but no longer exists.

Mount Delano

This mountain was named in 1872 by the surveyor Ferdinand Hayden for his immediate supervisor and America's first national park overseer, Columbus Delano (1809–1896), the Secretary of the Interior under President Ulysses S. Grant. Profiteering and corruption permeated the Interior Department during his tenure, and he was found guilty of negligence and incompetence in 1875 and forced from office.

The mountain was not a co-defendant, so the name remains.

Columbus Delano, ca. 1860. BRADY-HANDY PHOTO, LIBRARY OF CONGRESS.

De Loris Falls

The beautiful falls near Cooke City that is visible from the Beartooth Highway was named for De Loris Cole, a young lady from Cooke City whose father, "King" Cole, owned the local trading post. Unfortunately, the USGS is no longer naming all of the falls on their maps, but this lovely one does deserve mention.

Denny Lake

This is an error found on some older maps. A lake of this name can be found on the 2011 USGS map in a bowl on the north side of Mount Dewey and is a misspelling of Dewey Lake. (see citation) This has been corrected on more recent maps.

Derby Mountain/Creek/Gulch

Derby Creek, on the northeastern corner of the forest, enters West Bridger Creek on its way to the Yellowstone River. It was named for some squatters of that name who settled along the stream in the grasslands to the north of the national forest.

The **gulch** was formed by the creek, of course. The **mountain** was then named in 1918 because its multiple peaks are visible from so many points along the gulch.

In 2006 a lightning strike caused the Derby Mountain Fire that burned 223,570 acres and destroyed 26 homes and 20 outbuildings. It burned between Big Timber and Absarokee from the foothills to the Yellowstone River, and some of the effects are still visible along I-90.

Desolation Lake

One finds a whole series of these sad names for lakes that were applied in the latter part of the twentieth century—Desolation, Vengence, Trouble, Dreary, Nightmare, and others. It is really not known if the person who named these lakes was suffering from some serious depression or was having withdrawal symptoms. Harrison Fagg speculates that the names come from the miserable weather and the fact that "when the it moves in it can get really nasty up there."

This lake, on the south slope of Snowbank Mountain, is well over 10,000 feet. Montana fish biologist Pat Marcuson says, "My visits to Desolation always featured rain that was more like ice blowing at an unavoidable 45-degree angle."

Mount Dewey/Lake

James P. Kimball, on his 1898 survey expedition, climbed this peak and named it for his friend Admiral George Dewey, "the echo of whose valiant exploits at Manila reached the survey party at Cooke."

Admiral Dewey, 1899.

George Dewey (1837–1917) is best known for his victory at the Battle of Manila Bay during the Spanish-American War. During that engagement, the entire Spanish fleet was sunk, while the Americans suffered only minor casualties. He was promoted to the rank of Admiral of the Navy in 1903, the only American to have attained that rank.

Dewey Lake is in a bowl on the north slope of the mountain. It has been bothered with some name problems, having been misspelled as Denny on some earlier maps. It was also once incorrectly called Medicine Lake. In 1975, the Board on Geographic Names confirmed it as Dewey Lake, and moved Medicine Lake to a body of water about a mile to the northwest.

Dexter Point

This point overlooks the Yellowstone River, east of Pray, Montana. It was named for a John K. Dexter, a carpenter by trade, who had a squatters' title to his nearby ranch on Mill Creek. He lived alone and died in his cabin at about age 80 in 1886. The name was confirmed by the district forester in 1923.

Diamond Lake

The small lake north of Widewater and Horseshoe Lakes on the Fossil Lake quad is nameless on the USGS maps. It was called Diamond Lake for its shape by Montana Fish, Wildlife and Parks personnel and appears in some hiking guides, sometimes going by the name of Upper Horseshoe Lake. It is actually more of a teardrop in shape, but don't complain and enjoy this sparkling gem.

Lake Diaphanous

Something that is diaphanous is ethereal, or characterized by extreme delicacy of form, as in a painting of a diaphanous landscape. The poetic term describes this lake that is found on the Lake Plateau.

Dick Lake

Bob and Dick Lakes are found together north of Cooke City at the head of Lady of the Lakes Creek a half mile west of the Goose Lake jeep trail. The names are not for actual people but are a reference pair of a humorous bent. They sit just to the east of Mutt and Jeff Lakes and, like them, the Dick and Bob names are commonly seen together as an amusing pair.

Dick Randall Point

This point, overlooking the Yellowstone River at Cedar Creek near Corwin Springs, was named in 1992 to honor Dick Randall, the founder of the OTO Ranch.

James Norris "Pretty Dick" Randall (1866–1957), an Iowa native, came to Montana in 1884 as a cowboy. The terrible winter of 1886-1887 decimated the cattle herds, so Randall started working for Yellowstone Park where he was a guide and in charge of stage horses in the Upper Geyser Basin. In 1898 he acquired some 5,000 acres of land up

"Pretty Dick" Randall. MONTANA HISTORICAL SOCIETY.

Cedar Creek and created the OTO Ranch. He claimed that this was the first true dude ranch in Montana and one of the first in the West and hosted such notables as Gen. Otto von Hindenberg and President Teddy Roosevelt. He was known as "Mr. Dude Ranch" and "the father of dude ranching in Montana." Affected by the Great Depression, he sold it in 1934, and it then passed through several hands before falling into disrepair. When the Rocky Mountain Elk Foundation donated it to the Forest Service in 1990, the ranch buildings were restored, and in 1998 it was placed on the National Register of Historic Places and reopened to the public. (see Cedar Creek)

The point served to mark the entry to the ranch and was used as the backdrop for many tourists' photographs. Typical for the times, Randall called this rise "Nigger Head" to "honor" the OTO camp cook. That name was used locally but has disappeared and is best left forgotten.

Divide Creek/Divide Creek Lake

The divide between the Stillwater and the East Boulder Rivers hosts this lake and its creek, a tributary of the West Fork of the Stillwater River.

Dollar Lake

Dollar Lake is a swampy, shallow bit of water in the Sedge Creek drainage on the Fossil Lake quad.

Looking at this tiny one-acre lake on a sunny day from a ridge above the lake, one can see a nice, round shape with the shine of a silver dollar.

Dome Mountain

Named for its obvious shape, this mountain south of Emigrant near the Yellowstone River was first called Dome in 1878 by Ferdinand Hayden as he passed by on his way south to survey Yellowstone Park.

It had a brief time as Dailey Mountain for Ebeneezer Dailey's family, who ranched nearby (see Dailey Lake/Basin), but this is now a variant name and Dome is official.

The 6,200-acre Dome Mountain Ranch is a Western retreat and wildlife preserve that has been homesteaded by Thelma Gray and her family for over 95 years. It was the location of the original schoolhouse in the Paradise Valley.

Donelson Lake

Donelson Lake on the Beartooth Plateau was named for Roy Donelson (1886–1978), who came west from Illinois in 1904 on a doctor's recommendation. It must have been good advice as he lived to age 92. He had a lumber business and concrete plant in Red Lodge and served as alderman on the city council from 1945 to 1959, where he was its president for 10 years. Roy had a special-use permit from the U.S. Forest Service in 1927 that allowed him to build a summer home at Beartooth Lake, some 10 to 12 miles south of this lake that was named for him.

Dore Creek

This creek on the McLeod quad was named for the Dore family. Selvin E. Dore had one of the large ranches south of Big Timber and ran sheep up this creek. Among other documented Dore family members was a Riley whose name appears as a witness to a homestead application along this creek.

Mount Douglas

Edward M. Douglas was the geographer in charge of the U.S. Geological Survey of Montana in the late 1880s and made the first recorded attempt to climb Granite Peak in 1899. He was born in 1855 in Saratoga Springs, New York, and was educated at Columbia University. In addition to his time as Geographer in Charge of the Montana Survey, in 1903 he was appointed Geographer in Charge of the Rocky Mountain Section. He was known as an innovator in data gathering, recording, and computing.

Frank Tweedy and W.H. Leffingwell of the 1886 survey crew, who worked the Boulder watershed, were the first to climb this mountain that sits to the north of the Lake Plateau. They named it as a dedication to their supervisor.

Dreary Lake

Up on the Lake Plateau, and like its dreary cousins, Desolation, Vengence, Trouble, Abandoned, and Nightmare Lakes, this bit of water in the Flood Creek chain was named in the later twentieth century for the nasty weather that can be found in the high Beartooths.

It does not sound like a fun place to camp.

Drop Off Mountain

The 12,115-foot point above Jasper Lake and northwest of Spirit Mountain on the Silver Run Plateau is unnamed on official USGS maps. It first got this name when Harrison Fagg climbed all the peaks over 12,000 feet and put them on his 1978 climbers' map. It now appears on published peakbagger lists and websites.

Its vertical drop of over 1,500 feet on the east side gave it the name. Harrison Fagg mentioned that his hat blew off when he was up there and now remains as a tiny bit of humanity at the bottom of the "drop off."

Druid Peak

Druid Peak is in Yellowstone National Park, north of the Lamar Valley. It had an original name of Longfellow Peak that was given to it by Park Superintendent P.W. Norris to honor Jack Barronnette whose cabin and bridge were nearby. Gen. W.E. Strong said that Barronnette was "built like Longfellow's ship, for strength and speed." (see Barronette Peak)

The name Druid was attached in 1885 by members of the Hague survey. The reason was undocumented, but it may have been either because of its solitary location or for the Stonehenge-like rock formation on the eastern slope.

Both names existed for a while, but Druid was confirmed by the Board on Geographic Names in 1930.

Dry Creek

Montana is not wet country, so there are many intermittent or former streams called Dry Creek. For the area of this book, one can find five in Carbon County, five in Park County, two in Stillwater County, and four in Sweet Grass.

None are of any particular historical interest except the one in Carbon County along the Clarks Fork. Although outside of the area of this book, it was the site of the Ohio (later Marathon) Oil field, whose first well was drilled in 1929.

Dryad Lake

The *Dryas octopetala* flower, commonly known as the mountain avens, eight-petal avens, or white mountain dryad, gave its name to this lake in the Flood Creek chain.

It is a common alpine flower found in the high mountains, primarily on limestone outcrops. The plant is well adapted to cold country, growing its stems in mats close to the warmer ground. It is so prevalent and adapted to the cold that the three most recent glaciation periods in Europe are known as the "Oldest, Older, and Youngest Dryas" because the limit of the glaciers could be determined by deposits of *Dryas* leaves.

Some early maps had it misnamed Cimmerian Lake, which is nearby.

White dryad.

Dude Lake

A "dude" is a cowboy term for someone unfamiliar with life on the range. Places called dude ranches, where easterners would escape to experience Western life, were very popular in the early twentieth century, and Al Croonquist's Camp Senia on the West Fork of Rock Creek was one of the more famous of these. This lake was a favorite place where Al would take horseback parties, so he named it for his dudes in 1923.

Duggan Lake

According to one source, Duggan Lake was named for Fred Duggan, an attorney from Billings. He cut a trail up the East Rosebud to what was Duggan Falls (now Impasse Falls), and his lake sits just below these falls.

Another story claims that the name comes from the time when the Forest Service was blasting a trail up next to the falls above the lake. (see Impasse Falls) As large "duggans," or rocks, splashed down into the lake, Chuck Martin, the Forest Service crew chief, dubbed it Duggan Lake. Butte copper miners called false hanging or loose rocks, "Larry Duggans," so perhaps this is where he got this term for their "flyrock."

The fact that Impasse Falls was once called Duggan Falls supports the first story. However, you are allowed to choose between either of them, as both come from reliable sources.

Dutch Creek

Dutch was a common late nineteenth-century term for German immigrants because they spoke "Deutsch." This tributary of the West Fork of Rock Creek near Wild Bill Lake has two different stories given for its name, and both are based on this nickname.

O.J. Salo of Red Lodge said that it was presumably named for a bunch of Dutch (German) woodchoppers who worked this locality, among whom were Adolph Koenig and John Beital.

Another Red Lodge local, John Corey, says it was named in 1937 by Wild Bill Kurtzer, who had been herding cattle on this creek for a rancher whose nickname was Dutch. (see Wild Bill Lake)

Dyale Creek

This currently unnamed creek is a tributary of Lodgepole Creek and is in the vicinity of the former town of Limestone near Nye. It is listed on U.S. Forest Service records of the late 1930s and was named for E.F. Dyale, who homesteaded there.

Eagle Creek

The bald eagle, *Haliaetus leucocephalus*, is the national bird of the United States and is relatively common along the lakes and streams of southwest Montana. The mature bird has a dark brown body and white head. It is not actually bald, but the word bald derives from a Middle English word that meant "white patch."

Bald eagle. BACKCOUNTRY HORSEMEN'S ASSOCI-ATION, NATIONAL PARK SERVICE.

Its nests, seen on high snags or cliffs, are the largest of any bird, generally 3x5 feet with the largest on record being $9^1/_2$ feet wide, 20 feet deep, and weighing almost 6,000 pounds. (see Eagle Park/Creek in the Crazies chapter for its success as an Endangered Species)

Eagle Creek can be found just east of Gardiner, and the name goes back to at least 1883 when "One-Eyed" Parker had a ranch there. (see Parker Point)

East Fork Basin

The basin that this name refers to is on the East Fork of the Hellroaring Creek that flows into the Yellowstone River near Gardiner.

Eagle Nest Rock

The Yellowstone National Park stage drivers kept their passengers entertained with stories about the Park and its inhabitants, both human and animal. This rock is on McMinn Bench, about a mile south of the Park's North Entrance at Gardiner, and it was named by stage driver G.L. Henderson in 1884.

Osprey. NATIONAL PARK SERVICE.

The fact that the nest and the birds were actually fish hawks, or osprey, *Pandion haliaetus*, didn't seem to be a problem.

Echo Lake

There are two Echo Lakes. One lake is near Granite Creek and Peak in Montana, where the north ridge is said to be "mountain goat heaven." The other Echo Lake can be found on the Beartooth Plateau near Beauty Lake and Beartooth Butte in Wyoming. It is not stated which came first and which is the echo.

Edwards Gulch

Edwards Gulch holds one of the forks of Emigrant Creek along the northwest side of Mineral Mountain. A.C. Edwards filed a deed for his ranch in 1865 and patented the first placer claim on Emigrant Creek.

The gulch is mentioned by Livingston author David DePuy in his book about the Paradise Valley pioneers, but is no longer on USGS or USFS maps.

Eedica Lake

The Montana Fish, Wildlife and Parks website says that Eedica is from the Crow language and means "far away." That the word is in Crow fits with the fact that it is near both Little Face and Arrapooash Lakes, which were named for historic men of that tribe. At 9,700 feet, high in the East Rosebud, it is certainly far away. The actual Crow word for far away is *awatee*, but Native words are often shortened and corrupted when they enter the English language.

Ekwortzel Draw/Spring

Leonard Ekwortzel was born in Sweden in 1865 and emigrated to the U.S. in 1883. He first worked the mines at Cokedale, Montana, but moved to Columbus in 1892 where he met Julia Robinson from Nye. They married and moved near her family, taking a homestead near the confluence of the West Fork and Stillwater Rivers in 1896. Here they raised cattle, had a small store, and ran the post office. Leonard served on the Nye school board and the Stillwater Stock Growers Association.

His younger brother, Elmer, was born in 1869 and emigrated first to Chicago. In 1908 he came to Montana and homesteaded next to his brother. Leonard passed away in 1951, and Elmer died in 1959, but family members still ranch in the area.

Mr. & Mrs. Elmer Ekwortzel. JIM ANNIN COLLECTION, MUSEUM OF THE BEARTOOTHS, #172.

Elaine Sidley. EMILY COPELAND FAMILY PHOTO.

Lake Elaine

Lake Elaine sits in what was once known as the Big Basin near the Wyoming border on the Castle Mountain quad and was named by Larry Nordquist of the L bar T Ranch.

Elaine Sidley's husband, William, a Chicago lawyer, and his friend Frederick Kirk Copeland came west many summers to hunt and pack with Nordquist. They introduced him to other Chicago clients and helped him buy the land for the L bar T. In thanks he gave them each 15 acres, built a cabin, and named lakes for them. (see Copeland Lake) The Sidleys moved on and the Copelands bought their neighboring cabin and land. It remains now in the fifth generation of that family.

Ernest Hemingway came to the L bar T in the 1930s and stayed in the Sidley cabin. That is where he wrote much of his best work, including *Death in the Afternoon*, *The Green Hills of Africa*, and a good part of *For Whom the Bell Tolls*.

Elbow Creek/Lake

Elbow Lake is on the southern slope of Mount Cowen and has a dramatic waterfall that drops into it. The lake is the source of the **creek** of that name, which takes a right 90-degree "elbow" turn to flow into the Yellowstone River north of Emigrant.

There are two interesting historical tidbits involving this stream. Ralph Smith, a "hermit," had his homestead on Elbow Creek. Not a social character, he was known to walk all the way to Livingston when he needed supplies. Then there is the story concerning a homestead application involving a Mrs. Carlson. The hearing officer denied her application because he reasoned that she was too fat to get up the hill to the cabin.

The second **Elbow Creek** can be found in the Fishtail Creek country of Stillwater County. It, too, takes a 90-degree turn in its course.

Elephant Lake

The lake sits in the drainage off Sundance Glacier and Bowback Mountain, but there is no large elephant-like structure nearby. It is also not colored pink, so a flask was not involved. Perhaps it was named for a profusion of the elephanthead flower, *Pedicularis groenlandica*, which is common in the wet or boggy environments in our high mountains. This relative of the lousewort has modified petals that make the flower look like the trunk, ears, and head of an elephant.

Pedicularis groenlandica. PHOTO BY WALTER SIEGEMUND, WIKI CREATIVE COMMONS.

Elephanthead Mountain

This mountain is located at the head of Mission Creek, southeast of Livingston Peak.

Geologist Thomas Jagger called it "a strange looking knob" when he saw it in 1893, so the name refers to its shape (with a little imagination).

Elk Creek/Basin/Falls/Lake/Mountain

Elk, *Cervus canadensis*, is one of the largest members of the deer family. Their large numbers in the Custer-Gallatin National Forest has led to finding their name on many features.

Elk is a term that was poorly transferred from Europe by the early colonists. The Old World "elk" is what we in North America call the moose, and our elk most closely resembles the European red deer, *Cervus elaphus*, which is genetically quite distinct. In any case, elk is what our animals are called. They have been driven out on most of their natural prairie habitat by human activity and now are found in forest and forest edge lands where they feed

Bull elk bugling. PHOTO BY NEAL HERBERT, NATIONAL PARK SERVICE.

on grasses, plants, leaves, and bark. Hearing their fall bugling as the males assert dominance and attract females is a signature experience of the mountains.

There is an **Elk Lake** just to the south of East Rosebud Lake and the community of Alpine. It drains a short distance via an unnamed creek to the East Rosebud. In a 1916 photo, an old trapper's cabin can be seen along the shore. It is now long gone. John Branger, whose family started the TO Bar Ranch near Alpine, wanted it named Elizabeth Lake for his mother, but this was not accepted. Apparently there were not enough lakes named elk.

Another **Elk Lake** can be found on the Iron Mountain quad and empties via one of the Elk Creeks into the Boulder River. A 1943 map shows a dramatic waterfall from the exit of this lake, which is 800 feet above the valley floor. It is still there but no longer marked on the USGS map.

Elk Creeks abound. In addition to the one mentioned in the Boulder River country, there is one on the Enos Mountain quad that is in the East Boulder drainage, and another that starts at **Elk Creek Basin** on the south side of Hummingbird Peak and flows west to join Hellroaring Creek and on into the Park.

There are two **Elk Mountains.** One is along a ridge on Bowback Mountain, and the other is at the head of the Elk Creek on the Enos Mountain quad. This latter was named by William Henry Holmes of the 1878 Hayden survey expedition because he found it to be a favorite range for elk in the summer and fall.

Elk Horn Lake

Elk antlers are shed each winter, so there must have been some found near this lake. The lake sits among the Hellroaring Lakes in the Hellroaring/Rock Creek drainage on the east side in Carbon County.

There is another Elk Horn Lake, whose name is found only on Montana Fish, Wildlife and Parks documents. It is found on Beartooth Creek north of Beartooth Butte.

Ellis Mountain/Basin

Elllis Mountain and Basin is just south of Big Timber near Sliderock Mountain. It was named for W.D. Ellis, who was one of the early promoters of the ranch and stock industries in this part of Montana. Active from 1888 through the turn of the century, the Briggs-Ellis Ranch was run by his cousin, Marshall King, and had, by far, the largest wool output in Sweet Grass County— one-third of the total in 1897. Ellis retired and sold all but his King home to a Mr. Swanson in 1902, and it later became the Anneson Ranch.

Elpestrine Lake

This is a misspelling of the word "alpestrine," which means subalpine or growing at high elevations but not above timberline. Hikers' maps and Montana Fish, Wildlife and Parks documents and website spell it correctly.

W.D. Ellis. CRAZY MOUNTAIN MUSEUM.

The lake is located at nearly 11,000 feet on the south wall of Summit Mountain, which is actually high above subalpine country.

Emerald Lake

There are three lakes of this name whose color is due to the combination of the intense blue of the high-altitude sky and glacial flour suspended in the water.

The one that sits just to the north of Hicks Peak on the Upper Boulder River was named by the Forest Service in 1923 for the intense green color. It is the headwaters of Clear Creek.

The one in Stillwater County is by the West Rosebud and gave its name to the Emerald Lake USGS quad map.

The third Emerald Lake is in Wyoming near Beartooth Butte. This deep lake is a good trout fishery and was initially stocked in 1937 by workers on the Glacier Lake dam. Although across the Wyoming border, it continues to be stocked by the Montana fisheries people.

Emigrant Creek/Gulch/Peak/Townsite

The first "emigrants" were the people who arrived in Montana Territory in 1864 with the wagon trains led by John Bozeman and Jim Bridger.

In 1863 Thomas Curry was the first to discover gold in what he called Curry's Gulch. The following year he convinced some of the members of the wagon trains bound for Virginia City to come to his diggings. David Weaver, David Shorthill, and Frank Garrett were among these, and they made another rich discovery that led to a flood of "emigrant" prospectors, who renamed it Emigrant Gulch. There were placer mines all along the creek, and it has been said that gold worth more than $10 million was taken out in that first year. Placer mining and hydraulic sluicing continued for another 75 years, and in 1941 a huge dredging operation with what was then the world's second-largest dredge removed what was left of the placer deposits. It is no surprise that the Crow called this gulch *Ba'laaannuttuua* (where they get money).

The first settlement at Curry's Gulch was called Yellowstone City and had about 30 cabins and 300 miners. It was on the Crow reservation and was quite dangerous due to the narrow confines, winter conditions, and hostile Indians. The town was renamed Emigrant,

Emigrant Gulch, 1905. F.J. HAYNES PHOTO.

for the gulch, when it was moved out close to the Yellowstone River, and dredging has obliterated all traces of Yellowstone City. Because it was so far from transportation at that time, David Shorthill was quoted as declaring that "Emigrant Gulch had enough gold to starve to death." When the Crow Reservation boundary was moved east in 1885, and, with the arrival of the Yellowstone Branch of the Northern Pacific Railroad shortly thereafter, mining boomed again. The St. Julian mine that was founded up the gulch in 1904 was said by the *Livingston Post* to be "perhaps the richest strike ever made in a Montana gold mine."

The little town of Emigrant was quite active for the 75 years that the gold was coming out. It has now moved again, to a site across the river on the west side on U.S. Highway 89, where it is a quiet little gas station, tourist, and fishing stop.

Emigrant Creek is in the gulch and **Emigrant Peak,** which rises an impressive 6,000 feet from the valley floor, is along the southwest side of the gulch.

Enos Mountain/Creek

Enos Mountain and the creek flowing off it are in the East Boulder River country south of Big Timber. There is no information as to who this Enos was, but he got his mountain and his name on a USGS quad map.

Erratic Lake

This lake with a wiggly shape can be found on the southern slope of Snowbank and Castle Rock Mountains.

Estelle Lake

Estelle Lake is a widewater portion of Lake Creek in that cluster of lakes just to the north of the Montana/Wyoming border. Estelle herself remains one of the mystery women of the Beartooths.

Evergreen Mountain

Evergreen Mountain, in the Upper Deer Creek country to the west of Sliderock and Ellis Mountains, is covered with a pine forest.

It was once called Green Mountain, but this was changed in 1923 as there is a Green Mountain that is more prominent and located just a few miles to the west.

Falls Creek/Lake

With all of the elevation in the Absaroka-Beartooths, and with the many streams, you might expect to find a few **Falls Creeks.** You would be right.

Falls Creek Lake is found in a cirque on the north side of Summit and Snowbank Mountains. It is on a Falls Creek that flows through the lake and on north to Lake at Falls.

A second Falls Creek flows off Twin Peaks through Cataract Lake (which was once also called Falls Creek Lake) and on to the Stillwater River.

The Main Boulder River also has its own Falls Creek, which enters the river next to Two Mile Bridge.

Not to be left out, the West Boulder also has a Falls Creek that has a big falls where it enters the river on the Dexter Point quad. Kaufman Lake (see listing) was once called West Falls Creek Lake, but that was changed because that name got a bit crowded.

The west side of the forest near Emigrant also has a creek that was called Falls Creek by some. For a bit of variation, it is now Cascade Creek on the map.

Great Falls Creek

Great Falls Creek is part of the collection of Falls Creeks on the Main Boulder River. It enters that river about two miles south of Falls Creek and Two Mile Bridge. It also begins on the east of a divide, the other side of which is the head of the Falls Creek that goes to the West Boulder River. The actual Great Falls that gave the creek its name can be found after a hike of about a mile from the Boulder River trailhead.

Lake at Falls

Two nice waterfalls can be seen dropping into this lake. Falls Creek off Summit and Snowbank Mountains (see Falls Creek) has one of the waterfalls. East Rosebud Creek with its Charlie Falls just upstream from the lake is the other—good name.

Farley Creek/Lake

These features were named for Charles Farley (1854–1929), who came west from Mississippi in 1881. He initially worked for the 79 Ranch in Kansas, and, in 1882, trailed 6,000 head of cattle from there to the 79's Montana ranch. He had married Laura Porter in 1881 and they settled in Columbus, Montana, where he had a coal business, dray line, butcher shop, and smokehouse. Later in life, he moved again to a stock ranch near Nye. Farley was actually an alias for Andrew P. Wheat, and he resumed the Wheat name when "all was forgiven" back in Mississippi.

There is a bit of confusion with the names as Farley Lake and Farley Creek, which, although in the same general area, are not connected. **Farley Lake** lies to the south of Crazy Mountain and is at the headwaters of Lake Creek, which flows into Granite Lake on the Wyoming border. **Farley Creek** is northeast of Crazy Mountain and flows west from Hatchet and Jordan Lakes to Big Moose Lake, also on the Wyoming border. From there south in Wyoming it is called Crazy Creek. A 1937 map shows that Hatchet Lake was called Farley Lake at that time, and the current Farley Creek was called the East Fork of Crazy Creek. Confused? It should explain why the lake and creek are not connected but does not explain why the lake's name was moved but the creek's was not. A mystery.

Favonius Lake

Favonius means "favorable" in Latin and was one of the Roman wind gods who held dominion over plants and flowers and was generally equated with the Greek god Zepherus. His "return" in early February signaled the coming of spring in Rome.

The name was recommended by the U.S. Forest Service in 1942 "because, due to its location and the disposition of the surrounding mountains, the lake is continually blown upon by a west wind which is sometimes very strong and cold."

It is on the Pinnacle Mountain quad, and its outlet flows via Wounded Man Creek into the Stillwater River. Ed Ickerman, who had the Beartooth Ranch on the Stillwater, built the first trail to this lake, and named it after himself. That name and the local variant of Crow Lake were never recognized nor were they found on official maps.

Fawn Lake

Better than Bambi, this lake is up Crevice Creek near Jardine.

Fiddler Creek

The McDonalds of Columbus loved to play their fiddles and took them along whenever they went to their hunting cabin on this creek. The sounds of their playing gave it the name Fiddler Creek. It flows through McDonald Basin just south of Fishtail Butte on the Nye Road, which is where the father, M.M. McDonald, started his ranch with squatters' rights in 1886. One of the brothers, Richard, was still noted to be in the Columbus area in 1944. (see McDonald Basin)

Finger Lake

On a map, or from above, the shape of this lake on the Fossil Lake quad looks like an arm bent at the elbow with a finger pointed accusingly at Splinter Lake.

These two lakes form a fish environmental system where Finger has the best spawning grounds and Splinter has the best plankton for feeding. The hatching happens at Finger and the young fish wash downstream to Splinter where they grow big and catchable. (see Recroitment Lake and Production Lake)

Montana Fish, Wildlife and Parks calls it Hunger Lake, which was the name given it by fish biologist Pat Marcuson. He said that it was "not an official name, just a handle describing my state of affairs during one of my visits."

Fire Creek/Gulch/Lake/Ridge

Forest fires, common in pine forests, were the reason for the "Fire" names on this **lake and creek** due east of Emigrant on the south slope of Mount Cowen.

The **Fire Gulch and Ridge** in Lower Deer Creek country were also burned over by a fire many years ago.

Firewater Creek

Firewater refers to the "hooch" that was illegally distilled in the woods along this creek. It is found along the Main Boulder River near Chippy Creek, and the stills produced the liquor that was obviously used to serve the miners' and chippys' needs.

Fish Creek/Lake

Fly fishing has become a great sport in the Absaroka-Beartooths since the early miners and sportsmen started stocking the lakes with fish carried in metal pails and milk cans. Because of the isolated elevation, and the rapidly tumbling streams, almost all of the lakes were naturally fishless. Now, most have a healthy population with a staterun stocking schedule, primarily by airplane, that is almost industrial in size. The result has been a plethora of Fish, Rainbow, and Trout names on the lakes.

Of the **Fish Creeks,** one drains Trout (formerly Fish) Lake to Soda Butte Creek. A note in the Burlingame Archives at Montana State University grumpily says that it was "named for the dearth of fish—nothing but suckers." Another **Fish Creek** is near Mystic Lake and the West Rosebud and, hopefully, has a better trout population.

There are three **Fish Lakes.** One is a pond next to the Main Boulder River. Another can be found on Monitor Peak just upstream from Knox (Castle) Lake at the head of Bear Creek out of Jardine. The third, a very scenic lake, is near the Rainbow Lakes at the head of the East Fork of the Boulder River. It must be presumed that this latter's fishy population was considered more ordinary than those in the Rainbow Lakes close by.

Fisher Mountain/Creek

Fisher Mountain and Creek just north of Cooke City are thought to have been named for a George Fisher who was a longtime Cooke City miner. In 1885 he found a six-foot vein of silver that yielded $100/ton but netted him little because of the high shipping costs. He died of suicide in his cabin in 1916 with $500 in cash and a $17,000 bill of sale for his mines, apparently depressed at what he felt was too low a price. Interestingly, his headstone had two names, George Fisher and Jacob Bach. Apparently Fisher was an alias, as he had emigrated and served in the Civil War as Jacob Bach. He had no relatives.

Because of all the mining activity, the streams in this area have been found to be highly polluted, and the acid that gushed out of the adit of the McLaren Mine on Henderson Mountain sterilized Fisher Creek to a toxic pH of 2.9. It is now the site of a large, successful reclamation effort. (see Soda Butte Creek and Margaret Lake for details)

Fishtail Butte/Creek/Lakes/Plateau/Town

The town and creek get their names from the butte, which was named in 1883 by the Fowler brothers, James and John, who had a ranch nearby. **The butte,** a slim rocky ledge, has an unusual shape that looks as if a giant eagle dropped a fish headfirst onto the butte, burying it so that only the fish's tail protrudes at the top. It rises on the prairie just outside the national forest border on the corner of the Nye and Benbow Roads, above the little hamlet of Dean.

Both **East and West Fishtail Creeks** come off the **plateau** of that name to join near Dean and enter the West Rosebud farther on by the town of Fishtail. The **West Fishtail Lakes** are in a cluster at the head of West Fishtail Creek on the north side of Mount Wood.

The town, of course, gets its name from the creek that flows by the butte. It was established in 1892 after the Crow ceded this section of reservation land that year. Platted in 1913 by Joe and Addie Mason, it had, early on, a mercantile store, a post office, a hotel, and a flour mill. Chrome and platinum mining at the Stillwater Complex nearby at Nye has attracted residents and boosted the economy from the 1940s to the present.

Five Lakes

There are… five lakes (unless you count one more little pond) that are located in a group in the Bear Creek drainage on the east slope of Sheep Mountain near Gardiner.

Five Mile Creek

The creek is located about five miles from the little hamlet of Alpine. It is downstream and comes in as a tributary to East Rosebud Creek.

Fizzle Lake

This lake in the Broadwater drainage was originally called Windy Lake, and Montana Fish, Wildlife and Parks refers to it as Dead Horse Lake. Since two local residents called it Fizzle Lake, the Board on Geographic Names officially decided on Fizzle in 1985.

There is nothing in the citations to state why it was called Fizzle, but it probably comes from the definition, "to fail in a weak or disappointing way." It is presumed to refer to a less than successful fishing expedition.

The most famous Fizzle in Montana history is Fort Fizzle. This was erected in 1877 on the Lolo Trail west of Missoula by Capt. C.C. Rawn and the Missoula Volunteers and was designed to stop Chief Joseph and the Nez Perce in their flight from north-central Idaho. However, the Indians climbed a steep ravine behind the ridge to the north and simply bypassed the soldiers. The barricade was ridiculed as "Fort Fizzle." A partial reconstruction and historical site is located next to U.S. Highway 12 today.

Flat Rock Lake

Would you believe that there is a flat rock to be found in this lake on the Beartooth Plateau?

Flemming Bridge

A steel bridge on the Main Boulder Road crosses the river south of Chippy Creek. It was named for Ben Flemming, a homesteader, trapper, and postmaster who lived by the bridge. In 1933 he and a friend snowshoed up nearby Speculator Creek to set traps for marten. As Flemming crossed a snowslide he was killed by an avalanche. When his body was found in the spring, he was still holding two steel traps.

Flood Creek

Flood Creek is one of the major contributing tributaries of the Stillwater River, so the name comes from the high volume of spring meltwater. Formerly known as Hawks Creek as noted in 1961 Beartooth District ranger notes, the small widening of the Stillwater River here was also once known as Hawks Lake. The name of these miners was erased from the USGS maps when the creek was formally named Flood. (see Hawks Creek)

There is a spectacular, large waterfall just up from the confluence of this creek and the Stillwater River at the southern end of Sioux Charley Lake. It was once known as Dayton Falls for Dayton Farmer, an early trapper and packer who had a cabin nearby. It may seem a short hike on the map, but it is a difficult bushwhack. The USGS no longer lists many of the waterfalls on its maps, so this name can no longer be found, but the falls is indeed there. (see Dayton Cabin)

Flume Creek

A flume is a man-made channel for water where, in contrast to a trench or ditch, the sides are raised above the surrounding terrain. They were used extensively in hydraulic mining and for working placer deposits. This creek is south of Old Nye on the Stillwater River in what was big mining country. It provided the water for a flume.

Fly Lake

Fly Lake sits near that collection of humorously named lakes like Dick and Bob, Mutt and Jeff, and Molar and Incisor in the Sourdough Basin at the head of the Stillwater River. It is close to and paired with Spider Lake as a reference to the cautionary 1828 poem "The Spider and the Fly" by Mary Howitt. "Will you come into my parlor? Said the Spider to the Fly." Heh! Heh!

Forage Creek

This was good grazing land for the local stock, and the creek is found in flat country near Cooke City.

Forge Creek

A forge is a furnace used for refining metals. This creek is a tributary of the East Boulder River in a heavy mining area with Iron Mountain and the Mouat Mine nearby.

Fossil Lake

It is not stated which fossil was found by this lake north of Bald Knob and Mount Rosebud, but it gave its name to the USGS quad map. The limestone cap that still remains in the Beartooths comes from the Devonian Period, 400 million years ago. Where it has not been eroded off the base of granite, one can find many fascinating fossils. (see Beartooth Butte)

Foster Lake

The lake at the southern base of Druid Peak in Yellowstone National Park was named in 1931 for Fred J. Foster, who was in charge of the Park's fish hatcheries.

Fourmile Creek

There are two Fourmile Creeks in the Absaroka-Beartooths. One enters the Main Boulder River four miles from Hicks Park. The Fourmile cabin that is located here is in the Forest Service's cabin rental program from October to May.

Another creek of this name is a tributary of the West Boulder River some four miles upstream of the West Boulder Meadows.

Fred J. Foster. YELLOWSTONE HERITAGE AND RESEARCH CENTER, YRLL 19426.

Mount Fox

During his 1898 survey, James P. Kimball named this peak on the Cooke City quad for Dr. J.M. Fox of Red Lodge. Fox was the superintendent of the Rocky Fork Coal Company and arrived in Red Lodge in 1889. He was a trusted executive for Northern Pacific Railroad president Henry Villard, and befriended Kimball's party. (see Mount Maurice)

Fox Creek/Lake

Fox Lake is upstream from Widewater Lake at the end of the wagon road from Cooke City to Kersey Lake. It was probably named for another human, the Cooke City miner, Julius Fox, who was known to have been there in 1895.

There is a **Fox Creek** and campground just off the Beartooth Highway in the Wyoming section of the Absaroka-Beartooth Wilderness, and this particular fox name refers to a canine, the red fox, *Vulpes vulpes*, not the man. Red foxes are quite commonly found in Montana forests and, having adapted well to the presence of humans, are even seen in semi-urban environments. They are not all the classic red

Red fox. PHOTO BY NEAL HERBERT, NATIONAL PARK SERVICE.

of Reynard, as there is much natural variation and pups in the same litter may be red, silver, or gray. In the Beartooths, the foxes have developed a characteristic light blond coat with a sooty underfur. Locals call them "glacier foxes," and naturalists have wondered if they may not be a distinct subspecies.

Frederick Peak

Karl Telford Frederick (1881–1963) was a Harvard Law School graduate and New York City attorney who was an avid sport shooter and outdoorsman. He won three gold medals in the 1920 Olympics in pistol events, served as president of the National Rifle Association, was a member and president of the Boone and Crockett Club, and was also president of the Campfire Club of America.

Karl Frederick, ca. 1920. *ADIRONDACK ALMANACKE.*

He loved to come to the Lamar Valley in Yellowstone National Park to photograph wildlife. Because of his many visits and conservation work, this peak, just south of the Montana border, was named for him shortly after his death in 1963.

Frenchy Meadows/Creek

Joseph "Frenchy" Duret lived in the meadows of Slough Creek just north of Yellowstone Park. He initially prospected near Nye City, but soon turned to hunting, trapping, and guiding. In the 1890s he homesteaded in these meadows where in 1913 he married a local, Jennie McWilliams, and they raised cattle to sell in the local mining camps and to the coal miners at Horr. This is prime grizzly country and they can be quite a problem for a rancher. Frenchy claimed to have killed over 250 grizzlies, but in 1922 one broke loose from its trap and killed him. He was a nationally known guide and hunter and a friend of Teddy Roosevelt, so the Forest Service has set up a headstone and an historical marker near the site of his ranch that reads:

"Frenchy" Duret. YELLOWSTONE NATIONAL PARK, #36654.

"Joseph (Frenchy) B. Duret, Native of France"

"Pioneer, Park County trail blazer and nationally known hunter, trapper, and guide lost his life in hand-to-hand combat with a huge grizzly bear on June 12, 1922."

Frenco Lake

The lake can be found near Beckwourth Lake above Silver Lake in the West Rosebud drainage. It was named sometime around 1947 when the Boy Scouts of Columbus and Absarokee hiked in with its first planting of trout. Jerry French (1935–2015) of Columbus was one of those scouts, and Bill Koch and Earl Not, the adult leaders, used his nickname for the lake. Jerry was an active outdoorsman and worked as a teacher and a coach in various cities in Montana, and was later in the beverage business for Taylor and Ryan Distributing in Billings.

Fridley Creek

Frederick Francis (F.F.) Fridley was one of Montana's early pioneers. He and his wife, America, left Iowa in 1864 with a group of relatives in the Fridley wagon train bound for Idaho. They met up with John Bozeman, and the combined trains went up the Bozeman Trail to the Gallatin Valley where the Fridleys stopped. They pitched the first tent at what was to become the town of Bozeman and built the first family home in the Gallatin Valley that October. He had the Fridley Billiards Hall and Saloon and lived in Bozeman until 1876 when they moved to a ranch at Emigrant. The current town of Emigrant was variously called Fridley because he had the post office and the Fridley Station, which was close to the railroad tracks. He also built a bridge across the Yellowstone to attract miners to town. By 1911, all the names were consolidated as Emigrant. (see Emigrant Creek/Gulch/Peak)

The name Fridley is seen on several features, past and present, in the Paradise Valley. On the west side in the Gallatin Range is a Fridley Peak and a Fridley

Creek. The Fridley Creek in our area of interest is a tributary of Emigrant Creek that enters it about a mile south of White City in Emigrant Gulch. It was originally called Strickland Creek for Ben Strickland, one of the original settlers. (see Strickland Creek) The name was changed in 1962 because there is another Strickland Creek in Park County just to the south of I-90, where Ben's descendants lived.

The buffalo jump on Fridley Creek is an important archaeological site where many arrowheads and bone fragments have been found.

Fritter Lake

This lake can be found in the cluster of lakes near Crazy Mountain just to the north of the Montana/Wyoming border.

Older maps called it Hipshot Lake, and the currently unnamed smaller nearby lake was called Quyat Lake. These names refer to characters in the Stan Lynde comic strip *Rick O'Shay* that ran from 1958 to 1977, and whose Old West theme and humor were revered by Montanans. Two of the characters were Rick's best friend Hipshot Percussion and the boy Quyat Burp.

It is not stated why this lake was recently renamed Fritter. Perhaps it was because it is a good place to fritter away your time with a fly rod in hand.

Frosty Lake

Named more for the temperature than a talking snowman, Frosty Lake is just to the west of Metcalf Mountain on the Hellroaring Plateau. At 11,020 feet it is the highest of the named lakes in the drainage.

Froze-to-Death Creek/Lake/Mountain/Plateau

In the 1890s, John Cheney, Tom Hawley, and some fellow prospectors were working on the Stillwater and headed back to their cabin at Contact near the Upper Boulder. They were hit by a freak September snowstorm, and Cheney volunteered to go ahead to light a fire in the cabin, which stood by this creek. When the others arrived in the dark, Cheney was not there. His body was found the next day by this **creek,** froze to death. (see Hawley Mountain/Creek)

Other sources and ranger notes from the 1930s tell of a tie cutter who was found frozen in his cabin on this stream in 1882. This may have been another unconfirmed episode or may have been confused with the above well-documented report.

Froze-to-Death Mountain, Lake, and Plateau are quite a bit south of the above-noted creek and sit next to Granite Peak. The mountain has a long ramp on the west side that has all the aspects of a plateau, while the east side of the 11,775-foot peak is quite dramatically abrupt. The lake on the plateau drains into Phantom Creek and thus to the East Rosebud. There are no documented tales of people freezing to death, but it is high, cold country where the names of the summits reflect the harsh, ever-changing mood: Froze-to-Death, Tempest, Thunder. The author camped on the plateau late one August, suffered through a hail and lightning storm, and awoke the next morning to find the spring frozen.

This lake also established itself as a site in American literature when Ernest Hemingway included a real story about it in one of his novels. Hemingway's father killed himself with a Smith and Wesson revolver and Ernest's mother later mailed the gun to him. On a horseback trip from Red Lodge to the L bar T Ranch with "Chub" Weaver, he threw that gun into Froze-to-Death Lake. In his novel, *For Whom the Bell Tolls*, Robert Jordan, the protagonist, recounts toward the end of the book of how he dropped his father's suicide weapon into a mountain lake.

Frozen Lake

Do these names entice you to go swimming? Frozen Lake is at 10,000 feet along the Beartooth Highway in Wyoming and is the first lake that one comes to after crossing the west summit of the pass.

Fulcrum Lake

Bent like an L, this lake in the Sodalite drainage is obviously named for its shape. A 1992 hiking map and the Montana Fish, Wildlife and Parks references call it Mermaid Lake. This was certainly not due to its shape—so what did they see?

Fuller Gulch

William Fuller was the fellow for whom this gulch near the East Boulder mines was named. He was said to have been a respected citizen of the East Boulder Basin, about 60 years of age, and unmarried when he died of blood poisoning in 1900.

Gallery Lake

Those old enough can remember the television show *Howdy Doody* and Buffalo Bob's Peanut Gallery—the kids who sat in the bleachers on stage. The gallery here is a rock formation where the name comes from its appearance that fits the word's definition as "a balcony projecting from the back or sidewall of a hall or church which provides space for an audience or musicians." The lake is one of a series of lakes in the Russell Creek drainage near Lake of the Woods, south of Mount Rosebud.

Gardiner Town/River

The town and the Gardner River, originally called Warm Stream or Warm Springs Creek, were named for Johnston Gardner, a trapper who arrived around 1821 as part of the Ashley-Henry fur enterprise. He lived on the Upper Yellowstone for about 40 years and called the area Gardner's Hole. In 1870, the Washburn-Langford-Doane Expedition was exploring the area that became Yellowstone Park and named it Gardiner. It thrived with the arrival of the Northern Pacific spur in 1903 both as a tourist hub for the Park's North Entrance and as a place that served the miners who had discovered gold at nearby Bear Gulch (Jardine). Although the location was originally known as Gardner's Hole and that is how the river is spelled, the town is Gardiner with an "i." Legend has it that Jim Bridger, who was a Virginian, assisted Langford by describing the area. His southern accent made it sound like Ga-di-nah, and the misspelling was fixed in history.

Gardiner's town and post office was established in 1880, and by 1885 it had a population of 200, with 21 saloons, 6 restaurants, 5 general stores, 2 hardware stores, 2 fruit stands, 2 barber shops, 1 newsstand, 1 billiard hall, 2 dance halls, 4 houses of ill fame, 1 blacksmith, 1 milk man … and no churches.

It is now the thriving little town of about 1,000 people that houses the Yellowstone National Park Heritage and Research Center and serves tourists as the gateway to the North Entrance to Yellowstone Park, with the Roosevelt Arch and Mammoth Hot Springs right next door.

Gardner Lake

This lake is visible in a deep bowl three-quarters of a mile from the Beartooth Pass to the south of U.S. Highway 212. The trail to it is part of the Beartooth Loop National Recreation Trail.

Although the USGS and Wyoming citations do not identify this Gardner, and although it is well east of his hole and river, it seems probable that it was named for the Johnston Gardner who spent 40 years in the Upper Yellowstone. (see Gardiner town/River)

The name has become famous for the steep Gardner Headwall ski run at the Beartooth Basin Summer Ski Area where the Red Lodge International Ski Camp was held.

George Lake/Creek

This lake in the hills to the west of Emigrant was named for Joe George.

It was originally called Shorthill Lake for David Shorthill, who homesteaded to the west of the lake in 1873 and who, in 1868, was responsible for discovering the rich gold deposits in the Shorthill District up Emigrant Gulch.

People began calling it George Lake in the 1950s, probably because the George Ranch still existed at that time and the Shorthills no longer ranched there. Joe George arrived

Joe George.

in Montana in 1880 when he drove a wagon with supplies up from New Mexico and worked for David Shorthill. He was known to have filed a nearby coal claim in 1883, married Eleanor, one of the Shorthill daughters, and homesteaded by this lake next to his in-laws. Joe moved to California in 1944 and died in 1952.

The true **George Creek** is the little stream coming into George Lake, but the North Fork of McDonald Creek has also been called George Creek by some of the locals.

The interesting exposed examples of George Lake Marble, a fine brown weathering marble, can be found near the top of Black Mountain above the lake and along the ridges of the North Fork of Pine Creek.

Lake Gertrude

Gertrude Dimsdale Salo was the wife of Otto Jalmer (O.J.) Salo of Red Lodge. O.J. was Al Croonquist's friend who wrangled trips from Camp Senia and who helped stock many of the nearby lakes. (see Spirit Mountain) Mr. and Mrs. Paul Pierce, guests at Camp Senia, suggested the name for this lake along Timberline Creek since Gertrude was reported to be the first white woman to have visited it.

Ghost Lake/Creek

Steam rising in the early morning light must have reminded someone of a specter. Perhaps the contents of his hip flask aided his imagination.

Ghost Lake is found high up in the Sierra Creek drainage on the Beartooth Plateau south of Castle Mountain in Montana. Ghost Creek is in Wyoming and starts near the Beartooth Highway, just east of Muddy Creek, and flows south to enter the Clarks Fork. The creek's name has been present on the maps since 1897.

Gilbert Creek

A fellow named Gilbert was one of the first settlers in the Upper Clarks Fork country, and, after first squatting along this creek just south of the Montana/Wyoming line, he filed a homestead in 1880, and a formal deed was granted in 1915. It was originally run as a small cattle operation, but in 1925 Larry Nordquist, with the help of his friends and clients, Frederick K. Copeland and William P. Sidley, filed a mortgage deed and started the L bar T dude ranch. The brand and name L bar T came from the first and last letters of Lawrence Nordquist's name. (see Copeland Lake and Lake Elaine)

Lawrence Nordquist. COPELAND FAMILY PHOTO.

Glacier Creek/Lake, Little Glacier Lake

Glacier Creek is in the high country full of glaciers. It is on the west side of Iceberg, Sawtooth, and Wolf Mountains and drains Glacier Green Lake into the head of the Stillwater River.

Glacier Lake is the headwater for the Rock Creek that runs through Red Lodge. It is found on the Montana/Wyoming border, south of Metcalf and Rearguard Mountains. In 1936 the outlet was dammed with a 15- to 20-foot-high cement structure that created the largest lake on the southeast side of the Absarka-Beartooths. It is currently owned by the Montana Department of Natural Resources and Conservation and is run for irrigation by the Rock Creek Water Users Association.

Little Glacier Lake sits between Emerald and Glacier Lakes and is part of the same body of water as Glacier Lake, separated only by a small man-made barrier that was designed to restrict fish movement.

These lakes were first stocked by the miner Melvin E. Martin in 1920 (see Martin Lake), but since 1953, even though Little Glacier Lake is in Wyoming, the fishery has been the responsibility of the State of Montana.

Glacier Peak

This peak on the Alpine quad gets its name because it harbors two glaciers, Hidden Glacier on its northeast flank and Grasshopper Glacier to the west.

James P. Kimball, who led a survey expedition to the Beartooths in 1898, named it Mount Spofford for Charles A. Spofford (1822–1899), who was Henry Villard's private secretary and a member of the board of the Northern Pacific Railway. Spofford represented the Northern Pacific interests in Red Lodge before 1900, and the first hotel and brick building in town was initially called The Spofford. It was sold to Thomas Pollard in 1902 and renamed The Pollard, and is still the finest hotel in town.

For reasons not specified, the USGS changed the name to Glacier Peak in the 1940s, so the renaming of both the hotel and mountain has erased all reference to Mr. Spofford.

Glacier Green Lake

Glacier Green Lake formed in a cirque as a widening in Glacier Creek (see above), on the southwest side of Wolf Mountain.

The name comes from the result of glacial flour, a powder formed by the mechanical grinding of the rock by the base of a glacier—in this case, Wolf Glacier. The powder becomes suspended as cloudy water in the creeks, but when it arrives at the quieter water of a lake, the reflection of the blue sky creates a green or turquoise color.

Glissade Lake

A glissade refers to the act of sliding down a steep slope of snow or ice on one's feet—rather like skiing on your boots.

This lake is located just to the north of a steep wall on Summit Mountain where someone obviously enjoyed a glissade. Alternate sources call it Alice Lake, but Glissade is official.

Goat Lake

Mountain goat. PHOTO BY LARRY SCHNEIDER, WIKI CREATIVE COMMONS.

The white, shaggy mountain goat, *Oreamnos americanus*, is an herbivore and denizen of the high country. Its feet are well designed for traction on steep, rocky slopes, and its dense fur helps keep it warm in a forbidding environment. It is interesting that one can approach these animals quite closely from above, as the predators that they fear all come up from below.

This Hellroaring Plateau lake sits in a cirque on Spirit Mountain, and is next to another high country herbivore, Sheep Lake. Both lakes were once called Mountain Goat and Mountain Sheep Lakes, but the USGS has dropped the "mountain" for simplicity.

Gold Creek/Hill

Thar's gold in them thar hills! The **creek,** an obvious site of mining, is north of Red Lodge near Ruby Creek

The **hill** and mining site overlooks Placer Gulch on the Lower Deer Creek drainage.

Gold Prize Creek, Gold Run Creek

These two creeks parallel each other south of Emigrant. The name was applied by the district forester in 1923 and suggests that the gold rush or run was up the wrong creek and that those that hit the southern stream got the prize.

Golden Lake

The golden trout, not the metal, was the source of the name of this lake near Spirit Mountain. The golden trout, *Oncorhynchus aguabonita*, is a native of the Kern River in California, but has been stocked in several of Montana's mountain lakes.

The fishery for goldens in this lake died out some time ago and they were replaced by cutthroat trout. There is no move to rename this Cutthroat Lake, so Golden it remains. (see Lightning Lake and Sylvan Lake)

The Golf Course

There is a flat area near the Benbow Mine between Flume and Little Rocky Creek that collects the underground water seeping off the glaciers and snowfields of Mount Wood. This water keeps the grass lush and green, so the level area reminded the miners of a golf course.

Goose Lake/Creek, Little Goose Lake

The Canada goose, *Branta canadensis*, is ubiquitous throughout Montana. There are an estimated 5 million Canada geese in the U.S. with Montana hosting both the Pacific and Central flyways as well as its own group of over 50,000 nesting birds. The fact that it could be found at this lake at 9,865 feet is testimony to its hardiness.

Canada goose. PHOTO BY TOM KOERNER, U.S. FISH & WILDLIFE SERVICE.

Goose Lake sits at the end of a primitive jeep road north of Cooke City. The lake is now situated a half mile into the Absaroka-Beartooth Wilderness so the last bit of road to the lake is closed, but is a short, easy hike. The road was initially cut by unsuccessful miners from Cooke City, but became a frequently used wagon road when Amos Shaw started the Shaw and Powell Camping Company in 1898. He built Shaw's Camp at Goose Lake and led horseback tours to Grasshopper Glacier, which feeds into the lake via **Goose Creek**. Amos died in 1925, but his son, Walter, continued the business well into mid-century.

Active and productive mining began after 1905 when F.C. "Frank" Byrne and his partners discovered a copper lode. Byrne became president of the Copper King Mining, Milling, and Development Co., and a mine was started on the north end of the lake. All mining has now ceased, but scattered remnants of the Copper King workings can still be found. Other prospects showed promise for gold, silver, and platinum, and the photograph of Melvin Martin with his family at his Goose Lake chromium mine can be seen at the Martin Lake citation.

During their 1898 survey trek, James P. Kimball, A.B. Wilse, and A.B. Wood called the area around Goose Lake "Camp Misery" because of the persistently wet weather.

Little Goose Lake is just a mile upstream from Goose Lake near the head of Goose Creek. On the south end of the lake are the remains of Little Goose Lake Mine #1 on the west side and #2 to the east.

Gorge Creek

Gorge Creek, a tributary of the West Fork of Mill Creek, was once called Bear Creek. This name was a bit confusing as the more famous and larger Bear Creek at Jardine is just over the divide. Another name was needed, and in 1919, the

Absaroka National Forest people decided on Gorge Creek, as the stream flows through a narrow rock gorge. It was confirmed as official by the USGS in 1923.

Graham Creek

Graham Creek is just south of the mining town of Contact and was named for Amos and Mary Graham, who, although they worked this creek, had their homestead on Speculator Creek, 10 miles to the south. They were from Iowa where Amos worked for many years as a Missouri River pilot. In 1900, when he was 53, they decided to come to Montana and settled near Contact where they lived until their deaths—both in 1928.

The Gish Mine is located by this creek, and it worked the Chrome Mountain vein. It was started in 1915 by a brother of actresses Lillian and Dorothy Gish, who were film stars in the silent era from 1912 into the 1920s.

Granite Peak/Glacier/Lake/Range

To anyone who has been in this rocky country, it would not come as a surprise to find the "granite" name so common. Granite is a geologically old igneous rock of the basal layer that underlies much of the continental crust. Since most of the sedimentary layers have been eroded off the Beartooths, it is found everywhere. The name "granite" comes from its grainy, speckled look as *granum* is the Latin word for "grain."

The Beartooth Mountains were once known as the **Granite Range,** a name given to the mountains by the Cooke City miners, and the Beartooth Plateau was also called the Granite Plateau. The Board on Geographic Names certified "Beartooth" for the mountain range and plateau in 1930, but the term Granite Range is still on the USGS maps along the steep wall between Mount Wood and Mount Hague.

Granite Peak is the highest point in Montana at 12,799 feet and was first named by Arnold Hague in the mid-1880s when he directed the Yellowstone Survey for the U.S. Geological Survey. It was recently rated by *Backpacker Magazine* as "one of the toughest peaks to climb in the Lower 48," and has served as a challenge

Granite Peak from Froze-to-Death Plateau. PHOTO BY THE AUTHOR.

to climbers for many years. Edward Douglas had the first recorded attempt in 1899, and Fred Inabnit made five unsuccessful tries. The first to succeed was the district forester Elers Koch, who made the summit in 1923. (see Mount Douglas and Mount Inabnit)

Granite Glacier is on the north side of the peak and drains via **Granite Creek** into Big Park Lake on the Alpine quad. Because the creek's upper valley goes through the remains of a recent but now melted glacier, Elers Koch called it "The Valley of Desolation."

There are two **Granite Lakes.** The one in the cirque on the east side of Granite Peak, between it and Mounts Tempest and Peal, is obviously named for its location. What was once known as Upper Granite Lake is now called Lowary Lake. (see citation)

The other Granite Lake, once called Thunder Lake, is in a cluster of lakes that overlaps the Montana/Wyoming border. This area is part of the Beartooth Plateau, which, as mentioned above, was once called the Granite Plateau. Thus this lake's name is also for its location. It is unlikely that thunderstorms became less common, so the reason necessitating the name change to Granite is not known.

Grass Mountain/Creek

The Grass Mountain on the Sylvan Peak quad is rounded with a grassy summit above tree line.

The creek is not associated with the mountain but is a tributary of Lake Fork Creek.

Grasshopper Glacier/Lakes

The most famous **Grasshopper Glacier** can be reached by a trail up from Goose Lake and has long been a popular tourist destination. (see Goose Lake) In 1898, Anders Wilse of the Kimball Expedition climbed the mountain, which he named for himself and which lies just to the east of this glacier. On his return to camp he noticed the dark streaks in the moraine fringing the lower edge of the glacier. He brought a bottle of ice samples back, and they were seen to be grasshoppers, many perfectly preserved.

In 1914 a government entomologist determined that they were a form of migrating Rocky Mountain locusts, *Melanoplus spretus.* Several hundred years ago, many thousands of them were apparently caught in a snowstorm and forced down onto the ice. During the 1800s, massive swarms of these insects, many miles long, were seen on the Great Plains where their appearance was quite destructive. For unknown reasons, they became extinct with the last swarm seen in 1902 on the Canadian prairie. Jeffrey Lockwood theorizes that the extinction was due to destruction of the insect eggs by agricultural competition and plowing.

Not only have the locusts become extinct, but their little bodies, entombed in the ice, are disappearing as well. Global warming has caused a marked retreat of the glaciers, and, with exposure to air, most of the little bodies have decomposed. Like all of the glaciers in the Beartooths that are receding, the Grasshopper Glacier near Goose Lake is now only 89 percent of the size it was in 1940.

There is a second **Grasshopper Glacier** several miles to the east on the south side of Beartooth Mountain that was once called Martin Grasshopper Glacier. (see Martin Lake) This one, too, is shrinking and is now 62 percent smaller than it was in 1956.

Finally, a bit to the north of this is Hopper Glacier on a cirque on Medicine Mountain where more of the little bodies can be found.

The **Grasshopper Lakes** are just below the more famous Grasshopper Glacier noted above and serve as the headwaters to the West Rosebud.

Grassy Creek

This stream in the Slough Creek country flows through a grassy meadow into Buffalo Creek.

Gravel Lake

Way above tree line and near Till Lake, one can find this lake in the rocky, gravelly country on the south slope of Snowbank and Castle Rock Mountains. The gravel was created by the action of Snowbank Glacier, which left it in its moraines.

Grayling Lake

Thymallus thymallus or grayling is a member of the salmon family and is found in cold, rapidly moving, sandy or gravelly lakes and streams. Noted for its sail-like dorsal fin, it is very susceptible to competition from other fish and habitat change,

Grayling. U.S. FISH & WILDLIFE SERVICE.

and now Montana is the only place in the Lower 48 where it can be found.

James Simmons, a Wyoming Game and Fish biologist reported finding grayling at this lake near Beartooth Lake in 1941. However, the grayling have since disappeared, and brook trout are now the sole inhabitants.

Great Falls Creek/Lakes

Please see the citation on Falls Creek.

Green Lake/Mountain, Little Green Lake

The **Green Lake** in the Star Creek drainage near Cooke City was named by the rangers in the 1930s because "the Basin is covered with green lodgepole pine." **Little Green Lake** is its neighbor.

Another **Green Lake** can be found in a cluster of lakes just to the north of the Montana/Wyoming border in the rocky Sierra Creek drainage. Its name probably derives from the color that comes from glacial till. It is said to be very scenic, but with "abundant" mosquitoes.

The two **Green Mountains,** one north on the McLeod Basin quad and the other west near Pine Creek are also pine covered.

Greenough Lake

Greenough Lake is a half mile from the Greenough Campground south of Red Lodge along Rock Creek and the Beartooth Highway. It was originally a small spring-fed puddle, but the U.S. Forest Service constructed a dam in 1965 that created the larger lake that is seen today. The scenic Parkside National Recreational Trail passes next to Greenough Lake.

The lake and campground were named for the Greenough family. Benjamin Franklin, "Packsaddle Ben" Greenough, a Brooklyn orphan, made his way west in 1884 and worked as stagecoach driver, mail carrier, cowboy, and trail guide. His nickname was humorously applied by O.J. Salo when he saw Ben riding a packsaddled horse into town. He settled on a ranch near Red Lodge and his children became well known for their rodeo skills.

Called, "The Riding Greenoughs," Turk was the first to win the Triple Crown of Rodeo—the bronc riding championships at Cheyenne, Pendleton, and Calgary. Alice won four national women's saddle bronc championships in the 1930s and 40s and, according to legend, battled bulls in Spain, taught Roy Rogers and Dale Evans how to ride, and performed movie stunts while in her 80s. Alice, Turk, and sister Margie were inducted into the National Cowboy Hall of Fame in 1983. In the following generation, Deb was inducted into the Pro Rodeo Hall of Fame in 2018. He qualified for 13 consecutive National Finals Rodeos from 1988 to 2000, won the NFR average in 1992 and the bareback world title in 1993, as well as five circuit titles in Montana.

Marge Greenough. MONTANA HISTORICAL SOCIETY.

Griffin Draw

This draw near Nye was named for the Griffin family. A John Griffin had the original homestead entry in 1892, and a later John Griffin, probably the son, filed a nearby homestead stock raising permit on 80 acres in 1916, enlarging it with a further 320 acres in 1925.

Grizzly Creek/Peak

Grizzly. PHOTO BY MARY LEWANDOWSKI, NATIONAL PARK SERVICE.

Grizzly Creek is just north of Yellowstone National Park, and the rangers who recommended the name said, not surprisingly, that it was "named for a favorite haunt for the grizzly bear."

Grizzly Peak is just to the west of the town of Red Lodge and is the site of the Red Lodge Ski Area. This opened in 1960 with a Forest Service permit, and soon changed its name to Red Lodge Mountain Resort. Although officially Grizzly Peak, corporate and local publications have called it Red Lodge Mountain since 1965, and that is how it is commonly known.

Grouse Creek/Ridge

Male blue or sooty grouse in mating display. NATIONAL PARK SERVICE.

The **ridge** and **creek** on Iron Mountain in the Lower Deer Creek country was, according to rangers in the 1940s, a great summering place for the blue grouse and a favorite hunting ground in the fall.

There is a second **Grouse Creek** that enters the West Boulder on the Mount Rae quad.

Grouse are commonly found birds of the chicken family, *Galliformes*, that remain year around. The larger and more widespread of the grouse found in the Rocky Mountains is the blue, or sooty grouse, *Dendragapus obscurus*, whose habitat extends from the foothills to the tree line. Its smaller cousin, the ruffed grouse, *Bonasa umbellus*, is a bird of the deep woods and is found in aspen and coniferous forests.

Grove Creek

A grove is a small group of trees. This grove, and the creek of that name, is found south of Red Lodge and Mount Maurice on the eastern border of the national forest.

In 1893 it was reported to be the site of "rich and prolific gold and silver mines."

Gus Lake

Gus Lake, the northernmost of a series of small lakes that lead into the western arm of T Lake, is just north of the Montana/Wyoming state line. It was named by Ron Kent, a biologist for Wyoming Game and Fish Department. He did not say who this particular Gus was.

Once called Arctic Lake in earlier fishing guides, neither name is officially recognized by the USGS, but Gus appears on modern hiking maps and in fishing handbooks.

Mount Hague

Arnold Hague (1840–1917) was a geologist who worked for the U.S. Geological Survey when it first organized in 1879. He is most famous for his work in Yellowstone Park where he became geologist in charge of the Yellowstone Division in 1883. His book *Geological History of Yellowstone National Park* in 1888 is a classic.

Arnold Hague, 1892.
JACOB REICH.

The name Mount Hague, to honor him, was applied to this high 12,303-foot peak near Mount Wood by James P. Kimball and Anders Wilse during their 1898 survey of the Beartooths.

One of the amusing and interesting asides in a search for the source of names are some of the false legends that get passed on from one source to another. Although we have written proof from his own report that the name was applied by Kimball, a legend still persists, passed on by other writers, that it was for a Mrs. Hague of Cooke City, "who was well known and liked for her many good qualities."

Hairpin Lake

This long, squiggly lake has a twisty shape like an old-fashioned hairpin and can be found among the Hellroaring Lakes near Mount Rearguard.

Alternative, unofficial names of this and Hellroaring Lake are either Cliff or Bay Lake.

Hakel Gulch

Hackel Gulch can be found on Rock Creek just to the south of the town of Red Lodge. John Hackel is mentioned twice in the *Red Lodge Picket*—in 1892 for his marriage to Mary Albera, and again in 1902. No biographical information was given.

Hals Lake

Carl Hals was a surveyor for the Northern Pacific Railroad in 1882 and helped to plan a rail route to the mines of Cooke City. The line was to have gone through the Lamar Valley of Yellowstone National Park, so his team named this small lake at the base of Quadrant Mountain for him. Because of opposition from Gen. Phil Sheridan and other friends of the national park concept, Congress refused to approve and fund the rail project, so it was never built.

Hanlon Hill

Barney Hanlon was an old-time prospector who filed several claims from 1900 to 1905 in the Sheepeater Lode in the New World Mining District near Cooke City. He then moved west to Bear Gulch/Jardine where he, along with J.B. McCarthy, held

Carl Hals. YELLOWSTONE HERITAGE AND RESEARCH CENTER, YELL 9061.

the first patents of the Good Luck placer claim on Bear Creek. In 1907 he came to disrepute when he killed Tom Lannon, a "company miner," after a riot at Mrs. Welcome's Saloon. Lannon apparently had beaten Hanlon with a whipstock, and Hanlon in turn shot and killed him. What seemed self-defense disappeared when it was revealed at trial that Hanlon had been gunning for Lannon for weeks. He was sentenced to 30 years in Deer Lodge Prison.

The hill is just outside of Jardine.

Happy Jack Gulch

E.E. "Happy Jack" Aldrich (1841–1927) was one of the early cowboys in Montana Territory. Born in Iowa, he came west with his brother and family in 1873 and watched as they were all killed by Indians near Fort, Harney in eastern Oregon. He arrived in Montana in 1881 with W.F. McLeod, the first homesteader in the Boulder Valley, driving 125 head of cattle and 200 horses. He then worked as a cowboy for the 79 and 22 Ranches and later for W.D. Ellis. (see Ellis Mountain/ Basin) Eventually he established his own cabin and claim on Cherry Creek next to this gulch, which is on the Upper Boulder River just south of Big Timber.

Well liked, he was known for playing his fiddle

"Happy Jack" Aldrich, 1927. CRAZY MOUNTAIN MUSEUM.

at dances and was the rural postman in his area. It was in this latter role that he found the body of William Corker, who had been murdered near his cabin on Bovee Creek. (see Corker Canyon)

Harney Creek

This creek gets its name from the Harney family who settled on this creek in the good farming bench land six miles northwest of Red Lodge. J.F. "Francis" Harney was first noted to be in Red Lodge in 1892 and married Frankie Draper the following year. He filed a homestead on this creek in 1897 and was followed by his brother John in 1900. The ranch, which he called the Willow Grove Stock Farm, specialized in thoroughbred Holstein-Friesian cattle and Poland-China hogs. Francis died in 1897 and Frankie sold the ranch in 1902.

Harney Creek had a large enough collection of homesteads to have a school house in 1901.

Hatchet Lake

Its hatchet, or tomahawk, shape gives the name to this lake on the Montana/ Wyoming border.

This was once known as Crazy Lake, as it is on the west slope of Crazy Mountain, but on a 1937 map it appears as Farley Lake. Farley Lake is now over the ridge and drains south into Lake Creek. However, just to make things clear, Hatchet Lake is the headwaters of Farley Creek, which, you already know, is called Crazy Creek in Wyoming. Hmmm, this all sounds a bit crazy.

Hawks Creek/Lake

No raptors here; this creek was named for Jack S. Hawks, who in 1896 filed a claim on a vein of silver and lead that he found about six and a half miles up the canyon. The mine was later taken over by his brother Fred. Both were sons of William D. "Dad" Hawks, a Civil War veteran from Chicago who came and

Mr & Mrs. William D. "Dad" Hawks. JIM ANNIN COLLECTION, MUSEUM OF THE BEARTOOTHS.

homesteaded the Stillwater in 1897. Fred and Jack were two of his and Anna's nine children.

There is a small widening of the Stillwater River a mile above Tripod Hill that was known on older maps and Beartooth ranger notes as Hawks Lake. Neither the name of the creek nor of the lake remain on USGS maps but correspond exactly with Flood Creek and the widening of the Stillwater River at Cathedral Point. It seems a shame that the Board on Geographic Names has erased yet another historical reference from the Stillwater River country.

Hawley Mountain/Creek/Lake

In 1923 the **mountain** was named for this **creek** that flows around it on its way to the Boulder River. The creek's name comes from Thomas Hawley, who found gold in 1883, took out homestead papers in 1918, and tried raising Angora goats (that were all eaten by mountain lions). Said to be "as rugged as the peak," he walked the 60 miles to Big Timber in one day—at age 64. He was also one of the survivors of the Froze-to-Death Creek episode. (see that citation) Hawley sold his homestead to Ralph Jarrett, whose descendants still run it as the Hawley Mountain Guest Ranch. The final section of the creek where it drops into the Boulder is known as Hell's Canyon. (see that citation)

Although the names in these mountains tend to focus on the white pioneers and miners, archaeological explorations on the Hawley Mountain Ranch have found evidence of six prehistoric cultures; the earliest is some 7,000 years old.

Hawley Lake, along with Narrow Escape and Squeeze Lakes, are at head of Hawley Creek on the west side of Mount Douglas. These lakes are not officially named on the USGS map but can be found on other sources.

Fishing under Hawley Mountain. CRAZY MOUNTAIN MUSEUM.

Hayden Creek

This creek enters Soda Butte Creek via Woody Creek at Cooke City and honors Ferdinand Vandeveer Hayden (1829–1887), an American geologist who was instrumental in mapping the Yellowstone area. He first came west with the Raynold's Topographical Engineers expedition of 1860 and returned to Yellowstone Country in 1871 where he led the first federally funded geological survey into what was to become the national park. He was accompanied by the painter Thomas Moran and photographer William Henry Jackson. Their work

Ferdinand Vanderveer Hayden, ca. 1870. UNITED STATES GEOLOGICAL SERVICE.

along with Hayden's report were instrumental in convincing Congress to establish Yellowstone as the first national park. He returned to the Yellowstone area with his survey crew yearly until 1878, becoming well known to the local Indians, who called him "the man who picks up stones running." Trained as a physician, he served as a surgeon during the Civil War. However, his professor at Oberlin College had piqued his interest in geology and he spent the following 30 years out west, eventually becoming head of the Geological and Geographic Survey of the Territories. Ill health forced him to resign in 1886 and he died the following year.

Further evidence of his activity north of the Park will pop up throughout the citations in this book.

Haystack Peak

Named for its shape, this was originally called Monument Mountain. Edward M. Douglas called the current Monument Mountain Haystack Peak when he led his 1886 survey. It was used as a triangulation station. These names were official from 1893 to 1934 when the names were switched so that the six-foot-high stone survey cairn, or "monument," would be on the proper peak. Haystack is now a satellite peak that is one mile east of Monument Mountain.

Haywood Gulch

George H. Heywood (or Haywood) arrived in Red Lodge some time prior to 1890. He was first noted to have a "liquid establishment" (saloon) that moved to the Heywood Building, which he built in 1896. George was also active in civic affairs and was elected Justice of the Peace for Carbon County in 1894. In 1903 he patented a homestead south of the town of Red Lodge just to the southwest of Point of Rocks and Towne Point.

Heart Lake

There are three Heart Lakes in our area. Two are reasonably heart shaped—one just west of Fishtail and a bit south of Dean, and the other just south of the Montana/Wyoming border near the Beartooth Highway.

The third is vaguely shaped like the organ and is in a collection of lakes that includes Kidney and Liver Lakes on the Castle Mountain quad just north of the Montana state line.

Heather Lake

This small lake, unnamed on the USGS and National Geographic maps, is at the head of Wounded Man Creek in the Slough Creek drainage and deserves mention because of its ecological significance. It, and its neighbor to the southwest, Peace Lake, are two of the few lakes in the Absaroka-Beartooths with original native Yellowstone cutthroat trout. Almost all others have been planted. For this reason, the Montana state fisheries officials felt that it was important for identification reasons to give it a name. (see Peace Lake and Native Lake)

Pink mountain heather, *Phyllodoce empetriformis*, is a low-growing shrub with lovely dark pink bell-shaped flowers in clusters. Its cousin, western moss heather, *Cassiope mertensiana* (pictured), has scaly leaves and white

Western moss heather, *Cassiope mertensiana*. WALTER SIEGMUNDS, WIKI CREATIVE COMMONSE.

flowers, and both are common in the moist montane ecosystems of the northern Rocky Mountains. Their presence was convenient for naming this lake.

Heidi Lake

Heidi Lake is currently an unnamed body of water on the USGS maps between Thiel and North Hidden Lakes near the Montana/Wyoming border.

It is named on the Montana Fish, Wildlife and Parks and commercial hiking maps, but there is no information about this little Swiss girl.

Helicopter Lake

This is another of the lakes that is only on Montana Fish, Wildlife and Parks documents and is not named on USGS maps. Air drops to stock lakes were first started in the Boulder River country in 1939. This lake sits on a bench on the East Boulder Plateau above Hawley Creek and probably refers to the helicopters that were used—noisier, but a lot faster and easier than packing fingerlings in milk cans.

Hellroaring/Creek/Lake/Plateau/Mountain/Valley

Hellroaring was a popular expression used in the nineteenth century. Hellroaring Creek, in the Centennial Valley at the head of the Jefferson River, is the farthest point from the Gulf of Mexico on the Missouri/Mississippi River system. There is another Hell Roaring Creek that joins the Gallatin River north of Big Sky, and also one on the east side of the Crazies. Not to be outdone, the Absaroka-Beartooth area has three of them, all heading in different directions.

The first, and perhaps the most famous, arises halfway between Gardiner and Cooke City near Slough Creek and flows south past Hellroaring Mountain in the Park to join the Yellowstone River. It was the site of much of the early gold seeking activity in the area and was first found by Ansel Hubble, Lou Anderson, George W. Reese, and a Caldwell as they were prospecting along the Yellowstone in 1867. Hubble went ahead hunting, and when he returned mentioned that he had found a stream that "was a hell roarer." The name first appeared on a map when in 1871 Ferdinand Hayden placed it on his survey maps.

The second flows east as it comes from Mount Rearguard off the **Hellroaring Plateau** and down the southern side of the **Hellroaring Plateau Valley** past, of course, the **Hellroaring Lakes.** It enters Rock Creek near the Beartooth Highway a bit south of Red Lodge. There is a huge chrome deposit here that was first discovered in 1916 by a pair of prospectors who were working for J.F. Brophy of Red Lodge. Their Four Chromes claim in the Silver Run District piqued the interest of Melvin Martin in 1920, and before his death in 1937 he had located all of the other claims in the area. The chromium in the Hellroaring Mining District was first removed in World War II in a huge strip mine along the Mae West Curve of the Beartooth Highway, and later via a tunnel mine at the Hell Roaring Camp up on the plateau. All mining ceased after 1943 when the sea lanes opened up and cheaper, high-grade African ore became available. (see Martin Lake)

The third Hellroaring Creek gathers water from Red Lodge Creek and the East Rosebud Plateau and flows north to the East Rosebud, which enters the Yellowstone River near Absarokee, Montana.

Be sure that you have selected the correct creek for your hike or fishing trip or you will find yourself roaring, "Hell, I got the wrong one!"

Hellroaring Lake itself is one of the cluster of lakes by that name in the Hellroaring Creek Valley near Red Lodge, and old-timers called it and Hairpin Lake either Cliff or Bay Lake. Melvin Martin was the first to stock this lake (among many others) with fish between 1901 and 1905. Apparently fishing provided a nice bit of relaxation from the work in his mines.

Hells Canyon

Hawley Creek tumbles down this canyon to enter the Main Boulder River near the U.S. Forest Service Hell's Canyon Campground and Cabin. The Hells Canyon Trail switchbacks 1,100 feet up this steep, narrow defile. The grunt up is not heavenly.

Hemingway Creek

Ernest Hemingway, the famous American Nobel and Pulitzer Prize–winning author, spent five summers between 1930 and 1939 in Wyoming at Larry and Olive Nordquist's L bar T Ranch just south of Cooke City. (see Copeland Lake) There he hunted, fished, and did some of his best writing. During those summers he completed *Death in the Afternoon*, wrote *The Green Hills of Africa*, and did much of the work on *For Whom the Bell Tolls*.

Crazy Creek, which we know he fished, goes through the L bar T Ranch, and Hemingway Creek, in Montana, is a tributary of it.

Ernest Hemingway in Wyoming.

Henderson Mountain

A. Bart Henderson was one of the early prospectors along the Yellowstone River in the 1860s and is credited with the discovery in 1872 of the Great Republic Mine and the start of the New World Mining District south of Cooke City. His carefully kept journals are a great resource for information on those early mining years.

Henderson Mountain, which was named for him, looms north over the town and was also called the "Mountain of Ore" for the huge outcrops of copper and for the gold and silver that were mined. Daisy Pass is on its west shoulder where the profitable Homestake, Daisy, and Alice E. mines could be found.

A. Bart and his brother James also had a ranch at Cinnabar west of Gardiner that figured in the history of the area. In 1877 the Nez Perce were fleeing Gen. Howard and were about to cross the northern part of Yellowstone Park. A band of these Indians attacked the ranch to steal livestock. The two-hour gun battle that ensued left the ranch buildings burned to the ground. There were no casualties, and the fight ended when Lt. Gustav Doane arrived from Fort Ellis, chased off the Indians, and recovered the horses.

Hampered by the high costs of transporting the ore by wagon to the railhead at Cinnabar, much of the mining on Henderson Mountain stopped in the mid-1890s when the price of silver dropped. It resumed in 1914 when Dr. Gottwerth Tanzer sank a 2,100-foot shaft and started to build a huge power generator and smelter on the Clarks Fork at Cooke City. The construction was never finished, no ore was found, and Tanzer disappeared with the investment money. The McLaren Mines, which were started by Walter McLaren in 1933, opened a huge open pit mine on Henderson Mountain during World War II that expanded production of gold and copper. That mine was shut down in 1953 but left a devastated landscape and sterilized Fisher Creek to a highly acidic pH. (see Fisher Creek) In 1995 Noranda-Crown Butte announced plans to reopen the mines, and great public outcry ensued. The following year, a $68 million settlement was negotiated between the Clinton administration and the mining company to stop the mine and reclaim the land and waterway. The area is now under the protection of the Custer-Gallatin National Forest, and in July of 2019, after a $24.5 million cleanup of the McLaren Mine, the EPA declared the waterways fully reclaimed. (see Soda Butte Creek, Crown Butte, and Lake Margaret)

Hercules Pillar

This 1,000-foot cliff on Silver Run Peak rises above Timberline Basin at the head of Timberline Creek. It is not currently recognized by the Board on Geographic Names, so appears on none of the modern maps. However, it is found on U.S. Forest Service documents and maps of the 1930s. The pillar was named by Al Croonquist of Camp Senia, who was the first to climb it.

Herein Creek

The is no written or deed references to anyone called Herein, and this is most certainly a misspelling of the name Herem where the "m" became an "in."

There were, and still are, several Herems in the Stillwater country. The first appears to have been Arne (1850–1932), who emigrated from Norway and settled on Butcher Creek near Roscoe. Andrew (1879–1949) was also a Norwegian emigrant who came in 1896 and homesteaded with his wife, Hilda, along Beaver Creek near Absarokee in 1911. His brother Osmond (1889–1969) came to join him in 1907, and he and Katherine settled a few miles farther east. Mention of other Herems from a younger generation show up with oil and gas leases in 1953, and a quit claim deed by Larry Herem as recently as 2019.

Hermit Lake

The two Hermit Lakes in the Absaroka-Beartooths do not imply any particular person seeking solitude. Instead the name refers to lakes that are tucked off by themselves—good places for a hermit to hide out. One is below Castle Rock Glacier, and the other is in a cirque on the north slope of Two Sisters Mountain.

Hicks Mountain/Peak/Park/Lakes

Hicks Mountain is a 7,000-foot rise on the ridge that separates Deer Creek from the Stillwater River and is found a bit northwest of Nye. It was named for a Col. Walt Hicks who was the foreman of horses in Yellowstone National Park. From 1901 to 1906 he had a contract to winter the horses for $8 a head in Bad Canyon, which lies between this Hicks Mountain and Nye.

Hicks Peak is on the Main Boulder River and was named for a different man who settled **Hicks Park** during the mining boom at Independence in 1890. The little community of Hicks Park had a post office from 1892 to 1894, but now all that remains is the USFS campground of that name.

Walt Hicks. YELLOWSTONE HERITAGE AND RESEARCH CENTER, YELL 36876.

Upper and Lower **Hicks Lakes** are on the east slope of Hicks Peak. They are unnamed officially but can be found on hiking maps and Montana Fish, Wildlife and Parks publications.

Hidden Creek/Lakes/Glacier/Glacier Peak

A lot of hidden features can be found in the Absaroka-Beartooths, perfect for those who want to go seek the hard to find.

Hidden Creek is a mysterious little stream on the West Fork of the Stillwater River.

There are three **Hidden Lakes.** One is right next to Buffalo Creek, but is located slightly above a swamp and so is "hidden" from the creek. Another is on the Castle Mountain quad north of the Montana/Wyoming border and is hidden in a cluster of lakes. Nearby North Hidden Lake is cited next.

Hidden Glacier is hidden in a cleft between Mount Villard and Glacier Peak. It gave Glacier Peak its name, and some people are calling the 12,377-foot point on the ridge above this cleft, **Hidden Glacier Peak.**

North Hidden Lake

North Hidden Lake is also in the same cluster of lakes as the Hidden Lake on the state border. (see previous citation) It was formerly called Marmot Lake by local residents because of the many yellow-bellied marmots, *Marmota flaviventris*, found near the lake, and it appears as Marmot Lake on the 1986 and earlier USGS maps. (see Woodchuck Ridge in the Crazies chapter) However, the U.S. Forest Service field reports called it North Hidden Lake, and that rather ordinary name was adopted by the Board on Geographic Names in 1988.

An alternate name of Reini Lake can be found on some older maps and Montana Fish, Wildlife and Parks documents, but there is no citation as to why.

High Mountain

The rise near Dome Mountain in the Paradise Valley tops out at just under 8,700 feet, but it is "high" for the locality.

High Pass Lake

This lake is on a pass between Sierra Creek and Lake Fork Creek north of Granite Lake and the Montana/Wyoming border. There is no trail or pass noted on the USGS or hikers' maps after 1984, but it was there at one time.

Highline Trail Lakes

The Highline Trail is no longer found on maps but was previously in the northeastern part of Wyoming's Shoshone National Forest. These lakes were on that trail and sit just to the east of the current High Lakes Wilderness Study Area. This cluster of lakes forms the headwaters of Wyoming Creek, a short three-quarters of a mile south of the Wyoming/Montana border.

Hilleary Bridge

The bridge crossing the Main Boulder River near the Fourmile Ranger Station was named for "an obscure person" who was thought to have been a workman on the bridge.

Hilltop Lake

Hilltop Lake sits on the top of a gentle rise north of Cooke City. The original Hilltop Lake is now called Panhandle Lake, and the current Hilltop Lake is upstream from that. Both are on Goose Creek.

Hodges Mountain

Hodges Mountain rises to 11,000 feet southwest of Little Park Mountain. It holds the Corkscrew Lakes on its shoulder, and Corkscrew Creek flows from there to the upper Stillwater River. It is assumed that the Hodges referred to in the name was a prospector. This may have been the Woodson Hodges who, in 1903, filed a deed to land in Box Canyon near Fishtail on the Lower Stillwater.

Hogan Creek

The creek was named for the Hogans who homesteaded the ranchland north of the national forest near Roscoe, Montana. Thomas Hogan filed the first homestead in 1897, and he was followed by Mike Hogan in 1909, and a Mamie Hogan who filed hers a bit downstream in 1910. The creek originates in the national forest and flows out of the mountains past their ranches.

The Hole

A steep-walled cirque can be found above the North Fork of the Hellroaring Creek that goes into Yellowstone Park. It is obviously called The Hole for its shape.

Mount Hole-in-the-Wall

Mount Hole-in-the-Wall lies above East Rosebud Lake and the community of Alpine. It is another of those features named for a geologic formation.

Hopper Glacier

The original Hopper Glacier was on Castle Mountain and is now known as Castle Rock Glacier. The Hopper Glacier name was moved to the glacier that is a little farther north in the south cirque of Medicine Mountain—all part of the egg beater that hit the names on Castle, Summit, and Castle Rock Mountains.

More detail about the locusts can be found on the Grasshopper Glacier/Lakes citation.

Mount Hornaday/Creek

William Temple Hornaday (1854–1937) was one of the most famous naturalists of his day. He was the first director of New York Zoological Gardens, now the Bronx Zoo, and a pioneer on early wildlife conservation.

Hornaday was very interested in bison and collected them from Montana and Wyoming. He also compiled the first bison census in 1885 and found that there were only 285 wild bison in the U.S., most of which were in Yellowstone Park. He was said to have loved the Lamar Valley, so the mountain in that valley, just south of the Montana/Wyoming state line was named

William Temple Hornaday, 1906.

for him. The creek on the mountain, which had formerly been called Plateau Creek, was renamed for him in 1981. This avoided the duplication with the other Plateau Creek in the Park that is found on Two Ocean Plateau.

Horse Creek/Mountain

As one might suspect, with the horse being the main source of transportation in the West prior to automobiles, there would be several references to this animal, and that is true. Most of these were named for good places to graze horses, and most are out in the prairie. However, there is one Horse Creek on the Enos Mountain quad south of Big Timber, and another Horse Creek on its own Horse Mountain that flows into Hellroaring Creek near Gardiner. Both are within the national forest boundaries.

Horseman Creek/Flats/Lake

There is a peculiar figure resembling a horseman that can be imagined by looking at park and timber formations at the base of a hill north of Old Nye. This was noted in ranger notes in the late 1930s and gave the name to the creek, the flats, and the lake above it.

Horseman Flats is a triangular-shaped plateau, several thousand acres in size that sits some thousand feet above the Stillwater River, where its cliffs served the Crow as a pishkun. (see Buffalo Jump) **Horseman Lake** and **Creek** are passed along the trail up to the flats.

The lake has an alternate and unofficial name of No Ketchum Lake. Put your fishing gear away.

Horseshoe Mountain/ Basin/Lake/Creek

Horseshoe Mountain is on the Little Park Mountain quad and gets its name from a horseshoe-shaped basin on the southern exposure of this peak. **Horseshoe Lake** is round, so it is not named for its shape, but rather because it sits in the cirque on the floor of **Horseshoe Basin.** This basin was the site of mineral exploration in 1916 and again between 1926 and 1930, and relics of abandoned mining activity litter the basin. The lake has an old earthen dam that raises its level about four feet. It was made by the miners to power a hydraulic sluiceway that was used to expose the gold.

Horseshoe Creek is named for this mountain as well but comes out of Lake of the Woods on the mountain's north slope and flows northeast to the Stillwater River.

There are two other **Horseshoe Lakes** that actually have the C-shape of a horseshoe. One is on the Lake Plateau and is the headwaters of Upsidedown Creek near the Main Boulder. The other is above the West Boulder River on the Mount Rae quad and is at the head of Little Mission Creek.

Hubble Gulch

The gulch, off Dry Fork Creek and near the East Boulder River and mines, was named for Ansel Hubble (1837–1903), a frontiersman, Indian fighter, and trapper. Ansel was born in 1837, reputedly the first white child in Milwaukee, Wisconsin.

He arrived in Montana in the 1860s where he was one of the early prospectors on the Yellowstone River. During that time, he was credited with naming Hellroaring Creek near Gardiner as well as Slough Creek, and it was he who first found gold at Crevice in 1867. He was given the nickname of "Indian Fighter" because of two noted gunfights with both the Sioux and the Crow in 1875.

After his mine on the Stillwater was burned out by the Indians in 1884, he moved to the East Boulder and filed claims on this gulch near McLeod in 1894. His Morning Star and Pilgrim Lode claims produced some gold and nickel, but primarily copper, and were worked until shortly before his death. The area was active enough that a small town grew up that was named Hubble in his honor. It had a post office that ran from 1914 until 1933 but has now completely disappeared.

Ansel Hubble. CRAZY MOUNTAIN MUSEUM.

Huckleberry Creek/Gulch/Lake

Huckleberries, the fruit of several plants of the genus *Vaccinium*, are the favorite wild snack of hikers (and bears) in our forest.

There are two **Huckleberry Lakes.** One is north of Cooke City, east of Lulu Pass and above Goose Creek. The other, along with its creek of the same name, is on the off-trail route to Granite Peak from Mystic Lake. Both have lots of huckleberries along their banks.

A second **Huckleberry Creek** is in **Huckleberry Gulch,** which is just off Emigrant Creek and the Paradise Valley. This latter was the site of many claims and much gold activity.

Hudson Spring

Hudson Spring is located near Nye and was named for the four Hudson brothers of Saginaw, Michigan, who prospected and settled near there. John (1855–1893) came to the Shields River Valley with Bill Lee and a herd of cattle in 1878. In 1890 he squatted near Fishtail then established his ranch near Absarokee. Bob (1866–1952) had a ranch on Limestone Creek out of Nye and was the first settler in the Limestone Butte area where he ranched for over 50 years. He married an English emigrant, Emma Cooke,

Bob Hudson. JIM ANNIN COLLECTION, MUSEUM OF THE BEARTOOTHS, #1205.

and they died in the same year, after more than 55 years of marriage. Both John and Bob got the jump on the Stillwater country as they had squatted to wait until the survey showed that the Crow Reservation had been moved farther east. Of the other brothers, Ben (1863–1945) ranched near the Stillwater and Rock Creek but prospected near Nye. David, who also prospected near Nye, worked the 79 Ranch on the Stillwater.

Hummingbird Peak/Basin

Hummingbird Peak is a quadrangular mountain that sits just to the north of Yellowstone Park and has a USGS topo map named for it. There are basins located on all four sides—Telephone, Elk Creek, East Fork (of Hellroaring), and Hummingbird Basins. All, especially Telephone, were the sites of much mining activity.

Although there is no citation to explain why this mountain and accompanying basin were named for the little bird, Hummingbird is a popular name for mines. There was a Hummingbird Mine in Confederate Gulch near Helena, another in the Coeur d'Alenes in Idaho, and also one in the Klamath Mountains in Idaho. The Hummingbird Corporation is currently actively mining in Africa, and the Hummingbird Mine near Grand Junction, Colorado, was approved in 2017. There is no mining record on file with the State of Montana or the U.S. Bureau of Land Management, but there must have been a mine of that name in Hummingbird Basin, and the mountain's name would have come from the mine.

Hyman Creek

There is no confirmation of a Hyman in the homestead or mining records, but he must have been an early miner or trapper. Perhaps he was the builder of the "Bull Moose Cabin" on the wide flat area where Hyman Creek comes into Hellroaring Creek. This was noted on the 1943 Mt. Wallace quad north of Yellowstone Park, but the cabin no longer exists and the site is no longer noted on current maps.

Iceberg Peak

This is a fanciful name that just refers to the fact that the mountain is near both Grasshopper and Wolf Mountain Glaciers.

Imelda Lake

Imelda is another of the mystery women of the Beartooths. Her lake is on the north side of Wolf Mountain.

Impasse Falls

Harrison Fagg has said of Impasse Falls, "It is, without question, the most beautiful falls in the Beartooth area," and is impressive enough to be one of the few falls that the USGS records on a map.

It is found far up East Rosebud Creek just above Duggan Lake and was once called Duggan Falls. (see Duggan Lake) It was renamed Impasse Falls because of the steep cliff wall that prevented one from going any farther upstream. In 1962 the Forest Service decided that a trail, suitable for horses, was needed to connect the East Rosebud with the Fossil Lake country, which required blasting a trail up the sheer granite wall next to Impasse Falls. The crews were first supervised by Charlie Martin (see Charlie Falls), and after he was drafted into the military, it was completed by supervisor Blase DiLulo. The men who drilled the blasting holes were suspended by ropes and the whole chore took three years. No wonder they drove a gold spike to commemorate the completion of their efforts.

Mount Inabnit

Fred Inabnit. CRAZY MOUNTAIN MUSEUM AND MONTANA MEMORY PROJECT, MONTANA HISTORICAL SOCIETY.

Snow Glacier Mountain in the East Rosebud country had its name changed in 1929 to honor mountaineer and Beartooth enthusiast Fred Inabnit (1866–1928). Fred came to the U.S. from Switzerland with his parents at age three, moved to Ubet, Montana, in 1890, and settled in Billings in 1893. He was very civic minded and, in addition to his own business, served two terms as county treasurer, four as clerk of the district court, two terms on the city council, and seven years on the school board. He was a great outdoor enthusiast and explored much of the Beartooth region on foot. He made several unsuccessful attempts on Granite Peak and was with the group when Elers Koch finally made the summit. After his death, "for his services in creating public interest in the scenic splendors of these mountains," this mountain, the first that he climbed, was named for him. The memorial plaque dedicated to him was placed at East Rosebud Lake and reads: "This plaque was placed here by the friends of Fred Inabnit 1866–1928. A faithful official of Yellowstone County in whose honor this peak was named Mount Inabnit in recognition of his successful efforts to inspire others with his love and enthusiasm for these mountains whose silent depths and glorious heights he explored for many years."

Incisor Lake

The wild dentist was camped here as well. This lake, near Goose Lake, has the general shape of an incisor tooth, complete with the roots, and is next to Cavity Lake. Molar and Little Molar Lakes are in the same vicinity, but farther east. It is too bad that a ditch had not been dug between these lakes as it would have been a great opportunity to call it the Root Canal.

Independence Peak/Mine/Town Site/Pass

Gold was discovered in the 1860s near the Boulder River on what was to become the Independence Mining District, but, since the land was on the Crow Indian Reservation, the federal government ran the miners out. In 1882, after a new treaty moved the reservation boundary farther east, Elias Joseph "Joe" Keeney (1847–1938) got directions to the mines up the Boulder from "the spirits" that he saw in a trance. He staked claims to Big Spirit and Little Spirit Mines at a site that he named The Independence. The mountain, mine, district, pass, and town's names came

Joe Keeney. CRAZY MOUNTAIN MUSEUM.

from this. Mining boomed, with $42,000 in gold bullion produced between 1890 and 1893.

The town of Independence sprang up to serve the mines and miners in the Independence Mining District and the surrounding small towns such as Solomon City and Horseshoe Basin. At its peak it had a population of 400 to 500 men with another 300 in the surrounding area. There was a sawmill, seven stamp mills, two general stores, a restaurant, a blacksmith, a stable, two gambling establishments, and a house of prostitution (the only building made of sawn lumber boards), an electric power plant, and telephone service, but no schools or churches. The silver crash of 1893 and the cost of the five-day wagon trip to the railroad at Big Timber ended the boom, and the post office closed in 1895. In 1899, James Kimball noted in his survey report that Independence and Solomon City were "deserted mining camps," although small-scale work continued until 1905. All that exists today are a few tumbling cabins and mining relics.

Joe Keeney was quite the Western character, not only as a successful miner, but also as the source of legends. He was born in Oregon Territory in 1847 and came to Montana in 1875 with a herd of horses that he said were "wild." As he had no bills of sale for ownership, he was suspected of horse thieving and the Vigilantes ran him out of Helena. He had at least three wives, several paramours, and died in Livingston in 1938 at age 91, still telling tall tales.

Independence was also the location of one of the grislier tales in what was already wild mining country. In 1924, Ranger Harry Kaufman noted that a miner, Henry Hughson, had gone missing and he suspected murder. He called in the Sweet Grass County sheriff, Ed Brannin, and, when the law officers investigated, they found blood all over Hughson's cabin and a trail to the lake that looked like an apparent drowning. No body was found, but a man named Frank Lewis was suspected immediately because he was known to have had a disagreement with Hughson about a mining strike. Winter prevented further investigation, but when spring came the sheriff found that the bloody trail went by an old mining cut, or sump, and Hughson's body was found there, shot in the heart and and covered with piles of rock. Lewis was arrested and jailed in Big Timber. Before he could come to trial, he escaped the county jail and, in spite of a statewide search, was never seen again. Wild West country!

Sweet Grass County and the Boulder River area was also prime sheep-herding country in the early part of the twentieth century. On the east slope of Independence Mountain are three little lakes that celebrate the grazing allotments. They are unnamed on the USGS map, but they do appear on other maps where they are called Lamb, Wool, and Mutton Lakes.

Index Peak

Index and its neighbor, Pilot Peak, rise in dramatic welcome to visitors coming down the Beartooth Highway to the Northeast Entrance of Yellowstone National Park.

Bart Henderson was the first to record the name Index Peak when he put it in his journal in 1868. John Colter called it Finger Peak, and some of the early miners called it Dog Turd Peak; both were allusions to its shape. Thomas Moran painted Index and Pilot Peaks in 1871

Pilot and Inde Peaks from the L bar T. EMILY COPELAND FAMILY PHOTOGRAPH.

when he accompanied the Hayden Expedition, and they appear as they do now. It is thus thought that Colter's reference to a "finger" for Index Peak was for a taller point that looked like a raised index finger. It apparently fell after his visit in 1806, leaving just the knuckles or "dog turd" that we see now.

It is usually paired with its larger neighbor, Pilot Peak, and was once called Pilot Knob. The names Pilot and Index, perhaps because of mapping error, were often switched, but in 1937 the Board on Geographic Names determined that the taller, more southern peak was Pilot, and Index, which extends partway into Montana, was the shorter, northern one.

Indian Knife Lake

The lake, next to Otter Lake in the Russell Creek drainage, is round, not knife-shaped. One assumes that the name refers to an Indian artifact found there.

Ingles Creek

This creek, which enters the West Fork of Rock Creek by Wild Bill Lake, was named for an "old-timer" of Red Lodge who at one time cut timber on this creek. E.H. Ingles is recorded in the 1920 Carbon County census as a farmer.

Initial Creek

The USFS Initial Creek Campground is located where this creek joins the West Fork of the Stillwater River. It is the first tributary of the West Fork that one finds after entering the national forest but before coming to the wilderness boundary. Perhaps this could be the meaning of "Initial." Or perhaps it was because an illiterate miner marked or signed for his claim here with just his initials.

Iron Mountain/Creek

There are two Iron Mountains in the Beartooths, both in mining areas. Although iron has not been mined commercially, the name reflects the huge amount of that ore that is found in these mountains.

The most famous **Iron Mountain** overlooks the East Boulder River and is on that massive seam that extends northwest to southeast all the way from Contact on the Main Boulder, past Chrome Mountain, Iron Mountain, and beyond Nye to the Mouat and Benbow Mines on the Stillwater. (see Chrome Mountain and Contact Mountain) This Iron Mountain is part of the Boulder-Stillwater Divide, and is at the head of **Iron Creek,** where Ansel Hubble filed a claim in 1893, and where there was large-scale placer gold mining. The creek flows from Iron Mountain toward the West Fork of the Stillwater River.

There is another **Iron Mountain** on the northern edge of the Custer-Gallatin National Forest, to the north of Sliderock Mountain. The Knapp Mine is located on this mountain, and the fact that Gold Hill and Placer Gulch are nearby testifies to the ores located there.

Island Lake

The Island Lake that is most well known is on the West Rosebud just upstream from Mystic Lake and the power dam. When James Kimball camped here during his 1898 survey, he wrote that he found evidence of Indian occupation.

There is another small Island Lake just west of Fishtail, Montana, south of Dean, and a third is in Wyoming in the Little Bear Creek chain just north of the Beartooth Highway. The latter has a campground and boat launch and can be reached from the highway by way of a short gravel road.

Curiously, all three lakes have islands in them.

Ivy Lake

Ivy Lake is in the Wyoming section of the Absaroka-Beartooth Wilderness just south of the border in the Crazy Creek chain. The ivy plant is native to southern

Europe, northwestern Africa, and parts of Asia. Imported to America as an ornamental, it has become a serious invasive species is the western U.S. where the winters are mild. Winters in this part of the Rocky Mountains are not in the least mild, so the name must refer to a woman. The lake's name appears before 1937, but nothing is recorded or known about her.

Jardine

The town of Jardine is the site of one of the earliest, most profitable, and one of the longest-running mining operations in the Absaroka-Beartooths. Originally the small mining camp was called Bear Gulch and was the place in 1866 where Joe Brown discovered placer gold—and a burned, hairless bear cub. (see Bear Creek/Gulch)

A bit later, in 1870, Brown and James Graham struck gold-bearing quartz ore on Mineral Hill next to town, but development stalled as it was in the Crow Reservation. The 1882 cession by the Crow and the completion of the Northern Pacific Railroad from Livingston to Gardiner spurred activity. The Bear Gulch Placer Company was formed in 1884 and became the Bear Gulch Mining Company in 1898 when a common land-slide on Mineral Hill revealed one of the richest lodes in Montana. (see Mineral Hill)

Mrs. A.C. Jardine. YELLOWSTONE GATEWAY MUSEUM, 2006.044.2536.

In 1897, before the slide, Bear Gulch consisted of four log shacks. By 1900 it was one of the largest towns in Park County with 500 people, two 20 stamp mills, and a 40 stamp mill, the Revenue, which had 1,000-pound stamps capable of crushing five tons of ore a day. There were 130 residential and commercial buildings, telephones, electric lights, water and a sewer system, and a 200-pupil school. This new success deserved a higher-quality name, so the town's name was changed to honor A.C. Jardine, the secretary/treasurer of the Bear Gulch Mining Company. He was said to have been an excellent accountant with no claims to understanding mining. His wife, pictured, was supposed to have been the only cultured lady in Bear Gulch in 1898.

The mines changed hands several times with varying activity and names. Over the years of the area's continuous operation, until 1947, nearly a million tons of ore was treated and over 171,000 ounces of gold, more that 33,000 ounces of silver, and both copper and lead were recovered. In 1906 tungsten was recovered, and it was the first commercial source of that metal in the U.S. Gold production slowed, but the mines continued to produce the tungsten that was needed especially for military use, as well as arsenic trioxide, which was very profitable as an insecticide. Operations closed in 1948 after World War II, and many of the town's buildings were lost to fire and demolition. TVX Mineral Hill, Inc., briefly restarted gold mining in 1989, but closed for good in 1996. Business in Jardine is now primarily recreation and hunting.

On an amusing note, Jardine's cemetery is supposed to be the only one in Montana with a "Welcome" sign. It is the headstone for George Welcome, an early-day merchant and hotel owner who is buried there.

Jasper Lake

Jasper is a name that is derived from ancient Semitic languages meaning "a spotted or speckled stone." It refers to a semi-precious stone that can be highly polished and is used as ornamentation or as a gemstone. Ranger notes from 1961 indicate that it got its name because "the color of the lake is green and similar to the color of the stone worn in the breastplates of the high priest in Exodus 28:20."

It sits on the west slope of Spirit Mountain and is the headwaters of Tumble Creek, which explains its former name of Tumble Lake.

Jawbone Lake

There is no citation or information as to the reason for the name of this small lake that sits in a high cirque on the ridge between the West Rosebud and Pyramid Peak. The name appeared on maps sometime after 1937.

In the early part of the twentieth century, the term "jawbone" was used for "an attempt to persuade by force of one's position." Richard Harlow's Montana Railroad ran up Sixteenmile Canyon to the silver mines at Castle and on to Lewistown and the sheep and wool in the north Shields River Valley. It was known colloquially as "The Jawbone" railroad because of Harlow's vociferous promises and the company's perennially weak finances. (see Sixteen Mile Creek in the Crazies chapter) Perhaps someone camping at this lake was jawboning his companions.

Jay Lake

The name of the lake that sits in a cirque on the south side of Chalice Mountain near the head of Flood Creek refers to the birds that are so common in our mountains.

The Canada or grey jay, *Perisoreus canadensis*, is called the "camp robber" and is notorious for snatching unwatched chips or crackers. This is probably the bird for which the lake was named.

Canada jay.

However, we also have the less common crested, dark blue Steller's jay, *Cyanocitta stelleri,* which was named for Georg Wilhelm Steller, who sailed as the naturalist on Vitus Bering's expedition from Siberia to North America in 1741. His return with this bird skin confirmed that Bering was indeed the first to reach North America from the west, as crested jays were unknown in Eurasia.

Jeff Lake

Although this is thought by the author to be an excellent name, it is actually part of the humorous collection of lakes north of Cooke City. Mutt and Jeff Lakes are a pair of meadow ponds that can be found just off the Goose Lake jeep trail.

Mutt and Jeff was a long-running and widely popular American newspaper comic strip created by cartoonist Bud Fisher in 1907 about "two mismatched tinhorns." It remained in syndication until 1983. (see cartoon at Mutt Lake)

Jenny Lake

Jenny and Pat Lakes are widenings of Hemingway Creek just north of the Montana/Wyoming line near the Clarks Fork River and the L bar T Ranch.

Ernest Hemingway had quite the reputation as a lady's man. When he first came to Wyoming in 1930, it was with his second wife, Pauline, and he left after his last visit in 1939 with Martha Gellhorn, soon to become his third wife.

In spite of his various infidelities, no one seems to be aware of any association with a Jenny or a Pat, and these names appear before Hemingway Creek was placed on the maps. They, too, join the list of mystery women. (see Hemingway Creek)

Jewel Lake/Falls

This tiny jewel of a lake and its beautiful falls can be seen just as Pine Creek comes out of Pine Creek Lake on the Mount Cowen quad.

There is a second, and former, Jewel Lake near the head of the Middle Fork of Wounded Man Creek. Ed Ickerman of the Beartooth Ranch was the first to cut a trail to the lakes, and he called the small lake between Pentad and Sundown, Jewel Lake. It is now unnamed.

Jim's Gulch

The Jim of this gulch near the West Bridger Ranger Station on the Wildcat Draw quad is unknown, even to local sources whose ranch was nearby.

Jim Smith Creek/Mountain

This creek, which can be found southeast of Cooke City in Wyoming, has an interesting history.

Jim Smith, alias August Hild, homesteaded on the present B bar 4 ranch on the Clarks Fork. In the summer of 1912, he hired a local named Tony Rodoschek for some ranch work. They had a disagreement and altercation, so Smith ran him off without paying. Later Smith came to get some hay at the L bar T where Tony was working and Rodoschek shot him in the arm and he bled to death. Since Jim Smith was known as "an arrogant and aggressive type," Rodoschek was acquitted on grounds of justifiable homicide. The L bar T Ranch where Smith was killed is where Ernest Hemingway did much of his writing during his summer visits in the 1930s. Harry, the narrator of the book *The Snows of Kilimanjaro*, recalls this murder of Jim Smith. (see Gilbert Creek and Hemingway Creek)

Jim Smith Mountain was named for the same individual and sits a bit farther south in Wyoming.

Jimmy Joe Campground

The campground on the East Rosebud Creek road commemorates James "Jimmy Joe" Ayling (1904–1971), who was known as "The Hermit of the Beartooths." He was originally from West New York, New Jersey, and spent time in the Northwest Territories of Canada before coming to Red Lodge in 1925. Initially squatting on Forest Service land 18 miles up Rock Creek, he went over to the East Rosebud where he was caretaker for several cabins. He lived mostly by hunting and also as a noted "character" and tourist attraction around Red Lodge.

Joe Brown Creek

(see Brown Creek)

"Jimmy Joe" Ayling. CARBON COUNTY MUSEUM.

Johnson Creek

John P. Johnson patented a homestead on this creek near Dexter Point east of the Yellowstone River in 1899. In 1904 he enlarged his holdings with a further half section slightly upstream and closer to the mountains.

Jomaha Creek

Jomaha Creek runs down a very short gulch into Mill Creek near Montanapolis Spring. It is probably named for a mine that no longer exists.

Jordan Mountain/Lake/Pass

The mountain, and the lake and pass on its shoulder, are found on the Pinnacle Mountain quad map between the North and Middle Forks of Wounded Man Creek.

Although there is no clear citation as for whom it was named, it most probably refers to David Starr Jordan (1851–1931), who was a naturalist and the first fish investigator in Yellowstone National Park. During his day, he was known as the greatest living authority on fish. He was also a peace advocate, a teacher, and later became president of Stanford University.

Jorden Lake

This Jorden Lake, with an "e," probably refers to Allen Jorden, an early resident of Red Lodge. It sits in the cluster of lakes just north of Crazy Mountain near the Montana/Wyoming state line, with the name appearing prior to 1937.

Jungle Creek

This tributary of the West Boulder River was so named, according to ranger C.A. Butler, because of the dense second growth and windfall.

Lake Kathleen

In 1923 a district forester named this lake in the valley of the East Fork of the Boulder River at its confluence with Rainbow Creek. Further identification of the woman was not given in the ranger's notes. Perhaps she was his wife or sweetheart.

Kaufman Lake

Harry Kaufman (1881–1941), the first forest guard in the Absaroka Division of the Yellowstone Forest Reserve, was commemorated in this lake's name. Harry built the Main Boulder Ranger Station in 1905 where he and his wife Coral and their two children lived until ill health forced him to retire in 1941. The building is now a museum and represents what is probably the oldest existing facility in the U.S. Forest Service system. He also served as deputy supervisor and district ranger from 1909 to 1941 and patrolled throughout that time. Stories of his tenure are legendary. Among these are the fact that he was attacked

Harry Kaufman. USDA FOREST SERVICE, CUSTER-GALLATIN NATIONAL FOREST PHOTO ARCHIVES.

by Indians in the early years and had to carry a gun to fend off poachers. Harry is also the person who reported to Sheriff Ed Brannin that Henry Hughson from Independence was missing. (see citation under Independence for the murder story)

Coral was the daughter of George T. McKnight, who was a pioneer settler on the West Boulder River in 1886. (see Mount McKnight and Mount Rae) Coral raised her children and managed the Main Boulder Ranger Station, serving as administrative assistant and telephone operator for the many "spike box" phone lines set up throughout the wilderness. (see Telephone Basin)

The lake is at the head of Falls Creek below Boulder Mountain. It was known for many years as West Falls Creek Lake, but, since there are two Falls Creeks within a few miles of each other, the name was changed in 1953 to avoid confusion and to honor Harry Kaufman.

Kersey Lake

In 1897, Enos Kersey filed a patent on 160 acres at Kersey Meadows next to this lake. There, at the end of the wagon road north from Cooke City, he drained the meadow and grew hay for the many pack animals at Cooke. The hay was harvested in the fall but, because of the swampy conditions, he waited until the lake and wagon road froze solid in the winter, when he could haul the hay to town on sleds.

The 10-person Kersey cabin is available through the USFS rental program.

Keyser Brown Lake

Keyser Brown was a long-standing resident of Red Lodge where he served as judge from 1890 to 1900.

The lake was named in 1892 when he, along with his son-in-law Will McIntyre and a friend, Edgar Worman, went on a weeklong camping trip to Lake Fork Creek on Upper Rock Creek. In an article in the *Red Lodge Picket*, Judge Brown reports naming three lakes: Lake McIntyre for his son-in-law and group photographer, Lake Edgar for his friend Mr. Worman, and Keyser Lake. Keyser Brown Lake is still on the maps as a widening of Lake Fork Creek. The names of Lake McIntyre and Lake Edgar have disappeared and are now called the uninteresting First and Second Rock Lakes. As these individuals were of insufficient prominence, it is probable that the USGS just dropped their names from the official register.

Kid Lake

Kid Lake is in the high country on the drainage of West Rosebud Creek near Granite Peak. It is a great environment for the mountain goat, so the name probably represents a young kid of that species.

Of interest is that the U.S. Forest Service map spells it Kidd. This may be a misspelling, but there was a Kidd who had a mining claim in the New World Mining District near Cooke City in 1888. If the lake was named for an individual of this family, then the USGS did the misspelling, dropping one "d" and making it a goat.

Take your pick.

Kidney Lake

Our amusing anatomist (or was he a pathologist?) named this lake, along with neighboring Heart and Liver Lakes on the Alpine quad. Did he name it for the shape, which looks like a question mark or a very sick kidney, or did he pee in the lake?

Knife Creek

This short creek comes off the Red Rock Plateau to Grizzly Creek, and eventually to the Hellroaring Creek north of Yellowstone Park. It is not known where the "knife" name came from, but like Indian Knife Lake, it may represent a found artifact.

Knott Lake

Knott Lake is north of Cooke City, high in the drainage of the West Rosebud near LaVelle Lake. It was formerly called Castle Lake, but that name was moved to nearby Knox Lake (see citation).

Ralph Sanders of Billings, whose maps were the standard for hikers and anglers in the Beartooths in the 1980s and 90s, states that this lake was named recently for Earl Nott (1946–2009). James "Bridger Jim" Earl Nott was a life insurance salesman in Columbus and was very active with the Boy Scouts. As he was responsible for naming several of the nearby lakes for outdoorsmen from the Columbus area, it seems appropriate that his name is on this lake. Efforts to correct the misspelling have not been recognized by the Board on Geographic Names.

The fact that the USGS has kept the name Knott may reflect the fact that the name Proctor

J. Proctor Knott, ca. 1880. PHOTO BY MATTHEW BRADY, LIBRARY OF CONGRESS.

Knott was used in the Cooke City mining country. There was a Proctor Knott mining claim that was filed in 1890, and Proctor Knott was the name of a famous thoroughbred racehorse that ran in this part of Montana between 1888 to 1891. All of these names come from J. Proctor Knott (1830–1911), who was prominent nationally as governor of Kentucky from 1883 to 1887, a member of the House of Representatives, an opponent of railroad expansion, and a strong supporter of President Grover Cleveland.

Knowles Peak/Falls

Knowles Falls is on the Yellowstone River near the Black Canyon and was named for John S. Knowles. This early miner came to Montana in 1876 and originally worked a claim at Emigrant Gulch. He later built a cabin not far from these falls and mined Crevice Creek near Gardiner, one year making a strike worth $40,000. He left after 1886 when the army evicted all who were living and mining in the Park and moved to California in 1899.

Knowles Peak was named for a different person. It is located a bit north of Emigrant near Mill Creek and was named for Bill and Piercy (or Percie) Knowles. They built an open dance pavilion and a boardinghouse at Chico Hot Springs, and operated the resort from 1902 to 1912.

Knox Lake

Knox Lake is northeast of Jardine on the Bear Creek drainage and was named by Dick Randall of the nearby OTO dude ranch. It honors Al Knox, a friend of Randall's, who was the first person to ride from East Rosebud Lake to Cooke City on horseback, establishing the East Rosebud-Russell Creek Trail. (see Dick Randall Point)

The Board on Geographic Names did not agree with calling this Knox Lake. They once had it listed as Crystal Lake but officially changed it to the similarly uninteresting Castle Lake. Curiously, the USGS does name the Knox Lake Trail on the current Mineral Mountain quad map, and this trail passes right by what is now Castle Lake. The lake remains Knox Lake on the 2012 Gallatin National Forest map and on Montana Fish, Wildlife and Parks documents.

KooKoo Lake/Falls/Creek

KooKoo Lake, south of Bowback Mountain, was named by Al Croonquist and A.J. Salo in 1919. They were exploring a route to Cooke City along this previously unnamed creek when a horse fell off a cliff into the creek, was injured, and had to be shot. The packs were removed and rescued from the stream, and this led to the discovery of the falls.

Croonquist was reported as saying, "I'm coo-coo about those falls" and Salo suggested the spelling.

Laduala Creek

The creek is in Carbon County near the Montana/Wyoming border, and its name is clearly a misspelling of a local Red Lodge person. During the Carbon County coal mining boom there were a large number of Finnish emigrants who came to work in the mines. To this day, the Finnish community still has a number of people named Ladvala. The mapmaker must have been interchanged the "v" with a "u."

Barbara and Charles Ladvala, 1951.

Charles Ladvala, pictured at his marriage to Barbara, was a master carpenter and longtime Red Lodge resident.

LaDuke Spring

The LaDuke Hot Springs Resort was built in 1899 by the French-Canadian immigrants Celina and Julius J. LaDuke (1842–1927). It was located at this natural spring on the east side of the Yellowstone River near the coal mining towns of Aldridge and Horr/Electric. The locals from the towns provided some of the customers via a cable footbridge that crossed the river, while others came from the Yellowstone tourists who arrived by the Northern Pacific Railway spur that had a stop near the resort. It was successful for several years, especially with the addition of Dr. William Cogswell of Livingston as partner. However, in 1905, the LaDukes' four-year-old son, Lester, fell into a hot pool and scalded to death. The LaDukes left shortly thereafter and moved to Livingston, and the resort fell to ruin. Few remnants now remain. In 1909 the hot water from the spring was piped north to supply the resort of Corwin Springs. (see that citation) It, too, has had a varied career and has just reopened as Yellowstone Hot Springs, still using LaDuke Spring's water.

Lady of the Lake Lake/Creek

A lovely poetic name graces this lake that sits in a nice location north of Cooke City, just to the east of the Goose Lake jeep trail. However, the fact that it is situated between Mud and Swamp Lakes causes one to wonder.

These were called Lady Lake and Lady Creek on a 1937 map, but now carry the name of the Arthurian legend. The Lady of the Lake was the ruler of Avalon and plays a pivotal role in many stories. She is the one who gave King Arthur the sword Excalibur, enchanted Merlin, and raised Lancelot after the death of his father.

The USGS mapmakers forgot to put the name of the lake on the 2020 map, although the creek and trail by the lake are properly named. It is on the 2017 map and the GNIS website, so it should reappear on the next edition.

Lake of the Clouds

Situated in a scenic basin south of Mount Rosebud surrounded by 10,000-foot mountains, this lake seems to be high in the clouds. It is close to Lake of the Winds, and the view past its outlet deserves the lyrical name.

Lake Creek/Mountain/Plateau

Lake Creek starts at Granite Lake on the Montana/Wyoming border and wanders through a series of small lakes to join the Clarks Fork just south of the Lake Creek Campground on the Beartooth Highway. Its name comes from the series of lakes in its course, and it was one of the earlier named creeks in the area, already appearing on an 1897 map.

Lake Mountain is the high point on the **Lake Plateau,** which lies to the south of that mountain and is full of... lakes. Both the plateau and mountain are on the Boulder-Stillwater divide on the Mount Douglas and Tumble Mountain quads.

The lakes up on the plateau were important historically in the story of the fisheries in the Beartooths. In 1939, under the direction of John Schofield, the superintendent of Montana State Fisheries, these became the first lakes that were stocked by aircraft.

Lake at Falls

Two large waterfalls tumble into this lake, which is a widening of the East Rosebud. Charlie Falls is upstream, and the outflow from Martin Lake drops into its south side.

Lake Fork Creek

Lake Fork Creek can be found between the Hellroaring and Silver Run Plateaus flowing east into Rock Creek. It is called the Lake Fork (of Rock Creek) because it flows through several lakes along its way, including First and Second Rock Lakes and Keyser Brown Lake.

Lake of the Winds

At nearly 10,000 feet in the Russell Creek drainage, this lake is surrounded by meadows and has a windy exposure. It is found next to Lake of the Clouds.

Lake of the Woods

Would you expect lots of trees around this lake at the head of Horseshoe Creek? Good guess!

An early outfitter named Dayton Farmer had one of his cabins along the shore of this lake. His other cabin was mentioned earlier and was on the Stillwater River near Sioux Charley Lake. (see Dayton Cabin)

Lambert Creek

Henry Lambert and his wife, Mary, came west in 1889. They stopped for a while in the Black Hills where he hunted grizzly bears for bounty, but then moved on to Emigrant. There he traded his team and wagon for Heath's Deep Creek homestead, mined along this stream up Mill Creek that was named for him, and was a noted hunter and

Mr. and Mrs Henry Lambert. YELLOWSTONE GATEWAY MUSEUM, 2006.044.9197.

trapper. Perhaps he was too well noted, as he was arrested for poaching and gold panning at the head of the Gallatin River in Yellowstone National Park, had his equipment confiscated, and lost access to the Park.

LaVelle Lake

LaVelle Lake is high on the West Rosebud among those lakes that honor Stillwater County residents. It was named for Patrick LaVelle (1839–1912), who was an early promoter of the town of Columbus. He served with the New York 28th Infantry during the Civil War and afterwards worked for the Northern Pacific Railroad. In 1882, he and his wife, Maggie, moved to Billings where he worked in the NP yards. He went to Stillwater (now Columbus) in 1885 on railroad business and saw the opportunity for a hotel, which he built and called the LaVelle Hotel. He platted the town of Columbus in 1889, helped establish lighting in

Patrick LaVelle. JIM ANNIN COLLECTION, MUSEUM OF THE BEARTOOTHS, #533.

town, helped fund the first city water pipe, and became the first mayor in 1907. He was also a Yellowstone County commissioner and worked for the creation of the new Stillwater County.

Leaky Raft Lake

This lake is in the Sky Top country south of Granite Peak between Upper and Lower Aero Lakes. There must be a good story of a wet fisherman behind this name.

Lee Gulch

Lee Gulch is just south of Big Timber where it sits in the very northernmost section of the national forest on the West Fork of Upper Deer Creek. The Big Timber area is home to several Lees who are descendants of the Bill Lee who came to the Shields River country with John Hudson and a herd of cattle in 1878 and who filed his first "Ranch Claim" in 1880. (see Hudson Spring) There are many recorded Lee deeds in the Boulder River country from that time onward. F.W. "Fred" Lee was the most active of them with multiple claims filed for mining and water rights in the Boulder Mining District between 1884 and 1907. Thomas Lee was also mining, with a claim filed in 1888. Engebreit Lee lived closest to this gulch, just outside of McLeod, and died around 1904. Although there is no specific Lee deed, homestead, or mining record in the gulch itself, it may have been used in their mining or grazing activities, and it is assumed that it was named for one of these Lees or their many descendants.

Lennon Lake

Lennon Lake, which carries an alternate name of Wade Lake, sits among the cluster of lakes just to the north of the Montana/Wyoming border. Many of these lakes were named for several early Red Lodge residents. Although there is no citation for a specific Lennon on the lake, it is known that there was a Robert Lennon, a miner, who came to Red Lodge from Horr in 1893, and a Mrs. E.S. Lennon who had a boardinghouse in town in 1900. It is assumed that the lake takes its name from one of these Lennons or a relative.

Lewis Creek/Gulch

Lewis Gulch is located in the East Boulder Mining District on the north slope of Contact Mountain. It was named for a miner and his mine at the head of the creek. This was probably Frank W. Lewis, who was actively mining on the East Boulder between 1900 and 1907.

A different Lewis Creek can be found on Mount Douglas, a tributary of the West Fork of the Stillwater River. It is thought to have been named for Tom Lewis, who homesteaded in 1908 near Fishtail Butte and Dean, close to the mouth of the West Fork.

Lightning Lake/Creek

Obviously named for an impressive weather event, the lake sits in a large cirque on the north slope of Chalice Peak and empties via Lightning Creek into the West Fork of the Stillwater River. One of the several ponds at the lake's outlet was once called Little Lightning Lake, but this is no longer on the maps.

Both lakes are fishing favorites for the golden trout, *Oncorhynchus aguabonita*, which was introduced from its natural habitat in the Kern River of Northern California. That state now prohibits the capture and transport of the golden trout from its natural habitat, but it resides in several stable stocked-lake populations in the Montana high country. The Lightning Lakes are now said to be the best fishery in Montana for pure strain golden trout. (see Golden Lake and Sylvan Lake)

Lillis Lake

Lillis Lake is north of Cooke City on the Fossil Lake USGS quad. Dick Konizeski in his book, *The Montanan's Fishing Guide*, reports that this pond-type lake with swampy borders is fairly shallow and almost completely covered with lilies. Montana Fish, Wildlife and Parks' *Mountain Lakes Fishing Guide* also notes its late summer abundant vegetation. The name on the map almost certainly has too many "L"s and is a misspelling of "lilies."

Lily Lake

Larry Nordquist of the L bar T loved this lake, and it was a favorite spot to take guests for a ride and a picnic lunch in the 1930s. (see Gilbert Creek) One side is very shallow with a beautiful collection of water lilies, and the other has a good rock for swimming. It is just outside of the wilderness in Wyoming, and a gravel road off the Beartooth Highway now leads to the lake. (see Wagon Box Road) Some maps misspell it as Lilly.

Limestone Butte/Creek/Town

This mountain near Nye, except for its sandstone base, is said to be made entirely of limestone. The geologic formation gave its name to the creek that runs along it and the nearby town of Limestone. The town was settled by the Lowe, Holt, and Hawks families, and, from 1910 until 1953 Milton and Frances Lowe ran a general mercantile and post office there. It is now a ghost town with a number of buildings still standing.

Limestone Palisades

Palisades originally referred to the wooden stake barrier that was buried in the ground and used for defense—think of the old frontier fort. "The Palisades," the cliffs across the Hudson River that face New York City, were thought to resemble these wooden stakes, so, in the U.S., the word has come to mean a line of high cliffs. The Limestone Palisades is a long scarp on the north side of Grizzly Creek near the present Red Lodge Ski Area. It was the site of a CCC camp in the 1930s where the men lived when they built the Willow Run Ski Area. (see Willow Creek)

Limit Creek

Formerly Elk Creek, the name was changed in 1923 because "the name of Elk Creek is too numerous." The creek, a tributary of the West Fork of Mill Creek near Emigrant, has its head near the Limit Lookout, so that name seemed an appropriate choice. The Limit Lookout was present on the maps in 1937, but by 1947 it was no longer active, and it had disappeared completely by the 1961 map. The Forest Service no longer has historical records of the lookout and does not know why it was called "Limit."

Line Creek/Basin/Lake/Plateau

There are two Line Creeks.

One enters the West Rosebud next to the Custer National Forest boundary line. There was a chromite mining operation here during World War II.

The other Line Creek wiggles to and fro across the Montana/Wyoming state line at the far eastern end of the Custer-Gallatin National Forest. The creek flows through the **Line Creek Basin** where, in 1893, there was a productive asbestos mine. The **Line Creek Plateau,** which is situated a bit to the north in Montana, gets its name, of course, because it is the location of part of the creek. **Line Lake** straddles the state line just west of the creek.

Lion Mountain

Lion Mountain overlooks the West Boulder Meadows and was named for the cougar or mountain lion, *Puma concolor*. This cat has the largest range of any North American predator and is quite common in Montana. It is rarely seen, however, because of its secretive nature and nocturnal hunting habits. Its primary prey

Mountain lion. NATIONALPARK SERVICE.

is deer. Interestingly, it is not of the panther family but is more closely related to the common house cat.

Little Face Lake

Little Face (ca. 1845–1907) was a Crow leader whose Crow name was Mokene. He served as a scout for the 8th U.S. Cavalry and was employed by the U.S. military until his death. It was Little Face who was the first to hear of Custer's defeat at the Little Bighorn from the returning Crow scouts, and it was he who reported this to Lt. James H. Bradley. Bradley's historical notes are full of his conversations with Little Face and his tales on Crow history, creation myths, cosmology, and stories of The Land of the Hereafter. These notes remain an important part of the Montana Historical Society's archival extracts and were preserved by Columbus newspaperman Jim Annin in his book, *They Gazed on the Beartooth*.

Little Face, 1880. F.J. HAYNES, MONTANA MEMORY PROJECT, MONTANA HISTORICAL SOCIETY.

The lake is high up the West Rosebud, above Mystic Lake and next to Arrapooash Lake, which commemorates another Crow leader.

Little Pine Creek

(see Pine Creek)

Liver Lake

Another of the lakes in the anatomic collection with Heart and Kidney Lakes can be found on the Castle Mountain quad. The name is based on the shape and not to the fact that wild onions can be found growing along the shore.

Livingston Peak

Towering 9,314 feet to the south of the town of Livingston, Montana, and across the Yellowstone River, is the peak that was named for the town.

Used by the USGS as a triangulation point, it was originally called Old Baldy, or Baldy, for the vista that was created by a fire that had denuded the summit in the late 1800s. It is probably good that the name was changed as the top is now quite fuzzy green with a good stand of trees.

It also carried the name of Crow Test Peak, as men of that tribe had used it as a place for their vision quests.

The Northern Pacific Railroad reached the area in late 1882 and moved the former town of Benson's Landing to the present location. It was then renamed Livingston for Johnston Livingston, a stockholder and member of the board of directors of the railroad. In 1887 it became the county seat of the newly created Park County and is the business and governmental center of the area. Originally a railroad city with the Northern Pacific yards and locomotive repair shop, it has reemerged as a tourism, outdoor recreation, and gateway city to Yellowstone Park.

Mount Lockhart

Mount Lockhart is found on the Silver Run quad as a rise on the northeast ridge of the taller Whitetail Peak.

W.E. Lockhart was a longtime ranger and supervisor in the Beartooth National Forest, and the peak was named to commemorate him. However, in addition to the honor, there may have been a bit of irony and some fun generated by his subordinates. Lockhart climbed the peak in 1918 and broke his arm on the trip. While hurrying down, his horse spooked and ran off, and Lockhart had to walk all the way to town for medical attention.

After his time in the Beartooths, Lockhart was transferred to Choteau, Montana, where he became the supervisor of the Rocky Mountain Ranger District of the Lewis and Clark National Forest. Unfortunately, he was killed by a horse while leading a Boy Scout activity there.

W.E. Lockhart, 1926. USDA FOREST SERVICE, CUSTER-GALLATIN NATIONAL FOREST PHOTO ARCHIVES.

Mary Lake (see citation) was named for his wife.

Lodgepole Creek

The lodgepole pine, *Pinus contorta*, is one of the primary evergreens in the forests east of the Continental Divide. It has two types of cone. One is of the ordinary seed-spreading type, and the other, the sticky, resinous one, lies dormant on the forest floor until a forest fire comes through. The fire melts the resin and the cone springs open, scattering the seeds. This is why the lodgepole is the first conifer to emerge after a fire, and why it carpets the burned area. The creek is on the northeast corner of the national forest, and if you guessed that the tree was the reason for the name, you will need to guess again.

This tree grows tall and thin and is called the lodgepole pine because it was the favorite of the Plains Indians to use for the poles that supported their lodges (tipis). There is an old game trail that was used for years by the Indians when they crossed from the Stillwater into the Boulder Valley and on to Livingston. That trail, which goes along this creek, was called the Lodgepole Trail from an old Indian story. A raiding party of Piegan (Blackfeet) Indians had been in a fight with the Sioux over by the Rosebuds. They came up into this country and stole 400 ponies from the Crow, and, in their haste to leave, they traveled so swiftly that they scattered their lodge poles all along the trail.

Lone Elk Lake

This lake can be found in that rocky high country next to Rough Lake in the Sky Top country north of Cooke City. Lone Elk is a common Lakota surname, but this would be unusual country to find the Sioux, and no historical figures of similar name could be found for the area. This leaves us with the conclusion that someone saw a single elk... alone... by the lake.

Lone Lake

Lone Lake can be found north of Cooke City in a flat forested area near Lady of the Lake. It is not particularly alone as Round, Mud, and Corner Lakes are within a mile and are at the same elevation. It is, however, a bit farther south and deep in the forest.

Lone Ranger Lake

Lone Ranger Lake is a small pond that sits just to the north of Cimmerian Lake and drains into that lake. The lake is unnamed on the USGS map as it has not been recognized by the Board on Geographic Names. However, Montana Fish, Wildlife and Parks uses the name in their fishery survey, and it appears on some of the older hiking maps.

Was it named for a lonely USFS ranger? Wait! Who was that masked man? Hi-yo! Silver! Away!

Lonesome Mountain/Lake/Pond

Lonesome Pond reportedly has good fishing and can be reached up Monitor Creek on Mineral Mountain in the Mill Creek country near Emigrant. Apparently someone missed his friends on the fishing trip.

Lonesome Mountain, at 11,399 feet, dominates the view north of the Beartooth Highway. It gets its Lonesome name because it sits back and alone, a bit south of the main crest of the high Beartooths.

Lonesome Lake straddles the Montana/Wyoming border and is found, along with Abandoned Lake, on the southern flank of Lonesome Mountain. It drains through the chain of T and Grayling Lakes into Beartooth Lake by the highway.

Long Lake

Although there are more than 150 Long Lakes in Minnesota, the long and the short of it is that we only have two in the Absaroka-Beartooths.

Lonesome Peak. COURTESY RICK GRAETZ.

One is north of Cooke City on the Goose Lake jeep trail with Round and Corner Lakes nearby. It carries an alternate name of Lone Lake, which is probably just a misspelling.

The other is in Wyoming next to the Beartooth Highway. It is the first large lake that one sees coming west off the Beartooth Pass. Trailhead parking provides easy fishing access.

Long Mountain

This was so named because it is a several-mile-long ridge that extends west of Boone Mountain on the northern edge of the forest.

Looking Glass Lake

Looking Glass Lake in the Sky Top drainage is a good place to get a reflection of the sky, clouds, and surrounding mountains. It has also been called Mermaid and Stephanie Lake, but Looking Glass is official.

Lookout Mountain

There is no lookout on this mountain, but it provides an excellent panoramic lookout or view of the Bull Creek and Buffalo Fork Creek valleys.

Lost Cabin Creek

The cabin and the source of the name of this creek near the East Boulder River has been... lost.

Lost Creek

Not content with losing lakes, we have lost four creeks as well.

One comes out of the cluster of Lost Lakes above the West Boulder Meadows. It flows to the north from the West Boulder Plateau and was given that name because it disappears into a large hole in the mountainside. It reappears in the meadows farther down, just before entering the river. The Crow called this *Bilihu'ussee* ("Water does not come"). The Lost Creek Siphon Cave is here and was first explored in 2002.

The other three Lost Creeks, apparently difficult to find, are north of Cutoff Mountain, near Slough Creek, and on the north slope of Livingston Peak.

Lost Lakes

There are five "Lost" Lakes in the Absaroka-Beartooths. It is not that people have been careless with them, but four have been named because they are hard to find. The three Lost Lakes in a cluster above and east of the West Boulder Meadows are easy to find. They get their name from the creek that they head (see Lost Creek). Of the four that are difficult to find, one is in Fishtail country on the Emerald Lake quad, and another is just above East Rosebud Lake and the community of Alpine. It is sometimes called Hidden Lake. The third lake is downstream from Keyser Brown Lake on Lake Fork Creek near Rock Creek. It is in the woods and tucked against the wall of Mount Rearguard a few hundred yards from the creek, and was hard to find. It is currently a heavily used lake by hikers, so obviously it is no longer "lost." The fourth is just south of the Montana/Wyoming line draining via Gilbert Creek to the Clarks Fork. This last lake hides behind a little wooded pocket, and you won't know it is there until you stumble on it.

Lost Picket Creek

Pickets are spikes that were pounded into the ground to restrain horses when there was no suitable place to tie them. Some horse pulled one out and it was lost. The nuisance spent retrieving the wandering horse no doubt made enough of an impression to give the creek its name.

In the early part of the twentieth century, large chromium deposits were found between Lost Picket Creek and the Hellroaring Creek on the eastern side of the national forest.

Lowary Lake

This lake on the side of Granite Peak has variant names of Avalanche and Granite Creek Lakes, and the latter is still used by Montana Fish, Wildlife and Parks. The current name was apparently put on a U.S. Forest Service map by a Forest Service employee named Thad Lowary. The USGS picked it up off that map and continued the name by Board decision in 1987.

Lulu Pass

Lulu Pass is north of Cooke City and Henderson Mountain and leads to the mines around Scotch Bonnet and Fisher Mountains. A dirt road going over the pass still exists.

The rumor around Cooke City was that the pass was named for a mine and that the mine was named for one of Cooke City's "ladies of ill repute." This may well be true, but nothing further could be found about this "lady."

The author's father was wont to use the expression common in the early twentieth century, "That's a Lulu!" for something that was exceptional. If this is the case, the mine's name may have only referred to its rich mineral production.

Lundy Draw/Spring

The draw and spring near Nye were named for an original settler in the area, but nothing further could be found about him.

It is confused on some maps with Winge Draw, which is actually a bit to the east. (see citation)

M–K Campground

If you drive a few miles south of Red Lodge you will find this Forest Service campground just off the Beartooth Highway on the Main Fork of Rock Creek Road. The M–K is not a cattle brand but comes from Morrison-Knudsen, the Boise-based construction company that in 1931 was responsible for building the first 12 miles of the Beartooth Highway from Quad Creek south of Red Lodge to Twin Lakes. Their construction camp was on what is now the present campground.

Magee Creek

The Magee family settled on this stream near its junction with Elbow Creek south of Emigrant. The family cemetery is marked on the USGS topo map of the area and is located in a field on the bench above Elbow Creek. A local rancher has fenced in the plot, and this has preserved the unique handmade cement slab headstones, which have pointed tops for the men and rounded ones for the women. It is a poignant reminder of this pioneer family.

Maiden Basin/Falls

The reason for this name is unknown.

Perhaps the beauty of the falls reminded someone of a young maiden. It is just a bit north of the mining town of Jardine, so it might have been the site of some miner's maiden, or first, attempt at prospecting. This is just speculation.

Malin Creek

Malin Creek starts on Buffalo Mountain just north of Yellowstone National Park. It was named for four (of at least seven) Malin brothers—Amie, Norval, James D., and Harry N., who worked quartz placer mining claims on nearby Crevice Mountain during the period 1893 to 1898.

Amie and Norval were noted to be in Bozeman and the Upper Yellowstone Valley as early as 1870. Amie was clerk for Gallatin County from 1875 to 1878, and Norval served as a scout in Yellowstone Park in 1897. Norval moved to easier living in 1899 when he ran the Opera House Saloon in Livingston, and in 1905 he opened another saloon, Malin's Club, in Gardiner.

Margaret Lake

Sitting just to the north of the Montana/Wyoming line is a lake that was named for Margaret Ingeborg Reeb (1913–2005). She became famous and most deserving of this memorial because of her stance that forced the Clinton administration to reverse a permit to the Canadian Crown Butte/Noranda Mines Corporation that would have allowed the reopening of a large open pit mine on Henderson Mountain near Cooke City.

Margaret Reeb. MARGARET REEB COLLECTION, COURTESY LINDA HOLLAND.

Margaret was born in Walkerville, Montana, near Butte, the daughter of George "Morphine Charley" Reeb. Among the many interesting activities in life, she was a schoolteacher in Livingston and the Caribbean, headed the USO in Europe for the American soldiers after World War II, and, most importantly here, was dedicated to protecting her land north of Yellowstone Park. As the daughter of the reformed miner, "Morphine Charley," she inherited many old mining claims on Henderson Mountain in the New World Mining District, and gradually, throughout her life, acquired many others. She was incensed by the fact that she was not consulted during the initial negotiations that granted Noranda/Crown Butte permission to dig a huge open pit mine that would impact her property and the wilderness that she loved. As a landowner, her opposition was critical, and, supported by environmental groups, it finally resulted in the government's $68 million settlement that prohibited the mine and ensured the reclamation and protection of the land north of Yellowstone Park. (see Henderson Mountain, Fisher Creek, Soda Butte Creek).

Margaret died in 2005, but would have been delighted that her nephews were able to sell her mountain properties to the Trust for Public Lands, which then sold them to the Forest Service for permanent wilderness protection.

Mariane Lake

This long, irregularly shaped lake is near Otter Lake in the Russell Creek drainage. No information could be found as to who this Mariane was or why the lake was named for her.

Marie Creek

Marie Creek flows from the west side of Carbonate Mountain into Meatrack Creek.

Here is another of the women for whom we can find no reference. Perhaps she was a miner's love, or the sweetheart of one of the early rangers. You are free to invent your own story.

Marker Lake

Marker Lake is on the south side of Bowback Mountain and, at 10,870 feet, is thought to be the highest lake in Montana with a thriving fishery.

It was probably named for Hans Marker, a Danish immigrant, who was listed as living in Red Lodge on the 1910 census.

Marsh Lake

It will be left to the reader's imagination as to where this name came from, but the fact that it is near Wiedy and Swamp Lakes north of Cooke City may give a hint.

Marston Meadow

This meadow on Slough Creek was named for Charles Marston, a squatter who located here for a short time in the 1880s.

Marten Peak

Marten Peak is found south of Mount McKnight, and Ranger C.A. Butler said that it was named for the many pine martens found on the slopes. It was a favorite location for trappers, who harvested their fur in the early part of the twentieth century.

The pine marten, *Martes americana,* is a medium-sized member of the weasel family whose habitat is widespread throughout the pine forests of Canada, Alaska, the Northern Rockies, and the Pacific Northwest. Cute as it may be, it is, however, a fierce predator with a diet that consists primarily of voles and rabbits.

Pine marten. NATIONAL PARK SERVICE.

Martes Lake

Whoever named this lake was being a bit more erudite than the person who named Marten Peak, as *Martes* is the Latin name for the pine marten, *Martes americana.* This lake near the North Fork of Wounded Man Creek was named for that critter. (see Marten Peak)

Martin Lake

There are two lakes with this name, and both are on the Castle Mountain quad in Carbon County. The one to the north is in the East Rosebud drainage just to the north of Lake at Falls. The more southern Martin Lake is just to the north of the Montana/Wyoming line in the cluster of lakes in the Sierra/Falls Creek drainage.

One and probably both of these lakes were named for Melvin E. Martin who was a packer and prospector from Red Lodge, and who was known to be active near both

Melvin Martin and family at his mine. LINDA HOLLAND COLLECTION.

lakes. He and his wife arrived in the area in 1905 to seek their fortune in mining. He filed several chromite claims on the Hellroaring Plateau in the 1920s, and was involved in creating the Beartooth Highway in the early 30s, as it passed over his chromium mines. The photograph of him and his family was taken at his chromium mine at Goose Lake in 1927, demonstrating that he covered a lot of ground in the southern Beartooths. Grasshopper Glacier on Mount Rearguard was once called Martin Grasshopper Glacier for him. He also enjoyed fishing and was responsible for stocking many of the lakes west of Red Lodge.

Lake Mary

This lake, located near the West Fork of Rock Creek and just up a trail north of Quinnabaugh Meadows, was named for Mary Lockhart. Her father was Edwin C. Russell, the first supervisor of the Absaroka National Forest, and her husband was William E. Lockhart, who was also a ranger and forest supervisor. Mount Lockhart, appropriately, looks down the West Fork toward Lake Mary. (see Mount Lockhart)

Maryott Lake

John L. Maryott (1863–1945) arrived with his wife, Nellie, in 1886 and homesteaded their ranch near Rock Creek, two to three miles north of Red Lodge. He was one of the first to tap this creek for irrigation, and used a waterwheel to power the cream separator and butter churn on his dairy farm, which he called the Carbon County Dairy. Maryott became a director of the U.S. National Bank in 1914 and served as its vice president from 1916 to 1918.

The lake, with an alternate name of Felis "Cat" Lake, can be found in that cluster of lakes that is just north of the Montana line on the Castle Mountain quad.

Maurice: Mountain/Creek

Mount Maurice is the double-bump mountain just south of the town of Red Lodge. It was named for Dr. J. Maurice Fox, who came to Red Lodge with his wife,

Mary, in 1889 as the first supervisor of the Rocky Fork Coal Company. He was a Kentuckian who served the Confederacy in the Civil War and who later worked for Henry Villard of the Northern Pacific Railroad. The naming of the mountain is attributed to his three daughters, Nellie, Lockey, and Lillie, who climbed it with a group of friends in 1910. After christening the peak for their father, they became the first to register the climb by leaving their names at the top in the celebratory champagne bottle.

In 1935 the Princeton Geological Association purchased 120 acres on the slope of Mount Maurice where they built a lodge and research camp. In 1942 the property was transferred to the Yellowstone-Bighorn Research Association, which remains active to this day.

Maurice Creek flows off the mountain to enter Rock Creek.

McBride Lake

The lake that sits along Slough Creek in Yellowstone National Park was named for James McBride (1864-1942).

McBride came with the U.S. Army in 1886 when it was patrolling the Park and served as its chief scout. He remained after the formation of the National Park Service in 1916 as a ranger, then became chief ranger in 1920. He was stationed at Slough Creek from 1924 to 1927. McBride retired to Crevice Mountain in 1929, where he worked a gold mine. At that time, he was known as "the orneriest recluse on Crevice Mountain."

Jim McBride. YELLOWSTONE GATEWAY MUSEUM 2006.044.0859.

The image is from 1903 when, because of a friendship that developed when they were both at Medora, North Dakota, he became President Teddy Roosevelt's guide when he toured the Park.

His name also continues as the "McBride variant" of the Yellowstone cutthroat trout. This hardy native fish has been used to stock many of the lakes in the Absaroka-Beartooths.

McDonald Creek

McDonald Creek enters the Yellowstone River just south of Pine Creek. The McDonald family built a sawmill on this creek, and members of the family still reside in the Cinnabar Basin.

McDonald Basin

Malcolm McDonald, who was born in Ohio in 1852, started west working on the railroad and serving as an Indian scout. He prospected with William Hamilton,

"Skookum Joe" Anderson, and Ansel Hubble when they established the first mining claims in the Nye Basin. In 1886, he and his brother, Richard, established squatters' rights to a ranch and prospected at the head of Fiddler Creek in what became McDonald Basin, just east of Nye. Malcolm died in Columbus in 1926. (see Fiddler Creek)

McDonald Ditch

This irrigation ditch near the West Fork of Rock Creek and Red Lodge is noted on the USGS maps. It was named for the McDonald families who had homesteads along it and used the water to irrigate their land. Gideon McDonald arrived in 1892 and registered a patent a mile or two north of the ditch the following year. Mary McDonald had a desert claim in 1897, proved up, and patented a homestead for the whole of section 5 in 1904. The ditch runs through her section.

Mr. & Mrs. M.M. McDonald. JIM ANNIN COLLECTION, MUSEUM OF THE BEARTOOTHS, #14.

McKinsey Spring/Draw

The McKinsey Ranch is in the Lodgepole Creek Valley near Limestone and just outside the Custer-Gallatin National forest boundary. Both the spring and draw, however, are within the forest, and were named for these pioneers.

Mount McKnight/Lakes

Harry Kaufman was the first ranger of the Absaroka National Forest and named the mountain and its lakes for his wife Coral's parents. George T. McKnight settled on the West Boulder about 1886 and lived about seven miles southwest of the Main Boulder Ranger Station at the base of Mount Rae. (see citation) He had a mine that was just two miles south of the ranger station.

Mount McKnight and its lakes are a bit away from the McKnight homestead as they are found near the head of Davis Creek on the far reaches of the West Boulder overlooking Pine Creek and the Paradise Valley. The lakes are quite beautiful, but isolated and difficult to reach. They were once called Twin Lakes, but as there are three other Twin Lakes in Park County, McKnight became official.

One may find that George T. McKnight is referred to as George Knight in some references, as the current descendants have dropped the Mc.

McLeod Basin/Town

W.F. McLeod became the first settler in the Boulder Valley when he and "Happy Jack" Aldrich drove a herd of horses and cattle from Oregon in 1881. (see Happy Jack Gulch) The little town, first established as a mining settlement, was named for him. It had its first post office in 1886 and, when oil drilling accidentally reached geothermal water, a swimming pool was opened. It is now a resort town with basic services catering to outdoor enthusiasts in the Boulder River country.

The basin, good grazing country, sits just north of the national forest on the west side of the river.

McMinn Bench

The northern shoulder of Mount Everts in Yellowstone Park is next to the Montana/Wyoming state line and was named by army scouts as early as 1897 for Silas McMinn. He and E.C. Clark developed a coal mine there to supply the National Hotel at nearby Mammoth. The coal was of poor quality and because commercial ventures are not permitted in the Park, the mine was shut down and sealed.

Park Superintendent David Wear called McMinn "a drunken old reprobate, unreliable in every way." Be that as it may, McMinn has left his name on the maps.

Meadow Creek

There are many Meadow Creeks throughout the Custer-Gallatin National Forest, but the high, rocky Absaroka-Beartooths are not noted for meadows. Here there is only one Meadow Creek and it is on ranchland in the West Fishtail country on the northeast corner of the forest.

Meatrack Creek

Ranger notes of the 1930s report that the Indians in the early days used to frequent this watershed and hunt large game, the meat from which was dried and smoked on willow racks. Ranger Harry Kaufman, whose ranger cabin was on the Main Boulder, just four miles from this creek, wrote (ca. 1930) "These racks were still in evidence a few years ago."

Archaeological investigations have found a prehistoric camp on this creek that showed evidence of the production of tools and projectiles.

Medicine Lake/Mountain

Medicine Lake has been confused with Dewey Lake on older maps. A decision in 1975 established that Dewey Lake is on the southwest shoulder of Mount Dewey, while Medicine Lake is a bit farther to the northwest toward Pika Peak. It is currently unnamed on the 2020 USGS map, but since it is named on the 2017 map and occurs in their GNIS website, this is just an error of omission. It should reappear on future Fossil Lake quad maps.

Medicine Mountain is farther east on the Silver Run Peak quad.

The "medicine" of the Native Americans is a poor English translation of the concept of spiritual healing or renewal. Thus, the medicine of both the lake and mountain refers to a place where the Native Americans sought their vision quests.

Melody Lake

The National Geographic hiking map of 2013, and Montana Fish, Wildlife and Parks publications have the lake named, but it is not recognized by the Board on Geographic Names, so you will not see it on your USGS topo map.

It is not known what sweet song (or woman) generated the name of this widening in Farley Creek.

Memidgi Lake

This is an invented name for the man in Jim Annin's elaborate tale about how the Stillwater River got its name. In the story, as told by the Montana Historical Society, Memidgi and his lover Weeluna were forbidden to marry so jumped into the river and drowned in each other's arms. Where their bodies came to rest was seen as hallowed water, mistranslated as Still Water. It is a sweet story, but totally fictional. (see Stillwater River and Weeluna Lake)

Memidgi Lake is sited near Weeluna Lake upstream from Mystic Lake and the West Rosebud. It is near the historic site of the former town of Mouat, and is not far from Annin's home at Columbus. These two lakes are in one small collection of Indian names in the national forest, and are near Little Face and Arapooash Lakes, which were named for actual historic Native American individuals. Other than these and the name Absaroka itself, there are few names or references to the Crow people who inhabited the mountains from the Paradise Valley to Red Lodge and beyond. One must wonder why there are not more.

Annin spelled the name Nemidgi, which is what is found on the Montana Fish, Wildlife and Parks maps and website. The USGS has it officially as Memidgi. Can one truly misspell a fictional invention?

Mendenhall Draw

In 1881 Cyrus "C.B." Mendenhall drove 4,000 head of cattle to what became his ranch near Springdale on the Yellowstone River. It steadily expanded, and by 1906 he had 2,800 acres. When the ranch was at its peak, the Mendenhalls ran as many as 20,000 head of cattle and 5,000 horses. Later in life, C.B. operated Hunter's Hot Springs Resort at Springdale while his son Jim ran the ranch.

Cyrus "C.B." Mendenhall. CRAZY MOUNTAIN MUSEUM.

Part of the expansion occurred when the Crow lands opened up after the boundary was moved in 1892. His sons, James and Alfred, staked some of the earliest homesteads along the Rosebud, and this is where James formed the town of Absarokee and served as its postmaster.

The draw is on Mendenhall land.

Meridian Peak

The 110th meridian just west of Cooke City was the original eastern border of Yellowstone National Park, and this mountain sits almost exactly on the 110th meridian.

The meridian line is no longer important to the Park as the current eastern border was redrawn in 1932 to follow the crest of the North Absaroka Mountains to be more consistent with stream drainage patterns.

Metcalf Mountain

Lee Metcalf (1911–1978) served as representative for western Montana from 1953 to 1961, and was senator from 1961 to 1978. He held the position of president pro tempore of the Senate and used this office to shepherd the Wilderness Act of 1964 through Congress.

To commemorate this legislation and Metcalf's legacy, the mountain north of Glacier Lake on the Hellroaring Plateau was recently named for him.

Sen. Lee Metcalf. LIBRARY OF CONGRESS.

Meyer Mountain, Meyers Creek/Ranger Station/Pass

For reasons known only to the Board on Geographic Names, the mountain is Meyer and the creek, pass, and ranger station are Meyers. They all refer to the same person, a Mr. Meyers who had squatters' rights on the creek in the early part of the twentieth century.

The **ranger station,** which is a converted homestead, sits on Meyers Creek about two miles north of the ghost town of Limestone in the Stillwater River drainage.

Meyers Creek was, for years, called Squaw Creek. However, because the word is a derogatory term for a Native American female with unpleasant sexual connotations, all reference to "squaw" were removed from Montana maps in 2004. Since it flows by **Meyer Mountain,** that name was chosen as a substitute.

There could have perhaps been a better substitute name that would have preserved the Native American association with the original name. In the late 1800s, a group of five Indians was stalking a small elk herd that triggered an avalanche that killed three of the hunters. For years the widows and women relatives of the men who had been killed came here to grieve and pray for them. Because of the difficulty of the terrain, they didn't go all the way to Dead Indian Hill, but stopped here, one valley south. This regular gathering of Native American women generated the Squaw Creek name. It would have been nice to have found a better name to remember this very poignant and human behavior, especially for the Anglo-Europeans who have marginalized the Indians and too often profile their culture as ignorant, primitive, and cruel. (see Squaw Creek and Dead Indian Hill)

The pass, which crosses from the head of Meyers Creek in the Stillwater drainage to the Boulder River country, has also been changed from Squaw Creek Pass and is now called **Meyers Creek Pass.**

Mid Mountain, Middle Mountain

Although this peak is Middle Mountain in the USGS Geographic Names Information System website, it is Mid Mountain on the USGS Fossil Lake quad map. This probably doesn't matter as it is a rather mundane name that just refers to the fact that the mountain is midway between the Aero Lakes and the Clarks Fork along the Broadwater River.

Middle Ridge

This ridge lies between the Hellroaring Creek that flows into Yellowstone Park and its Middle Fork. Since it overlooks this Middle Fork it is... Middle Ridge.

Mill Creek/Pass

Mill Creek, called Big Pine by the Crow, is the largest tributary of the Yellowstone in the Paradise Valley/Gardiner area, and, like most of the Mill Creeks in Montana, was named for a sawmill that was located there.

John J. Tomlinson arrived in 1864 with the parts for a circular saw that he erected here, the first sawmill in Park County. Lumber was produced in 1865 to serve the needs of the Yellowstone City/Emigrant miners, and also went into the construction of Mackenzie boats to float the Yellowstone, the fastest route to the outside world. However, the first boat carrying disappointed miners was ambushed by Indians, killing one of the passengers. The Indian danger and poor returns in gold convinced Tomlinson to relocate his family. So in 1867, they moved to the Upper West Gallatin near present-day Gallatin Gateway where he started a more successful milling

J.J. Tomlinson. YELLOWSTONE GATEWAY MUSEUM, 2006.044.1777.

operation. Before leaving, his wife gave birth to a son, Philo, who was said to be the first white child born in Montana east of the Bozeman Pass.

Mill Creek provided the miners access to mining country east of Emigrant, and, during Prohibition, was the site of numerous moonshine stills. Following the creek up and over **Mill Creek Pass** also provided a route from the Mill Creek country to the West Boulder.

The Mill Creek Ranger Station near Snowbank Campground was built in 1914 and still remains as one of the locations in the Forest Service's cabin rental program.

Another small Mill Creek can be found on the far southeastern edge of the Custer-Gallatin National Forest south of Red Lodge and Mount Maurice.

Mill Draw, Mill Fork Creek

Also named for the sawmills that were located there, **Mill Draw** is near Red Lodge, and **Mill Fork Creek** is on the northern end of the Custer-Gallatin National Forest by Little Mission Creek.

Miller Mountain/Creek

Miller is a common surname in English, but unlike our Mill Creeks that came from the sawmills, this name developed in the Middle Ages for the man who ran the water mill that ground the grain into flour.

One **Miller Creek** flows into the Main Boulder River and was named for a local land-owner. Because he was a German immigrant, it should have been called Mueller Creek, but his name was mispronounced by the neighbors.

The other **Miller Creek** is on **Miller Mountain,** a ridge on Henderson Mountain just north of Cooke City where the creek parallels the Daisy Pass Road. These features were named for one of the early prospectors, Adam

Adam "Horn" Miller. YELLOWSTONE GATEWAY MUSEUM.

"Horn" Miller (1839–1917), who was born in Bavaria and came to the U.S. to work on the railroads. He went up the Missouri in 1854 on a trading company keelboat and had settled in Emigrant by 1864. Along with A. Bart Henderson and others, he was credited with the first discovery of gold in the area north of the current Yellowstone Park and, for over 40 years, from 1870, he mined on his mountain at his Josephine, Stump, and Shoo Fly Mines. Said to be over six feet tall, "Montana's Toughest Man" and "strong as a moose," his obituary described him "as a man of sterling character, a man without enemies of any kind, and a citizen who had a kind word for everyone." (also see image in Introduction page vi)

Camp Minanagish

This church camp on the Boulder River was founded in 1929 by the Congregational Congress (United Church of Christ). They decided to call it "Singing Waters," which, when translated into the Crow language, came out *Mimanagis,* which was corrupted into Minanagish.

Mineral Hill

Just outside and east of the town of Jardine is this rich hill, a remnant of some very successful mining. James Graham and "Uncle" Joe Brown discovered the quartz vein on the hill in 1870. Since this was still on the Crow Reservation, mining was stalled. However, when the reservation border was moved east in 1882, mining on it picked up. Then a natural landslide in 1898 revealed one of the richest lodes ever found in Montana, and things really boomed. Although the ownership changed hands several times, this hill was essentially the hardrock part of the Bear Gulch Mining Company of Jardine. Profitable mining activity continued off and on, depending on the veins and the economy, until the last mine, operated by TVX Mineral Hill, Inc., shut down in 1996.

The big mine on Mineral Hill was recorded as the Revelation but was usually referred to as the Sowash for one of the memorable characters of the area. Zackwell "Red" Sowash was among the group of miners that made the first discovery of gold on Crevice Mountain just south of Jardine. He mined on Mineral Hill, and later moved to Cooke City where, in 1884, his saloon was found to be in the Park and was "removed."

Mineral Mountain

There are two of these, both obviously named for their mineral deposits.

One is in the Cooke City mining area and is located a bit west of town.

The other is on the Mineral Mountain USGS quad at the head of Emigrant Creek. Gold was initially discovered there in 1887 and was mined by D.C. Lilly at his St. Julian Mine. The ore was assayed as high as $368 in gold and $40 in silver per ton, but despite these promising reports, the mine's development was slow due to lack of capital. Later, Peter Clauson drove a 560-foot tunnel into the mountain, finding only molybdenum, which was worthless at that time.

Mini Lake

A tiny lake, just a widening of Flood Creek in the Stillwater system, is found a few hundred feet upstream from Bill Lake. It is not recognized by the USGS or USFS nor is it on their maps. This mini omission is corrected on Montana Fish, Wildlife and Parks documents.

Mirror Lake

One Mirror Lake is on the Lake Plateau a bit to the east on a tributary of Rainbow Creek. It was named in 1923 because "it reflects the mountains which surround it."

The other is north of the Beartooth Pass in Wyoming where its drainage flows off the east side of Quintuple Peak into Rock Creek.

Misery Creek

Sounds like fun!

The creek, once known as Greenough Creek, was apparently re-named by Ben Greenough (see Greenough Lake), who was on a pack trip near here and was caught in a storm where he got very cold and wet. In camp, he said, "This is misery!" so the creek acquired that name.

Mission and Little Mission Creek

According to the 1868 treaty between the United States and the Crow Indians, the government was to erect a schoolhouse or mission building along this creek that is located near the Yellowstone River about eight miles east of Livingston. It was not a religious site, and the mission or school building was never built. An army installation, an extension of Fort Ellis in Bozeman, was built here and called Fort Parker for I.N. Parker, who briefly taught the Crow children there before his early death. This probably qualified it as the "school," but since the primary business was administrative, it was also called Crow Agency. This was only open the five years, from 1869 to 1874, and was closed when the reservation boundary was moved east and the Second Crow Agency was opened on the Stillwater River near Absarokee. Fort Parker burned to the ground about a year after it was built and was replaced by an adobe building. This, too, disintegrated with abandonment, the winter weather, and rains, so now all that is left are some corner posts marking where the fort stood. The fort's location can be visited at an interpretive site created by Undaunted Stewardship about a quarter mile south of the I-90 freeway off the Mission Creek Road exit.

The Crow called Fort Parker the Deer Creek Agency because it was across the Yellowstone from the Shields River, which they referred to as Deer Creek. The Crow called Mission Creek *Bah-re-ah-shoo-ah*; *Ahsh-ke-aht* or Skull Creek for the large number of human skulls that had been found there. Skull Creek was also the name that William Clark gave to this stream on the expedition's return trip to St. Louis. The story behind this name was that these skulls belonged to a party of trappers who were killed near the creek. There is no historical reference to such a massacre, so, if true, they must have been French-Canadians as it occurred prior to 1806 when Clark passed by.

One of the first white settlers on the creek was George Bruffey (1842–1928), who had left Missouri for Colorado and then Virginia City, Montana, to avoid the Civil War. He settled on Mission Creek and started his ranch that he called the 63 for the year he arrived. He named the small community of Bruffey for himself and was postmaster, on the school board, and served one term in the state legislature. The ranch is now the Triangle 7.

Little Mission Creek was named in 1932 and is a tributary of Mission Creek.

Moccasin Lake

There are two Moccasin Lakes.

The one at the headwaters of the East Boulder River is just over Meyers Creek Pass. This was once called Squaw Creek Pass, where the widows of the men killed in the avalanche on Dead Indian Hill went to grieve and pray for the men.

The other Moccasin Lake is in the Broadwater drainage on the shoulder of Mid Mountain. It is not particularly shaped like a moccasin footprint, so it is assumed that Indian or trapper artifacts must have been found here.

Molar Lake, Little Molar Lake

These humorous lake names appeared in the Broadwater drainage about 1995, with Incisor Lake nearby. From surrounding heights, or on a map, they appear tooth-shaped, roots and all.

Monitor Peak/Creek

Locals relate that the mountain, which sits at the head of Sixmile Creek south of Emigrant, is called Monitor Peak because "you can see everything from there and it can be seen from everywhere." It was not used by the Forest Service to monitor wildfires as it is a very difficult climb to the top.

The **creek** was named for the mountain. It was initially called the West Fork of the West Fork of Mill Creek, but in 1922 this was deemed too cumbersome and changed.

The recently reintroduced wolves in Yellowstone Park have developed several packs outside of the Park. One of these is called the Monitor pack for its territory on and around this mountain.

Montanapolis Springs

The springs are up Mill Creek from Emigrant and were discovered in the 1880s by Walter and J.D. Matheson, who had had an interest in Chico Hot Springs.

The water from the springs is naturally carbonated and laxative, which they thought was therapeutic and resembled that from Apollinaris Spring in Yellowstone National Park. A spa was started, and in the 1930s C.L. Smith built a lodge that he called the Diamond S, and Joe Simmons had a little store and cabins. Most of the buildings have now been torn down.

Monument Peak

The 1886 surveyors led by Edward M. Douglas erected a six-foot-high stone monument as a triangulation station at the summit of this mountain. Douglas originally called this peak at the head of the Boulder River, Haystack Peak, and that was official until 1934. Haystack is now a satellite peak about a mile to the east, and this became Monument Peak for the structure on top.

Moon Lake

There is a good view of the north side of the Bear's Tooth spire from this lake.

It is located in a cirque on Mount Rearguard but is not moon shaped. One must hope that the name comes from the astronomical view of our lone satellite, and not some camper's dysfunctional behavior.

Big Moose Lake, Little Moose Lake

Both of these lakes on Montana's southern border drain south into Crazy Creek in Wyoming. They were once called the Crazy Lakes as they are part of the Crazy Creek chain and are essentially swampy widenings of that stream.

The moose, *Alces alces*, is the largest member of the deer family. Its broad palmate antlers and solitary be-

Alces alces, moose. YELLOWSTONE NATIONAL PARK, #11702.

havior set it apart from other deer. They inhabit boreal forests, lakes, and boggy areas and are common in the mountains of Montana. The word moose was borrowed from the indigenous eastern Algonquian languages and means "twig eater." They like to eat willows and in summer they graze on pond grasses, so one might antici-pate finding them feasting in the shallows of these lakes.

Morning Star Peak

This mountain is at the head of Skookum Joe Canyon on the northern side of the Custer-Gallatin National Forest and was formerly called Squaw Peak. With the removal of the derogatory term "squaw" from the Montana maps in 2004, the state legislature, in partic-ular Rep. Henri Mann, a Cheyenne elder, submitted HB421 that recommended this name to the USGS.

Morning Star. DETAIL FROM A PHOTO BY EDWARD S. CURTIS.

Morning Star (1810–1883), translated from the Cheyenne *Vooheheve*, was also called Dull Knife, the name that he was given by the Lakota (Sioux). Following the Battle of the Little Bighorn, he allied with the Sioux, but a U.S. Army raid destroyed over 200 lodges and killed or captured 700 horses. This forced his band's surrender, and they were transported to

Oklahoma. Facing disease and starvation, Dull Knife and Little Coyote led two groups of the Cheyenne on an escape north on foot. Unfortunately, many of Dull Knife's band were killed and the rest captured near Fort Robinson in Nebraska's Sand Hills. Morning Star and the remaining survivors were eventually allowed to settle on a reservation near Fort Keogh in Montana. Chief Dull Knife College on the Northern Cheyenne Reservation at Lame Deer, Montana, was named in his honor.

Morris Creek

Morris Creek near Roscoe, Montana, was named for Robert O. Morris (1850–1907). He was born in Pennsylvania and came to Montana in 1883. Initially settling on the Upper Yellowstone, he moved in 1886 and was one of the first to gain a foothold on the former Crow Reservation with squatters' rights on the East Rosebud. He developed a successful ranch, founded the little town and post office of Morris in 1901, and served many years as justice of the peace. Robert was also elected to the first group of county commissioners for Carbon County, and in 1904 formed the Rosebud Oil Company that explored that area. He married Nancy Brown in 1884 and, when the Postal Service insisted on a

Robert and Nancy Morris, 1894. JIM ANNIN COLLECTION, MUSEUM OF THE BEARTOOTHS, #35.

name change for the town of Morris because of confusion with Norris in Madison County, it was Nancy who came up with the name Roscoe—her favorite horse.

Mosquito Lake/Peak

The lake is currently unnamed, so the name is unofficial and of local usage. The fact that it is near Swamp, Wiedy, and Marsh Lakes assures that it is a good habitat for this pesky bug.

Mosquito Peak overlooks the South Fork of Wounded Man Creek. This irritating little insect is all too common and was first mentioned in Anglo-European writings on Montana by William Clark when, in July of 1805, he noted in his journal that "musquitors verry troublesome" near the Three Forks of the Missouri.

Mountain View/Creek/Lake

The small community of Mountain View and the mine are located directly west of Nye, Montana, with the "view" toward Black Butte and the mines east of Old Nye. The ore found at the Mountain View Mine was discovered in 1886 and it is now the location of one of the modern Stillwater Mine operations.

Mountain View Lake is on private mining claims and is partly manmade with water piped in from the south. It, and a small community on its shore, were once known as Mouat. (see Chrome Mountain for William Mouat's story)

Mouse Lake

The mouse name for this small lake east of Columbine Pass appears on the maps after 1944. It was not noted whether the name comes from the small size of the lake or the little creatures that infested the campsite.

Moze Gulch

This gulch near Chico was named for J.J. Moze, one of the original miners at Emigrant. He appeared officially in 1888 when he registered a mining claim in the Mill Creek District. The name Moze has also been used as a location on county mining claim notices in an area close to Emigrant, so it is probable that J.J. worked this as well.

Mud Lake

Mud Lake is north of Cooke City in a flat area near Lady of the Lake and, in spite of the unattractive name, sits in a beautiful location. As the name suggests, it is not recommended for swimming—unless you are trolling for leeches.

There is a tiny lake nearby that Montana Fish, Wildlife and Parks calls Upper Mud Lake or Schoolmarm Lake. There must be a good story behind this latter name, but it is not explained, and neither of this lake's names are recognized nor cited by the USGS.

Muddy Creek

Muddy Creek, in the Wyoming section of the Absaroka-Beartooth Wilderness, gives its name to the USGS quad map of the area. Almost all of the tributaries of the Clarks Fork are clear, but this creek flows through a flat, swampy area where it picks up much clay, the same clay that is found on nearby Clay Butte.

Mutt Lake

Paired with Jeff Lake, these two meadow ponds lie just off the Goose Lake jeep trail north of Cooke City. They are humorous allusions to Bud Fisher's comic strip, *Mutt and Jeff,* that ran from 1907 until 1983. This was the first of the newspaper funnies that was published as a strip of panels instead of one single picture. Thus it was the first "comic strip." (see Jeff Lake)

Mutt and Jeff, 1926. CARTOON BY BUD FISHER.

Mystic Lake/Mountain

The big lake just beyond the end of the road up the West Rosebud was first called Long Lake, but the reason for the change from Long to Mystic in 1918 has become a bit of a mystery.

The Montana Historical Society in its book and website, *Montana Place Names from Alzada to Zortman*, states that the lake's name is credited to a surveyor for the Montana Power Company whose last name was Mystic, and who, in 1918, helped the company launch its effort to dam the lake to generate hydroelectricity. Montana Power Company comes in again in ranger notes from the 1940s where it is claimed that the name came in 1918 from the company surveyor, who was unnamed. He is said to have called it Mystic because of the mystery concerning the lake's true depth.

The utility company did put in the power station in 1918 just downstream from what was a natural lake, and in 1926 they dammed the lake to further raise the reservoir level. That station remains in operation today, and when the dam added 40 feet to the depth of the lake, it also created the largest lake in the Absaroka-Beartooth Mountains.

Mystic Mountain is at the headwaters of the West Rosebud and gets its name because the creek on its flank flows into Mystic Lake. At 12,080 feet it just barely makes the list of peaks over 12,000 feet.

Narrow Escape Lake

This small lake is currently unnamed on USGS and Forest Service maps, but the name is used by Montana Fish, Wildlife and Parks and can be found on some hiking maps. It is a long, slender body of water jammed between two ridges at the headwaters of Hawley Creek on the west side of Mount Douglas and just above Squeeze Lake. Tight fit up here.

There is no citation as to who had the narrow escape or what occurred.

Native Lake

Prior to the arrival of the miners and horse packers, almost all of the lakes in the southern Beartooths were barren of fish since the tributaries of the upper Clarks Fork were too tumultuous for fish to migrate upstream to spawn. Most of the lakes that are now fished got their original populations from people who brought pails or milk cans full of fry on horseback or mule to "plant" in these lakes. As a result, these lakes are now populated with non-native brook or rainbow trout. This lake was one of the few that had a "native" population of Yellowstone cutthrout trout.

It can be found north of Beartooth Butte near the Montana/Wyoming border.

Natural Bridge Falls/Draw

About a mile north of the Main Boulder Ranger Station at the end of the paving on the Boulder Road is the site of a well-maintained Montana state park with an excellent scenic trail. Here the river disappears down a 100-foot drop through a large hole into a channel through the soft limestone and then reemerges a few hundred yards downstream. The Indians called it "The place of the diving water." Unfortunately, the "natural" stone arch, or bridge, which was left by earlier erosion, collapsed on its own in 1988. Today, as the river dives into its hole, it is creating new bridges.

When one follows the Forest Service's Nature Trail with its interpretive signs, one learns about the limestone cap still present in the Absarokas but eroded off by glaciers in the Beartooths to the east. Here, some 340 million years ago, limestone, some thousands of feet thick, formed in a shallow sea. One can see evidence of wave action preserved in the rock, as well as fossils of crinoids (sea lilies) and brachiopods. This limestone also weathers into beautiful formations such as the Lionhead formation that is visible across the river. (see Baker Mountain)

Navajo Tarn

A tarn is a small mountain lake, and this one can be found on the south slope of Castle Mountain.

Remnants of the limestone cap on the Beartooth granite can be stained many colors by dissolved mineral salts, particularly the reds and oranges from the iron oxide. This lake was named for the surrounding rocks that resemble the colors found in the beautiful Navajo rugs.

Needle Lake

The name of this tiny lake to the north of Two Sisters Mountain first appears in 1928. As it is quite round, the name cannot refer to the shape. It is found in forested country on the Two Sisters branch of Flood Creek, so the name must be from the pine needles seen floating on the water.

The Needles

The formation called The Needles is located on The Needles USGS quad midway on the Boulder River, just to the east of Boulder Mountain. Frank Tweedy, who was with a survey crew in 1895, is said to have gotten the name from some prospectors. Although there are no spires on this peak, apparently the alternating series of gullies and aretes on the northern side gave the impression of needles.

New World Gulch

In June of 1870, A. Bart Henderson, Adam "Horn" Miller, James Gourley, Ed Hibbard, and others were prospecting in the Clarks Fork/Soda Butte drainages near present-day Cooke City and found gold. They staked their claims and called it the New World Mining District. It is primarily located on Miller and Republic Mountains and was a very rich strike with over 3,000 patented and unpatented claims. Unfortunately, transportation was a problem. The ore had to be hand-sorted from the waste, then bagged and taken by mule to Cooke City. From there it went by wagon to Cinnabar/Gardiner where it was loaded on train cars to the smelter in East Helena. As a result of these overhead costs, the net profit for the small operations was marginal.

Nichols Creek/Peak

The Nichols brothers, Charles and William, aka "Hunter Bill," were trappers, prospectors, and woodchoppers who cut mine props here in the 1890s. Their cabin was on this creek near the present-day Red Lodge Ski Area.

The creek comes off Nichols Peak, which shares a ridge to the west of Grizzly (aka Red Lodge) Peak where the ski resort is located.

Night Lake

There is no citation to explain why this lake is called "Night." It is about 100 yards upstream from Island Lake in the Little Bear Creek chain just north of Beartooth Highway.

Nightmare Lake

This lake is in a cirque above 9,000 feet off Woodbine Creek and up from the Stillwater River. It is another of the lakes whose name seems to come from the weather, like Desolation, Vengence, Trouble, and Dreary Lakes. Afternoon thunderstorms are common in the higher elevations of the Beartooths, and it can get nightmarishly nasty.

No Bones Lake

There is no information to explain the curious name of this lake that is found north of Cooke City.

Mount Norris

Philetus P. Norris (1821–1885) was the second superintendent of Yellowstone National Park, serving from 1877 to 1882. He did much to promote and develop the Park, hired Harry Yount to be the first ranger, and named many features. Shamelessly, several, like the geyser basin, were after himself. His name on the mountain that is now Dunraven Peak, near the pass on Mount Washburn, was removed, and he is left with this less impressive peak in the northeast corner of the Park north of the Lamar Valley.

Philetus Norris. YELLOWSTONE NATIONAL PARK, #6338.

North Fork Basin

Triple North Fork points! The North Fork Basin is at the head of the North Fork of Clover Creek, which is the head of the North Fork of the Hellroaring Creek that flows south into the Park.

Nugget Lake

The name of this lake, on the West Rosebud drainage, reflects on the gold mining that was so prevalent in the Beartooths.

Nurses Lakes

This cluster of 11 lakes sits on the northern edge of the Custer-Gallatin National Forest, high on the northern end of the Boulder Plateau just above Taylor Flats. Local sources believe that these fishless lakes were named for a person, and that would most likely be Anna Hauge. She filed a homestead patent for the northeast quarter of section 29 and the northwest quarter of section 30 in 1922, which includes all 11 of the lakes. It is assumed that Anna was trained and worked as a nurse.

Nye Town /Creek/Basin/Falls

In the late 1860s Ansel Hubble and Joseph "Skookum Joe" Anderson were the first to discover ore along the upper Stillwater River, but were unable to work it as it was on Crow land. In 1883 Jack Nye, along with Ephriam, Jimmy, and Jonas Hedges, returned with "Skookum Joe," located copper, lead, and nickel deposits nearby, and staked their claims. Jack Nye then formed the Stillwater Mining Co and sold the claims to the Minnesota Mining and Smelting Company. In 1886 a small smelter had been assembled and Nye City grew to a population of 300-400 people with 11 saloons, two stores, a commissary, six restaurants, a boarding-house and an assay office. However, a government survey revealed that Nye City was actually three miles into the new Crow Reservation land, so the Department of the Interior shut down their operation, the mining equipment had to be removed, and by 1889 Nye City was abandoned. The Crow's further cession of 1,800,000 acres of the reservation in 1892 reopened homesteading, claim staking, and mining in the area, and the town of Nye reappeared but was now relocated a couple of miles downriver from Old Nye. That small community has continued and has been associated with mining ever since. It had 272 residents in the 2010 census, a school, church, fire hall, bar, and post office all spread along several miles of County Road 419, the Nye Road. There are currently also some recreational housing developments, as well as agricultural cattle, hay, and sheep operations. Old Nye is no more, just a Montana FWP picnic area. However, mining has always been prominent, with the Benbow and Mouat Mines producing much-needed chromium during the World Wars. These mines are still very active and can be seen across the river from the Nye Road where the Stillwater Mines, the largest employer in the county, is extracting ore rich in chromium. It is also the only site in North America for platinum and palladium. The huge, modern Stillwater Mines processing plant is right next to the road on the west side of the river at the south end of what was once Old Nye.

Nye Basin is a local term for the big bowl-shaped area on the Stillwater Plateau that is the headwaters of **Nye Creek.** As the creek leaves the plateau, **Nye Falls** drops over a precipice, falling some 500 feet before entering the Stillwater River at Old Nye.

Nymph Lake

Situated among the other "bug lakes" on the Fossil Lake USGS quad along with Copepod, Cladocera, Spider, and Aquarius, this lake also has a fly-fishing connotation.

A nymph originally referred to several of the minor Greek deities that were associated with woods, water, and other natural features. The term was taken up by biologists to refer to the immature form of insects, and now anglers create artificial flies that look like these nymphs—to tempt the wily trout.

The former name of Leo Lake is no longer recognized.

Pheasant tail nymph. WIKI CREATIVE COMMONS.

Octopus Creek

So what is this? We have bears and deer, fishes by the score, bugs, birds, and snakes, but never since the Devonian seas covered this land has an octopus been found in the Northern Rockies.

Actually, the name comes from the map. A series of creeks come together into the Stillwater River at the same place—Horseshoe, Octopus, Glacier, and Clarks Creeks and the Stillwater River to the north and south. The appearance on the topo map looks like the arms of an octopus—or rather a sextopus, but you get the idea.

Oliver Draw

George Oliver, who was an early-day cattleman, homesteaded where the Meyers Creek Ranger Station is now. He had a line cabin at the mouth of this draw near Bad Canyon north of Nye.

Oly Lake

There is no citation or other information on this high lake on Dewey Mountain near Dewey Lake. It must be assumed to have been named for a Scandinavian emigrant miner, and not a can of beer.

Omega Lake

Omega is one of two lakes that sit in a cirque on the north side of Medicine Mountain, and it is certainly not shaped like the last letter of the Greek alphabet.

The name makes more sense when you know that the small, nearby, presently unnamed lake was once called Alpha Lake. They then become "the alpha and omega," or the beginning and the end—the essence of alpine beauty.

Oregon Mountain

John Spiker was an early prospector who lived in the Gardiner area but would go back and forth to his other home in Oregon. He named this mountain that reminded him of his warmer winter place. It lies just east of the rich diggings on Crevice Mountain, with which it shares a ridge.

Otter Lake

The North American river otter, *Lontra canadensis*, is a semi-aquatic member of the weasel family that is commonly found in the lakes and streams of the Northern Rockies. They feed primarily on fish, supplemented with an occasional crawfish or frog, and are quite social, living in family groups. It is fun to watch them in what appears to be a purely playful sliding on their bellies down to the stream.

Otters in Yellowstone. PHOTO BY JIM PEACO, NATIONAL PARK SERVICE.

The lake is on the south slope of Summit Mountain.

Ouzel Lake

The American dipper or ousel, *Cinclus mexicanus*, lives along many of our streams, and, obviously, near this lake south of Bald Knob and Fossil Lake. The dipper name come from these wren-like birds' habit of bobbing in the water. Because they have dense feathers and blood that can store oxygen better than other birds, they are able to submerge for up to 10 seconds while they walk along the bottom feeding on insect larvae.

Ousel. ILLUSTRATION BY JOSEPH WOLF.

Ovis Lake

Ovis Lake, sometimes called Sheep Lake, is on a shelf on the northeast side of Sheep Mountain. *Ovis* is the Latin word for sheep, so *Ovis aries* is the domestic sheep, and *Ovis canadensis* is the Rocky Mountain bighorn sheep. (see Sheep Mountain and Ram Lake)

Owl Lake

Although owls are one of the primary avian predators in our forests, their presence here is not the reason for the name of this body of water up on the Lake Plateau.

Montana's Department of Fish, Wildlife and Parks has done an extensive study of the lakes in the Absaroka-Beartooths, which has included hydrographic mapping of the lake beds to assess fish spawning habitats. Pat Marcuson gave the lake this name in 1969 because the map of the underwater contour lines created an owl-like shape.

Oxide Mountain

Oxygen forms stable chemical bonds with almost every element except gold and platinum to form oxides. Most of the earth's crust consists of solid oxides, and perhaps the most commonly known and easily recognized are iron oxide, or rust, and silver oxide, which is tarnish. The term, and this mountain's name, thus reflects many of the minerals that the prospectors were searching for.

The mountain was a scene of a great deal of mining and overlooks the Broadwater River.

Pablo Lake

This tiny little lake sits west of Fossil Lake and is immediately south of Basin Lake. Its name is not recognized by the USGS, but it is on other maps for a very obvious reason. Basin Lake is called Picasso Lake by some because of its shape, so this is... Pablo Picasso. (see citation at Basin Lake and map at Picasso Lake)

Packsaddle Butte

The term "saddle" in the mountains refers to a shallow ridge between two higher points that looks like a horse's saddle. A packsaddle has a tall cross buck on either end to tie on the gear that the pack horse or mule will carry, and thus has a deeper saddle.

Packsaddle Butte is on the very northeast corner of the Custer-Gallatin National Forest near Ramshorn Peak. The topographic lines on the map display the typical wide figure 8 that saddles create.

Paddle Lake

This lake in the Sodalite to Broadwater drainage was named for its paddle-like shape.

Palisades

(see Limestone Palisades)

Palmer Creek/Mountain

Palmer Mountain is just to the north of Crevice Mountain in the rich mining area near Cooke City. It was named for the Palmer brothers, who were prospectors and who also worked as Yellowstone Park stagecoach drivers.

Palmer Creek flows east between Palmer and Crevice Mountains to enter Bear Creek south of Jardine and was known by that name prior to 1892. In that year the *Livingston Enterprise* reported that a pipe had been constructed to divert water from the creek to the mill at Crevice, which was to help with ore separation.

Panhandle Lake

Panhandle Lake, near Cooke City, was named for its shape. It was called Hilltop Lake in 1937, but Hilltop is now a lake that is a bit farther east toward Goose Lake.

Big Park, Big Park Lake, Little Park Mountain

The dictionary defines a park in the western U.S. as a broad, flat, mostly open area in a mountainous region.

Big Park is such a flat area along the Stillwater River at the confluence with Herein Creek. It is on the Little Park Mountain USGS quad about 12 miles south of Woodbine. The Big Park Ranger Station was once located here, but was burned in the Fires of '88 and not replaced. The 1937 Merino map had another Big Park in the basin around Lake Elaine near the Wyoming border. This name is no longer recognized by the Board on Geographic Names and is not found on current maps.

Big Park Lake is somewhere else entirely. It is in a large park-like meadow along Granite Creek, above the hamlet of Alpine in the East Rosebud drainage near Lake at the Falls.

Little Park Mountain is high in the Beartooths east of Big Park and the Stillwater River. There is no Little Park that can be found on the maps, but perhaps there are some smaller flats that carry this as a local name. A USGS quad map is named after this mountain.

Park Rapids

It is rare for a rapid to garner a mention from the USGS. One exception are these rapids in an unnamed creek just east and above the Granite Lake in Wyoming near the border with Montana. Although the rapids are dramatic, part of the creek flows through a flat park.

Parker Point

Parker Point is north of Jardine at the head of Eagle Creek. It was named for Jim

"One-Eyed" Parker, who in 1920 filed a homestead for his ranch on Eagle Creek just below this point. He also worked as a hunting guide and his wife ran the Cottage Hotel in Gardiner.

Parker raised pigs at the ranch and sold the meat to the miners at the coal mines at Aldrich. He also trapped bears and sold that meat as "poor man's pork." How does one know the difference, and how did you know what you got?

North Pass Creek Spring, South Pass Creek Spring

These springs that feed the creeks are located along the pack trail that goes from Castle Creek over a pass on the shoulder of Meyer Mountain and on to Meyers Creek.

Passage Creek/Falls

Passage Creek starts just east of the West Fork of Mill Creek near Emigrant. It was called a "passage" because the trail along the creek was a natural way to get from Emigrant to the Hellroaring Plateau.

One of the more popular day hikes in the Absarokas is to beautiful **Passage Falls** at the junction of Wallace and Passage Creeks. Betsy Counts had a cabin near these falls. (see Counts Creek)

Pat Lake

Pat Lake is a widening in Hemingway Creek just to the north of the Montana/Wyoming line. It is not known who either the Pat or the Jenny of the lakes along this creek may be. Ernest Hemingway had a reputation for infidelity, even shedding his second wife during his time at the L bar T Ranch. However, these names are not mentioned in the books and papers on Hemingway's time in the Yellowstone high country, and the women's names appear on the lakes in 1937, before the creek became Hemingway.

They now join our group of other mystery women lakes.

Pavement Pass

Pavement Pass is no longer on any map but its unusual geological formation still exists in the high country north of Cooke City. It branches off of the Russell Creek Trail on the route that the Kimball expedition took to Mount Dewey.

He named it "Pavement" in 1898 because of "the remarkable tessellation of granite blocks, worn by ice and water to the smoothness of a city pavement."

Peace Lake

The small lake—unnamed on the USGS and National Geographic maps—is at the head of Wounded Man Creek in the Slough Creek drainage. It is listed here because it is important to Montana Fish, Wildlife and Parks, who gave it the name. Peace Lake, and its neighbor to the northeast, Heather Lake, are two of the few lakes in the Absaroka-Beartooths, with original native Yellowstone cutthroat trout, ones that migrated up from the Clarks Fork River on their own. Almost all of the other lakes with fish have been planted. (see also Native Lake and Heather Lake)

Mount Peal

Mount Peal, at 12,414 feet, is the ninth tallest peak in Montana, but the exact derivation of its name remains clouded.

There are some people who have said that it was "most certainly" named for the famous mineralogist Albert Peale (1849–1914). He worked for the U.S. Geological and Geographic Survey of the Territories from 1871 to 1879 and was on several of his friend Ferdinand Hayden's survey expeditions, where his 400-page treatise on the thermal features of Yellowstone was definitive. He continued as geologist for the USGS from 1882 until 1898 when he became paleobotanist for the National Museum. During his geological work he had his name placed on two mountains in Utah and Idaho as well as Peale Island in Yellowstone Lake. However, neither Hayden's notes nor Peale's several biographies mention this mountain in the Beartooths, and his surname ends, unlike the mountain, in an "e."

The high peaks around Granite Peak, Peal's immediate neighbor, are known for collecting huge storm clouds, so perhaps it was the reverberating peals of thunder that generated the name of this peak. This would fit with the bad weather mountains and lakes up there like Vengence, Desolation, Dreary, and Froze-to-Death Lakes and Thunder and Tempest Peaks.

Peanut Lake

Peanut can be a synonym for small. The name may come from this, but the little lake on the Fossil Lake quad is also peanut shaped.

Pebble Creek

One of the more popular hiking trails in the northeast corner of Yellowstone Park follows along Pebble Creek. The creek starts on the side of Wolverine Peak and flows into Soda Butte Creek west of Cooke City.

The 1872 Hayden Survey crew named it White Pebble Creek for the light sedimentary stones found at its headwaters. In 1878, the third Hayden Survey shortened it to Pebble Creek.

Pentad Lake

Pentad comes from the Greek word meaning "five," and there are five drainages coming into or leaving this lake at the head of the Middle Fork of Wounded

Man Creek. It has a rather irregular shape, so, as Pat Marcuson says, "How you perceive the points depends on what you put in your coffee."

Ed Ickerman from the Beartooth Ranch originally called it Crazy Mule Lake. He was the first to blaze the trail to this lake and was bringing fish to stock it. A mule, possibly as a result of a bee sting, ran into the lake with its panniers full of buckets of fish and drowned. That mule's skull sat on a large rock at the lake's outlet for years, but the skull and the unique name are both now gone.

Phantom Lake/Creek/Falls/Glacier

Phantom Glacier drains into **Phantom Creek,** which passes through **Phantom Lake** and to the East Rosebud.

John Branger of the OT Bar Ranch out of Alpine named the lake in the early part of the twentieth century. There is an odd formation in the cliff above the lake that to him appeared to be some sort of spooky woman, or, as Harrison Fagg describes it, "a spirit-looking thing." The creek, falls, and glacier's names come from the lake.

Phelps Creek

Once misnamed Phillips Creek, the spelling of this creek was corrected to Phelps in 1957. George W. Phelps, one of the early prospectors and hunters, had a ranch on this creek north of Gardiner. He came to Montana in 1863 and initially settled at Grasshopper Creek near Bannack. In 1864 he accompanied the James Stuart expedition that prospected the Upper Yellowstone, was reported to have found placer gold near Gardiner, and spent many years prospecting at Jardine, Montana. In 1881 Phelps was working as a scout for Park Superintendent P.W. Norris exploring the Park and Norris called him, "our intelligent, observant mountaineer comrade." He continued to work for the Park after 1881 where he supervised the building of the Park roads.

Picasso Lake

Officially this is Basin Lake, but hikers looking at the topo map have seen a Picasso-esque profile, and that name has developed quite a following. Pablo is the tiny, unnamed pond in the lower right-hand corner. Pablo Picasso is more interesting, don't you think? (see Basin Lake and Pablo Lake)

Picket Lake

A picket here refers to a pointed stake as in a picket fence. In the West, a stake that is driven

Picasso and Pablo Lakes. DETAIL FROM 2020 USGS FOSSIL LAKE QUAD MAP.

into the ground and used to tether a horse is called a picket or picket pin. It can also be used as a verb, as in "to picket your animal." The area near this lake on the south slope of Summit Mountain was used as a horse camp.

Picket Pin Creek/Lakes (North and South) Mountain/Canyon

As noted above, a picket pin is a stake, often metal, that can be driven into the ground so that a horse's picket rope can be attached and the animal tethered. "Skookum Joe" Anderson, a prospector, built a road into **Picket Pin Canyon** in 1892 and found an iron picket pin driven into a tree, so he used that to name the creek. The name was originally for this creek that flows into the Stillwater River, and the name of the lakes, canyon, and mountain come from the creek.

Pierce's Pond

In 1919 O.J. Salo of Red Lodge named the small pond that sits under the hogback and upstream from Timberline Lake for his friend Paul Pierce. Although noted by the U.S. Forest Service in the 1930s, the name has not been recognized by the Board on Geographic Names and does not appear on modern maps.

Pika Peak

The pika, or coney, *Ochotona princeps*, is common to the high rocky slopes in the mountains. Its distinct high-pitched whistle and mouse-like shape generate a delightful encounter for most hikers. Pikas are actually close cousins to the rabbit and have been called rock rabbits. They do not hibernate, but spend the summers gathering grass and flowering plants to store in their rocky burrows for winter feed.

Pika. PHOTO BY EMILY MESSNER, NATIONAL PARK SERVICE.

The pika's thick fur is designed to protect it in its cold alpine environment, but can become a lethal problem if exposed to temperatures above 78 degrees Fahrenheit (25.5 C). As a result of global warming, they seem to be migrating higher and the population is decreasing, particularly in their more southern ranges. Some environmentalists feel that they are threatened, but pikas have not yet been so listed.

Pika Peak is a common name in Montana, and this particular one is in rocky country just southeast of Granite Peak and Cairn Mountain.

Pilot Peak/Creek

(see image under Index Peak)

Pilot, and its partner Index Peak are in Wyoming and just southeast of the Northeast Entrance to Yellowstone Park and Cooke City, where their distinctive profiles have guided miners, trappers, and Indians for years. Highly visible from U.S. 212, they provide a beautiful and dramatic welcome to tourists entering the Park from the Beartooth Highway.

John Colter was supposedly the first to have called it Pilot Peak in 1806, but the name's first written record was by prospector A. Bart Henderson, who put it in his journal in 1868. Pilot and Index are on the same ridge, and before 1900 the names were reversed; in fact, they were switched back and forth on various maps from 1873 to 1930. That latter year the USGS, perhaps from a mapping error, did a final switch, putting Pilot as the southern, pointed peak. This was confirmed by the Board on Geographic Names in 1937, and that is what we see today. Pilot is the taller glacial horn carved by four glaciers into a pointed finger, and Index is its shorter northern neighbor. Is that clear? If not and you switch the names, you will have joined many other geographers.

Lake Pinchot

Up on the Lake Plateau is "the Crown Jewel of the Lake Plateau," Lake Pinchot. It was named to honor Gifford Pinchot (1865–1946), who served as the first chief of the U.S. Forest Service from 1905 to 1910. A close friend of President Teddy Roosevelt, and two-time governor of Pennsylvania, Pinchot set the tone for the Forest Service for decades to come.

Gifford Pinchot, 1909. PHOTO BY PRIRIE MCDONALD.

With his often repeated principle that "conservation is the foresighted utilization, preservation, and renewal of forests, waters, lands, and minerals, for the greatest good of the greatest number for the longest time," he put conservation of the forests high on America's priority list. His program of planned use and renewal demonstrated the practicality and profitability of managing forests for continuous cropping, and his pioneering vision continues to be a model for the Forest Service today.

Big Pine Basin/Creek, Little Pine Creek, Pine Creek, Pine Creek Lake

There are lots of pine trees in the Absarokas, particularly on the Paradise Valley side. **Big Pine Basin and Creek** and **Little Pine Creek** are tributaries of Sixmile Creek south of Emigrant.

Pine Lake, which sits in a cirque beneath Black Mountain, and just plain Pine Creek, which drains it, are a bit farther north near Pray, Montana. This latter creek was named early on for the strip of pines that extend from the Absaroka Mountains to the Yellowstone River. The hike along the creek up to the lake is strenuous, but the mountains and the waterfalls at the lake make for special scenery. Thomas Leforge, whose 1928 *Memoirs of a White Crow Indian,* as told by Thomas P. Marquis, had a cabin at the mouth of Pine Creek.

The creek flows through the little community of **Pine Creek,** an area that was heavily burned by a forest fire in 2012.

Piney Dell

Piney Dell was one of the original resorts on the Beartooth Highway south of Red Lodge. It was built as a homesteader's log cabin in the 1920s, but in the 1930s Dr. J.C.F Siegfriedt of Red Lodge opened it "as a cultural center for music and dance from the old countries and as a community meeting place." The coal mines near Red Lodge hired many immigrants to work them from a variety of different countries, and Siegfriedt used this cabin as he tried to find ways to break down the barriers between the nationalities.

The Piney Dell still exists as an upscale restaurant, part of the Rock Creek Resort just south of town.

Pinnacle Mountain/Lake

Pinnacle is an obvious description of the mountain's shape, and descriptive enough to have the USGS quad map named for it.

Pinnacle Lake, named unofficially, sits on the western side of the mountain at the very head of Slough Creek.

Pipit Lake

Pipits, genus *Anthus*, are small birds that are distributed worldwide and are found generally in grasslands from sea level to the alpine tundra. Their plumage is drab, tending from brown to a faded white.

The lake is on the Lake Plateau in the birder's section.

Nilger pipit. PHOTO BY NISHAD H. KAIPPALLY, WIKI CREATIVE COMMONS.

Lake Pisces

This fishy lake is found on the north slope of the Two Sisters.

Pisces is the Latin plural for fish, and is an obsolete English taxonomic name that now, like Ichthes, is just a general term for these creatures. However, the use of this name is probably better than repeating another Fish or Trout Lake.

The sport of fishing lures many visitors to the Beartooth high country, but the use of this Latin word can cause a bit of confusion with the astrological term. The other Pisces that many people know is the constellation in the Zodiac and the sign in the horoscope that covers the period from March 15 to April 14. People born under this sign are supposed to be incorrigible romantics and, obviously, the term is totally unrelated to this lake.

Placer Basin, Basin Creek, Placer Gulch

A placer is defined as a deposit of sand or gravel in the bed of a stream or lake that contains particles of valuable minerals. Placer mining is the simplest form of gold mining, and it finds actual gold rather than the ore. Typical placer mining uses panning, a rocker, or the more efficient sluice box with its riffled bottom to separate the gold from the sand. In all cases the sand is washed and the heavier gold settles to the bottom. This is particularly useful for single or small groups of men, but does not yield the quantity that finding and smelting ore does.

Placer Basin is located near the head of the East Boulder River where Forge Creek comes in. The basin is in the Natural Bridge Mining District and was the district's most heavily prospected area.

Placer Gulch can be found on the north side of Sliderock Mountain. Since it sits directly under Gold Hill, one can appreciate that it, too, was a site of much mining.

Placer Basin Creek also comes from another basin that was a good placer mining location. It flows into Sixmile Creek just to the south of Emigrant.

Planaria Lake

Here our naming scientist has come up with a lake that brings back memories of college biology laboratories. Cut these worms in two, either lengthwise or crosswise, and they grow back as two identical worms.

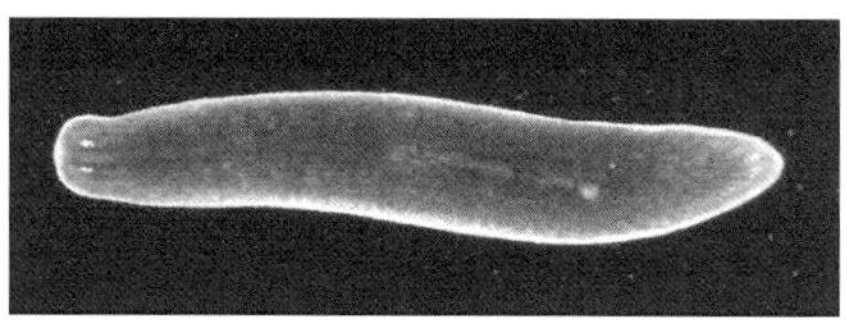

Planaria torva. HOLGER BRANDL ET AL, *NUCLEIC ACID RES.,* ISSUE 44, JAN 4, 2016.

Planaria are flatworms of the Class Turbellaria, and are common to much of the world, living in both saltwater and freshwater ponds and rivers. It would not be surprising that the person naming this lake found these flatworms in the water or under a log by the shore. It also is rather a long, thin lake that has a bit of a planarian shape.

Some maps have it as Planana Lake, but this is just a misspelling where the "ri" became printed as an "n."

The lake is on the Castle Mountain quad just north of the Montana/Wyoming border, and on the same creek as Snail and Shrimp Lakes.

Plateau Creek

This small tributary of Lake Creek comes off the Silver Run Plateau.

Mount Pleasant

Mount Pleasant is not recognized by the USGS. However, peak baggers want to record everything over 12,000 feet that they have climbed, so this 12,006-foot point, actually a 196-foot bump on the Mount Peal plateau, appears on the climbing maps.

Pleiades Lakes

In Greek mythology, the Pleiades were the seven daughters of Atlas and Pleione. When Orion began to pursue them, Zeus made them into stars and placed them in the sky. The Pleiades star cluster is found just to the right of the constellation of Orion in the night sky, with seven stars visible to the naked eye. It is the closest star cluster to earth and the most easily seen.

This group of seven little lakes is in a basin north of the Montana/Wyoming border and just north of Crystal Lake on the Castle Mountain quad. Since the Pleiades star cluster is also known as the Seven Sisters, one can understand where the name came from.

Pneumonia Lake

There are several lakes like Dreary, Vengence, Misery, and the like that reflect the nasty weather that can hit the high country. This lake shows the result of that exposure.

Poacher Basin

On the 1947 USGS map, about a half mile north of the Yellowstone National Park boundary, on the upper East Fork of Coyote Creek, is a small basin labeled "Poacher." The basin is no longer noted on any map, but there is a Poacher Trail on the USGS Needles quad map that goes right through that area. Poaching, or illegal hunting, was rampant after the formation of the national park in 1872. This was one of the main reasons that the U.S. Army was assigned to patrol the Park from 1886, and why it stayed until the Park Service was formed in 1916. One wonders if there is more of a story here.

Pocket Lake

Downstream from Kaufman Lake on Falls Creek and up a bit to the west is a small lake that sits in a mountain pocket. It is not on USGS or hiking maps, but the name is used by Montana Fish, Wildlife and Parks.

Pole Creek

The many Pole Creeks in Montana come from the logging that was so prevalent. It refers to a stand of trees that were large enough to cut for poles or fence posts, but too small for lumber. This one is north of Gardiner and is a tributary of Bear Creek.

Porcupine Draw

Assistant Ranger T.F. Hogg named this draw near Nye in 1917. It is not stated why they were so honored, but these rodents of the Family Erithizontidae are quite common and are notorious

Porcupine. PHOTO BY ED AUSTIN, NATIONAL PARK SERVICE.

for chewing axe handles and motor belts, and other nuisance behaviors. Perhaps that brought them to his attention.

The sharp, protective quills of the porcupine are the bane of your dog, and have been dyed and used in decorative traditional Native American quillwork. The name porcupine comes from the Latin *Porcus*, meaning pig, and the animal is also called the "quill pig."

Prairie Creek

The Stillwater River flows through some flat country northeast of Nye as it heads north to more hospitable ranching country. This creek joins it at the Stillwater Bridge in prairie-like surroundings.

Prairie Dog Creek

Prairie dogs are burrowing ground squirrels of the genus *Cynomys* and are found in large colonies throughout the western prairies. Although rodents, the "dog" in their name comes from their barking warning call. The term has been in use since at least 1774, and Lewis and Clark called them that in their journals. The genus name, *Cynomys*, comes from the Greek words for "dog mouse."

The Stillwater River opens to the prairies after Nye, and this creek joins that river near the Nye cemetery.

Prairie dog. NATIONAL PARK SERVICE PHOTO.

Prairieview Mountain

Prairieview Mountain is on the Alpine quad north of Phantom Creek. It was first named Mount Fairview, but apparently the view was more prairie than fair.

Pray

Although the Church Universal and Triumphant has established itself in the southern Paradise Valley, the name of this unincorporated community does not have a spiritual basis.

In 1909 Valentine Eggar established a rail siding, small store, and post office five miles north of Chico along the Northern Pacific's branch line from Livingstone to Gardiner. He wanted to call it Eggar, but the Postal Service refused as it was too close to Edgar, another Montana town. As a substitute, it was named Pray in honor of Charles Pray, who, as

Charles N. Pray. MONTANA MEMORY PROJECT, MONTANA HISTORICALSOCIETY.

Montana's congressman from 1906 to 1911, was responsible for many of the small post offices in the state. Pray later went on to a distinguished 33-year career as a federal judge in Montana.

Princess Lake

There is no citation to identify the young royalty for whom this pretty little lake was named. It is located along the rather difficult off-trail approach route to Granite Peak that follows Huckleberry Creek up from Mystic Lake. One might assume that it honors the efforts of a youngster whose father led her up that way.

Production Lake

This lake in the Sky Top drainage was named by the Montana state fisheries people because it is a good brook trout factory, with excellent spawning beds that produce them in great numbers. However, the food supply is more restricted, so they tend to only reach the 7- to 10-inch size. Since this lake is just up from, and connected to, Recroitment Lake, which has poor spawning sites but where the food supply and subsequent growth is excellent, these two lakes make a biological system. There is reproduction in one and the recruitment of huge growth in the other. (see Recroitment Lake)

Prospect Lake

A "prospect" is a mining term that refers to a place that is being explored for mineral deposits, and this is where the term "prospector" comes from. The name of the lake clearly relates to the rich mining around it rather than the view.

The fact that the lake sits in a private mining inholding wilderness exclusion on the southwest side of Boulder Mountain probably explains why it is absent on the USGS and Forest Service maps. However, it can be found on the 2013 National Geographic hiking map of the Absaroka-Beartooth West.

Pruitt Park

Pruitt Park is another of the private mining inholdings in the national forest and can be found between the East and West Boulder Rivers. The name is official on the maps, but there is no USGS citation, so it must only be assumed that the name comes from the Pruitt who started and worked the mine there.

Puddle Lake

Between Beauty and Anvil Lakes near the head of the Stillwater River is a tiny lake—a puddle. It only carries that name on the Montana Fish, Wildlife and Parks fisheries documents, and does not appear on the USGS or National Geographic hikers' maps.

The Pyramid, Pyramid Mountain, Black Pyramid Mountain

Frank Tweedy was the first to publish **The Pyramid's** name on his 1893 map. He is thought to have gotten the name from local miners, who called it that because its four-sided pyramidal shape resembles those in Egypt. The mountain sits on the far eastern end of Mill Creek on the divide to the Boulder and has a USGS quad map that is named for it.

Pyramid Mountain is not The Pyramid. Rather it is a pyramidal point at 12,151 feet that sits on the flat saddle on Mount Wood above the West Fishtail Lakes. It was first named by mountaineers who climbed it.

The color and shape gave the name to **Black Pyramid Mountain.** It, then, gave its name to another USGS quad map. It is on the eastern edge of the Custer-Gallatin National Forest where the Beartooth Highway crosses into Wyoming.

Quad Creek

The first steep climb of the Beartooth Highway going south from Red Lodge heads out of the Rock Creek Valley with four big switchbacks that ascend along the drainage of this creek—thus it is "Quad" Creek.

The gneiss exposed here is some 3.3 billion years old, some of the oldest rocks in North America.

Quaker Spring

Quaker Spring is found just to the west of the hamlet of Limestone, west of Nye and at the head of a small, unnamed stream that flows into Lodgepole Creek. The area was heavily homesteaded in the early twentieth century. Milton C. Lowe and his wife Francis were the first. In addition to farming, they ran the Limestone General Store and Post Office from 1910 until 1953. Their land included this spring. The name of the spring suggests that they were Quakers, members of the Religious Society of Friends. (see Limestone Butte/Creek/Town)

Quinnebaugh Meadows

These flat meadows on the West Fork of Rock Creek were named by Ranger Arthur M. Baum in 1917. The name is a purely poetic description and comes from the Mohawk Indian word for meadow and falls. Because of its beauty, with the meadow and stream framed by the high alpine mountains, it is a popular hiking destination and is frequently photographed.

It was once the site of a proposed dam, which, fortunately, was never built.

Quintuple Peaks

The long mountain ridge between Rock Creek and the Beartooth Highway can be easily seen from the north side of the Beartooth Pass. There are five peaks that extend along the ridge, and thus the name becomes Quintuple.

The tiny lake that is found on the west side of the mountain carries the unofficial name of **Quint Lake.**

Rabbit Gulch

Rabbit Gulch is a steep-walled valley on the southeast side of Chalice Peak in the Flood Creek/Stillwater drainage. At 9,000 feet it would be at the upper limit of the rabbits' rather ubiquitous habitat, which includes

Cottontail rabbit. NATIONAL PARK SERVICE ILLUSTRATION.

everything from meadows, forests, and grasslands to deserts, wetlands, and your vegetable garden. All rabbits are Lagomorphs and are related to pikas and hares in the Family Leporidae, of which there are over 60 species. The several species of cottontail rabbits, genus *Sylvilagus,* are native to North America, but one also commonly sees domestic rabbits that have gone wild. These latter are descendants of the European rabbit, *Oryctolagus cuniculus,* which has been introduced throughout the world.

Rachel Lake

This lake that was formerly called Wall Lake was named for Rachel Spogen of Red Lodge. It is just a bit upstream from Spogen Lake, named for Leo of an earlier generation. (see Spogen Lake)

Mount Rae

Rachael McKnight and her husband George settled on the West Boulder around 1884 where they had a ranch on the south side of the mountain that was named for her. They were the parents of Coral Kaufman, who lived with her husband, Harry, the first ranger, at the Main Boulder station, just two miles from the McKnights. It is interesting that early reports refer to the family name as McKnight, but it changed, losing the "Mc." Current family members use Knight. (see Mount McKnight)

Rainbow Creek/Lakes

There are several Rainbow Lakes and one creek, all named for the rainbow trout, *Oncorhynchus mykiss.* This is a non-native fish that was introduced for sport and has become extremely successful, often crowding out the native cutthroat trout.

The **creek,** a tributary of the East Fork of the Boulder River, is just east of Baboon Mountain and Independence. The **Rainbow Lakes** are a collection of small lakes at its head, seven of which have a successful rainbow trout population.

The second **Rainbow Lake** is a large body of water near the head of the East Rosebud. In 1914 John Branger of the TO Bar Ranch at Alpine, a forest officer, and two others carried buckets of fish from East Rosebud Lake to stock this lake.

Branger was asked to name the lake, and he wanted to christen it for his wife Rosina. However, as she was still living (a rule that was often broken), he was told that he had to choose something else, so he used the rainbow trout that they had planted.

There is a third **Rainbow Lake,** which is close to Gardiner and, after the annexation of the Cinnabar Triangle in 1929, is now within Yellowstone Park. It was once called Chadbourn Lake. In a common move, the USGS removed an early piece of history from the map and replaced it with a fish. Allen Wright Chadbourn (1842–1943) came to Montana in 1882 with his wife Dolly, and shortly thereafter purchased a ranch south of Stephens Creek near the towns of Cinnabar and Gardiner. He started the Yellowstone Park Transportation and Camping Outfit, which had a fleet of Concord stagecoaches, ran camping and saddle trips, and provided transportation within Yellowstone Park, until 1901 when he sold the business and ranch to George W. Wakefield.

Ram Lake/Pasture

A ram is the term for a male sheep, and this lake, in a cirque between Mount Wood and Pyramid Mountain, is prime habitat for the Rocky Mountain bighorn sheep, *Ovis canadensis.*

Bighorn ram near Tower. PHOTO BY DIANE RENKIN, NATIONAL PARK SERVICE.

Ram Pasture is on the plateau just to the north of Index Peak. The males of the Rocky Mountain sheep could be found here, and the sound of their horns banging together during the rut would have been most impressive. (see Sheep Mountain/Creek/Lake)

Raspberry Creek

There must have been some good eating for the miners near Chrome Mountain on the Main Boulder. Raspberry Creek, just upstream from the Flemming bridge, is next to Bramble Creek. Both raspberries and brambles (blackberries) are members of the *Rubus* family, and are common in Montana and famous for their delicious fruit.

Ratine Creek, Rattin Camp or Rattine

Ratine Creek comes off the Line Creek Plateau to join Rock Creek at Rattin Camp on Beartooth Highway just south of Mount Maurice and the town of Red Lodge. Of course, the USGS spells it Ratine, and the Forest Service spells it both Rattine and Rattin, but the man's name, according to Red Lodge voter registration records, was Pietro Rattin. He was an Italian immigrant who mined in the area from 1908 to 1928.

Ravin Lake

Ravin Lake, named for the bird, is in the Flood Creek chain west of the Stillwater River. Although it is misspelled Ravin by the USGS, commercial hiking maps and Montana Fish, Wildlife and Parks websites and publications have it spelled correctly as Raven Lake.

The raven, *Corvus corax*, is widespread throughout Montana. It is a very intelligent creature, and studies of its interesting behavior have been the topic of several recent books. You may see the dominant, breeding pair soaring together, but are more likely

Raven. PHOTO BY KENT MILLER, NATIONAL PARK SERVICE.

to see and hear the flock (unkindness) of juveniles that noisily call their buddies to the food that they have found. There is also a well-studied theory that ravens have developed a cooperative relationship with wolves. The high-flying ravens can easily spot deer and elk and will draw the wolves to their prey. Since a raven's beak cannot pierce hide, the birds then wait nearby to feast on the carcass that the wolves have opened up.

Raymond Lake

A tiny lake sits above Lake Kathleen and the East Fork of the Boulder River. It is officially unnamed by the Board on Geographic Names, but the name Raymond is used by Montana Fish, Wildlife and Parks. Perhaps this Raymond, one of our unknown men, was an FWP employee.

Mount Rearguard

Standing a bit south and away from the main ridge of the 12,000-footers in the Beartooths is this 12,155-foot mountain—which presents as a "Rear Guard."

Recroitment Lake

Recroitment is a USGS map misspelling of Recruitment, which describes its function and is the name seen on all other maps. The lake, near the Sky Top Lakes, is linked by a small stream to Production Lake, and both are part of a brook trout "system." Recruitment is a receiver lake where little brookies from Production Lake come downstream to grow large on its abundant zooplankton. It is not a good lake for spawning and reproduction, so that is why these two lakes are considered a linked system. (see Production Lake)

Red Lodge (Town)/Mountain/Creek, Red Lodge Creek Plateau

The names of all of these features come from name of the **town,** which is the county seat of Carbon County and is located on the eastern edge of the Absaroka-Beartooth Mountains at the eastern end of the Beartooth Highway.

Originally the town was called Danville, and was settled in 1882 when the Crow Indian Reservation was moved farther east. Two years later, when they wanted a post office, the Postal Service insisted on another name and Red Lodge was the choice. The reason behind this name is as varied as there are historical sources. Some say it was because the Crow Indians of the Red Lodge clan camped in the area and painted their council tipis with red clay. Another story refers to the fact that there is an outcropping of reddish rock on a mountain west of town that looks like a huge red tipi. This is much too obvious. Others say that it was just that there were "a lot of red men" living in the area. Perhaps the most interesting is that the name was adopted from the Crow, who called the place "Bad Lodge" (mistranslated "Red") for a batch of spoiled meat that ruined a celebration. Whatever the actual reason for the name, it beat out the other options—Rocky Fork, Coalville, and Villard. The latter would have been interesting as the Northern Pacific Railroad might have anchored both ends of the Beartooth Highway since Henry Villard followed Jay Cooke as the president of that railroad in the 1880s. (see Cooke City) In any case, Red Lodge it is.

"Yankee Jim" George discovered coal here in 1866, but the location on the Crow Reservation prevented active development until 1887 when the Rocky Fork Coal Company began mining. Much of the coal was sold to the railroad, but this ended in 1925 when diesel and electric power reduced their need for coal. With the decreased demand and some serious mine disasters, the mines closed in 1932. The town had a population of about 5,000 at its peak, but declined rapidly. With the construction of the Beartooth Highway in the 1930s, and the Red Lodge Ski Area in 1960, tourism became the primary activity, and the town now numbers about 2,500.

Butcher Mountain is the high point on the **Red Lodge Creek Plateau,** which is considerably west of town and situated just east of the East Rosebud. **Red Lodge Creek** comes off the plateau where it drains the foothills to enter Rock Creek near Joliet, Montana.

Red Lodge Mountain is just south of town on U.S. Highway 212 and is the location of the Red Lodge Ski Area. The mountain is officially Grizzly Peak and the USGS does not recognize the name Red Lodge Mountain. However, since 1965 the ski area has called it Red Lodge Mountain on all of its corporate and local advertising, so that is how it is known to most.

Red Mountain

The color of this mountain prompted local usage, so in 1923 a district forester applied "Red" to the rocky point between Dailey Basin and Slip and Slide in the Paradise Valley.

It was once called Stands Mountain as it overlooks Stands Basin. When Joe married Molly Dorgan in 1907, she felt Joe's place was too high and cold, so they moved to Sixmile Creek, and left his basin and mountain. (see Stands Basin)

Red Rock Lakes/Plateau

The plateau is south of Summit Mountain on the Castle Mountain quad. The lakes are on this plateau and get their name from the nearby rocks that have been stained red by iron oxides.

Red Storm Lake

It seems that a stormy sunset gave this lake its name. It is located near Lake Elaine in the cluster of lakes near Crazy Mountain and the Montana/Wyoming line.

The alternate and unofficial name is Midnight Lake.

Redfield Lake

The lake is a thousand feet above and directly overlooks the West Boulder River, but it drains to the northwest into Little Mission Creek. It was named for Fred Redfield, who patented a homestead near this lake in 1905. His brother Frank homesteaded the adjoining section.

Reed Lake

This small lake is in a swampy area just north of the Montana/Wyoming border near Rock Island Lake. It is sometimes called Lower Vernon Lake and is really little more than a marsh.

Reeves Lake

William W. Reeves was noted to have a ranch on the West Rosebud in 1902 and appears in the 1910 Red Lodge census. The Reeves Ranch sits a short distance from the shore of this lake.

Lake Reno

This lake, which is just south of the Montana/ Wyoming line, was named for Maj. Marcus Reno (1834–1889). He served in the Civil War and then later with Lt. Col. George Armstrong Custer and the 7th Cavalry. During the Battle of the Little Bighorn he maintained a defensive position about four miles away and did not support Custer on the battlefield. This action was a source of great controversy for many years. However, in 1879 Judge Advocate General W.M. Dunn concluded, "I concur with the court in its exoneration of Major Reno from

Maj. Marcus Reno, ca 1876. PHOTO BY DAVID FRANCIS BARRY, DENVER DIGITAL LIBRARY.

the charges of cowardice which have been brought against him… The suspicion or accusation that Gen. Custer owed his death and the destruction of his command to the failure of Major Reno, through incompetency or cowardice, to go to his relief, is considered as set to rest."

In 1967 his remains were reinterred with honors at the Custer National Cemetery at the Little Bighorn Battlefield.

Republic Mountain/Peak/Creek/Pass

Republic Mountain rises over Cooke City and Soda Butte Creek and was the site of one of the great mineral strikes in Montana. Traditionally, the discovery is attributed to A. Bart Henderson in 1872 in what became the New World Mining District, but a variety of people were involved. In 1883, Maj. George Eaton invested $300,000 and formed the Republic Mine that gave the mountain its name, and mining boomed. It is said that by 1885 the mine had produced tons of lead-silver bullion, but high freight charges due to the lack of rail access, and the drop in the price of silver shortly thereafter, cancelled much of the profit.

There is a bit of confusion with the "Republic" name because **Republic Peak** is a separate summit that is just a few miles due south of **Republic Mountain.** Republic Mountain is outside of Yellowstone Park and just to the south of the town of Cooke City, whereas **Republic Peak** is partly in Yellowstone Park, where the Park's eastern border passes directly over the peak.

To make matters more difficult, **Republic Creek** flows north off Republic Peak and collects streams off the eastern side of Republic Mountain before it enters Soda Butte Creek at Cooke City.

The Republic Pass Trail stretches from Cooke City south along Republic Creek to Republic Peak where it goes over **Republic Pass** to meet the Cache Creek Trail in Yellowstone Park.

Richel Lodge

This historic dude ranch, Richel Lodge, was located just 12 miles from Red Lodge at the confluence of Rock Creek and Lake Fork Creek. Herbert and Marian Richel obtained a U.S. Forest Service Special Use Permit in 1921 and started a small family resort on 29 acres. In 1935, after the completion of the Beartooth Highway, they developed the property further

Mr. and Mrs. Herbert Richel. CARBON COUNTY MUSEUM.

and built a lodge with a dance hall and dining room that could hold 500 people. There were 11 rooms in the lodge and 13 cabins on-site, with a waterwheel to provide electricity.

Herbert operated it until his death at age 83 in 1948, and Marian continued for some time after that.

The resort burned down in 1966 and is now just a historical site on the meadow with a campground and RV park.

Rigler Bluffs

These bluffs on the Yellowstone River south of Dick Randall Point were named for the nearby Rigler family ranches. Therien, or Paul, Rigler (1863–1909) was born near Innsbruck, Austria, and emigrated to the U.S. in 1890. He came to Montana in 1893 to work the mines at Cokedale, then moved to Aldridge in 1896. After working the Aldridge coal mines, he opened a saloon and boardinghouse in 1903. In 1909, just before he died, he bought the Cutler ranch where the family raised prized shorthorn cattle. His descendants continue to live in the area to this day.

Mr. & Mrs. Paul Rigler with brother-in-law. YELLOWSTONE GATEWAY MUSEUM, #2006.044.0588.

The ranch is on the east side of the river, but since the school was at Aldridge, across the river, a cable was strung so the kids could pull a cable car across to get back and forth. Sounds like more fun than the old yellow school buses of today.

As an aside, and characteristic of nineteenth-century orthography, the surname was originally Rigben. This became Rigbe, Rigbey, Riggslar, Riggler, Regler, and finally Rigler. Rigler is how all the descendants spell it today.

Rimrock Lake

The name refers to the dramatic rimrocks in the steep, narrow canyon of the East Rosebud where this lake is found. The lake formed as backup from a big rockslide that created a natural dam.

Robble Lake

The south slope of Castle and Snowbank Mountains is high, rocky, alpine country that is well above tree line. Here, above 10,000 feet, one finds Gravel, Till, and Robble Lakes in a line on the Snowbank Glacier drainage. Their names reflect the effects of that glacier's erosion and the different sizes of rock found in the moraines, but Robble? This appears to be a mapmaker's misspelling of Rubble.

Robertson Draw

Robertson Draw is near Line Creek and the Montana/Wyoming line on the far eastern edge of the Custer-Gallatin National Forest. It was named for George

W. Robertson and his wife Ina, who first homesteaded and ran sheep here around 1900. The Robertsons later dug a ditch to divert water from North Line Creek to this draw, which was still in use in 1985. Several Robertsons still live in the area.

The human-caused Robertson Draw Fire was the first large Montana wildfire of the 2021 season. Its 30,000 acres and close proximity to the town of Red Lodge made it a worrisome and dramatic event.

Robinson Spring/Draws (North and South)

The spring and draws are situated just east of the Stillwater River and a bit north of Limestone Creek and the town of Nye in an area where several of the "draws" were named for the early ranchers—Ekwortzel, Hudson, Stanley, Winge, Lundy, Russell and others. (see those citations) The Daniel W. and Nancy Robinson family settled by these springs in 1925.

First and Second Rock Lakes

These two lakes are upstream from Keyser Brown Lake on Lake Fork Creek near Red Lodge.

In 1900, after a long fishing trip, Judge Brown named them for his companions. Lake Edgar was for his friend Edgar Worman, who owned a paint store in Red Lodge; and Lake McIntyre was for his son-in-law, the trip photographer. The names were unofficial and were not accepted by the Board on Geographic Names, so by 1937 they had become officially First and Second Rock Lakes on the maps. The unique presence of rocks in the lakes was apparently more important than the early pioneers and fishermen.

Rock Creek

The most well-known Rock Creek runs from the Hellroaring Plateau through the town of Red Lodge to go on to join the Clarks Fork of the Yellowstone. It is the stream that the Beartooth Highway follows south of town before ascending up the Beartooth Pass. The original name of the stream was from the Crow, who called it the Swiftwater River, and William Clark's 1814 "Map of the West" calls it the Ap-sahro-ka River for these Crow Indians. Capt. William F. Raynolds' map of his 1860 exploration calls it Baudin's Fork, and that name derives from a story that he heard from his guide, Jim Bridger. Apparently a French-Canadian trapper named Bodah was killed by the Blackfeet on this stream in 1836. These names all surrendered to Rocky Fork, for its bed of boulders, which was the name that the mountain men used. As the Rocky Fork, it gave its name to the Rocky Fork Coal Company and Mines that put Red Lodge and Carbon County on the map. The name was shortened to Rock Creek in the 1890s, and that is now the official name. (see Red Lodge)

There are two other Rock Creeks in the area. One is just north of Yellowstone National Park and a little to the west of the Absaroka-Beartooth Wilderness border. It is a tributary of Lake Abundance and Slough Creeks. The second is a short stream in the Wyoming section of the Absaroka-Beartooth Wilderness that drains into the Clarks Fork east of the Park.

Rock Island Lake/Butte

Oh, the Rock Island Lake is a mighty fine lake
Oh, the Rock Island Lake is the Lake to find
This lake is a bit east of Colter Pass on the Beartooth Highway, and its Butte is right on the Montana/Wyoming line. There are several islands in the lake that are… surprise… rocky.
Git yer ticket at the station for the Rock Island Lake.

Little Rocky Creek

This Rocky Creek is unrelated to the Rock Creek near Red Lodge. It flows from the Nye cemetery to the Stillwater River, and is near where Thomas "Chalky" Benbow discovered chromite ore and developed his mine in 1905. (see Benbow Mine and Stillwater Mine)

Rock Tree Lake

A tree grows from the rock in this lake on the south slope of Summit Mountain.

Roosevelt Lake

President Theodore "Teddy" Roosevelt (1858-1919) served as the 26th president of the United States from 1901 to 1909, and in that position he championed conservation and established many new forests, monuments, and national parks, and created the U.S. Forest Service, as well. It seems appropriate that this lake near the Stillwater River was named to honor him as it is in the Custer-Gallatin National Forest and the Absaroka-Beartooth Wilderness, with Yellowstone National Park just to the south.

President Theodore Roosevelt. LIBRARY OF CONGRESS.

Rosebud Mountain/Lake/Creek/River

This stream was named well before Orson Wells' 1941 movie, *Citizen Kane.* In fact, all of these terms relate to the myriad of wild roses, *Rosa woodsia,* that grow along the banks of the creek. The name was first recorded in English by William Clark, who called what is now the Stillwater River, the "Rose bud river" when, on their return journey on July 19, 1806, his party stopped at its mouth. He probably got the name from the Hidatsa during their North Dakota winter camp. The Crow are close relatives to the Hidatsa, and their word for the stream is *Bichkapa'ashe,* which means "Rose Hip River."

For unknown reasons the names have changed over the years. The Stillwater was originally a tributary of Clark's **Rosebud River.** However, the names were switched so the main river is now the Stillwater and the smaller tributary is **Rosebud Creek.** This latter forms with the confluence of East and West Rosebud Creeks by the town of Absarokee and joins the Stillwater River near Columbus, Montana.

The East Rosebud, which flows through the hamlet of Alpine and East Rosebud Lake, was called the Big Rosebud River by Ferdinand Hayden on his 1871 map. The East Rosebud has been threatened with at least three proposals for dams, the most recent in 2011. Fortunately, it was given Wild and Scenic River status in 2018 and is now protected. The West Rosebud starts from Grasshopper Glacier and goes through Mystic Lake and the power station. It was formerly the Little Rosebud River, but probably has more water in it now than the (Big) East Rosebud does.

East Rosebud Lake was initially Armstrong Lake, for Maj. Henry Armstrong, the Crow Indian agent, who purchased 105 acres there in 1894. He left in 1899 after a devastating fire and sold the property to a group of Billings bankers. In 1912 they, along with investor Christian Yegen, renamed it East Rosebud Lake, built a lodge, and formed a non-profit association to grant leases for cabin sites along the lake. This grew into the small community that local dude ranchers John and Rosina Branger named Alpine. (see Alpine)

There is also a tiny **West Rosebud Lake** that is just a widening in the creek. It is so small that the name is not printed on the map, but it is indeed official and is cited on the USGS website.

Mount Rosebud, a spur on the west ridge of Mount Dewey near Fossil Lake, is at the head of East Rosebud Creek.

Round Lake

More irregularly square than round, this lake is in the geometry class of lakes along with Long and Corner Lakes on the Goose Lake jeep trail north of Cooke City.

The USFS maintains a rental cabin by the lake.

Rough Draw

The broken ground in this draw at the head of Mission Creek created the name.

Rough Lake

This lake is in the rocky, alpine Sky Top country north of Cooke City, just below Granite Peak. It is a bit east of the Aero Lakes, but there is no designated trail.

The irregular shoreline and high winds that stir up

Rough Lake. PHOTO COURTESY RICK GRAETZ.

rough water have been suggested as the source of the name. Other sources, however, say that its name comes from the rough and difficult cross-country scramble that is necessary to reach it.

Roundhead Butte

Named for the shape of a knob at the top, this butte gives its name to a USGS topo quad and sits just north of Yellowstone National Park. No, Cromwell's army never made it to Montana.

Ruby Creek

There are two creeks of this name. One is a tributary of the Main Boulder River and the other is south of Red Lodge on the far eastern edge of the Custer-Gallatin National Forest.

Miners who were panning for gold would often find garnet chips, a semi-precious stone that is common in our mountains. Its red color reminded them of rubies.

Russell Creek/Lake

Dave Russell was a buffalo hunter and rancher who settled on the nearby Buck Ranch in 1882.

Russell Lake is at the head of Russell Creek, which flows into Fox Lake, the northernmost of the Crazy Lakes. The creek was known as the North Fork of Crazy Creek as late as 1937.

Rydberg Lake

Among the collection of Hellroaring Lakes is this shallow, rocky lake that is just a wide spot in Hellroaring Creek where it comes off the Hellroaring Plateau.

Bob Anderson, in his 1997 book on the Beartooth country, states that it was named for P.A. Rydberg, curator of the herbarium of the New York Botanical Garden. He collected in this area of Montana in late 1890s.

However, it seems more likely that it was named for a B. Rydberg who was Red Lodge public administrator in 1900 and had a business as a jeweler and watchmaker in the post office building. He was a friend and hunting companion of David Smethurst, and Rydberg Lake is right next to Smethurst Lake in the Hellroaring Lakes chain. (see Smethurst Lake)

Sacrifice Mountain

There is a 12,027-foot point near The Pyramid and Mount Wood that mountaineers have unofficially named Sacrifice Mountain. The name comes from a large block of granite on the top that they thought looks similar to the sacrifice table found in a Mayan temple.

It is a name that is not recognized by the Board on Geographic Names, so you will not find it on your topo map.

The Saddle

This unofficial, local name refers to the low ridge between Pilot and Index Peaks, where Index appears as the saddle horn and Pilot—just looks uncomfortable. (see image under Index Peak)

Saddleback Mountain

There are two separate peaks at 10,635 feet and 10,876 feet with a low ridge in between that gives this mountain the appearance of a saddle. It is northwest of Alpine on the same ridge as Prairieview Mountain.

Saderbalm Creek/Lake/Ponds

The creek and lake were named for Nels Soderholm, so this is another misspelling on your map. In 1908 Nels and his wife Elizabeth had one of the first stores in Cooke City where they ran the post office and lived in an apartment above the store. When the Beartooth Highway was completed in 1935, business improved, and they installed the first gas station between Red Lodge and Gardiner.

Nels was quite the winter traveler. One of his regular adventures was to ski from Cooke City over Daisy Pass to Lake Abundance for the mail. A postal employee from Nye had a cabin there where the two would rendezvous and exchange their mail sacks. Nels also trapped marten and would snowshoe to his trap line, which ran along the Stillwater River and up this creek.

Saderbalm Lake is on the north side of Tumble Mountain at the head of the creek. Early U.S. Forest Service maps call it Sodderholm Lake, further confirming that the name comes from Nels.

Sage Creek

There are many Sage Creeks in Montana as the big sagebrush, *Artemisia tridentata*, is one of the dominant plants of the plains and foothills. This Sage Creek in is the Pine Creek country, just up from the Paradise Valley. During Prohibition there were reportedly many moonshine operations along this creek that produced liquor for the miners. One doubts that it had a sage-like flavor.

Sawmill Gulch

This gulch is on the Wildcat Draw quad off Blind Bridger Creek on the northern edge of the Custer-Gallatin National Forest. Sawn lumber was an essential of pioneer life, and almost all of the early mills were water powered. The owner of this particular sawmill is not known.

Sawtooth Mountain/Meadow/Lake

The **Sawtooth Mountain** in Montana is north of Cooke City near Goose Lake and Grasshopper Glacier.

There is also a **Sawtooth Mountain, Meadow, and Lake** that is in Wyoming in the Shoshone National Forest and directly south of the Beartooth Pass. It was the site of F.I. Johnson's Sawtooth Camp, which was serviced from Red Lodge. He built it in 1921 and ran it until his retirement in 1937. Johnson was followed by a variety of owners, but, since it required a 16-mile car ride, followed by another 11 miles on horseback, the lease was not renewed when it expired in 1960. The Forest Service burned the lodge, cabins, and corral in 1970.

Obviously, all of our many Sawtooth Mountains and Ranges were named for their jagged profile.

Scat Lake, Little Scat Lake

These lakes are found just north of Summit Mountain, and their small creek drains into Lake at Falls on the East Rosebud.

Scat is a word that comes from Greek and means dung, or the droppings of animals, particularly carnivores. This does not make these lakes sound very inviting.

Schoolhouse Gulch

Dutton School is on this gulch's creek near its confluence with the Main Boulder River.

When the U.S. Congress passed the Land Ordinance of 1785, it required that all lands outside of the then-existing states had to be surveyed prior to being sold or opened to settlement. The standard way to do this was to divide the land into square miles called sections, each containing 640 acres. Six by six, or 36 sections, then became a township, and section 16 was designated "school land" with proceeds going to support local schools. The result of this provision was the funding of schools and increased literacy for small rural communities like Dutton, way up the Boulder River.

Schoolmarm Lake

(see Mud Lake)

Scotch Bonnet Mountain

Apparently the early miners thought that this mountain looked like a tam o'shanter.

It can be seen just to the right as one goes up the Lulu Pass road north of Cooke City and was part of the New World Mining District. The Glengarry Mine (another good Scottish reference) was on the east slope of this mountain. The mine was closed in 1934, but the adit became the source of much of the acidic and metals pollution of Fisher and Soda Butte Creeks. Recent mitigation efforts have resulted in eliminating this.

Second Creek

Basin Creek is the first, and this is the second creek south of the West Boulder Meadows.

Sedge Lake/Creek

Sedge Lake is second of three lakes at the headwaters to Sedge Creek, a tributary of the Broadwater River.

Sedges, Family Cyperaceae, are relatives to rushes and grasses, which they resemble. They differ from these others in that the stems are triangular in cross section and the leaves are arranged spirally in threes. They are widespread, but are generally associated with wetlands and poor soils. They can obviously be found near this lake and creek.

Seeley Creek

This tributary of Rock Creek can be found just south of the town of Red Lodge.

It was named in 1889 for a Mike Seeley who was a prospector and the local butcher. Ranger notes from the 1930s note that some of his prospect holes were still in evidence at that time.

Senal Lake

Al Croonquist and his wife, Senia, started the dude ranch called Camp Senia on the West Fork of Rock Creek in the early part of the twentieth century. This lake was named for both of them: Senia and Al.

Senia Creek, Camp Senia Historic District

In 1914 Al Croonquist of Red Lodge married Senia Pollari, and in 1917 started construction of the dude camp on the West Fork of Rock Creek that he named for her. The first cabin was completed in 1919, and he went on to build a total of 18 more buildings. It was a very popular destination that could accommodate up to 40 guests and profited from the eastern fondness for the dude ranch experience. Al built on this and helped organize and became secretary of the Dude Rancher's Association and initiated the *Dude Ranchers* magazine. The ranch went bankrupt when the Great Depression destroyed Croonquist's clientele, and the camp closed in 1935. The cabins were sold to private individuals in 1938 under USFS leases and have been listed on the National Register of Historic Places. Several were unfortunately burned in the forest fires of 2008.

Senia Pollari Croonquist. CARBON COUNTY MUSEUM.

Al Croonquist went on to become the Billings district manager for Northwest Airlines and died in a small plane crash in 1938. Senia and their daughter, Senia Hart, were focal points for the arts in both Billings and Red Lodge.

Sentinel Falls/Rock

In 1916 Assistant Ranger T.F. "Shorty" Hogg named these falls on the West Fork of Rock Creek for Sentinel Rock, which sits high above the falls and gives a view for many miles down the canyon.

The rock was named by a troop of Boy Scouts that Al Croonquist took there on a hike.

September Morn Spring/Lake

The spring is on the Wildcat Draw quad near Wildcat Springs. The lake is much farther to the southeast on Lake Fork Creek and is just upstream from Keyser Brown Lake.

The name September Morn comes from a painting by French artist Paul Chabas done in 1912. It pictures the morning waters of Lake Annecy in

September Morn, 1912. PAINTING BY PAUL CHABAS.

Upper Savoy and a local peasant girl. The painting won Chabas the Medal of Honor at the 1912 Paris Salon and was sent to New York the following year where it was exhibited in a gallery window. This caught the eye of Anthony Comstock, head of the New York Society for the Suppression of Vice. He stormed into the store and roared, "There is too little morn and too much maid!" and demanded its removal. The ensuing controversy spread across the country, with opponents and defenders. As a result, the image of *September Morn* popped up on everything from calendars and postcards to candy boxes, cigar bands, bottle caps, suspenders, and much more. The painting still hangs in the Metropolitan Museum of Art.

Shadow Lake

There are two Shadow Lakes, one off Armstrong Creek above East Rosebud Lake, and the other off the West Fork of Rock Creek north of Whitetail Peak. The names obviously come from the shadows that grace the waters in the morning and evening.

Shaft House Creek

This intermittent stream north of Gardiner reflects the hardrock mining there.

A mine shaft is the long, typically vertical hole that gives access to the mine. The shaft house held the works for the elevator and the fans that provided ventilation.

Sheep Mountain/Creek/Lake

Both of the mountains and the lake were named for the many Rocky Mountain bighorn sheep, *Ovis canadensis,* that were found in great numbers there. In the late nineteenth and early twentieth centuries it is estimated that there were about 2 million of these wild sheep in southwest Montana. They were common enough to be frequently seen and provided the main food source for a band of the Shoshoni who called

Rocky Mountain bighorn sheep. PHOTO BY KIM KEATING, U.S. FISH & WILDLIFE SERVICE.

themselves the Sheepeaters. Diseases introduced by domestic sheep have totally decimated the population, and they are now only an occasional and special sighting. Recent attempts to introduce bighorns with more disease resistance has met with some success.

The two **Sheep Mountains** are each on the Gardiner and Cooke City quads. The **lake** is in a cirque on Spirit Mountain on the Silver Run Peak quad and is next to Goat Lake. Earlier maps called it Mountain Sheep Lake, but by 1986 it had become just Sheep Lake.

Domestic sheep were a critical part of the economy of Sweet Grass and the other counties that surrounded the Absaroka Range. In 1900 it is estimated that over 100,000 domestic sheep grazed these mountains, but Forest Service restrictions designed to prevent damage from overgrazing gradually reduced the numbers. By 1978, when the Absaroka-Beartooth Wilderness was formed, only two allotments numbering 1,200 ewe/lamb pairs remained to be "grandfathered." The last one ended in 2003.

The prevalence of sheep, both domestic and wild, in these mountains is attested by the fact that there are seven *Sheep Creeks* in Park County, one in Sweet Grass, four in Stillwater, and two in Carbon County. Seven of these can be found in the area covered by this book.

Of the Sheep Creeks named for the domestic flocks, the one that comes off the Silver Run Plateau to Rock Creek was used as the route to the plateau for local Red Lodge sheepherders. Of the other Sheep Creeks that were named for domestic herds, one was in the West Boulder Valley, another in the East Boulder River country, the third was near Nye and Limestone Creek, and the fourth was near Slip and Slide in the Paradise Valley. All were reachable from the plains where the sheep flocks were wintered.

The Rocky Mountain bighorns get their creeks as well. The Sheep Creek near Cooke City was named around 1890 for a mountain sheep that was killed there, but there is no information as to the hunter's name. The seventh and last Sheep Creek is near Gardiner/Jardine and was also known as a "good place for hunting Mountain Sheep."

Sheepherder Peak/Lake

The names of **Sheepherder Peak** and the **lake** on it are evidence of the importance of domestic sheep grazing in the early twentieth century. The peak is at the head of the Boulder River where the sheepherders built a large rock cairn to pass the time. It, and evidence of stone wall wind shelters, can still be found. The Boulder River flows north from the peak to the town of Big Timber on the Yellowstone River, which at one point in the early twentieth century was the largest wool shipping point in America. (see Big Timber)

Independence Mountain, known for its mining, is just north of Sheepherder Peak. On its east slope are three small lakes that are known locally as Lamb, Wool, and Mutton Lakes.

To show how widespread domestic sheep were in this part of the country, there is also a **Sheepherder Lake** in Wyoming, just north of the Beartooth Highway.

Shelf Lake

The lake can be found on a high bench in a cirque on the southwest wall of the Hell Roaring Plateau and is therefore on a "shelf."

Shell Creek/Mountain

Ranger Harry S. Kaufman, the first ranger appointed to the Absaroka National Forest in 1905, had this mountain and creek in his district on the West Boulder. He noted that "numerous petrified shells and small fossils are annually found on the mountain crest and slopes."

Shelter Lake

Montana fisheries specialist Pat Marcuson says that at this elevation in the Sky Top drainage, shelter is hard to come by—the lake has "no trees, just big rocks under which to wait out a cloudburst."

Shepard Mountain

The mountain rises above and to the southwest of East Rosebud Lake. Unlike the mountains, lakes, and streams named for the sheepherding business, this mountain was named for a person. The name is spelled incorrectly, but it was named for Russell E. Shepherd, who enjoyed coming up to his cabin at Alpine which has a view of this mountain. In the early twentieth century he was the president of the Billings Land and Irrigation Company and the Merchants National Bank, and the small town of Shepherd, Montana, was named for him, too.

Sheridan Creek/Point/Campground

Sheridan Creek and **Point** are about seven miles south of the current town of Red Lodge. In 1872 Gen. Phil Sheridan went on an inspection tour of Yellowstone National Park and wanted to catch the train at Billings for his return to Washington, D.C. In order to avoid the long detour that followed the Clarks Fork, he took the advice of an old hunter named Shuki Geer and took his 120-man detail over the Beartooths. The unmarked track apparently went along the route of the current Beartooth Highway, and **Sheridan Campground,** where Sheridan Creek joins Rock Creek, is supposed to be where he paused.

Gen. Philip Sheridan, ca. 1865. PHOTO BY MATTHEW BRADY.

Gen. Philip Sheridan (1831–1888) was a Civil War hero and protégé of Ulysses S. Grant. He commanded the cavalry corps of the Army of the Potomac and was responsible for the defeat of Jubal Early's Confederate army and the subsequent destruction of the Confederacy's breadbasket in the Shenandoah Valley. His cavalry maneuvers around Lee's army also contributed the the surrender at Appomattox.

After the Civil War, Sheridan was appointed to head the Department of the Missouri when the Plains Wars subdued the Indian tribes. He became general-in-chief of the U.S. Army in 1883, and in 1888 was promoted to the 5-star rank of General of the Army.

Sheridan was personally and professionally interested in Yellowstone Park. He lobbied Congress for its formation as a park, and sent Lt. Gustavus Doane to escort the Washburn Expedition of 1870, and Maj. John Barlow to accompany Ferdinand Hayden's 1871 survey party. He and his colleagues also worked to repeal the permit that would have allowed the Yellowstone Park Improvement Company to build a railroad up the Lamar River and develop 4,000 acres within the Park. Sheridan was the one who initiated the order that sent the army into the Park in 1886, where they remained for 20 years controlling and protecting it until the National Park Service was formed in 1916.

Ship Lake

Also misspelled, this lake south of Bowback Mountain does not refer to any sailing vessel. Instead the lake was named for E.N. Shipp, who was a photographer for the Northern Pacific Railroad and National Geographic. He was on a photographic expedition in 1923 where Al Croonquist led a party of forest officials, the photography group, and personnel from Camp Senia to this lake.

Shorthill Creek/Lake

Shorthill Lake and Creek east of Emigrant are now named George Lake and Creek for Joe George. Originally they were named for David Shorthill (1831–1914), who had the initial ranch on this lake. Joe George worked for him, married his daughter, and also ranched at this lake. Because the Shorthills moved away, it gradually became known as George Lake, and in the 1950s the name was officially changed. (see George Lake/Creek)

Although Thomas Curry was the first to find gold at Emigrant Gulch in 1863, it was David Shorthill who found the richer deposit farther upstream and started the gold rush to what became called the Shorthill District. He and his wife Margaret homesteaded by this lake in 1873.

David Shorthill. YELLOWSTONE GATEWAY MUSEUM, #2006.044.1584.

The Shorthill cemetery remains at the lake, but David and Margaret took another 160-acre homestead along the Yellowstone River where his family continued ranching. They are now in the seventh generation in the Paradise Valley.

Shorty Creek

This creek is on the Boulder River just south of Chippy Park and the Chrome Mountain mines. Because the creek flowed through their ranch, it was named for two brothers, prospectors of rather short stature.

Shrew Lake

Shrew Lake is located in a cluster of lakes just north of the Montana/Wyoming border near Crazy Mountain. Either seeing these little creatures or the tiny size of the lake may have brought on the name.

Water shrew. U.S. FISH & WILDLIFE SERVICE PHOTO.

Shrews, Family Soricidae, are little mouse-like mammals that have long, pointed noses. They are actually not rodents, do not hibernate, and are more closely related to moles and hedgehogs. Because they are so small, they are rarely seen, but are quite common and found worldwide in many habitats, where they serve as prey for raptors, weasels, and the like. One species, the American water shrew, *Sorex palustrus*, traps air bubbles in its fur so is able to "water walk" and dive under the surface for insect larvae, their principal food. After a 15-second or so hunt, the bubbles pop them back to the surface. Shrews are also able to find their prey with their unique ability to echolocate with a series of ultrasonic squeaks.

Shrimp Lake

Although nearby Snail and Planaria Lakes would make one think that this name is another of that frenetic biologist's contributions, its name appeared prior to 1930 and was actually named by fishermen. It reflects the abundance of freshwater shrimp found in its waters.

The fairy shrimp, *Anostraca*, are a group of small crustaceans that are widely distributed from deserts to ice-covered mountain lakes, and even in Antarctic ice. (See Copepod Lake and Cladocera Lake)

Sienna Lake

Sienna is a pigment widely used by artists and gets its name from the Italian city of Sienna where it was produced during the Renaissance. Raw sienna is a yellowish brown, but when heated it becomes reddish brown and is called burnt sienna. This lake is on the east slope of the Two Sisters near the Stillwater River and was named for the color of the nearby rocks.

Sierra Creek

Sierra comes from the Spanish word *serra* for "saw," and is used to refer to a jagged mountain range. This creek comes off the Beartooth Plateau to Granite Lake at the Montana/Wyoming border. Its high, rocky environment must have reminded someone of the High Sierra country in California.

Silt Lakes

Silt is fine sand or clay that is deposited by running water to form a sediment. It is found in these two small lakes that are widenings in the upper reaches of the West Fork of Rock Creek between Medicine and Sundance Mountains.

Silver Creek/Basin/Lake/Pass

The name is a reflection of both the sky and the mining activity. Silver was commonly found along with the gold strikes and, although subject to large market fluctuations, was sometimes more profitable.

There are three **Silver Creeks** in the Beartooths. One is next to the town of Silver Gate near the Park's Northeast Entrance. Another is a tributary of Buffalo Creek that flows into the Park. The third comes out of **Silver Basin** into the North Fork of Hellroaring Creek, which also enters the Park.

There are also two **Silver Lakes.** One is up from Mystic and Island Lakes in the West Rosebud, and the other is south of Boulder Mountain at the head of Fourmile Creek.

Silver Pass crosses the knife-edged ridge that forms the main east/west backbone of the Absaroka Range. The Hi Ho Silver Trail over this pass leaves the Silver Lake Trail where Fourmile Creek comes out of Silver Lake, goes over the pass, and drops into the valley of the East Fork of Mill Creek.

Silver Falls Creek

Named for its sparkling falls rather that the sparkle of the metal, the creek comes off the Hellroaring Plateau to Lake Fork Creek.

Silver Gate (Town)

In 1932 John L. Taylor and J.J. White started the town as a purpose-built place for tourism. They felt that with its position just one mile from the new Northeast Entrance Station to Yellowstone Park, and with the completion of the Beartooth Highway due in three years, it would be a perfect location to serve these new visitors. With its log construction and alpine village appearance, the little hamlet has been a good gateway to the Park, but with only 30 year-round residents it may not be the commercial success that the founders envisioned.

Although there was much mining in the vicinity, and one of the Silver Creeks enters Soda Butte Creek nearby, the metal is not where the name comes from. Taylor's daughter says that the name actually comes from its gateway position and her father's impression of the "silver haze" that seems to hang over the surrounding mountains.

Silver Run Peak/Plateau/Lakes/Creek

Lee Corey, who was the first ranger on the east side of the Beartooth National Forest, named the **peak** and plateau in 1896, but records do not show the reason why he gave it this name. The peak is the fifth highest in Montana at 12,477 feet and has its own quad map.

The **plateau** is the high country between the West Fork of Rock Creek and Timberline Creek. In 1916 two prospectors from Red Lodge found the first chromite there at the Four Chromes claim. During the next 20 years M.E. Martin located all of the other chromium deposits on the plateau, and mining them has continued off and on ever since. (see Martin Lake)

Silver Run Lake is at the headwaters of Timberline Creek on the north side of the plateau. Silver Run Creek comes off the east side of the plateau.

Silver Tarn Lake

A tarn is a small mountain lake, and this one is just south of Beartooth Mountain. The name comes from sky as it is reflected in the water.

Silver Tip Creek, Silvertip Creek, Silver Tip Ranch

The grizzly bear, *Ursus arctos horribilis*, is "grizzled" like an unshaved mountain man because of the lighter-tipped guard hairs found on the sides and hump. These lighter hairs are also responsible for the bear's other nickname—"silvertip." There are three Silvertips in our area, and all are quite separate geographically.

Silver Tip Creek (two words) is in Wyoming and flows north to the Clarks Fork.

Silvertip Creek (one word) is a tributary of the Boulder River on the Chrome Mountain quad.

The Silver Tip Ranch is on on Slough Creek just north of the Montana/Wyoming border, and is adjacent to Yellowstone National Park. It was originally homesteaded by G. Milton Ames in 1913. That first spring, he shot eight grizzly bears, and that probably contributed to the ranch's name. It was later bought by Burton C. "Bob" Lacombe, who was one of the original 1917 rangers, and who then became the chief buffalo keeper at the Lamar Buffalo Ranch. In 1923, the Bliss family, who were from the House of Morgan on Wall Street, acquired it. "Hellroaring" Jim Anderson was their ranch manager. (see Anderson Ridge) This private ranch later added Frenchy Duret's place (see Frenchy Meadows) and is still in operation with access only by horse or wagon from the Slough Creek Campground in the Park.

Sioux Charley Lake

The long widening of the Stillwater River three miles south of the end of the Nye Road at Woodbine had been called Sioux Charley Lake for years. It carries a long history, but for unknown reasons the Board on Geographic Names decided to remove the man's name from the maps and their website after 1996. It is officially now unnamed, but remains in local use, and that name is still found on the 2013 National Geographic hiking maps and the USFS Stillwater Trail signs.

It is unfortunate that the name was removed as it represented one of the long-time early characters of the Stillwater country, and is also a reflection of problems created by the Indian/White interaction during the Plains Wars.

Sioux Charley, whose real name was unknown, was a white child that had been adopted by the Sioux and raised by them. This probably means that he was either kidnapped or captured after his family was killed in a raid. Like many of these cultural amalgams, he did not fit well in either society, so he retreated to the forest, became a trapper, and built a cabin on this lake. During the many years that he lived at his cabin, he maintained the wagon road and the mail route between the Stillwater mining towns and Cooke City.

Sixmile Creek

This creek is about six miles south of Emigrant Gulch and was prospected at the same time—the mid-1860s. It remained an active mining area for many years, and in 1900, Frank McGuire, while hunting up this creek, found a particularly rich quartz lead. Floyd and John Counts were among the early homesteaders here (see Counts Creek), and this is also where Joe and Molly Stands moved in 1907, and where they spent their remaining years. (see Stands Basin)

Skeeter Lake

This shallow lake is in a swampy area to the east of Granite Lake on the Montana/ Wyoming border. Although it is not recognized or named by the USGS, it is on the hikers' maps and on Montana Fish, Wildlife and Parks documents. The omission kind of bugs this author.

Skookum Joe Canyon

The canyon on Sheep Creek in the East Boulder country was named to commemorate the man.

Joseph Richard "Skookum Joe" Anderson (1835 or 1843–1897) left his home, which is reported to have been in Ontario, Paris, England, or Norway at the age of 16 and traveled to Puget Sound, Washington Territory, where he lived among the Chinook Indians. It was this group that gave him the name "Skookum," which means "good" in their language.

He came to the Yellowstone country around Billings, Montana, in 1865 and started prospecting the Absarokas in 1870. Some credit him with being the single most influential person to open up the mining industry in Montana. He discovered the rich Spotted Horse Mine near Maiden in the Judith Mountains east of Lewistown, helped open up the Castle Mine near White Sulphur Springs, located iron mines on the Stillwater that are yet to be developed, and his copper discoveries with "Horn" Miller on the Stillwater helped the Nye City boom of the 1880s. When he was hospitalized in Billings with a terminal illness, he told his partner, I.D. O'Donnell, "We've got it at last, richest thing in Montana." He promised to draw a map the next day, but passed away during the night. Despite many searchers and numerous leads, the lode has never been found.

The Skookum Joe Trail followed the old Mountain Shoshoni Indian Trail that skirted the north side of the Absaroka Mountains, then went up the Stillwater

River and over to Red Lodge where it connected to the Meteetse Trail. This continued into Arapaho country in Wyoming and on south to Colorado and the Platte River.

Skull Lake

There are other Skull Lakes in Montana where actual Indian or trappers' skulls could be found many years after a fight. This Skull Lake in the Sodalite drainage is much more benign.

Looking down at the lake from one of the surrounding 10,000-foot ridges, or on a topo map, one can see that it exhibits the outline of a skull.

Sky Pilot Mountain/Lake

Although "sky pilot" was miner's slang for an itinerant preacher, the name of this peak and lake comes from the common name of the beautiful, blue high-alpine flower, *Polemonium viscosum.* It is often seen in profusion on the higher elevations on the east side of the Beartooth Plateau, and its other common names are sticky Jacob's-ladder and skunkweed—for the smell of its crushed leaves.

Sky Pilot, *Polemonium viscosum.* NATIONAL PARK SERVICE PHOTO.

The 12,047-foot **mountain** is just to the west of Beartooth Mountain at the head of Lake Fork Creek. **Sky Pilot Lake,** the headwater of the creek, is on the mountain's east slope, and Hopper Glacier is on its north flank.

Sky Top Lakes/Creek/Glacier

These series of lakes, the creek, and the glacier are certainly near the top of the sky, as they hunker in the canyon between Mount Villard and the southern base of Granite Peak, both high points on the Beartooth Plateau.

Sliderock Mountain/Lake

Sliderock Lake was found by hydrologic survey to drop 245 feet below the surface of the water, the deepest lake in the Absaroka-Beartooths. It is in a steep-walled cirque on the east side of Mount Rearguard at the head of Hellroaring Creek and its series of Hellroaring Lakes.

Sliderock Mountain is on the quad map of that same name. It can be found on the northern edge of the Custer-Gallatin National Forest in the Upper Deer Creek country near Iron Mountain and Gold Hill. This is good mining country and was worked early on by a Roy Harris. Somewhat later, in the 1930s, Henry Billman had a mine here as well.

Both the mountain and the lake were named for the frequent rockslides found there.

Sliding Mountain

In earlier mining days, this was known as Slide Rock Mountain and worked by Joe Stands and Peter Bair in the 1890s. (see Stands Basin). Since it duplicated the name of a similar mining mountain to the east (see above), a new name was needed. The name Sliding Mountain was submitted by Will C. Barnes and accepted in 1923. It is actually not so much a mountain as a ridge of three peaks near Big Pine Creek and Dome Mountain on the Paradise Valley side of the Absarokas. However, the new name was deemed appropriate and accepted by the Board on Geographic Names, "because of a geologic formation with many faults and rock slides."

Slip and Slide Creek

This creek enters the Yellowstone at the Slip and Slide fishing access site in the Paradise Valley.

The name appeared long before the children's hosed-down yard slide and does not come from some wet miner. It comes from the numerous landslides along the creek.

Slip and Slide Creek also carries the names of some of the prominent settlers of the upper Yellowstone River. Hugo Hoppe was one who homesteaded here before moving on to promote of the town of Cinnabar. It was later homesteaded by "Buckskin Jim" Cutler, and his family sold their place to Paul Rigler in 1909. (see Rigler Bluffs, and Cutler Lake and Cinnabar in *Bozeman's Backyard*)

Slough Creek/Lake

One of the first prospecting parties of the Upper Yellowstone came in 1867 and contained Lou Anderson, George W. Reese, and Ansel Hubble, among others. Hubble was sent ahead to scout and upon his return was asked about the next stream up ahead. "Twas but a slough" was his reply, and that is what it is called to this day. The name is appropriate as it flows through long, swampy meadows before entering Yellowstone Park.

Slough Creek is the site of several historic events on the Upper Yellowstone. Jim Bridger and Osborn Russell were known to have hunted beaver there as early as 1837. The Silver Tip Ranch, now an upscale dude ranch, was started around 1913 and is located on this creek, just a spit north of the Park boundary. This was also where, in 1890, Frenchy Duret established his homestead and is where he was killed by a trapped grizzly in 1922. (see Anderson Ridge, Silver Tip, and Duret Meadows)

Several references say that it was named for Lt. John Slough, a soldier of Troop 1, 2nd U.S. Cavalry, who got lost in the valley in 1873. This was six years after

Hubble named it and two years after it appeared on Hayden's 1871 survey map, but years later, Slough was still convinced that the stream was named after him.

Slough Lake, no relation to Slough Creek, is farther east and is a wide spot in the Armstrong Creek that flows into East Rosebud Lake. As one would imagine from its name, the lake is shallow and the area around it is quite swampy.

Smethurst Lake

Hellroaring Creek flows through the collection of Hellroaring Lakes before joining Rock Creek south of Red Lodge. Smethurst Lake is one of the Hellroaring Lakes and was named for David Smethurst, who had a ranch near the lower end of Hellroaring Creek. He was born in England in 1855 but emigrated to the U.S. and is first noted when he filed homestead patents on his ranch on Upper Rock Creek in 1894. In addition to his ranch, he owned and worked the Miner's Mercantile store in Red Lodge, was elected county administrator in 1902, and served on the Montana State Board of Sheep Commissioners.

Jim Smith Creek/Mountain

(see Jim Smith Creek—under Jim)

Smith Coulee, Smith Coulee Spring

Francis (Frank) "Midnight" Smith (1842–1931) was from Colorado where he served in the Union army and participated in the 1864 Sand Creek Massacre against the Cheyenne and Arapaho. He married Abigail Ward in 1869, moved to Washington, then came to Montana in 1893 driving a herd of

Mr. & Mrs. F.M. "Midnight" Smith, 1867. JIM ANNIN COLLECTION, MUSEUM OF THE BEARTOOTHS, #253.

200 shorthorns. In 1907 they settled at the Midnight Ranch east of Old Nye near the Beehive School, on what was considered one of the better spots in the valley. He wintered his cattle and horses in Smith Coulee on the south side of Bad Canyon Creek and had a line cabin below the spring.

Snail Lake

Garden snail, *Heli pomatia*. PHOTO BY JURGEN SCHONER, WIKI CREATIVE COMMONS.

Biology students take note. Snail Lake is on the south slope of Summit Mountain near Planaria and Shrimp Lakes. There are many species of snails, all of the Order Gastropoda, that are found world wide in most habitats. All have spiral shells and a single foot—their close relatives without shells are slugs. Some are gill bearing and found in water, some are terrestrial with lungs, and some have both. They are quite common in the Custer-Gallatin National Forest, where their white, dead shells can be seen scattered next to many of the forest trails.

Snake Lake

Montana Fish, Wildlife and Parks is the only agency to list this little lake. It sits in the outlet stream between Lonesome Lake and T Lake in Wyoming. Since it is not particularly snake-like in shape, one of the fisheries people must have seen something slither.

Snow Lakes/Creek

The Absaroka-Beartooths were once called the Snowy Mountains, so you would suspect that there would likely be certain features that referred to snow. You would be right, as there are two Snow Lakes, three Snow Creeks, as well as Snowball Lakes, Snowbank Mountain, Glacier, and Lake as well as Snowslide Creek and Gulch, and a Snowy Peak, too.

The **Snow Creek** and **Lake** that most people know is on the East Rosebud upstream from Alpine. It is here that the plaque honoring Fred Inabnit was placed in 1929 after his death. (see Mount Inabnit) Ranger notes from the 1930s state that the name came "because of the exceptionally heavy fall of snow which usually occurs at the head of the creek."

There is another **Snow Creek** that comes off the Silver Run Plateau to Rock Creek near Richel Lodge. Of the other **Snow Lakes,** one is on the Cooke City quad high up near the end of the Goose Lake jeep trail, and the other is at 10,400 feet on the Beartooth Plateau just south of the Montana/Wyoming line.

Snowball Lakes

The Snowball Lakes are a collection of small, round lakes at 10,000 feet that can be found above Mystic Lake and its power station in the Huckleberry Creek drainage. It should be of no surprise that Cold Lake is just around the corner.

Snowbank Mountain/Glacier/Lake

Snowbank Mountain, at 12,084 feet, is on the long ridgeline between Summit and Castle Rock Mountains. The glacier is on the east slope of the mountain, and the lake is on the mountain's south slope. In the 1930s, Snowbank Lake was the body of water on the north side of Snowbank Mountain. This is now Summit Lake, and Snowbank Lake was moved to the south side. It is all part of the confusion from the shuffling of the names of the mountains and lakes on this ridge. (see Castle Rock and Summit Lake/Mountain)

There are two other Snowbank Lakes, one in the Hellroaring Lakes chain and the other on the north slope of Mount Dewey; both are obviously fed by meltwater.

Snowslide Creek/Gulch

Snowslide Creek enters the Main Boulder River at Hicks Park. **Snowslide Gulch** is near the East Boulder Mine on the southern slope of Morningstar Mountain, where its stream flows down into the Dry Fork of the Boulder River.

Snowslides were obviously prevalent, but there were no reports of avalanche deaths here. (see Speculator Creek/Lake)

Snowy Peak

Ferdinand Hayden used this name on his first 1871 map of these mountains. Just like the Snowy Mountain Range, the miners in the Independence mining camp were the ones that were supposed to have named this peak. It apparently came from the deep snow and the slides that tumbled down onto the road at the base of the mountain.

Snyder Lake

Snyder Lake is just off the Beartooth Highway and can be found next to Sheepherder Lake just north of Little Bear Lake.

Snyder was a Wyoming ranger in the Sunlight Basin. His son established a dude ranch there, and this lake was named for that family.

Soda Butte, Soda Butte Creek

Soda Butte and the creek next to it were named in 1870 by the early prospecting party of A. Bart Henderson, Adam "Horn" Miller, and James Gourley who were on their way to the rich strikes near present-day Cooke City. Henderson wrote in his diary, "...this creek has a very singular butte some 40 feet high, which has been formed by soda water." Like Liberty Cap at Mammoth Hot Springs, it was created by mineral precipitation from a now dormant hot spring. Although the minerals in the tower are not soda (sodium salts) but calcium carbonate from dissolved limestone, the historical name has been kept.

Soda Butte. PHOTO BY THE AUTHOR.

Soda Butte Creek starts just east of Cooke City and follows U.S. 212 through the town and then on to flow along the Northeast Entrance Road into the Park to where it joins the Lamar River. Because effluent from the mines in the New World Mining District north of Cooke City drain into tributaries of Soda Butte Creek, it became one of the most polluted streams near any national park. It is said that it was so toxic that fish could not be kept alive in its waters more than 24 hours. Fortunately, the Clinton administration's 1996 settlement with Crown Butte/Noranda Mining, in addition to the reclamation of the McLaren and other mines on Henderson Mountain, also provided $25 million to clean up the waters of Soda Butte Creek and its tributaries. In July of 2019, a celebration was held to declare that mining close to the Park is now forbidden, that the waterways are now clean, and that all are under the protection of the Custer-Gallatin National Forest and Yellowstone Park.

There is a hot spring along Soda Butte Creek that P.W. Norris, the second park superintendent, who served from 1877 to 1882, said "is the legendary spring of the surrounding Indian nations for the cure of the saddle-galls of horse, or arrow or other wounds of warriors, and besides has properties similar to those of Arkansas Hot Springs that will soon fatten man or animal using it." Curative it may have been, but S. Weir Mitchell, who visited Yellowstone in 1879, wrote, "I do not distinctly recall all the nasty tastes [that] have affected my palate, but I am quite sure that this is one of the vilest. It was a combination of acid, sulphur, and saline, like a diabolic julep of Lucifer matches, bad eggs, vinegar, and magnesia. I presume its horrible taste has secured it a reputation for being good when it is down."

The Soda Butte Ranger Station is located on the Lamar River a couple of miles west of where the creek joins that river. It has been retired and is now called the Buffalo Ranch, which is used as a teaching facility by the Yellowstone Institute.

Sodalite Creek/Lake

Sodalite is a royal-blue mineral that occurs in igneous rocks that crystallized from sodium-rich magmas—thus the "soda." It is widely used as an ornamental gemstone.

This creek is on the Fossil Lake quad in the Broadwater drainage northeast of Cooke City, and the lake is in a long, slender canyon at the head of the creek.

Sourdough Lake/Basin

Sourdough Basin is directly southeast of Courthouse Lake near the head of the Stillwater River, and contains Sourdough, Spider, Fly, and Aires Lakes.

Sourdough has been used as a leavening agent for bread for most of human history. Because the bread is made by the fermentation of dough using naturally occurring lactobacilli and yeast, a small amount of the dough can be reserved and easily carried to provide for the next day's loaf. During the 1849 California gold rush, French bakers brought the technique to San Francisco, and it was adopted by the miners for its ease of carrying. From this, the term "sourdough" came to be used to refer to an old-timer or an experienced prospector. Since the basin and lake are in the mining country near Cooke City, it was an appropriate reference to this activity.

Spaghetti Lake

This thin, wiggly, spaghetti-shaped lake is on the Wyoming/Montana border between Copeland and Granite Lakes. It is another those lakes that are unrecognized on the USGS map, but used by Montana Fish, Wildlife and Parks and some hiking guides.

Specimen Creek/Falls

According to ranger notes of the 1930s, the specimens referred to in this name were "peculiar mineral formations and Indian relics" that were found at the head of this creek.

It is a tributary of the Hellroaring Creek that goes into Yellowstone Park and is the source of the name on the Specimen Creek USGS quad map.

Speculator Creek/Lake

Both the lake and creek are on Boulder Mountain where the creek flows east to meet the Main Boulder River just south of Chippy Park. Although Bill Schneider, in his book *Hiking the Absaroka-Beartooths*, wryly speculates that some old miner couldn't spell spectacular (for the scenery), the name actually derives from the Speculator Mines that were found along this watershed. Their name certainly defines mining, as it means "to invest in property or other ventures in the hope of gain but with the risk of loss."

Amos and Mary Graham, longtime residents of the Contact mining area, homesteaded on this creek in 1916. They also bought the ranch on nearby Shorty Creek and had property on Graham Creek just south of Contact. (see Shorty Creek and Graham Creek)

Although Snowslide Creek is just a few miles south, the only recorded deaths from snowslides in this area were on Speculator Creek. In 1921 Ben Fleming, a trapper, was buried in an avalanche. When his body was found the following spring, he was still holding two steel traps. Several years later, John Nordby, who was in the group that found Fleming's body, was also killed by a snowslide in the same area.

Spider Lake

As this lake is near Cooke City and right next to Fly Lake, one might think it part of the biological list of lakes, which it is not. Rather it is part of the set of humorous pairs like Mutt and Jeff, Dick and Bob, and Molar and Incisor Lakes.

It refers to the poem "The Spider and the Fly" by Mary Howitt that was published in 1828. The opening line, "'Will you walk into my parlor?' said the Spider to the Fly," is a cautionary tale of seduction and the use of flattery and charm to disguise true intentions. Heh! Heh! Heh!

Spirit Mountain

The Board on Geographic Names does not say why this mountain to the south of Mount Rearguard and Beartooth Mountain was recently renamed Spirit

Mountain. In 1961 a group of climbers from the University of Wyoming named it Mount Salo, and that is the name that is still found on some climbing maps.

It is a bit sad that Salo's name has been abandoned, as he was an important figure in Beartooth country in the early part of the twentieth century. Otto Jalmer, "O.J." Salo (1895–1977) grew up in Red Lodge where he worked at the post office and family store. He later became the supervisor of Carbon County Welfare and was a good friend of Al Croonquist at Camp Senia, where he spent summers as a guide and wrangler. He went on many pack trips out of Camp Senia, named several lakes, and helped Croonquist and the Forest Service by transporting milk cans full of fish to stock many of the east-side lakes.

Spirit Mountain, a difficult climb, is visible from the Beartooth Highway. It is still seen as a shrine by Salo family members.

Splinter Lake

Ouch! This long, narrow lake is found next to Finger Lake in the Broadwater drainage.

Sometimes misnamed Sliver Lake—you get the idea—Finger Lake points at it accusingly.

Much like Production and Recroitment Lakes (see those references), Finger and Splinter are a fish growing system, with the spawning hatchery in Finger and the excellent planktonic food in Splinter.

Mount Spofford

James P. Kimball named this mountain for one of his backers during his 1898 survey. Charles August Spofford (1822–1899) was Henry Villard's private secretary, so this was probably an appropriate name, as it stands close to Mount Villard. However, the Board on Geographic Names, for unstated reasons, renamed it Glacier Peak some time prior to 1947. (see Mount Villard and Glacier Peak)

This is just another instance of the Board erasing history from the mountains. C.A. Spofford was a man of some importance in the Red Lodge area in the late nineteenth century as he was on the board of directors of the Northern Pacific Railroad and oversaw their interests as controlling partner in the Rocky Fork Mining Company. The first building in downtown Red Lodge, and the first brick building in town, was built by the coal company and was called the Spofford Hotel. It was renamed the Pollard in 1902 after it was sold to Thomas Pollard.

Spogen Lake

Spogen Lake can be found on the Castle Mountain quad just north of the Montana/Wyoming border and was named for Leo Spogen (1898–1986). Leo was born in Belt, Montana, and came to Red Lodge where he taught in the Carbon County High School from 1928 to 1940. He was then appointed postmaster and held that position until his retirement in 1968. Leo was also an officer of the Red Lodge Rod and Gun Club in the 1930s, where he worked on planting trout in the Clarks Fork country and up toward this lake. (see Rachel Lake)

It sits in a cluster of lakes in the Martin Lakes Basin along with Martin, Whitcomb, and Wright Lakes and has also carried the name Little Falls Lake for the spectacular waterfall between it and Wright Lake. Jason Rhoten, who writes for Montana Fish, Wildlife and Parks, has called it "one of the prettiest spots in the world."

Spread Creek

This little creek is a tributary of the East Rosebud in the flat area north of East Rosebud Lake and the vacation community of Alpine.

Since it comes quickly out of a narrow canyon before leisurely wandering across the meadows, the name certainly refers to its course. There are other Spread Creeks in the West, such as the one in the Tetons of Wyoming, and all are similar with a widening and braiding of the channel where it slows.

Spring Creek

Unsurprisingly, there is a spring at the source of this creek, enters Rock Creek near Richel Lodge south of Red Lodge.

Squaw Creek/Pass/Peak

Squaw Creek was a poignant name for the creek where the women came to pray and grieve for their men who were killed in the avalanche on Dead Indian Creek. Because of the derogatory implications of the word "squaw," all references to it were removed from the Montana maps in 2004, and that caused this stream to be renamed Meyers Creek. (see Dead Indian Creek and Meyers Creek)

Squaw Pass connected the Main and West Forks of Meyers (formerly Squaw) Creek. It appeared on the 1939 Mount Wood quad, but it is now unnamed and is without a marked trail.

Wyoming, not as politically correct as its northern neighbor, still has a **Squaw Peak** and **Creek** just south of Jim Smith Creek and the L bar T Ranch. Like the Grand Tetons farther south, which means "Big Breasts" in French, Squaw Peak was said to have been given its name because it reminded an old miner of a woman's breast, with the top knob looking like a nipple.

Squeeze Lake

A small, currently unnamed lake is squeezed into a narrow canyon at the headwaters of Hawley Creek. It is just upstream from Narrow Escape Lake on the south side of Mount Douglas.

It is not recognized by the Board on Geographic Names so is not found on the USGS or Forest Service maps. However, it does exist on hiking maps and in Montana Fish, Wildlife and Parks documents.

Stands Basin

Joe Stands arrived in Emigrant in 1890, mining up Emigrant Gulch, filing claims in 1913 and 1915, and working a claim on Sliding Mountain with Peter Bair. After he left the Sliding Mountain claim, he was employed by the Daileys on their ranch south of Emigrant as a cook and as a cowboy working cattle. (see Sliding Mountain and Dailey Basin/Lake)

He squatted a homestead in this basin in 1893, which is close to Dailey Lake. When he married Molly Dorgan, she found the basin too high and cold for her, so they moved to a homestead on Sixmile Creek where they spent the rest of their lives.

Molly and Joe Stands. YELLOWSTONE GATEWAY MUSEUM, #2006.044.1709.

The current Red Mountain was once called Stands Mountain because it overlooks his basin. (see Red Mountain)

Stanley Coulee

Edward Stanley ran a coal mine on the lower end of this draw that is located near Nye and the Stillwater River.

Star Dust Lake

This tiny dot of a lake is on the other side of Goose Creek from Star Lake near the head of the Stillwater River. It was obviously named for its starry neighbors.

Star Lake/Creek

At high altitude and away from the pollution and lights of the cities, the stars are brilliant, and they obviously impressed some of the early explorers.

Star Creek comes out of Astral Lake north of Cooke City. One of the **Star Lakes** is on the Goose Lake road about ½ mile west and 200 feet above Astral and is the headwaters of the Stillwater River. It is rather star shaped—as if drawn by a five-year-old with a crayon.

There is another **Star Lake** that is a widening in the West Rosebud that was caused by a rockslide. It is not far from the other stars and a bit north of Grasshopper Glacier. It has five small bays, so it, too, can be considered almost star shaped.

Stash Lake

The source of the name is not stated, but it must be assumed that it is like various Cache Creeks where someone had stashed some equipment. It is found near the Sky Top Lakes in the Broadwater drainage.

Stepping Stone Lake

The prior name of Rain Lake has never been accepted by the Board on Geographic Names, who preferred Stepping Stones. It is in the Sky Top drainage, with numerous islands and obvious rocks in the shallows.

Stillwater River/County/Complex/Gorge/Plateau

The Stillwater River is one of the primary tributaries of the Yellowstone River and, along with the Boulder River and Rosebud Creeks, gives access to the interior of the Absaroka-Beartooths from the north.

This river runs through, and provides the name for, **Stillwater County,** which was formed from portions of Yellowstone, Sweet Grass, and Carbon Counties in 1913. Columbus is the county seat and its only incorporated town.

The town of Columbus itself was originally called Stillwater when it was started by Horace Countryman. He had a store there, a stage stop known as the Eagle's Nest, and a watering hole that the miners called the Sheep Dip Saloon for the quality of its liquor. In 1893, when the Northern Pacific Railroad came through and made the town one of its stops, the name was changed to Columbus so as not to duplicate the NP's Stillwater stop in Minnesota. (see LaVelle Lake) The Columbus sandstone quarry was active in the late 1800s and supplied the stone for the state capitol building in Helena. It closed around 1910, and the economy is now primarily agriculture, mining, and outdoor sports.

The **Stillwater Complex,** partway south on the river, refers to a rich mineral band of igneous material that intruded into the basement rocks. It was discovered in 1883 by Jack Nye and Jimmy and Jonas Hedges and was known to contain copper, nickel, and chromium. Gold and silver were what the early miners were after, but the Benbow, Mouat, and Gish Mines were particularly aimed at the chromium, which was essential during both World Wars. Rhodium, copper, nickel, and iron were also found, and in the 1970s geologists discovered platinum and palladium in a 28-mile-long vein that is one of the few sources of these minerals outside of Russia and South Africa. The Stillwater Mining Company, the largest employer in that part of Montana, is now actively extracting those minerals.

The naming of the **Stillwater River** is a bit of a convoluted story and the source of many legends and fictitious tales. The Crow called it *Ahr-nah-puma-ta,* or "Where the Buffalo Jumped Off," which actually refers to that part of the river near Nye where an archaeologically important pishkun or buffalo jump exists. They apparently also called the lower reaches the Rose Hip River, because that is the stated reason that Capt. William Clark called it the Rosebud River when the Corps of Discovery passed by in 1806. According to Lt. James Bradley's notes from his Crow interviews of 1876, they called the current Rosebud Creek *Itch-keep-pe,* meaning "still," or "quiet water," for the many beaver dams and numerous quiet pools near its source. For unknown reasons, the names were switched in the late 1800s and the main channel became the Stillwater, with the Rosebud the smaller tributary. Of the several legends about the name, the one that has persisted and is even related in Montana Historical Society publications is Jim Annin's poignant story. Jim was the editor of the Columbus newspaper, and in 1916 published the tale of the two Indian lovers, Memidgi and Weeluna, who were forbidden to marry. It is a long involved story, but briefly, the two were devastated by the decision, and, deeply in love, they jumped into the river and drowned in each other's arms. Where the bodies came to rest was called "the hallowed water," mistranslated as Still Water. It is a nice story, but, according to Crow sources, is a complete fabrication. My favorite tale, however, comes from local rancher Ralph Southworth. He tells about an Indian who made a long trip exploring up the river. When his friends asked him how far he had gone, he said, "Four sleeps." Asked if there was water in the stream that far up, he replied, "Yes, still water." Hmmm, yes, it is so.

The actual name of the river comes from a more ordinary source. It ascribes the naming to John Bozeman, whose trail in 1864 came along the south side of the Yellowstone River and crossed a quiet, sandy ford that the Indians called *Biliinneete,* or "No Current." Although this is the true derivation, it not as cute as the others.

The **Stillwater Gorge** is found at the end of the Nye Road just a few steps south of the Woodbine Campground. The Stillwater Trail follows the river south for many miles, but the first half mile is carved from the rock wall of the gorge and is one of Montana's most spectacular wilderness hikes. The cleft squeezes the river into a narrow, roaring, boiling maelstrom that is particu-

Stillwater River. RICK GRAETZ, USED WITH PERMISSION.

larly impressive with the early summer snowmelt. Even though there are quiet sections of the river like Sioux Charley and Hawks Lakes, after seeing this gorge, one cannot imagine why anyone would ever call it the Still Water.

The **Stillwater Plateau** sits above and to the east of Woodbine and the upper reaches of the river.

Storm Creek/Lake/Mountain

The **Storm Lakes** are in the big bowl found between Granite Peak and Mystic Mountain with Glacier Peak and Mount Villard at the head. It is in the highest part of the Beartooth Mountains, so finding storms is a given.

Storm Mountain is farther west and sits just to the north of Little Park Mountain. **Storm Creek** flows north off the east shoulder of the mountain to join the Stillwater River south of Cathedral Point. Ranger notes of the 1930s justify the name "because of the generally stormy appearance of the atmosphere around this peak."

On June 20, 1988, near the mouth of Storm Creek, a bolt of lightning hit a dead pine tree. Because the previous three years were extremely dry, and because of high winds, a massive forest fire blew up. It merged with the fires in Yellowstone National Park to the south and burned the rest of that summer, finally being extinguished by the snow. The "Fires of '88" consumed nearly 3 million acres of beautiful forest land, which is just now beginning to appear recovered.

Strawberry Creek

Strawberry Creek is a bit north of Emigrant and enters the Yellowstone River at the Loch Leven fishing access site.

The wild strawberry, *Fragaria virginiana*, is found throughout the Rockies from the plains to subalpine zones. Its tart flavorful little berries and the three toothed leaflets look all the world like a miniature version of the cultivated fruit. In fact, it is the original parent of 90 percent of all commercially grown strawberries.

This is, of course, mining country, and two 1895 gold claims, the Mehach and the Strawberry, were located near this creek, and that is where its name came from. The mine's exact site is currently unknown, but is probably east of the wilderness boundary.

One of the first homesteaders along this creek was George A. Allen, whose family stayed for several generations. He married a daughter of David Shorthill, and developed some fame as one of the people who guided President Theodore Roosevelt around Yellowstone Park during his 1903 tour. (see Shorthill Creek/ Lake and McBride Lake)

Strickland Creek

Ben Strickland was a discharged Civil War veteran who came up the Bozeman Trail in 1864 with the Stanford Train and settled in Yellowstone City (Emigrant). He did some mining, but worked primarily hunting to supply meat to the miners, and was noted for mediating between the miners and the Indians. He married Nancy Jane Dailey, Ebeneezer's daughter, in 1868 (see Dailey Lake), and in 1874 they homesteaded on the creek that bore his name. The first schoolhouse in the Paradise Valley was on their property, and the first sermon was preached there.

Ben Strickland. YELLOWSTONE GATEWAY MUSEUM, #2006.044.1589.

    This creek, a tributary of Emigrant Creek, is now called Fridley Creek (see that citation) because there is another Strickland Creek in Park County, just south of I-90 where the current Strickland descendants live.

Suce Creek

Suce Creek is in the northern part of the Paradise Valley near where the Yellowstone River is crossed by the Carter Bridge. It was named for a Suce (also spelled Souce or Soos), a Mexican who married into the Crow tribe and lived there in the 1870s. He is mentioned by Thomas Leforge in his *Memoirs of a White Crow Indian*, as well as by Andrew Garcia in *A Tough Trip Through Paradise*, both classic first-person accounts of early Montana history. He prospected with George Huston on the Firehole River in what was to become Yellowstone National Park, was employed as a scout by the U.S. Army, and was one of the people who retrieved John Bozeman's body.

    Prior to Suce's arrival, the bench south of Suce Creek was settled by Iremus "Trapper" Haynes. This was in the 1840s and would have made Haynes the first settler in Park County.

Sugarloaf Mountain

Prior to the latter part of the nineteenth century when sugar cubes were introduced, refined sugar was produced and sold as a firm, tall cone with a rounded top that required sugar nips to break off smaller pieces. That characteristic shape is reflected in the names of these two mountains—one on the Roundhead Butte quad north of Yellowstone Park, and the other on the Sliderock Mountain quad in the northeast corner of the Custer-Gallatin National Forest.

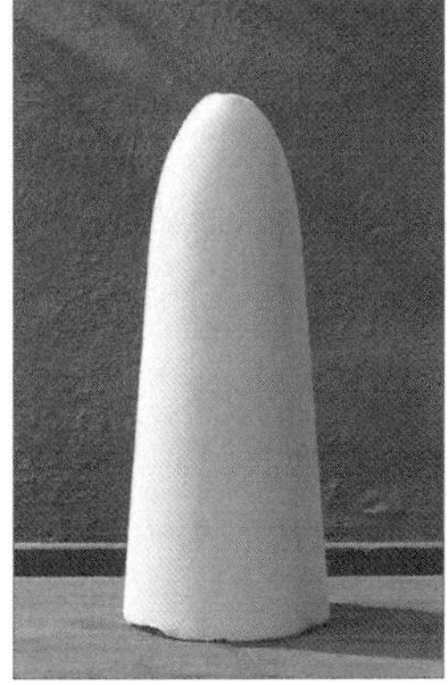

Sugarloaf. PHOTO BY PETR ADAM DOHNALEK, WIKI CREATIVE COMMONS.

Summerville Lake

The name of this lake in the Sierra Creek drainage just north of the Montana/Wyoming border was placed prior to 1937. It is just a poetic description.

Summit Lake/Mountain

The high peak got an obvious name, but indecision as to which mountain was really the Summit caused some early confusion. Castle Rock Mountain was known as Summit Mountain prior to 1937, and today's **Summit Mountain** was Castle Rock. Now Snowbank Mountain is on the same ridge between Summit and Castle Rock Mountains, and **Summit Lake** was previously known as Snowbank Lake. However, the present Snowbank Lake is now the one on the south side of Snowbank Mountain, and the former Snowbank Lake is now Summit Lake, even though it is on Snowbank Mountain's north slope and somewhat east of Summit Mountain. Got that? Don't argue or ask for explanations. Just accept what is on your USGS Castle Mountain quad map because that is what is now official according to the Board on Geographic Names.

Sundance Mountain/Lake/Pass/Glacier

O.J. Salo (see Spirit Mountain) named the lake in 1919. He was up with employees from Camp Senia stocking the lake with buckets of trout fry and was impressed with the scene of the sun dancing on the ripples of the lake.

Sundance Lake is just to the west of **Sundance Pass,** which is between Mount Lockhart and **Sundance Peak** on the Silver Run Peak quad. The pass, on the trail between the East Rosebud and Rock Creek has been described as the most beautiful point in the Beartooths.

Sundance Peak got its name from Forest Supervisor James Whitham's survey of the area in 1914–1915 and can be found on an early 1918 map. Although the names are the same, and they are near each other, Forest Service notes confirm that the source of the names of the lake and peak are different. The pass's name could have been from either. There was a lot of sun dancing in their eyes up at that high elevation.

Sundance Glacier was once called Horseshoe Glacier and is on the north wall of Castle Rock Spire next to Castle Mountain. This, as you might suspect, reflects the fact that Castle Mountain was once called Sundance Peak. That name has been moved to another mountain to the northeast, but the glacier was left behind. And you are not surprised that Castle Mountain is on the same name-shuffling ridge as Castle Rock, and Summit and Snowbank Mountains, right? (see Summit Lake/Mountain and Castle Mountain)

Sundown Lake

The lake with this rather romantic name is the second lake north of Pentad Lake at the headwaters to the Middle Fork of Wounded Man Creek. One can imagine an August evening, sitting by your tent and watching the sun set. Ed Ickerman of the Beartooth Ranch and great-uncle of Billings mountaineer and legislator Harrison Fagg, named several of the lakes in this area. He called this one Mearl Lake for his nephew, Mearl Fagg, Harrison's father. The Board on Geographic Names has not accepted any of Ed's names. (see Pentad Lake)

Sunken Rock Lake

This is a descriptive name for the lake near Jordan Mountain and Pass on the Lake Plateau. It has a large submerged rock on its northeast shore.

Sunset Peak

Sunset Peak is northwest of Cooke City on the northern border of Yellowstone National Park. It sits along a ridge with Wolverine Peak between Miller and Mineral Mountains.

The western slope has a flat surface for the sun to play on at sunset.

Surprise Lake

Surprise Lake is in the Sodalite backcountry. Pat Marcuson says that it takes a skillful horse and a talented rider to weave through all of the barriers, so finding it is a "surprise."

Lake Surrender

This lake is in the Flood Creek chain between Cimmerian Lake and Rabbit Gulch. Although details of her are not known, it was formerly called Sherril Lake. The name was changed when a Montana Fish, Wildlife and Parks crew nearly surrendered when driven crazy by the mosquitoes that swarm the meadow around this lake.

Lake Susanne

Lake Susanne is just north of Castle Mountain and remains one of the mystery women of the Beartooths.

Susie Creek

This creek, along the northern edge of the Custer-Gallatin National Forest in the Boulder River country, was homesteaded by Frank and Harold Blanchard in 1919 and 1921. Presumably Susie was a daughter of those families.

Swamp Lake/Creek

One Swamp Lake heads the creek of that name and is a tributary of Picket Pin Creek near the former settlement of Limestone.

There is a second Swamp Lake in a boggy area north of Cooke City which can be found near Weidy and Marsh Lakes.

Mosquito heaven!

Lake Sylvan/Peak

Sylvan is defined as something consisting of or associated with woods, or wooded. It comes from Sylvanus, a minor Roman woodland deity.

The **peak** is the highest point on the East Rosebud Plateau. The **lake,** on the flank of the peak, is one of the best golden trout, *Oncorhynchus aguabonita*, fisheries in Montana. Since it has continued to maintain a healthy self-sustaining trout population, it has been used to stock numerous other lakes in the state. These beautiful fish are close relatives to the rainbow trout and have golden flanks with red horizontal bands along the lateral lines. They are native only to the Kern River area in the Sierra Nevada of northern California but have been transplanted throughout the northern Rocky Mountains.

T Lake

Named for its T-shape, the lake is found downstream from Lonesome Lake on the Beartooth Plateau just into Wyoming.

Taylor Flat

An old trapper named Taylor worked this country in the 1880s and gave his name to these flats. A Kathleen Taylor, presumably his wife or daughter, filed a federal land patent for these flats in 1900. It is drained by Grouse Creek and is found just off the West Boulder River on the very northern border of the Custer-Gallatin National Forest next to Burrls Flat.

Telephone Basin

Telephone Basin lies just to the south of Hummingbird Peak and was the site of a number of early gold mines. It was named for a telephone line that was laid up to a "spike box" telephone in 1893. This line to Telephone Basin was a temporary one for communications

Ranger Harry Kaufman at a spike box. CRAZY MOUNTAIN MUSEUM.

with the mines and got to within 10 miles of Independence and the mines there.

The first of the many Forest Service lines was strung from the Main Boulder station to Jardine and Hellroaring. Ranger Harry Kaufman, who began his service in 1905, strung many miles of lines and installed spike boxes for communication within the forest. His wife, Coral, was the operator and ran the switchboard from their home at the Main Boulder Ranger Station. These spike lines were used until the 1950s when they were replaced by radios, which were more useful and required less maintenance.

Tempest Mountain

Tempest Mountain is next to Granite Peak and Froze-to-Death Plateau, and near Thunder Mountain. Tempest and Thunder reflect the fact that, at this high location, violent summer afternoon thunderstorms are common. The author found his hair standing on end when he was caught in an impressive hail and lightning storm on this peak late one August.

Tepee Mountain/Creek/Spring

A tepee is a conical tent made of animal skins that are supported on slender poles. It was the primary residence of the Plains Indian tribes as it could be folded into a travois and moved from one encampment to another. (see Travois Creek) The word has been adopted into English from the Lakota (Sioux) language with "tipi" the preferred spelling—except by the Board on Geographic Names, which uses "tepee," and the U.S. Forest Service, which spells it "teepee." Go figure.

Tepee Mountain overlooks Contact on the Main Boulder. The mountain was probably named for the triangular shape that resembled the conical Plains Indian lodge.

Tepee Creek and Spring form a small tributary of Bad Canyon Creek near Nye on the Stillwater River. This creek, as with many other Tepee Creeks throughout the Custer-Gallatin National Forest, was named for the wikiups that were found nearby. Like the tipi, a wikiup is also a cone of sticks. It is covered with skins or branches, but it is not a tipi because it was a temporary structure where the sticks were just piled together and left in one location. They served as shelter for the local migratory Mountain Shoshoni, but were also used by other tribes as hunting huts or as rest sites. The cones were mistaken by the whites as the remains of tipi poles, so the creeks were actually misnamed. Although most were built in the nineteenth century, a few wikiups can still be found in more remote parts of our forests.

Thiel Lake/Creek

Thiel Lake is in the cluster of lakes near Crazy Mountain just north of the Montana/Wyoming line. It is believed to have been named for a Mr. Thiel of Clark, Wyoming, not far away down the Clarks Fork. **Thiel Creek** is west and north of Red Lodge on the Bare Mountain quad.

The Thiels are a well-known local family with many descendants still in the area. The variant name Tiel is seen on some maps, but Thiel is the correct spelling. The original Red Lodge Thiels came from Wisconsin in the 1890s and homesteaded on or near **Thiel Creek.** Peter was the eldest brother and was the clerk of the local school district in 1900. Anthony was ranching in the area in 1893, and both he and the youngest brother, William, were listed as "farmers" in the 1900 Red Lodge census.

Thompson Lake/Creek

Thompson Creek flows from the lake of that name into the West Fork of Mill Creek north of Emigrant. Locals say that the lake was named for a Leif Thompson who had a cabin by the lake "long ago." He had no descendants. This man's legal name was Christian P. Thompson, who was recorded as filing for water rights from the creek in 1890.

The creek had a former name of East Creek, but it was changed in 1922 as it was close to the East Fork of Mill Creek and the Board on Geographic Names didn't want any confusion.

Three Creeks

The single creek comes off the east slope of Marten Peak, but has three channels where it enters the West Boulder River.

Three Sisters Creeks/Bluff or Cliffs

There are three ridges, each about the same size, on this bluff that overlooks the East Rosebud downstream from Alpine—thus "Three Sisters." Each has a draw with a creek, which are unnamed on the current maps, but are locally called the Three Sisters Creeks for the ridge that they come off.

Throop Lake

Once known as Swede Lake, this lake, in the cluster of lakes just north of the Montana/Wyoming border, was posthumously renamed to honor George L. Throop of Red Lodge "in recognition of his mountain travels." George worked as a guide in the Beartooth Mountains, and he was the president of the Red Lodge Rod and Gun Club in 1936 when the club had a project to plant trout in the lakes of the Clarks Fork drainage. He and A.O. Whitcomb personally took 16,000 trout into Glacier Lake that summer when the Rod and Gun Club planted over 325,000 trout in the Beartooth country. (see Whitcomb Lake)

Thunder Mountain

This meteorologically named mountain is on the Silver Run Peak quad to the west of Red Lodge. It is in the area of Granite, Froze-to-Death and Tempest Mountains, where violent thunderstorms occur almost daily during warm summer afternoons.

The Thunderer

The mountain overlooks Soda Butte Creek in the northeast corner of Yellowstone National Park and was named by Arnold Hague's 1885 survey crew. Park engineer and historian Hiram M. Chittenden wrote in 1895 that it was "seemingly a great focus for thunderstorms."

Tibbs Butte

Tibbs Butte is visible to the south of the Beartooth Highway and is passed as one hikes the Beartooth Loop from the top of the pass along the Beartooth National Recreation Trail.

The name comes from a Tibbs who ran sheep up here with John Tolman in the early 1900s. (see Tolman Point/Mountain/Flat)

It is the current site of a uranium mine, although there has been no production and little activity other than routine claim maintenance.

Tie Creek

In 1880 the timber along this creek was cut for ties for the Northern Pacific Railroad that was coming across Montana.

It is on the north side of the mountains in the West Boulder River/Mission Creek country where logging is still a consideration. A Forest Service timber sale was blocked in the 1990s and further development has been halted as the area is part of the Montana Wilderness Bill, which is currently stranded in Congress.

Tie Cutter Gulch

This gulch is farther east than Tie Creek, on the Sliderock Mountain quad, but the name is similar because it, too, was an area logged for railroad ties.

Till Lake

Till Lake is found next to Gravel Lake on the south side of Snowbank and Castle Rock Mountains in the drainage off Snowbank Glacier. The name of this lake comes from glacial till, a geologic term for the jumbled glacial sediment found as piles of gravel on the moraines left by the glacier.

Timberline Mountain/Creek/Lake

Timberline Lake was named in 1916 by Ranger Art Baum because it is located in a bowl of scrub whitebark pine right at timberline, the altitude above which no trees grow. **Timberline Creek** flows out of the lake through a wooded corridor below Silver Run Peak down to the West Fork of Rock Creek near Camp Senia. The lake was stocked by A.J. Salo and Al Croonquist in the 1920s, and was used by James Kimball and his 1898 survey party as a base camp on their attempt to climb Mount Dewey.

Ê**Timberline Mountain** is quite separate as it is on the far western border of the Absaroka-Beartooth Wilderness just south of Pinnacle Peak between the Stillwater River and Slough Creek. It rises well above the tree line, so the timberline is visible on its flanks.

Tinker's Hill

The cemetery for Gardiner, Montana, is on this hill, located just one mile inside the Park boundary. It is owned by the Gardiner Eagles Club and is the only non-federal land within Yellowstone National Park.

The cemetery was established in 1880, and one of the first burials was John Hartz, a tinsmith, or "tinker." One source says that he died of a head injury after being bucked off a horse. Another says that he was crushed to death when his wagon fell on him as he was trying to grease the wheels. In either case, his grave gave name to the hill.

Tolman Point/Mountain/Flat

Located south of Red Lodge near Richel Lodge and the Beartooth Highway, the flat, point, and mountain were named for John Tolman, who at one time ran cattle in the area.

Tolman was born in 1861 in Assam, India, to missionary parents, returned to the U.S. in 1864, and first worked for the huge Dilworth Cattle Company in Kansas City. When Dilworth expanded to Red Lodge in 1882, Tolman drove cattle there and became that division's manager. After Dilworth's death in 1886, he bought the company, one of the largest in the state. He was elected to the Montana state legislature in 1903–1912, served on the State Board of Livestock Commissioners, and was vice president of the Red Lodge State Bank. Has son, Bronson (1902–1986) married Charles Wright's daughter and continued the ranch after his father passed. (see Wright Lake)

Tomato Can Gulch

This was a local name that ranger notes from around 1940 say was "probably related to the fact that pack trails came through here and littered cans etc." It is on the northeast section of the forest in Deer Creek country on the Sliderock Mountain quad.

Tommy Creek

This creek was named on older maps, but is no longer recognized by the USGS. It joins the West Rosebud a couple hundred yards downstream from the Mystic Lake power plant and just upstream from Chicken Creek.

It was named for Tommy Fosvedt, a Montana Power employee who lived and worked at the dam for 17 years and established his semi-permanent camp on the flats by this creek.

Towne Gulch/Point

Although one source says that this was named because the town of Red Lodge can be seen from this point on the West Fork of Rock Creek, this is probably not the case.

In 1888 George H. Towne (1844–1914) was getting timber from the mountain for his sawmill, which was located on the south side of Red Lodge. George came to Montana in 1867, built the first house in Red Lodge, worked the Bridger Coal Camp, married Viola Moore, and died in 1914 at age 70. His activity there, and the spelling of his surname, make him the most likely source of the gulch's and point's name.

Trail Creek

There are two Trail Creeks in the Absaroka-Beartooths.

One is a tributary of Fourmile Creek and the Boulder River. The trail along this creek connects Fourmile with Meatrack Creek and is uniquely called the Trail Creek Trail.

The other Trail Creek drains the East Boulder Plateau to the West Fork of the Stillwater. There is no trail marked along this creek on the more recent USGS and hikers' maps, but it was probably named because its entry to the West Fork is crossed by a pack trail.

West Trail Draw/Spring

The trail between Trout and Bad Canyon Creeks goes up this draw north of Nye. The springs are there, too, and are near Wildcat Springs on Wildcat Draw.

Trail Lake

Both the Granite Lake Trail and the Beartooth Creek Trail form a loop via the Green Lake Trail near the Montana/Wyoming border. As it passes from Wright to Green Lake, the hiking trail courses along the edge of... Trail Lake.

Trapper Lake/Creek

Forest Service notes from 1923 say that the name was suggested by the presence of an old trapper's tipi that was located on the shore of this lake. Later reports say that it was a camp or a cabin, but there is no information about the trapper himself, and the structure is long gone.

The creek comes out of the lake and flows west to the West Boulder River.

Travois Gulch

This was another of those 2004 name changes where the derogatory term "squaw" had to be removed from the Montana maps. The creek in the gulch is a tributary of Dead Indian Creek and was formerly called Squaw Creek/Gulch to remember those women who came to grieve and pray for their men, the dead

Stump Horn's Cheyenne family using a travois, 1890. PHOTO BY CHRISTIAN BARTHLMESS.

Indians who had been killed by an avalanche while elk hunting. Maintaining a Native American reference, the Board on Geographic Names chose to substitute Travois Gulch.

The word travois comes from the French word *travail,* which means "an arduous journey." It was a transport device used by the Plains Indians, who lacked wheels, and consisted of two poles that were joined by a frame and pulled by an animal. Initially these were small poles dragged by dogs, but when the Indians acquired horses in the mid-eighteenth century, tipi poles were used and that allowed for much larger loads.

Triangle Lake

There are, or were, two Triangle Lakes on the Silver Run Peak quad map. The one with three sides that is still on the maps is up by Bowback Lake on the West Fork of Rock Creek drainage. The other was just to the north of Glacier Lake on the Montana/Wyoming border. It was named on the USGS maps through 1986, but rules (often broken—note Falls and Wounded Man Creeks) state that there cannot be two features of the same name on the same quad map. As a result, this rather triangular-shaped lake currently has no name on the USGS map. Just to keep you on your toes, the National Geographic hikers' map and Montana Fish, Wildlife and Parks documents still call it Triangle Lake, but you can figure this out.

There is a third Triangle Lake that is a bit farther west and can be found on the Castle Mountain quad to the northeast of Otter lake on the south slope of Summit Mountain. It, too, is generally triangular in shape.

Tripod Hill

This 6,107-foot hill rises 200 feet above the Stillwater River where it is joined by Flood Creek. It gives an excellent view of the canyon and was, as the name implies, used by surveyors. The name is mentioned in ranger notes of the 1960s but was erased from the maps prior to 1985.

Triskele Lake

A triskelion or triskele is a figure consisting of a triple spiral with rotational symmetry. The word means "three-legged" in Greek and can be represented by three bent human legs on the circle.

Triskelion.

The earliest creation of the triskele goes back to the Neolithic era and appears on the Newgrange Irish kerb-stones, which are thought to originate around 3200 BC. It became popular in Celtic culture from 500 BC onward. While believed to represent forward motion to understanding, it is also thought to evoke the Celtic interpretation of the three realms of material existence: earth, water, and sky; or to represent the three worlds: spiritual, physical, and celestial.

The symbol has lost some of its luster recently as it was appropriated by the Nazis and became a significant hate symbol, particularly as it was used by the South African white supremacist Africaner Weerstandsbeweging in the 1970s. The lake's general three-lobed shape can be described as a triskele.

Trouble Lake

Located near the head of Flood Creek, this lake's name, like Desolation, Vengence, Dreary, Abandoned, and Nightmare Lakes, appeared on the maps after 1945. The depression that caused the person to give these lakes such cheery names is not explained, but is thought to relate to the weather, which can be very nasty at this elevation.

Trout Creek/Lake

Trout Creek is near Wildcat Springs, and there are two **Trout Lakes.** One is on the upper Boulder River and the other near Soda Butte. This latter lake was apparently first called Trout Lake by A. Bart Henderson, one of the early Cooke City miners. In his 1871 diary, he claimed it was the most beautiful little lake and "is full of the finest trout." By the 1880s it was called Fish Lake, either for the good fishing or for Park Assistant Superintendent Edmund Fish, or both. It later reverted again, becoming established as "Trout" because it was an egg collection site beginning in 1910 and the Park trout hatchery was situated there from 1922 to 1951.

One of the Park's tragedies occurred on this Trout Lake near Soda Butte in 1918 when Sgt. Arthur S. Brewer and Pvt. Victor Manterfield were fishing and drowned after their boat overturned.

The second Trout Lake is right next to the Main Boulder River and the Fourmile Guard Station. It has also been called Bray's Pond and Lost Lake, and is easily accessible from the Main Boulder Road. It is regularly stocked with rainbow trout.

Temptation, 1919. PAINTING BY A.P. SPEAR, *ARTS AND DECORATION*, MAY 1920.

Tucker Creek

This creek in the Slough Creek country was named for a Mr. William Tucker who filed a mining declaration here in 1881. There is no further information on him in the newspapers or ranger notes.

Tumble Mountain/Creek, Tumble and Little Tumble Lakes

The **mountain** gets its name from the **creek's** wild action as it tumbles off its mountain down into the West Boulder River.

The lakes are at the headwaters of the creek on the west slope of Tumble Mountain. **Little Tumble Lake** is a bit upstream of **Tumble Lake,** and neither are on the USGS map as they have not been certified. However, you will find them on the National Geographic hikers' map and on Montana Fish, Wildlife and Parks documents.

Turco Pond

Antoine J. "Tony" Turco brought his family from Nevada in 1910 and patented a homestead just east of Nye. The pond is on his ranch land.

Lake Turgulse

This lake with its fascinating name is found in a basin on the Froze-to-Death Plateau along with Froze-to-Death and Brent Lakes. It is well known,

A.J. "Tony" Turco. JIM ANNIN COLLECTION, MUSEUM OF THE BEARTOOTHS, #2000.

as it is used as a base for climbs of Granite Peak and Mount Peal. The name was not noted on Merino's 1937 Top of the World Map, and Turgulse is not a word in the Crow language, but no one has yet been found who knows where the name comes from.

Tuscarora Creek

Tuscarora is a common name for rivers in the East and for mines in the West, so this creek was probably named for a mine in the vicinity. It comes off Carbonate Mountain to join Bridge Creek then on to the Main Boulder River.

Tuscarora is the name of an Indian tribe whose members can currently be found in North Carolina, New York, and Ontario. The were traditionally found around the Great Lakes in the eighteenth century and, being Iroquoian speaking, were accepted in 1722 as the sixth nation of the Iroquois Confederacy.

Twin Island Lake

This lake is just to the east of Fossil Lake, between Molar and Russell Lakes, and is listed on the USGS topo maps of 2000 and earlier. The lake is still there, but since 2011, no name has been attached to it on the USGS maps and it has been removed from the Geographic Names Information System website with no explanation. Perhaps they were embarrassed by the fact that there are three islands in this lake, even though the two southern ones could be considered twins.

Twin Lakes

There are three sets of Twin Lakes.

The ones on the Fossil Lake quad are south of Russell Lake and just above Russell Creek. Looking down into the basin, they do indeed appear to be twins.

The second set of Twin Lakes is more well known. They sit just north of the Beartooth Highway in Wyoming and were an important landmark in the highway's construction. Section A went from Red Lodge to Twin Lakes, and Section B from these lakes to the L bar T Ranch on the Clarks Fork. They are easily seen from the highway just southwest of the 45th parallel marker, and their proximity to the road makes them a goal of day anglers. They were first stocked with fish in 1924 when two names from the early history of the area, O.J. Salo and "Packsaddle" Ben Greenough, packed them in.

These Twin Lakes on the Beartooth Highway have, since the 1940s, taken advantage of the altitude and the persistent snow well into summer to attract skiers looking for adventure. In 1957, the High Road Summer Slalom held its first race on the Gardner Headwall. The nearby headwall above Twin Lakes is the site of the Red Lodge International Ski Camp where, starting in 1966, Austrian Olympic medalists Pepi Gramshammer and Anderl Molterer, and U.S. National Junior coach Erik Sailer trained future Olympic racers. (see Gardner Lake)

Initially served by a steep uphill trudge and later by a makeshift rope tow driven off the rear wheel of a Jeep, the Beartooth Basin Summer Ski Area currently operates under a Forest Service permit on 600 acres with two platter-like Pomalifts that were installed in 1994. The racers' summer ski camp has continued under the auspices of the local Silver Run Ski Team.

The third set of Twin Lakes is a tiny pair in the Stillwater drainage just off Fishtail Creek south of Dean. They are maintained for irrigation, and the old headgate and irrigation structures have recently been improved.

Twin Outlets Lake

East Rosebud Creek goes from Dewey Lake to Twin Outlets Lake before continuing down to Impasse Falls. There is an S-shaped wiggle as the creek exits the lake where there appears to have been a double outlet. There is now only one, as the southern bay blind ends. There was, however, clearly a second, or twin, outlet in the past.

Twin Peaks

This prominent landmark in the Stillwater mining district was called Squaw Saddle Butte by the Crow Indians. It was a very descriptive and appropriate name for a double summit but could not be used after 2004 with the removal of all the "squaw" references in Montana. Perhaps "Woman's Saddle" would have been a more interesting and acceptable name and would have kept the Crow reference.

Two Bits Lake

Two Bits Lake is situated on the west side of Beartooth Mountain and has also been called Tuesday Lake.

A "bit," now popularized with the Bitcoin cryptocurrency, first came to use in the U.S. in the colonial period when the Spanish *reale,* or dollar, was a common unit of currency. These were also known as "pieces of eight," and a bit was 1/8 of a reale. With the adoption of decimal currency by the U.S. in 1794, there was no longer 1/8 of a dollar, but there was a quarter of a dollar, or 25 cents, which was colloquially called "two bits." The term remains in the language, and its secondary meaning is probably the derivation of the name of this lake—something of small worth or importance.

Two Mile Bridge

Because the bridge crosses the Main Boulder River two miles south of Contact near the Falls Creek Campground, it was given this unique name.

Two Sisters

The mountain was named in 1925 for the dual peaks that overlook the Stillwater River. It was mistakenly called Twin Sisters on earlier maps, but this was corrected in the 1950s.

Upsidedown Creek

The Upsidedown Creek Trail leads east from Hicks Park on the Main Boulder and goes up to the Lake Plateau. Its steep ascent and numerous switchbacks attest to the creek's precipitous fall of some 2,000 feet in a mile and a half. Descending this stream will leave you upside down.

Van Dyke Spring

Lewis Henry Van Dyke came to Montana in 1885 and settled first on Cedar Creek north of Gardiner. He opened a meat market in the coal mining town of Horr/Aldridge and was also the beef supplier for the hotel concessionaires in Yellowstone Park. In 1904 he acquired the Chadbourn Ranch from George Wakefield, which lies between Stephens Creek and Gardiner. (see Rainbow Lake) He opened a large butcher shop in Gardiner, which ran until 1922, then moved north to Livingston where he served as a Park County commissioner in the 1930s.

Varve Lake

Varve Lake, on the south slope of Castle Mountain, at 10,466 feet, is the second-highest fishery in the state of Montana.

Varve is a geologic term that refers to an annual layer of sediment or sedimentary rock that forms in brackish or fresh water. While it usually refers to one whole layer, it can also mean an exposed series of layers, and it is this latter meaning that attaches to this lake. As one looks east across the lake, the cliff side opposite appears as a whole series of laminated layers that looks like a giant stack of pancakes.

There is an alternate name of Forsaken Lake that appears on some maps. Fortunately, the USGS has applied this more interesting scientific description instead of the grim reminder of some hiker's love life.

Lake Vengence

This lake can be found in the north cirque of the Two Sisters. It is another with Desolation, Trouble, Dreary, Forsaken, Abandoned, and Nightmare Lakes that are thought to represent the nasty weather that can be found in the high mountains. The word's misspelling is correct according to the USGS.

Verdigris Creek

Verdigris, from the French for gray-green, is the common name for a pigment that is usually obtained through the application of acetic acid to copper. It is also the natural patina formed when copper, brass, or bronze is weathered by exposure to air or seawater.

The name of this creek on the Stillwater River near the Mouat Mine at Woodbine comes from the fact that the Stillwater mining district had much exposed copper that weathered to this color. It is said that in the 1890s 3 percent copper ore could just be loaded into wagons without mining.

Vernon Lake

The specific Vernon who gave his name to this lake near the Montana/Wyoming border just east of Cooke City could not be found. The name appears before 1937, so it is possible that it comes from Professor J.L. Vernon, a Bozeman teacher who absconded with the school's library funds in 1873. He reappeared in Montana shortly thereafter claiming that he had discovered gold on Wolf Mountain, which is north of Cooke City near Goose Lake. Showing that you can fool some of the people some of the time, he raised funds for an expedition out of Cooke City, but ran off with the money and disappeared before they got to any gold.

Mount Villard

James P. Kimball climbed and named this mountain during his 1898 survey of the Beartooths. As was typical for that time, he honored one of the nation's wealthiest capitalists, an investor in the Red Lodge coal mines, president of the Northern Pacific Railroad, and one of his backers. It is one of Montana's highest peaks at 12,329 feet and is found just west of Granite Peak.

Henry Villard. WIKI CREATIVE COMMONS.

Henry Villard (1835–1900) was the epitome of the American emigrant and capitalist. He was born Ferdinand Heinrich Gustav Hilgard in Bavaria and, after clashes with his father over politics, was sent to a semi-military academy in France. He ran away from that as a teenager and emigrated to the United States where he changed his name to avoid being sent back to Europe. In the U.S. he started as a war correspondent, but became interested in railroads. During the 1870s he acquired several of them, but his greatest coup was buying the Northern Pacific Railroad after Jay Cooke's bankruptcy. During his ownership he completed the transcontinental route by driving the gold spike at Gold Creek, Montana, in 1883. He was a strong promoter of Thomas Edison and established what was to become General Electric Corporation. Returning to his journalism roots, he also acquired the *New York Evening Post* and *The Nation.* (see Hilgard Peak in *Bozeman's Backyard*)

Vogel Lake

Vogel Lake's name came with the scramble of names among Summit, Snowbank, and Castle Mountains and Lakes. It was known as Summit Lake on the 1937 maps, but when Snowbank Lake was changed to Summit Lake, this Summit Lake needed a new name. (see Summit, Castle Rock, Castle, and Snowbank Mountains for the rest of the naming gymnastics)

Vogel Lake was an appropriate choice as Ernest Vogel was a good friend of Fred Inabnit (see Mount Inabnit) and, along with Sierra Club mountaineers, was credited with the second successful ascent of Granite Peak.

Wagon Box Road

Wagon Box Road is a dirt track that is found as a short spur north of the Beartooth Highway along Lake Creek. It was named for a wagon box that served as a coffin and burial site for Frank Hammitt.

The Shoshone National Forest was the first forest signed into law in 1891, and in 1898 Frank was hired to serve there as one of the first six forest rangers appointed in the U.S. He died in 1903 at age 34 either by accident or suicide when he fell 1,000 feet off a cliff on nearby Antelope Mountain. One of his friends recovered the body and put it in his wagon box, which was taken to this site. The box was placed against a steep rock wall and boulders were carefully put around the sides and rocks placed on top. Remnants of the box and site still remain.

In 1938, some 35 years later, the CCC placed a memorial to Hammitt at the base of Antelope Mountain on Wyoming Highway 296 where Crandall Road follows Russell Creek. There is some question as to whether some of Frank's remains may also have been buried near the memorial site.

Wall Lake

There are two Wall Lakes. One is north of Cooke City near Goose lake, and the other is on the Beartooth Plateau just south of the Wyoming line. Both are named for the steep cirque wall behind the lake that leads to a rather vertical shoreline.

Mount Wallace/Creek

Henry Cantrell Wallace (1866–1924) was the Secretary of Agriculture, first under President Warren G. Harding, then under President Calvin Coolidge after Harding's death. The U.S. Forest Service is a division of the Department of Agriculture, and thus was under Wallace's supervision. He died in office in 1924, and the following year the Forest Service suggested that this peak be named **Mount Wallace** in his honor. It is a prominent point at the head of Mill Creek with magnificent views of the Paradise Valley.

Henry Cantrell Wallace. PHOTO BY GEORGE GRANTHAM, BAIN COLLECTION, LIBRARY OF CONGRESSS.

Interestingly, his son, Henry A. Wallace, followed his father's footsteps and became Secretary of Agriculture, Secretary of Commerce, and Vice President under President Franklin Delano Roosevelt.

Wallace Creek is named for the mountain that it is on.

Wand Lake

Wand Lake is south of Mount Rosebud near Lake of the Woods. It has a prior name of Amphitheater Lake because the box canyon in which it is found is shaped like a Roman amphitheater. It is a narrow, bent lake with an irregular shoreline that someone must have thought looked like a magic wand. Perhaps the "wand" is the orchestra conductor's baton that was used for a performance in the amphitheater.

Wapiti Mountain

Wapiti is another name for elk. The word arrived in English around the mid-nineteenth century from the Shawnee words meaning "white rump." The 9,413-foot mountain of this name is located southwest of Red Lodge where Rock Creek and the Beartooth Highway swing around its eastern and southern flank.

War Eagle Mountain

This was named for the War Eagle Mine, one of Chalky Benbow's claims, which can be found near Bridge Creek on the north slope of this mountain. The claims are a bit east of Nye and on a nine-mile dirt road that goes south out of Dean. (see Benbow Mine)

Washburn Mountain

A fellow named Washburn had a ranch in the vicinity of the Meyers Creek Ranger Station, and Meyers Creek flows around the south side of Mount Washburn.

Washoe Creek

Washoe was a common name in the nineteenth-century West and comes from the Washoe Indian tribe that lived on the Nevada/California border. This tribe gave its name to a creek in California, and to a valley, creek, and the county in Nevada where Reno is the county seat.

This creek is near Red Lodge in coal mining country. The Anaconda Company had interests in Washoe, Nevada, and called their smelter in Anaconda, Montana, The Washoe. When they opened their Red Lodge coal mine in 1907, they formed a company town they called Washoe, and the nearby creek was named for the town.

Washtub Lake

The lake is located on the western slope of Mid Mountain above the Broadwater River. One must ascribe its name to its oval shape rather than the cleanliness of the miners.

Weasel Lake

Least weasel. PHOTO BY STEVE HILLEBRAND, U.S. FISH AND WILDLIFE SERVICE.

The small lake that is located on the north slope of Oxide Mountain near the head of the Sodalite drainage gets its name from these commonly seen predators of the genus *Mustela*. Weasels have long, slender bodies that are perfectly adapted for pursuing their primary prey, rodents, down their holes. They are active in the winter in the subnivean world, when they can be seen in their beautiful, white ermine phase.

West Chippy Creek on the Boulder River had a brief run as the more polite **Weasel Creek,** but that name didn't stick with the miners, so it formally reverted to West Chippy. The cluster of small lakes at its head are all officially unnamed, but are sometimes called the Weasel Lakes. (see Chippy Creek)

Weeluna Lake

This little lake is found up the West Rosebud, above Mystic Lake and, appropriately, next to Memidgi Lake.

Weeluna is the name of the beautiful Indian maiden in the story that Jim Annin, the owner and editor of the *Columbus News,* wrote in 1916. According to him, she lived by the Stillwater River and was in love with Memidgi, a great hunter, but the wedding was not to be. There are various versions of what came next. The version from the Montana Historical Society says that they were forbidden to marry, so jumped into the river and drowned in each others arms. In Jim Annin's own book, he says that after finding the elk that saved her tribe from starvation she died of exposure. When her burial platform blew into the river in a storm, Memidgi jumped in to save her body and died in a mudslide with Weeluna in his arms. Where the bodies came to rest was called the hallowed water, and was mistranslated as Still Water.

This is a lovely story that was given credence by the fact that Annin published the authentic Crow legends of Little Face that had been recorded by Lt. James H. Bradley in the 1870s. Perhaps the fact that Annin translated Weeluna as "Little Moon" would give you a clue, but the author's Crow sources state that Annin's story is pure fabrication.

Wepler Cabin

This cabin is noted on the USGS Sliderock Mountain quad and can be found in the Iron Mountain Mining District on Ellis Mountain in Deer Creek country.

It may have had its start as a mining cabin, but it is now used primarily as a retreat and hunting cabin. There are Weplers of several families and generations in the area north of the Absaroka-Beartooths, and I am told that this cabin is owned by the Weplers of Rapelje.

Whirlpool Creek

This is an obviously wild, swirling stream. It can be found on the north slope of Castle Rock Mountain.

Whitcomb Lake

Whitcomb Lake is found on the Castle Mountain quad in the Martin Basin cluster of lakes along with Martin, Wright, and Spogen Lakes, and is just to the north of the Montana/Wyoming line.

It had earlier names as Robin and Hunter Lake but is now named for Arnold O. Whitcomb (1909–2004), who came to Red Lodge from Minnesota in 1925. He had a wrecker service, sold Willy's Jeeps, and owned Whitcomb's Oil and Gas, the oldest

A.O. Whitcomb. CARBON COUNTY MUSEUM.

Mobil Oil dealer in Montana. Many of his relations are still listed in the Red Lodge census.

A.O. was an active member of the Red Lodge Rod and Gun Club, and in 1936, the year that the club planted 325,384 trout in the Beartooth country, he and George Throop took 16,000 trout into the Glacier Lake area. (see Spogen Lake and Throop Lake)

White City

The former White City is now a ghost town up Emigrant Gulch above Chico with only one building of the busy miner's hamlet remaining. It was started by Billy Carr, who patented the Hy-Grade Placer machine that was used in hydraulic mining. With it he basically power washed the gulch for the remaining placer gold, and the remnants of the pipeline and the scars from the hydraulic mining can still be seen.

His mining camp, which had a power plant and running water, was known as "White City" because all of the log cabins were whitewashed. Carr gained some notoriety for organizing a trust in his Hy-Grade Mine, which he supposedly over-sold many times. Many considered it mail fraud, but he was never prosecuted.

White Draw/Spring

Dudley White (1875–1957) arrived in Montana in 1905 and filed a homestead in 1915 on Lodgepole Creek near Nye in the Limestone Butte country, just south of

Bad Canyon. He ran cattle on what he called the Lodge Pole Ranch and owned the land on the lower portion of White Draw. The spring is up this draw.

Whitetail Peak

Whitetail Peak, the fourth-highest mountain in Montana at 12,548 feet, sits to the north of Beartooth Mountain across Lake Fork Creek.

Dudley White. JIM ANNIN COLLECTION MUSEUM OF THE BEARTOOTHS, #187.

There are two stories as to the source of this mountain's name. It was first recorded on a map in 1918 that came from Forest Supervisor James Whitham's survey of the area in 1914–1915. It apparently was said to have come from the ice- and snow-filled couloir that drops several thousand feet down the mountain, giving it a "white tail" year-round.

A more interesting story comes from "Packsaddle" Ben Greenough of Red Lodge. (see Greenough Lake) In 1940 he claimed that he shot the tail off a white-tail deer, *Odocoileus virginianus*, on this mountain. That is a bit of a stretch as the peak is over 12,000 feet and way out of this deer's usual habitat of river bottoms, grain fields, and

White-tailed deer. USDA PHOTO BY SCOTT BAUER.

foothills. However, Greenough was one of the great characters of the eastern Beartooths, so his tale needs to be remembered.

Whittaker Spring

This spring can be found at the head of Bad Canyon Creek just east of the former town of Limestone and northwest of Nye. It was named for Charles Whitaker, an early settler who obtained the deed to his ranch land there in 1925. Note that the official name is misspelled with two "t"s.

Wicked Creek

Wicked Creek is in the Mill Creek Mining District north of Emigrant. An early ranger wrote, "It is as wicked a creek that I have ever tried to descend."

Widewater Lake

The name of this lake comes from a large widening of Russell Creek on the Montana/Wyoming border. It drains into Big Moose Lake and thus into the Crazy Creek system.

Widowed Lake

The lowest lake in the Desolation Lake chain, Widowed is another of the depressing names that were supposedly generated by the nasty weather in the high country.

Wiedy Lake

With Marsh, Swamp, and Mosquito Lakes nearby in the Broadwater drainage, this is either a misspelling of weedy or a bad pun on some poor fellow's name. The USGS does not specify. As one might assume, it is a "high density" mosquito area.

Wild Bill Lake

Hickock didn't get farther west than Deadwood, South Dakota, so scratch that romantic notion. This Wild Bill was William Kurtzer, a hermit who held squatters' rights to the area around this lake starting in 1902. It is a short, easy drive from Red Lodge to the West Fork of Rock Creek Road where he dammed the lake's outlet, stocked it with whitefish, and rented flat-bottomed boats to anglers. When he died in 1935, the land reverted to the federal government. The U.S. Forest Service restored it in 1978 with a lovely picnic area, a half-mile National Recreation Trail, and a disabled-accessible boardwalk with fishing docks. It is stocked with catchable-sized rainbow trout four times a year—just prior to holidays.

Wild Bill Kurtzer, photo from Red Lodge, *Saga of a Western Area*. USDA FOREST SERVICE, CUSTER-GALLATIN NATIONAL FOREST PHOTO ARCHIVES.

Wildcat Draw/Spring No 1 and No 2/ Mountain/Lakes

Wildcat Draw and Springs are on the quad of that name in the northeast corner of the national forest. Wildcat Mountain and Lakes are on the Pinnacle Mountain quad in the Wounded Man Creek country.

Although wildcat wells refer to oil wells drilled in an area not known to have an oil field, this is hardrock mining country where the similar term is a prospect. Thus these features get their name from the common name for any of several smaller members of the cat family. In this location, it would be referring to the bobcat, *Lynx rufus,* rather than its larger but more secretive cousin, the Canadian lynx, *Lynx canadensis.* (see Cat Creek)

Wildness Lake

Ed Ickerman, from the Beartooth Ranch, named it Wilderness Lake for its remote location near Lake Wood and Mount Hague, which are found a bit east of his ranch. It was known as Wilderness Lake on the USGS maps through 1996, but for reasons unknown, it became Wildness Lake on the 2011 map and has remained so. Although the location is in the Absaroka-Beartooth Wilderness, and the word "wildness" properly refers to teenage behavior, the Board on Geographic Names website has kept it officially Wildness. One must suppose that this change was originally a misspelling that reflected upon the cartographer's behavioral issues with his adolescent daughter, and the problem spilled over into his work.

Willow Creek

Willow Creek was obviously named for the willows that grow along its banks. Willows are any of the nearly 400 species of the genus *Salix* and are very common along Montana's streams and boggy meadows where they serve as a major food for elk and are important in preventing streamside erosion.

Prior to World War II, the Rocky Fork Mining Company had a logging camp here to provide props for its mines.

Ski Run Road is just outside of the town of Red Lodge and goes up along this creek to the ski resort. The former Willow Run ski site was built here by the CCC in the 1930s and existed from 1941 to 1958, until the larger and better Red Lodge Mountain Resort supplanted it.

Willow Park

The flat, swampy area along the Clarks Fork of the Yellowstone River is called Willow Park for its dominant vegetation. It is just north of the Beartooth Highway in the Wyoming section of the Absaroka-Beartooth Wilderness.

Bud Hart had his cabin here. In 1931 he got into an altercation at a Cooke City bar with Les Lightener and Walt McCall where a couple of shots were fired. No one was hurt, but Lightener and McCall set out for Hart's cabin at Willow Park to settle the score—or were claim jumping. Bud shot and killed them both and was acquitted on grounds of justifiable homicide. (see Lake Abundance/Creek)

Mount Wilse

Anders Beer Wilse (1865–1949) emigrated from Norway to Seattle in 1890 where he worked as a surveyor, engineer, cartographer, and commercial photographer. He was hired by James P. Kimball in 1898 to accompany his expedition to the Beartooths and was assigned to "prepare a map of the Granite Range [Beartooths] with the aid of photographs, a plane table, a barometer, and a compass." His photographs, published in the *Bulletin of the American Geographic Society of New York*, became quite famous. During the

Anders Wilse, 1892. PHOTO BY BOYD AND BRAAS.

expedition, he climbed this peak to get a photograph of Grasshopper Glacier, and named it for himself.

He left the U.S. in 1900 for a visit to Norway and never returned.

Windy Gap/Glacier

The gap between Sundance and Castle Mountains was known as **Windy Gap** on a 1937 map, but that name is no longer found on the current maps.

Windy Glacier sat to the east of the gap but is now just labeled "Snowfield."

Winge Draw

This draw is on the northeast corner of the national forest and was named for Peder Winge. Born in Norway in 1882, he came to the U.S. in 1900, and to Columbus, Montana, in 1908. There he operated a livery stable and drove the stage from Absarokee to Limestone. He filed a homestead at this draw in 1923 and married Benton Serrett in 1929. His descendants still ranch in the Fishtail area.

Peder Winge. JIM ANNIN COLLECTION, MUSEUM OF THE BEARTOOTHS, #158.

Wolf Mountain/Glacier/Lakes

Wolf Glacier, and **Wolf Lake** below it, are on **Wolf Mountain** north of Cooke City, where they are the headwaters of West Rosebud Creek.

The mountain's name first appears on a 1947 national forest map, but it was named in the early twentieth century by the miners at nearby Goose Lake who saw an occasional wolf on the flanks of the mountain. (see Lake Vernon) The gray or timber wolf, *Canis lupus*, was the dominant predator with a large population in Montana throughout the early years of white settlement. However, loss

Cool wolf. PHOTO BY HANS STRICKLER.

of habitat and human conflicts with bounty killing and poisoning led to their extinction in the state in the 1930s. Listing as an endangered species was the beginning of their natural recolonization around Glacier National Park in 1979. Then in 1995 and 1996, wolves were reintroduced to Yellowstone National Park and their population rapidly increased. They have now spread and there are several packs active north of the Park in the Custer-Gallatin National Forest. They can once again be seen occasionally on the flanks of Wolf Mountain.

Wolf Voice Lake

Wolf Lake is on the east side of Wolf Mountain. Wolf Voice Lake is on its north side. How great to be able to hear a pack howling again.

Wolverine Creek/Pass/Peak

Wolverine Peak is located at the extreme northeast corner of Yellowstone Park where the Custer-Gallatin National Forest and the Absaroka-Beartooth Wilderness meet, and it is from here that the Stillwater River starts its northward journey.

Wolverine Creek flows the other direction, south off this mountain, to join Slough Creek just north of the Park boundary. The Lost Wolverine Trail, which goes from Daisy Pass over **Wolverine Pass** on the saddle of the north shoulder of this mountain, was one of the main routes used by Cooke City miners to prospect around on this mountain as well as the Wolverine Creek and upper Slough Creek country.

The wolverine, *Gulo gulo* (Latin for "glutton") is the largest member of the Mustelid or weasel family. It is found in northern boreal forests, is quite solitary, quite ferocious, and is endangered because of loss of habitat. Its stocky frame makes it look like a small bear, and its coloring has led to its nickname of "skunk bear."

Wolverine. NATIONAL PARK SERVICE.

Mount Wood/Lake

At 12,649 feet Mount Wood is the second-highest peak in Montana. As the high point of the Stillwater Plateau it looms over that river and the Beartooth Ranch. The Beartooth Ranch's proximity has given rise to an incorrect assertion about the source of the mountain's name. Byron Wood homesteaded the ranch in 1892, and some people felt that the peak was named for him. However, A.B. Wood was with James P. Kimball on his 1898 survey of the Beartooths, and he and Anders Wilse climbed it that summer. Kimball, in his report, says that he named it "in honor of my friend and companion, who took the elevation, and whose aid and energy in mountain-work many of the more important results of the survey are to be ascribed." (see Mount Wilse and Woodbine Falls/Creek)

Wood Lake is on the shoulder of the mountain and drains via Lake Wildness into Woodbine Creek. Woodbine Creek (see below) certainly was named for Byron Wood, and the creek from Wood Lake to Lake Wildness, now unnamed, was once called Cora Creek for Byron's wife. These facts would lead one to conclude that Wood Lake got its name both from Byron Wood as well as from A. B. Wood's mountain that it sits on.

Woodbine Falls/Creek

Byron Wood was a Cooke City miner who came to the Stillwater River country in 1892 and homesteaded a ranch across the river from this creek and falls. Not wanting to use his own name, and because the creek comes off Mount Wood, he used the woody vine, false Virginia creeper or grape woodbine, *Parthenocissus vitacea*, that is commonly found in Montana.

Woodbine, *Parthenocissus vitacea*. MISSOURI DEPARTMENT OF CONSERVATION FIELD GUIDE.

Wood's ranch started as a 40-acre homestead that expanded and changed from a cattle operation to a dude ranch. Wood sold it in 1921 to Ed Ickerman, who renamed it the Beartooth Ranch. (see citation)

Dramatic **Woodbine Falls** can be seen from the Nye Road near the Beartooth Ranch entrance. A short and well-maintained 1.4-mile out-and-back trail to the falls starts at the Woodbine USFS campground at the end of the road. Woodbine Creek, which tumbles precipitously off the Stillwater Plateau, has created a 280-foot waterfall that is one of the tallest in Montana.

John Mouat relates the story of the "Legend of Woodbine Falls." In it a Blackfeet warrior named Big Nose kidnapped the Crow maiden Pretty Bird. Her father and friends caught up with him at the top of these falls, and he was shot with an arrow and fell into the water. His body was never found, but when the water in the falls is reduced due to drought, the rock behind it is exposed. At a place about three-quarters of the way down, an image like the Indian Head nickel can be seen in the rock—all that is left of Big Nose.

Woods Gulch

Ranger notes from the 1930s assert that this was not named for a person but came from what the local settlers called the area. Before the formation of the Beartooth (now Custer-Gallatin) National Forest in 1908, this gulch was burned over and lots of dead wood and pitch posts were left.

Woody Creek

"This is the perfect time to panic!" No, really, Woody from the movie *Toy Story* was never known to have been sighted here, so the name must come from the large number of trees along the banks.

Wounded Man Lake/Creek

There are two Wounded Man Creeks and one Wounded Man Lake. All are in the same general vicinity.

Wounded Man Lake is the headwaters of the North Fork of the creek of the same name. According to the 1900 *Tri-County Atlas* and restated in the Forest Service notes of the 1930s, the lake was supposedly named because an old trapper and miner was badly injured by a bear near the lake.

The **Wounded Man Creek** that most refer to is a tributary of the Stillwater River and drains the area from Pinnacle Mountain north to the Lake Plateau. The story for this is also in the 1900 *Tri-County Atlas* and from Beartooth Ranger District notes of 1960. In that account, a Northern Pacific Railroad survey crew was caught in a forest fire near the creek in 1887 or '88 and one of the members, a Peter Ginsterblum, suffered a skull fracture. His crew took him by stretcher to Old Nye where Dr. Line was summoned from Columbus, but Ginsterblum died before the doctor could arrive. Both stories may be correct as one refers to the lake and the other the creek

This was apparently not a healthy part of the Absaroka-Beartooths as there is a second **Wounded Man Creek** just to the south of Pinnacle Mountain and the South Fork of (the other) Wounded Man Creek. This one, however, is part of a different drainage, as it flows west off the mountain to Slough Creek. No particular story could be found as to the man or his injury that generated the name of this creek. It may well have been confused as the site of the Ginsterblum accident.

Wright Gulch

Wright Gulch is near the East Boulder Mine north of Contact Mountain and was named for a William Wright. He initially came to Montana as a federal government Indian agent, then joined W.C. Officer and his crew as they scouted the route for a railroad from Bozeman to Miles City. One of the first to take up ranching in the Boulder Valley, he also participated in the Boulder gold rush and had a cabin and worked his mine on the west ridge of this gulch between 1893 and 1901. He disappeared shortly thereafter and was believed to have drowned while trying to cross the Yellowstone River.

Wright Lake

Charles E. Wright (1867–1915) gave his name to this lake that sits in the cluster of lakes in the Martin Lake Basin south of Red Lodge on the Wyoming border. The spectacular waterfall between Wright and Spogen Lakes is well worth the visit.

Wright originally came to the area in 1884 to work the huge Dilworth Ranch east of Red Lodge, and followed John Tolman as its foreman in 1892. In 1896, after the Dilworth Ranch folded, he and his brother, Fred, filed for homesteads in the East Rosebud Canyon. Charles was active in community affairs and was elected treasurer of Carbon County in 1900 and served two terms. He married Ida Lamport, the daughter of the manager of the Bear Creek Coal Mine in 1901, and they moved to their Mountain View Ranch closer to town. He died tragically in 1915 at age 48 when lightning struck, killing both him and his horse. Charles and Ida's daughter married Bronson Tolman. (see Tolman Point/Mountain/Flat)

Wrong Lake

There is no Wright Lake nearby. Since this Wrong Lake is on the west slope of Courthouse Mountain in the upper Stillwater River country, one might think that the officers of the law who worked Courthouse Mountain were out to right some wrongs. Hmmm…

The name's true derivation actually does involve Courthouse Lake. A Montana Fish, Wildlife and Parks summer employee was sent to Courthouse to do a scheduled stocking. He got confused and placed the fish here, in the wrong lake.

Wyoming Creek

Reflecting the location near this state's border with Montana, the creek starts about three-quarters of a mile south of the Wyoming line near the Highland Lakes Trail. It then flows north into Montana to pass under the Beartooth Highway and join Rock Creek near Greenough Lake.

Yankee Jim Canyon

Ferdinand Hayden called this canyon "Butter Keg" for a cask that was lost down the cliffs. However, the longtime presence of the toll road keeper and noted character soon had everyone calling it his canyon.

Yankee Jim at his cabin.
PHOTO COURTESY MUSEUM OF THE ROCKIES.

"Yankee Jim" George came to Montana in 1863, prospecting first at Bannack but moving to the region of Yellowstone Park as early as 1866. That year he discovered the coal deposits near Red Lodge, but they were on the Crow Reservation and could not be developed, so he worked as a meat hunter for the Crow Agency. By 1873 he had squatted in this canyon, a narrowing of the Yellowstone River gorge just north of present-day Gardiner.

A year earlier, A. Bart Henderson, John Curl, Joe Brown, and "Horn" Miller had built a road that ran along a travois trail on the west side of the river. It was designed to supply the miners at Cooke City, but when they failed to get a federal charter to charge a toll, they abandoned the scheme. Yankee Jim took it over and got the authorization for the toll road in 1879. He ran it until 1910 when Park County bought it and made it a public right-of-way. Although his cabin and toll road were on the west side of the river, most people now know the canyon from the Absaroka side as U.S. Highway 89, built in 1950, goes along the east side.

Yankee Jim, always known as "the most luridly picturesque liar in the Northwest," was brought to international fame in 1899 by Rudyard Kipling's book, *From Sea to Sea: Letters of Travel*. It described his trip from India to England via America, and in it, he devoted a complete section to Yankee Jim. Kipling described him as "a picturesque old man with a talent for yarns." And also thought that he was "a whopping liar."

Jim left the canyon in 1920 to spend the remainder of his old age with his brother in California.

Yodel Lake

This little lake at the head of the West Fork of the Boulder River is high on the side of Mount Cowen. It is not recognized by the USGS, and the name is only found on Montana Fish, Wildlife and Parks documents. It is, however, a good place to let forth with your Swiss warble.

Z Hill

This is an unofficial name for a hill near Gardiner, Montana, that came from the appearance of the switchbacking wagon road that ran up it.

Although it is no longer named and the switchbacks have been replaced by a modern road, it is mentioned for an event in 1899. Maurice A. Burke, the general manager and an engineer for the Bear Gulch Mining Company, was riding with Alfred Blair in a buggy from Jardine to Gardiner when the horses ran away down the hill. The buggy overturned and Burke died of head and neck injuries.

Z Lake

Apparently, Zorro must have been around when this lake was created. The Board on Geographic Names changed the name from Shallow Lake to reflect its Z shape.

Mount Zimmer/Lake/Creek

Mount Zimmer sits to the north of Cooke City near Goose Lake. Along with Iceberg Peak, it holds the neve, or firn, at the top of Grasshopper Glacier. If you follow the Lady of the Lake Trail north from Colter Pass, you will come to the **Zimmer Creek** Trail, which follows that creek to **Zimmer Lake** on the east side of Zimmer Mountain.

The *Butte Semi-Weekly Miner* reported in its January 14, 1888, edition on a mining consortium that was formed in 1881 of Northern Pacific Railroad executives and eastern capitalists "for the purpose of discovering and developing mines at the head of the Clark's Fork." A Charley Simmer was sent out the following spring to prospect for the company, and "made a number of locations, including a lofty granite peak in the Bear Tooth range which still bears the name Simmer Mountain." When the Kimball Survey Expedition went through in 1898 it was already known as Mount Zimmer. Although the name of this mountain most probably refers to a misspelling of Charley Simmer, it could also be referring to W.T. Zimmer, one of the old Cooke City miners who, in the late 1880s, had a claim on the Maclean quartz lode a few miles to the south. There were only a few claims subsequently filed on Mount Zimmer itself, and none were successful.

Zoeteman Lake

Peter Zoeteman (1888–1973) was born in the Netherlands and emigrated to America with his parents at age 14. He married Laura Schnitker in Billings in 1920, and, after moves to Red Lodge and Meeteetse, Wyoming, they came to Nye in 1948. Their descendants continue to live in Montana's Beartooth country.

The Zoeteman ranch is on the bluff overlooking the Stillwater River just west of Nye, and this lake is on their property.

THE CRAZIES

Day Greets the Crazy Mountains. PHOTO COURTESY RICK GRAETZ.

The Crazy Mountains are one of the largest exposed blocks of igneous rocks in the world. They rise out of the prairie north of Big Timber and the Yellowstone River and, being an "island range," are not connected to any other mountain ranges. They were formed by an intrusion of magma that pushed up into the central Montana plains, an isolated thrust without volcanos. Geologically isolated as they may be, the Crazies are still high, containing 23 peaks over 10,000 feet, and their rise of 7,000 feet from the Yellowstone River to the summit of Crazy Peak is one of the most dramatic in Montana. They are also rugged because, protruding above the continental glacier, they were not flattened. Thus, their smaller montane glaciers were able to create the scattered high cirque lakes and jagged contours of the peaks that are seen today.

The Crazies' geographic position, rising high off the prairie, exposes them to some wild winds. The stark rocky profile, windy conditions, and unpredictable weather led the Crow to call them *Awaxaawippiia*, the "ominous" or "mad" mountains. Mad was translated as "crazy," and the name was in common use by the 1870s.

There are various other legends for the source of the Crazy Mountains' name. The most prosaic is that it was due to the profusion of locoweed or crazyweed at their base. But the most interesting is the one professed by the Montana Historical Society website, *Montana Place Names from Alzada to Zortman*. This story reflects Capt. William Raynolds topographic map of 1860 where he was the first to call them the Crazy Woman Mountains. His name refers to an undocumented story of a white woman whose wagon train was attacked by Indians and her husband and children were all killed. She went insane with grief and wandered into these mountains to haunt the Indians.

Whatever the true origin of the name, they are the Crazy Mountains, a place of vision quests for the Native American and a wild place of nature and spiritual revival for the modern Montanan.

Amelong Creek

Amelong Creek is on the far eastern border of the national forest and is a tributary of Big Timber Creek. It was named for Christopher Amelong, a miner from Melville, who filed for water rights in 1888.

Once known as North American Creek, the name was changed in 1975 to avoid confusion, as it is found just to the south of American Creek.

Bald Ridge

The Bald and Baldy names populate the mountains of southwest and central Montana. A few are above tree line, and the rare hill was cleared by logging, but the majority were, like these ridges, denuded by fire. One of the two Bald Ridges in the Crazies is found on the Rimrock Divide topo and overlooks the Bozeman Fork of the Musselshell River on the northwest corner of the national forest. The other is a northern extension of Sugarloaf Mountain on the upper reaches of the South Fork of the Shields River.

Basin Creek

A "basin" is just that, an area that looks like an old-fashioned washbasin. In geologic terms, it is a circumscribed area within which the rock strata dip toward the center. This creek can be found near the beginning of Sweet Grass Creek and starts in Wolf Park, which is located in a typical basin.

Bear Mountain/Spring

As is probably appropriate for the top of the food chain, there are 31 features named "Bear" in the eight Montana counties covered by this book. This particular **mountain** is on the northwest edge of the Crazies next to Scab Rock Mountain. It has also been locally known as Three Peaks (but is unrelated to the Three Bears in the children's story).

Black bear. NATIONAL PARK SERVICE PHOTO.

Bear Spring can be found at the head of Station Creek on the northeast side of the Crazies.

The black bear, *Ursus americanus*, is the most widespread of North American bears and is found throughout the continent in almost all heavily vegetated and forested areas, and even some semi-urban environments. It is omnivorous, medium-sized at around 200 pounds, and, although named "black bear," also comes with brown- and cinnamon-colored fur as well. Of the same genus, *Ursus*, as the grizzly, they are only distantly related.

Beley Lakes

The Beley homestead is on Swamp Creek on Raspberry Butte near the southwest corner of the national forest. The lakes, at 6,300 feet, are nearby.

The family came early to Park and Sweet Grass Counties. Frank Beley registered a deed in the town of Big Timber in 1887, was mayor of Livingston in 1894, was sheriff in 1902, and also served as Park County commissioner. There was a Beley Saloon and liquor store that Louis Beley started in Big Timber in 1901, which remained an active business through the first part of the twentieth century. Hans Beley, who was born in 1910, had his ranch on Big Timber Creek.

Bennett Creek

Manford E. Bennett (1860–1922) arrived from Iowa in 1879 during the time of the Shields River Valley boom and was honored with his name on this creek that is about three miles upstream from his registered homestead on the Shields River. He was president of the Citizen's State Bank of Clyde Park, was unmarried, and ranched his whole life at this site.

A Forest Service guard station was once located on Bennett Creek, but was moved after a land exchange that was negotiated in 2006.

Big Elk Creek

(see Elk Creek)

Big Timber Peak/Canyon/Creek/Falls/Town

Back in the nineteenth century, some of the largest cottonwood trees in the Yellowstone Valley were found at the mouth of this creek. This gave the name to the creek, and the names of the town and mountain come from the **creek**.

William Clark's detail of the Corps of Discovery passed by here on their return to St. Louis on July 18, 1806. He called the place North and South "Rivers Across" because Big Timber Creek from the north and the Boulder River from the south join the Yellowstone at nearly the same place. The creek starts in **Big Timber Canyon** between Granite and Conical Peaks and comes out on the eastern side of the mountains to head south toward the town. There was once a ranger station on the creek that served as the district headquarters for the southeast Crazies, but this no longer exists.

Not to be confused, there is another named Big Timber Canyon on this creek. It is found just east of the national forest before the creek swings south into the prairie toward the town.

Big Timber Peak is on the east side of the Crazies just south of the creek.

The **town of Big Timber** was originally a trading hamlet and post office called Dornix, which is a Gaelic word meaning "smooth flat stones," and suggests a hand-held rock that is good for throwing. Hmmm, there must be a story behind this. Dornix only existed for a year. When the Northern Pacific Railroad was built through Montana in 1882, the town became a scheduled stop and they moved it a few miles, renaming it Big Timber for its location along the creek. The area of the former townsite of Dornix with its 1895 log cabin and barn was acquired by Big Timber in 1999 and is now a city park. Big Timber became the county seat of the newly formed Sweet Grass County in 1885 and was a major wool shipping point. In the late nineteenth and early twentieth century it was called "the wool capital of the world," as evidenced in 1886 when some 2 million pounds of wool shipped out on the railroad—one of the largest wool export points anywhere. The loss of free grazing, and the Forest Service's restriction on grazing allotments, has greatly reduced the wool volume. However, sheep and wool still remain an important part of the economy, and the name of the Big Timber High School's sports teams, the Sheepherders, reflects that.

Billie Butte/Creek

Billie Butte and nearby Davey Butte are on the west side of the national forest and overlook the Shields River. They were named for the Hamilton brothers, whose family came in 1883 and who were prominent stockmen in the northern end of the Shields River Valley. Active in local affairs, their aunt, Adda Hamilton, was elected the Park County superintendent of schools in 1884 and '86.

The **Billy Creek** that flows from Bald Ridge to Sixteenmile Creek on the north side of Woodchuck Ridge in the northwest corner of the Crazies was named for this William Hamilton as well. This Billy Creek and person is not to be confused with the creek of the same name that can be found east of the Crazies. It enters Sweet Grass Creek near Melville, Montana, and lies outside of this study area.

Bitter Creek

Bitter Creek is a tributary of Smith Creek on the western side of the Crazies. There are many Bitter or Alkali Creeks in Montana, and the name comes from the water's taste. Alkali is a term for the dissolved salts of sodium carbonate, or soda, that are picked up from the sedimentary rock that the stream passes through. It has a high, or alkaline, pH and, besides the bitter taste, can seriously harm plant growth.

Black Butte

Black Butte is on the eastern edge of the national forest between Otter and Amelong Creeks. The Crazies are formed from igneous rock, which tends to be black—think lava. The exposure of the black rock was the reason for the name of the butte.

Black Mountain

This mountain on the west side of the Crazies and on the east ridge of Sugarloaf Mountain was named by the Forest Service prior to the 1930s. Ranger Erwin A.

Schilling's notes say that "the summit has a very black rocky formation and is also covered with a dense tree growth whose shadows give it a black appearance. On sunny days the shadows are especially noticeable during early morning and immediately after sunset."

The South Fork of Shields River starts on its west slope.

Blackaby Creek

The Blackaby whose name is attached to this tributary of the South Fork of American Fork Creek is not identified, and there are no deeds or claims under that name in the Sweet Grass County records. However, there were several people of that name in the area, and they were probably related to the source of this name. The *Harlowton News* mentions a Lizzy Blackaby in 1901, as well as a Joe Blackaby who was a sheepherder for W.B. Cooley and who committed suicide in 1913.

Interestingly, the U.S. Forest Service map calls the road along this creek to the east near Rein Lake, the Blackberry Creek Road. It leaves one to wonder whether the road or the creek is misspelled.

Blacktail Creek

The black-tailed deer is a subspecies of the mule deer, *Odocoileus hemionus.* It was once found as far east as Montana and Wyoming but is now restricted to the Pacific coast from Alaska to northern California.

In the 1930s, the Forest Service reported that the area around this creek on the east slope of Lebo Mountain "was a good feeding ground for the blacktail deer, and had good hunting."

Blue Lake

Obviously named for the way it reflects the color of the high alpine sky, the lake had a bit of a name confusion with its close neighbor, Granite Lake. It was known as Blue Lake on a 1933 map, but sometime thereafter it became Granite Lake. Apparently the Forest Service worker who carried the signs up Big Timber Creek put them on the wrong lakes. This was understandable, as both lakes are at the head of the creek and next to each other in a cirque on the eastern side of Granite Peak. However, it was not corrected until former district ranger Al Roemer and rancher and author Spike Van Cleve both confirmed the proper names in 1975. It is those correct names that are seen on the signs, maps, and lakes today.

Box Canyon on the Bozeman Fork of the Mussselshell River

The Box Canyon on the Bozeman Fork of the Musselshell is in the very northwest corner of the national forest near the head of that river. It fits with the definition of a box canyon with its rather flat bottom and steep walls.

Box Canyon of the Sweet Grass

This "Box Canyon" is not seen on the USGS nor Forest Service maps. However, it is in local use and documented in communications to the USGS by author and rancher Spike Van Cleve.

Sweet Grass Creek flows through prime sheep raising country north of Big Timber, and sheepmen would herd their flocks up the creek to good grazing in the national forest. It is not really a "box canyon" as it is not blind ended and Sweet Grass Creek flows through it. But this narrow, steep-walled defile prevented them from reaching the flat grazing farther up at the head of the creek. To get around it, the herders had to go up the South Fork of American Fork and cross a saddle to the North Fork of Sweet Grass Creek where they could then reach the good grazing upstream of this canyon.

Bozeman Fork of the Musselshell River

The Musselshell River is one of the major streams that drain a large part of central Montana to the Missouri River to the north. Although the town of Bozeman is south and on the other side of the Bridger Range, it gave its name to the Bozeman Fork of this river, which begins in the very northern part of the Crazies and flows along its northern edge

Lewis and Clark put the "Muscle Shell" name on their maps when they passed the mouth on May 19, 1805, as they ascended the Missouri. They were told by the Hidatsa, where they camped that winter, that it was called *Mahtush-ahzha*, meaning "Mussel-shell," and referred to the freshwater mussels found there. It became properly spelled as Musselshell in 1975.

Bruin Creek

This is just another way to have a Bear Creek that is a little different from the 14 other "Bear" names in this book. It enters Sweet Grass Creek flowing north off Conical and Granite Peaks.

Buck Creek

There are lots of "Deer" names in the Custer-Gallatin National Forest, so it is only reasonable that one of them is a "buck." Fawn Creek is over a few ridges to the northeast and also is a tributary of the Shields River. It is not known where the Doe went.

Buzzard Creek

Buzzard Creek flows east off Cinnamon Mountain to join Big Elk Creek out on the prairie, and was named for the very common turkey vulture or buzzard, *Cathartes aura*. These birds are found throughout Montana and are scavengers that feed almost exclusively on carrion. They are typically seen circling on thermals as they cruise in search of their next meal. Buzzards are distinguished from the other large, soaring raptors such as hawks and eagles by their small, bald, red heads; and by the fact that, while soaring, the wings are held in a dihedral, or shallow forward V.

Campfire Lake

Campfire Lake is at the head of the Middle Fork of Sweet Grass Creek and serves as the midway stop on the popular hiking trail that crosses the Crazies from Half Moon Campground on Big Timber Creek to the Ibex Ranger Station out of Clyde Park. By a curious error of omission,

Turkey vulture. PHOTO BY WALLACE KECK, NATIONAL PARK SERVICE.

there is no Campfire Lake on the 2020 USGS Campfire Lake quad. Apparently the cartographer neglected to place the name of the lake on the map. It is Campfire Lake on Forest Service maps, on all of the previous USGS maps, and is confirmed at this location on the Geographic Names Information Service website, so this will certainly be corrected in the near future.

The name and good camping bring to mind images of roasting marshmallows under a starry sky. Actually, no; this name was given to the former Hindu Lake because of a forest fire in the early part of the twentieth century. Kelly Wagner, a Forest Service worker, was camped by the lake, and when he left he had not fully doused his campfire. The fire flared with the wind, and the entire area around the lake was burned.

Cascade Lake

This pretty lake sits in a cirque of an unnamed 10,000-foot peak north of Granite and Big Timber Peaks.

Its outlet creek tumbles down a series of cascades to join Hell Roaring Creek.

Castle Creek

Located on the northernmost part of the Crazies, this creek joins the Middle Fork of Cottonwood Creek at the eastern base of Mount Elmo. It was named for nearby rock formations.

Cave Lake

Cave Lake is in a glacial cirque on the north slope of Conical Peak and serves as the headwaters for Milly Creek.

Many of these high mountain lakes are fed by springs that form from the meltwater of the glaciers and winter snows. Some of the water percolates down until it hits an impermeable rock layer where it then flows horizontally, emerging on the side of the mountain as a spring. If the flow is great enough, a cave will form.

This is reported to be a good fishing lake, and the Montana state record golden trout, *Oncorhynchus aguabonita*, was caught here by Mike Malixi in July 2000. It was a huge 23.5 inches and 5.43 pounds. (see Sylvan Lake in the Absaroka-Beartooths section)

Cinnamon Peak/Creek/Spring/Cave

Cinnamon Peak is in the far northeast corner of the national forest lands in the Crazies. The creek is intermittent and flows north off the mountain of the same name. In the past it was confused on some maps with Spring Creek, which is one drainage to the north. That has been corrected on all current maps. The Cinnamon Spring is on the peak's southeastern slope.

All of these features' names come from the mountain and its color that is formed by iron oxide.

Clear Creek

This is clearly a pretty stream. It joins the Shields River near its origin in the northern Crazies.

Comanche Creek

The Comanche were the dominant tribe of the southern Plain, occupying the lands from eastern New Mexico to southwestern Kansas, and including most of northwest Texas, western Oklahoma, and northern Chihuahua. A powerful tribe, they hardly came near central Montana. So why did they get their name on this creek?

Comanche in 1887. PHOTO BY JOHN C. GRABILL, LIBRARY OF CONGRESS.

Actually, it was not the Indian tribe, but a horse. Comanche was ridden by Captain Keogh, who was with Lt. Col. George Armstrong Custer at the Little Bighorn Battle on June 25, 1876. Custer's entire detachment was killed and Comanche was the sole survivor. He was found, badly wounded, by U.S. soldiers two days after the battle, nursed back to health, and retired. He continued as a bit of a mascot for the 7th Cavalry for the rest of his life. Comanche died at Fort Riley, Kansas, at age 29 and was one of only four horses to be given a military funeral with full military honors. His taxidermy mount can be seen today at the University of Kansas's Natural History Museum.

Comb Creek/Butte

Comb Butte rises up on the prairie near the Musselshell River. Ranger Erwin

A. Schilling reported that the butte's name came from its unique appearance, suggestive of a rooster's comb. The creek gets its name because it passes by this butte after it leaves the northernmost part of the Crazies. It flows north to enter the Musselshell River near Lennep, Montana.

Conical Peak

Don't laugh. It's not spelled with an "m." This mountain really does have the archetypal conical mountain shape of children's drawings. It is located along the Big Timber Creek Trail to Campfire Lake and Trespass Creek. Although high, at 10,751 feet, it is an easy climb that will reward you with wide, stunning views from the middle of the Crazies.

Cottonwood Creek/Lake

There are two Cottonwood Creeks in the Crazies. Both were named for the cottonwood tree, *Populus trichocarpa*, which is so common in the riparian habitats of Montana. The tree is a close cousin to the aspen, which prefers dry slopes, while the cottonwood is found on stream banks and in wetlands.

The most commonly known **Cottonwood Creek** headwaters at **Cottonwood Lake** between Conical and Wilsall Peaks and flows southwest out of the Crazies to meet the Shields River at the town of Clyde Park. Just before it arrives at Clyde Park the creek passes Moolsh Hill, which is the Anglicization of the Salish word for cottonwood. In the early part of the twentieth century, this stream had three names—it was Glacier Creek for the upper three miles, Pine Creek near Clyde Park, and Cottonwood in the middle. In 1925 the Board on Geographic Names consolidated them so that all of the branches became just one Cottonwood Creek. An excellent trail to the lake leads from the Ibex Ranger Station at the end of the road out of Clyde Park. This lovely lake sits in a steep glacial bowl at timberline with Grasshopper Glacier in a hidden pocket above the lake. Carcasses of a swarm of locusts that were killed in a blizzard some 200 years ago are found scattered on the melting surface. (see Grasshopper Glacier)

The second **Cottonwood Creek** flows from Virginia Peak north out of the Crazies where it joins Lost Horse Creek. Its West and Middle Forks pass on either side of Mount Elmo.

Coyote Creek

The coyote, *Canis latrans*, is the most common canine predator in North America. While the wolf was exterminated in most areas, the coyote population has increased, as they were more versatile and adapted to human modification of their

Coyote howling. U.S. FISH & WLDLIFE SERVICE.

environment. It is thought that the coyote was originally an animal of the plains, but it has expanded its range and now can even be found in some urban situations.

In Native American folklore, Coyote is the trickster and uses humor and deception to poke fun at social conventions. The wise hiker avoids coyotes carrying anvils or sticks of dynamite.

This creek is a tributary of Sweet Grass Creek in its upper reaches and joins the names of the other common creatures in our forest—deer, elk, eagles, bears, and the like.

Crandall Creek

Crandall Creek comes down from Loco Mountain to the upper Shields River. According to the U.S. Forest Service, it was named for a "Mr. Crandall, an early settler." This was Edgar B. Crandall, who first appears on the pages of the *Big Timber Pioneer* in 1899 and over the years was noted to have helped Sheriff Falang chase Kid Royal, collected bounty for coyote pelts, and sheared sheep on the Bruffy ranch. He sold his place on this creek to a D.H. Marsh in 1917 and retired to a rooming house in Big Timber. In May of that year he had been drinking in a saloon and disappeared. Although his body was never found, none of his effects were missing from his room, and, after two months, it was concluded that he accidentally fell into the Yellowstone River and drowned.

The Crandall Creek Cabin is in the U.S. Forest Service rental program and can be found at the end of a road from Wilsall near the Shields River Campground.

Crazy Peak/Lake

Outside of the 12,000-foot peaks around Granite Peak in the Beartooths and Hilgard Peak in the Madisons, Crazy Peak at 11,204 feet is the highest point in Montana. It gets its name, obviously, as the dominant peak of the Crazy Mountains.

The mountains were called "mad" by the Crow Indians because of their rugged appearance and their wild winds and weather. Mad was apparently mistranslated as "crazy" rather than "angry." It was on this mountain in 1859 where Plenty Coups (1848–1932), the great Crow chief, went for a youthful vision quest. Tradition says that he foresaw the buffalo disappear and

Plenty Coups, ca. 1908. PHOTO BY EDWARD S. CURTIS, LIBRARY OF CONGRESS.

the white men and their cattle take over the land, and it was from this vision he knew that the survival of the Crow depended on siding with the whites. They allied with the U.S. against the Sioux and Cheyenne, their traditional enemies, and never did make war on the Americans. Plenty Coups was so revered by his people that after his death no other person was deemed worthy to become a full chief.

He was also well respected by the white culture and was asked to represent Native Americans at the dedication of the Tomb of the Unknowns after World War I.

Crazy Lake is well above timberline on the south slope of Crazy Peak, where it forms the headwaters of the South Fork of Big Timber Creek. It had a variant name of Whirlwind Lake that rancher and Western writer Spike Van Cleve wanted to make official. He suggested calling the smaller lake that is a few hundred yards downstream Crazy Lake. Because of Crazy's long location on the maps, the Board on Geographic Names rejected his request. Crazy Lake remains where it is, and the smaller lake is currently unnamed. Whirlwind is only of historical interest.

Crow Creek

Crow Creek is a small tributary of the Middle Fork of Cottonwood Creek just east of Virginia Peak. Although this was formerly Crow Indian country, the fact that it is across Cottonwood Creek from Eagle Creek suggests that it was probably named for the very common bird, *Corvus brachyrhynchos*, the American crow. All black in color and somewhat smaller than its cousin the raven, *Corvus corvax*, the crow is omnivorous and quite successful, with an estimated population of 31 million in the U.S. These birds mate for life and tend to be found in large family groups. They are among the more intelligent animals and have been observed using tools to obtain food.

American crow. PHOTO BY ANDREA PUTNAM, NATIONAL PARK SERVICE.

The term crow is also used more broadly as a synonym for any bird of the genus *Corvus,* of which there are many species, including ravens and magpies, both of which are also common throughout Montana.

Daisy Dean Creek

Forest Service notes from 1940 quote Ben Stevenson, a Harlowton resident, saying that the name comes from an event in 1881. A young woman by the name of Daisy Dean was riding with a companion when their horses became mired down crossing this stream—so it became known as Daisy Dean's Creek.

There is no further reference to this woman, but Daisy Dean was not an uncommon name in the late nineteenth century. It was particularly popular in the South and has continued to the present day with names of actresses, singers, songs, and even the title of a play. In Montana, there is a Daisy Dean Creek and campground north of Martinsdale, and this creek in the Crazies east of Wilsall, both of which have Daisy Dean Ranches on them. There was also a horse named Daisy Dean who was reported to have raced in eastern Montana in 1899.

All of these names probably stem from the popular ballad, "Daisy Deane," that was composed by Lt. T.F. Winthrop and James Ramsay Murray in a Civil War camp. It has been recorded many times, most recently in 2016, and was the theme music for the *Little House on the Prairie* television series. The lyrics of the song reminisce about meeting Daisy Deane in a flowery meadow in springtime with the birds singing, and how she outshone the flowers. The scenery has faded and Daisy is reported to have died, but the singer's memory of her is still fresh and his love for her remains.

"None knew thee but to love thee thou dear one of my heart."

Davey Butte

Please see the reference to Billie Butte. Both buttes are near each other and refer to William and David Hamilton, who were brothers in a pioneer family that ranched on the north end of the Shields River Valley.

Dead Horse Lakes/Creek

The Dead Horse Lakes are two tiny things at the head of the creek of the same name. It flows from the southeast slope of Sunlight Peak a short distance into the Middle Fork of Sweet Grass Creek. It must be presumed that the hunter had to walk out.

Deep Creek

Deep Creek is a very common stream name in Montana, and the name is obvious for the creek's flow. This one is a tributary of the Shields River on the western side of the Crazies on the Virginia Peak quad.

Deer Creek

There are deer everywhere in Montana, with the name appearing 16 times on various features in the counties covered by this book. This one happens to be on a creek in the very northern edge of the Crazies in the Lewis and Clark National Forest. Ranger B.P. Martin said in 1936 that the name comes because, at one time, white-tailed deer were numerous in this drainage.

Devil Creek

The author had a devil of a time trying to find the source of this name. Perhaps it was called this because of the devilishly steep drop down the east side of Granite Peak. The head of the creek starts near Big Timber Creek, but rather than turning south, it flows east from the Raspberry Butte quad toward the Grossfield Ranch in Sweet Grass County.

Diamond Lake

The vaguely diamond shape gives name to this small lake that drains into the South Fork of Sweet Grass Creek. If the diamond that you bought your sweetheart looked like this, you might be in for some trouble.

Druckmiller Lake

Joseph E. "Ed" Druckmiller, who is described as "a mountain man," discovered this lake above Blue Lake at the head of Big Timber Creek, and has had his name on it since about 1885. In addition to being a "galena and sulfite" (lead and silver) miner, he was a fisherman as well, and he was known to be responsible for stocking the Blue/Granite/Thunder/Crazy Lakes. He also worked for the USFS at Benchmark on the Rocky Mountain Front and had a sawmill on Big Timber Creek. He married Maude, the proprietress of a Wilsall hotel, in 1907. She filed for divorce in 1915.

Dry Creek

This is not the Pacific Northwest. There are five Dry Creeks in Park County and eight in Sweet Grass County. Of the two in the Crazies, one can be found on the Lena Creek quad draining the west side of the mountains, and the other is on the east side just to the south of Sweet Grass Creek.

Duck Creek

Duck Creek drains the southern side of Fairview Peak and heads to the Yellowstone River. The ducks don't paddle the rapids, so were most likely found nesting in the quieter reaches close to the river.

Dugout Creek

The name of this creek comes from a primitive building called a dugout that was used by homesteaders on the Montana prairie in the nineteenth and early twentieth centuries. This was essentially an earth home that was dug into a hillside and partially buried. It saved on lumber, which was scarce outside of the forest, and was "more modern" than a sod hut as the wooden front wall could hold a real door and window. There are lots of Cabin Creeks in the forest, and this is the prairie form that helps us remember what the pioneers endured.

Eagle Park/Creek

Once in danger of extinction, the bald eagle, *Haliaetus leucocephalus*, was moved to "threatened" in 1995, and removed from the threatened and endangered wildlife list in 2007. It is now common in Montana, and, with fish its primary food, is particularly frequent along rivers and streams. The DDT found in the fish in their diet damaged their eggs, and along with loss of habitat, there were fewer than 500 breeding

Bald eagle. JOHN JAMES AUDUBON.

pairs in 1963. Conservation efforts and the banning of DDT generated a remarkable recovery, with nearly 10,000 pairs noted in 2007, and many more now. In 2020 it was estimated that there were 150,000 bald eagles in the U.S.

There is an **Eagle Creek** in Meagher County that comes off Virginia Peak to the head of the Middle Fork of Cottonwood Creek.

Another can be found on the east side of Granite Peak as a tributary of Big Timber Creek.

Eagle Park is farther north on the east side and is seen as a flat area along Sweet Grass Creek. The name was erroneously omitted from the 2020 USGS map, but is confirmed on their website and the Custer-Gallatin National Forest map. Ranger Emory Wilson noted that in 1890 there was "a drove" of eagles here with some huge nests. Settlers went up the creek and shot the nests to pieces. (see Eagle Creek in the Absaroka-Beartooths section)

Elk Creek, Elk Lake, Big Elk Creek, Little Elk Creek

Elk Creek is on the western side of the Crazies and comes off Sugarloaf Mountain to join the Shields River at Wilsall. It is of historical interest because it is where Samuel O'Neill Cox Brady, called Alphabet, had a huge ranch. In 1907 he reportedly owned or leased some 6,700 acres on the east side of this creek where he ran 5,000 sheep and 60 head of cattle.

Elk Lake is a wide section of Park Creek that enters **Big Elk Creek** as it comes off Loco Mountain. Big Elk drains the eastern sides of Loco, Lebo, and Cinnamon Mountains and joins Cinnamon Creek out east on the prairie on its way to the Musselshell River. It was once misnamed Alkali Creek since a ditch out on the prairie connected Big Elk and Alkali Creeks. This was corrected in 1974 and it is now all officially Big Elk.

Little Elk Creek starts over a ridge just to the west of its big brother, but flows north off Cinnamon Mountain to enter the Musselshell west of where Big Elk/Cinnamon comes in.

There is also an **Elk Mountain.** It is south of Ibex Mountain and just outside of the national forest borders.

The elk, *Cervus canadensis*, is one of the largest members of the deer family. During the Lewis and Clark Expedition, they were reported in large numbers on the prairie. However, hunting and human habitat competition have now generally limited their range to forest and forest edges. In mountainous regions such as the Crazies, they follow the

Bull elk. WIKI CREATIVE COMMONS.

melting snow to higher elevations in the spring, and migrate down to the valleys for shelter and better browsing in the Winter. With all the elk names found here, you can be assured that there is good elk hunting around the Crazies.

Mount Elmo/Creek

There is no citation or reference to tell us what gave this mountain on the northeast side of the Crazies the name of Elmo.

It was a not uncommon name in the latter part of the nineteenth century. There is a Lake Elmo Park near Billings and a town of Elmo near Flathead Lake in northwestern Montana where the latter's name is a corruption of the Salish/Flathead word for "inlet on the lake." St. Elmo's fire is a weather event where a thunderstorm can create a glowing discharge around a sharp object such as a ship's mast and seeing it was thought to be a bad omen or a sign of divine judgment.

We know for certain that the name did not come from a red Muppet. But was it from the Flathead Indians who hunted buffalo on the plains northeast of here, a strange form of lightning, or just a guy's name? We will probably never know.

Fairview Peak

This peak, on the quad of the same name, is on the southern end of the Crazies with lovely views south to the valley of the Yellowstone River and the Absaroka Mountain Range beyond.

Fawn Creek

Fawn Creek comes west off Lebo Peak to join the Shields River near its start. Buck Creek joins that river a bit farther downstream, but we do not know where Mama Doe went.

Forest Lake/Creek

Where the Middle Fork of Cottonwood Creek flows north out of the Crazies, one finds **Forest Lake,** a widening of this creek, in a flat marshy basin to the east of Virginia Peak.

Forest Creek joins this Middle Fork of Cottonwood Creek about a half mile downstream of the lake. The U.S. Forest Service's Forest Lake cabin is located near this junction.

Forty Creek

The reason behind the name of this creek, a tributary of the West Fork of Cottonwood Creek in the northern Crazies, is unknown.

Glacier Lake

During the last ice age, the Crazy Mountains were left uncovered by the large, flattening continental ice fields. Instead, they were home to many smaller montane glaciers that carved cirques into the steep, jagged peaks, leaving many small glacial remnants and lovely tarn lakes.

Glacier Lake is at the head of the South Fork of Sweet Grass Creek and is in such a cirque. It is on the southwest slope of Conical Peak where it is surrounded by several small glaciers high above that create the waterfalls that feed it.

Goat Mountain/Creek

Goat Mountain was named for the mountain goats, *Oreamnos americanus,* that frequent its slopes. A native to the Rocky Mountains and Cascade Range, the Rocky Mountain goat is the largest animal found in high-altitude habitats. They generally remain above the tree line, but can occasionally be seen at lower elevations when they descend for mineral licks.

Mountain goat. NATIONAL PARK SERVICE.

The mountain was once confused with Scab Rock Mountain, which lies just to the north. **Goat Creek** flows off Goat Mountain and along Scab Rock Mountain to join Smith Creek. The creek gained some notoriety during Prohibition when Brad Wilson's grandfather had a still on it.

Granite Peak/Lake

"Gigantic granite formations" were the reason that this peak was given this name by the Forest Service. It was confused on some older maps with Conical Peak, and, although very close, Conical is actually two miles northwest of Granite.

Granite Lake is in that cluster of lakes on the south slope of Granite Peak at the head of Big Timber Creek. Granite and Blue Lake were once confused with each other when a Forest Service worker put the trail signs on the wrong lakes. Both were also variously called Thunder Lake, which is close by. In 1975 the Board on Geographic Names, with the advice of forest ranger Al Roemer and Spike Van Cleve of the Otter Creek Ranch, certified them in the present order. Granite is upstream and west of Blue Lake, and Thunder Lake is a widening of the outlet of Blue Lake, sitting just above Thunder Falls.

Grasshopper Glacier

After a lovely, long hike up Cottonwood Creek from the Ibex Ranger Station out of Clyde Park, one can camp at Cottonwood Lake and walk up to this glacier.

The grasshoppers are actually the now extinct Rocky Mountain locust, *Melanoplus spretus.* A swarm of them migrated over the Crazies some 200 years ago and were forced down on the ice by a storm. Their little bodies were frozen into the glacial ice and can be seen when the summer sun melts the surface snow of winter. Common and easily visible when the author camped at Cottonwood Lake in 1986, climate change has caused a 90 percent reduction of the glacier in the past 16 years. Unfortunately, the melting exposes the little bodies, which then decompose and disappear. (see Grasshopper Glacier in the Absaroka-Beartooths section for more information on *Melanoplus*)

Grouse Creek

Grouse Creek is a tributary of the northern Cottonwood Creek, which it enters just downstream from the Forest Lake Ranger Station south of Mount Elmo. Although there is only one Grouse Creek in the Crazies, the forest is full of these birds.

The blue, or dusky grouse, *Dendragapus obscurus*, is the one most often seen in the mountain forests, although their smaller cousins the spruce grouse and ptarmigan are also occasionally found. Montana also hosts the prairie, sage, and ruffed grouse at lower elevations, and all are

Blue grouse in mating display. NATIONAL PARK SERVICE.

of the family Galliformes, like the barnyard chicken. Nicknamed "fool's hens," these birds nest on the ground and can be found waddling and clucking down the trail as they try to lead hikers away from the eggs or chicks.

Hell Roaring Creek

Hell Roaring Creek is a tributary of Sweet Grass Creek that starts between Conical and Granite Peaks. It was also called Cascade Creek, a name that was used by the U.S. Forest Service around 1945, while Hell Roaring showed up on the county maps. Both names refer to the noisy, steep descent and were used on different maps until Hell Roaring, established to be the usual name in local use, was certified as correct by the Board on Geographic Names in 1975.

Hell Roaring must have been a popular expression in the late nineteenth century, as there are so many creeks of this name in southern Montana. In addition to this one in the Crazies, there is one in the Centennial Mountains of Madison County, one that flows into the Gallatin Canyon from the Madison Range, and the three in the Absaroka-Beartooths. A lot of Hells a Roaring here!

Hidden Lake

Hidden Lake, also called Fish Lake, can be found at the headwaters of the Middle Fork of Big Timber Creek. It is tucked away in a high cirque just below the glacier on the east side of Crazy Peak. It is well hidden, and it is hard to find unless you know where to look.

Honey Run Creek

According to local landowners and residents, this short creek that arises at Spruce Springs on Woodchuck Ridge and flows into Sixteenmile Creek "has always been known as Honey Run Creek." The exact reason is not clear.

Honey Run was not uncommonly used as a name for streams in the latter part of the nineteenth century, with examples found in Ohio with a nice park and waterfalls, in Missouri at Lake of the Ozarks, in Pennsylvania, and in northern California where its covered bridge was recently lost to a forest fire. The published story behind the California creek is that a couple was walking nearby and disturbed a bee's nest. "Run, Honey! Run!" cried the man, and the name stuck.

Until 1974 when Honey Run was confirmed, it had a period where it was also called Turkey Creek. The actual Turkey Creek is farther southeast near the head of the Shields River. (see citation)

Horse Creek

Horse Creek comes out of the Crazies on the western side and joins the Shields River just south of Wilsall, Montana. Early notes from the Forest Service say that it got its name because the area was frequented by numerous crippled horses that had been turned out by their owners.

The extension of the creek up its northern fork was called Horse or Horsefly Creek but was confirmed as the North Fork by the Board on Geographic Names in 1917. The Middle Fork had been called Pitch Creek, and the South Fork was Bear Creek, but these became plain old forks of Horse Creek by Board decisions in 1974 and 1975.

Because the creek flows through good ranch country near Wilsall, there were several pioneer families who homesteaded here and whose families remained in the area. Isaac Mather, who worked for the Northern Pacific Railroad, homesteaded on this creek in 1901. His son, Dallas Mather, married Minnie Cowan of Fort Benton and homesteaded next to his father. Dallas also started a sawmill operation at the head of this creek around 1899. John Killorn, who emigrated from Ireland and England, was also one of the early homesteaders.

Ibex Mountain

This prominent peak on the west side of the Crazies was called Ibex by the early settlers. Ranger E.A. Schilling said in 1940 that this was apparently because in the early days in Montana, people thought that they saw wild European sheep here. What they saw was probably the Rocky Mountain goat, as the ibex, genus *Capra*, from which all domestic goats are descended, is not found in North America. Furthermore, the ibex is a brownish-gray with long recurved horns, but then, the American bison doesn't look much like a water buffalo either.

The Ibex Ranger Station was built in 1939 and is now in the USFS cabin rental program. The only trail that crosses the Crazies and that goes via Campfire Lake to Big Timber Creek starts here.

Iddings Peak

Joseph Paxon Iddings (1857–1920) was a prominent late nineteenth-century geologist and petrologist who in 1880 entered the service of the United States Geological Survey. It was in that capacity that he joined the 1894 survey crew that did the first topographic maps of the Crazy Mountains. He later became professor of petrology at the University of Chicago and was honorary curator of petrology at the U.S. National Museum. Iddings Peak honors him.

Joseph Paxon Iddings, *Popular Science Monthly*, vol 72. WIKI CREATIVE COMMONS.

Indian Creek

Of course, this was all originally "Indian country," but a group of Indian tipis that the early white settlers found along its course gave name to the creek. It is in the northernmost part of the Crazies and is a tributary of the Bozeman Fork of the Musselshell River.

Kid Royal Mountain

The southernmost peak in the Crazies was named for Mike Hall, aka Kid Royal. Sweet Grass County was formed in 1895, and in 1901, when Oscar Fallang became the new sheriff, he vowed to clean out the nest of horse thieves that populated the northern end of the county. Kid Royal was the most famous of these, and reading about him in contemporary issues of the *Big Timber Pioneer* newspaper is quite entertaining. The editor treated him with a certain bemused forbearance and said that "Kid Royal was probably the shrewdest horse thief Montana has ever known. He is an expert horseman, a good judge of horseflesh, and has, no doubt, stolen more horses in this state than any other man." He also wrote that Kid Royal never carried a gun, and that "he was harmless in every way except his inability to keep away from a rope with a horse tied to it." Hall himself claimed that he was really a good man, but that a horse thief had switched souls with him.

In any case, he proved to be Sheriff Fallang's biggest headache, and for nearly 20 years he kept stealing, getting caught, escaping, stealing, and getting caught again. Since this was a more civilized time in the West, he was never at risk for hanging, but he did keep the lawmen busy. He was first sentenced to Deer Lodge prison after a trial for horse theft in 1890, and again in 1902, and was released after three years. That year, 1905, he again stole a horse and saddle and was arrested, convicted, and sent back to Deer Lodge. While there, two years later, he was transported by train to testify at a trial of one of his accomplices, Arthur Charlesworth. He managed to escape, fully manacled, by jumping out of the window of the moving railroad car's toilet room. He came back to Sweet Grass County, was sighted with a herd of stolen horses and tack, and led Sheriff Fallang and a posse on a 250-mile chase all the way to Twin Bridges where he was recognized and arrested by Sheriff Deadmond of Broadwater County. An excellent rider, Fallang claimed that Kid Royal was "elusive as a flea." Jailed again in Big Timber, he was convicted and sentenced to 14 additional years plus the original eight. While in jail in Big Timber awaiting transfer to prison, Undersheriff Dell Whitney went uptown to get a shave. A bit of a dandy, Kid Royal always kept a metal comb in his back pocket, so he used that to unscrew the transom over the door, got out, stole some horses tied nearby, and made good another escape. Of course, he was caught again and sent back to Deer Lodge. En route by train, he once again tried diving out of the moving train's window. The deputy, however, was wise to his tricks, and grabbed him by the pants and pulled him back in.

With such a colorful career, one would have thought that someone would have made a movie of his escapades. However, he had two Hollywood failings. There was no recorded love life, so no part for Katherine Ross. Also, he did not die in a blaze of gunfire with the Bolivian army. Rather, he studied veterinary medicine in prison, was a model inmate, and, upon parole, went straight. He worked as a miner and practiced as a vet in Contact on the upper Boulder River where, in 1921, he died in bed of pneumonia.

Lebo Peak, Lebo Fork

Lebo Peak is in the northern Crazies just to the south of Loco Mountain at the point where Sweet Grass, Meagher, and Park Counties meet. It gives its name to several important geologic features and a former town, but no one seems to know where the name comes from, and the Montana Historical Society merely states "unknown."

The **Lebo Fork** comes off the gap between Lebo Peak and Loco Mountain and is a fork of Big Elk Creek. It is the only other Lebo in the national forest, but there several Lebo features just outside of the forest. A large irrigation reservoir built in 1908 is called Lebo Lake. It is southeast of Two Dot and fed by a Lebo Creek. There was even a town of Lebo that had a post office from 1913 to 1933 and was a stop on the Milwaukee Rail Road where many of the new Scandinavian emigrants got off to find their homesteads in northern Sweet Grass County. The post office was run from the homestead home of Mandius and Ellen Teig whose son still lives on the property. It was never a real town, but had a school, church and cemetery and was recognized as a populated community by the USGS until 1972. Almost all of the other homesteads in the area except for the Tiegs failed and were bought out so that nothing but the house and the name of the location now remains.

Lebo also persists in current natural history as the Lebo Pack of wolves. These are descendants of the wolves that were introduced into Yellowstone in 1995 and who spread to the Crazies as a new pack in 2008. There is also a geologic stratum in Montana that is called the Lebo Formation that contains many fossils dating back to the Paleogene period (from 66 to 23 million years ago).

It seems unusual that something like Lebo that has generated so many other names has no history. This author's own suspicion is that this is an English phonetic misspelling of the French name LeBeau or LeBeaux. In 1885 Canada experienced the Northwest Rebellion led by Louis Riel that tried to establish land rights and political autonomy for the Metis, those of mixed Cree and French Canadian heritage. The rebellion was put down and Riel was captured and hanged. Afterwards, many Metis fled south and settled along the Rocky Mountain Front and in Musselshell country on the plains north of the Crazies. Although many of these people were rounded up and returned to Canada by the 10th Cavalry in 1886, some of the Cree and Metis remained in self-contained communities until 1910. By 1930 their land had been completely taken over by ranchers and homesteaders as the U.S. Government did not recognize their squatters' rights nor homesteads and the land was given to emigrants and American citizens. Most of the Metis drifted into towns and ranch labor, and, though they disappeared as a culture in the state, the echo of French-Canadian names remains on the maps and among Montana's population.

Lena Creek

Louis and Anna (or Bertha) Bird, who emigrated from Germany in 1883, homesteaded near the current Porcupine rental cabin from 1904 to 1920. This branch of Porcupine Creek was named for their daughter, Lena Bird. And, no, there is no record of her marrying an Ole.

Little Elk Creek

(see Elk Creek)

Loco Mountain/Creek

Loco is from the Spanish word for insane, and this allusion to "crazy" may be a Spanish reference for this mountain toward the northern end of Crazy Range.

However, other authors presume that the name comes from the presence of large amounts of locoweed at the foot of this mountain. Locoweed is a common name used for several plants of the genus

Locoweed. NATIONAL PARK SERVICE.

Oxytropis and *Astragalus*, wild peas. Locoweed is quite toxic to horses, sheep, and cattle, either by producing its own toxins or by absorbing selenium from the soil, which causes "blind staggers." One, called milk vetch, is particularly poisonous as it makes its own toxin, locoine, which can cause a type of insanity in humans called locoism. This effect is known because extracts of vetch were used in some frontier patent medicines. The term locoweed now just refers to its effect on livestock.

Lodgepole Creek

This creek, unnamed before 1923, passes through a lodgepole pine forest before joining the Shields River.

Pinus contorta, the lodgepole pine, is one of the dominant conifers in the mountains east of the Continental Divide. It gets its common name because its straight, thin trunk was the preferred tree that the Plains Indians used for their tipi (or lodge) poles. This interestingly contrasts with the Latin scientific name, which translates as "twisted pine." That name is explained by the fact that the first specimens were collected and named by the U.S. Navy's 1838 Wilkes Expedition led by Lt. Charles Wilkes. This was a voyage of discovery and was the first scientific government expedition to the Pacific Northwest and Columbia River since Lewis and Clark. In addition to charting all of the places they had been and establishing U.S. claims to the country, the explorers gathered thousands of specimens of plant and animal life. The pines were necessarily the coastal subspecies that had been buffeted by Pacific winds, which caused their contorted, or twisted, trunks.

Lodgepoles are also the first conifer to reseed after a forest fire. They have a resinous cone that can lie unharmed on the ground for years. When a fire sweeps through the area, the heat melts the resin and the seeds pop out of the cone to start a new forest.

If the trees surrounding you have the long needles of a pine tree that are bundled in pairs, you are in a lodgepole forest.

Lone Lake

Named for its location, Lone Lake is in a high, remote cirque north of Cottonwood Creek and Lake at 9,300 feet and sits just to the west of Conical Peak.

Lost Horse Creek

Lost Horse Creek exits the Crazies into the prairie to the north. The name must represent a cowboy's misfortune.

Lost Lake

The little, hard-to-find lake can be found at 9,000 feet high above Crazy Lake near the head of the South Fork of Big Timber Creek.

Makey Creek

Makey Creek was once called the North Fork of American Fork Creek, which exits the Crazies to the east. It now represents a small tributary of that North Fork and is located a bit upstream from Spring Creek.

Although there are no federal homestead or Sweet Grass County records under this name, it is known from *Big Timber Pioneer* articles that an E. Makey and a Leroy Makey lived in Melville during the first two decades of the twentieth century. Makey Creek lies just west of that town, so the name probably refers to their activity.

Meadow Creek

Meadow Creek starts between Billie and Davey Buttes in the northern Shields River country and joins that river near the Meagher County line. The meadows that it passes through were good grazing country.

Walter Hill (1885–1944), the youngest son of Great Northern

Walter Hill in his library, ca. 1905. MINNESOTA HISTORICAL SOCIETY.

Railroad magnate J.J. Hill, came to Montana in 1910 as a remittance man buying up homesteads. He gathered quite a bit of land along Meadow Creek and established the Hill Ranch in 1919 where he spent his later years. Hill was a colorful character in Montana as he spent his money freely. He bought up huge acreages near Ekalaka and Broadus in eastern Montana as well as several purebred cattle herds. He also purchased and renovated Corwin Hot Springs in the Paradise Valley, which had a brief resurgence as a plunge, bar, and dance hall in the 1920s. He divorced his first wife in 1921 and married Livingston local Pauline Gibson. They divorced in 1927 and, on the same day, he married another Livingston woman, Mildred Richardson. He died in Livingston in 1944 and is interred in the family plot in St. Paul, Minnesota.

Mill Creek

Like so many Mill Creeks in Montana, this tributary of the Upper Shields River was named for the sawmill located there. The owner was not recorded, but these mills were essential to provide cut lumber for the towns, mines, ranches, and homesteads. Because of transportation problems in the early era, they needed to be located near water power and close to both the timber source and the market. In the counties covered by this book, there are at least five Mill Creeks, and one Sawmill Creek.

Miller Creek

The two forks of Miller Creek exit the national forest on its northeast corner and enter the Musselshell River a bit west of Two Dot, Montana.

Although it starts in the Crazy Mountains, it gets its name from an 1899 prairie homestead. Frederick Miller patented 160 acres near Two Dot that year, and in 1900 expanded his holdings along the creek to include an entire section.

Milly Creek

No information could be found as to who this Milly was.

Miners Creek

Miners Creek, a tributary of the South Fork of American Fork, gets double "mining" credit. Ranger L.H. McLean wrote in 1936 that it was named for an old prospector by the name of Miner who mined along this stream in 1919.

Moose Lake

Beautiful Moose Lake is in a timbered valley near Campfire Lake at the head of the Middle Fork of Sweet Grass Creek.

The moose, *Alces alces*, is the largest member of the deer family and is quite common in the mountains of Montana. They are particularly fond of aquatic vegetation, so finding one wading in this lake and naming it for the species

Bull moose. PHOTO BY MIKE LOCKHART, U.S. FISH & WILDLIFE SERVICE.

would not have been unusual. Moose tend to be found either solitary or in small groups and are rarely bothered by human presence. However, stay away from a cow and her calf. More people are injured in Alaska by moose than bears. (see Big and Little Moose Lakes in the Absaroka-Beartooths section)

Muddy Creek

This creek with an uninviting name starts in the northernmost part of the national forest to the west of Cottonwood Creek. It picks up its mud when it flows through some swampy land where it comes out onto the prairie.

Musselshell River

When Lewis and Clark wintered in North Dakota, the Hidatsa told them about this river that they called *Mahtush-ahzhah,* which meant "Mussel-shell" for the freshwater mussels found there. When they passed the mouth of this river as they ascended the Missouri on May 19, 1805, they gave it the name Muscle Shell in English.

This important river originates in the Crazies and heads east to drain much of central Montana before turning north to join the Missouri in the Fort Peck Reservoir. The spelling was changed to the more proper, but less amusing, Musselshell in 1975.

Oasis Lakes

Twin Lakes are on the north slope of Granite Peak at the head of Big Timber Creek, and the cluster of small lakes some 500 feet above and north of Twin Lakes are the Oasis Lakes. There are no palm trees, and notes from the USGS and Spike Van Cleve do not say why, at 8,766 feet, this was considered an oasis.

O'Hearn Creek

O'Hearn Creek was confused on earlier maps with the North Fork of American Creek, which is actually a bit south of it. Both are tributaries of American Creek. No claim or deed records remain of an O'Hearn, but local residents remember him to be a miner in the area.

Otter Creek

River otters, *Lontra canadensis*, are large members of the weasel family that can be found throughout North America. Their habitat has been reduced due to the actions of humans, but they are common in the lakes and streams of wild Montana. Primarily fish eaters, it is a pleasure to watch family groups swim together in summer or playfully slide down snowy slopes in winter.

River otter in Yellowstone. PHOTO BY JIM PEACO, NATIONAL PARK SERVICE.

Otter Creek was once called Medicine Bow Creek and sits to the north of Black Butte as a tributary of Sweet Grass Creek.

Spike Van Cleve (1912–1982) was a local rancher and noted author, whose book *40 Years Gatherin'* remains popular. He was raised on the family's Lazy Bar K dude ranch in Big Timber Canyon, but developed his own ranch here, along Otter Creek.

The Park, Park Creek

In the western U.S., a "park" is defined as a broad, flat, mostly open area in a mountainous region.

The Park is a flat area below Spruce Springs at the head of Honey Run Creek.

Park Creek flows through Elk Lake to join Big Elk Creek at a big, flat "park."

Pauline Creek

Pauline Creek flows into Cottonwood Creek east of Ibex Mountain near the town of Clyde Park. Nothing specific could be found about Pauline herself, but a place that locals call Pauline's cabin is situated along this creek.

Pear Lake

Pear Lake was named for its pear shape. It can be found above timberline between Iddings and Granite Peaks, and its outflow drops into Granite Lake and thus on to Big Timber Creek.

Pig Creek

Just why this tributary of Deer Creek in the northernmost part of the Crazies is called Pig Creek is unknown. As it is just south of Lennep and the more populated agricultural area around the Musselshell River, it may have been the site of a pig farm.

Porcupine Creek

Porcupines, *Erethzontidae*, are arboreal rodents that are distinguished by their spiny quills, which were used by the Native Americans for decoration and are the bane of your dogs. *Porcus* is Latin for pig, and an alternative name for these animals is "quill pig." These critters are very common throughout Montana, so there are several creeks named for it. The Porcupine Creek in the Custer-Gallatin National Forest is on the west side of the Crazies and comes off Bald Ridge to go to the Shields River.

Porcupine. PHOTO BY MARY HARRSCH, WIKI CREATIVE COMMONS.

Porcupine Butte is on the prairie to the east of the mountains and guards the front of the Crazies. From a distance it does rather resemble a porcupine, but is not in the national forest.

The Porcupine Ranger Station along this creek was rebuilt after a fire in 1914 and served as the headquarters of the Shields District until the 1930s. It is now in the cabin rental program. An alternate trailhead to access Trespass Creek and the route that crosses the Crazies via Campfire Lake to the Big Timber side is found by this Porcupine Creek station. It also is the start of the brand-new (2021) Porcupine Lowland Trail #267 to the Ibex Ranger Station. This was recently renovated on public lands to avoid six miles of private property.

Among the early settlers were Louis E. Green and his wife, Bertha, who lived next to the ranger station from 1904 to 1920. Eberhardt Becker, who emigrated from Germany in the 1880s, set up the Becker Hereford Ranch on Porcupine Creek just to the west of the national forest. They raised purebred registered shorthorn cattle and, although Eberhardt died in 1909, the ranch continued into the third generation of Beckers until his grandchildren sold it in 1973.

Rapid Creek

Like so many of the streams in the Crazy Mountains, this short creek drops quickly over rocky rapids. It joins Cottonwood Creek just east of Trespass Creek.

Raspberry Butte

Raspberry is the common name for several spiny, woody perennial plants of the genus *Rubus.* Cultivated commercially, it has a delicious fruit. They are very common throughout Montana and, certainly, can be found on this butte. However, the name does not come from the presence of this plant. Rather, in 1918, the name was applied to this butte because of its round, knobbed shape that resembles the raspberry fruit.

Rock Lake/Creek

Rock Lake, the largest of the Crazy Mountain lakes, is at the head of Rock Creek and is surrounded by talus rocks and snowfields. It sits high up at 8,797 feet between Wilsall, Iddings, and Granite Peaks, and its creek exits the Crazies to the south, where it bends west to join the Shields River near the town of Clyde Park. It is a good fly-fishing stream, and the hike up the Rock Creek Canyon leading to the beautiful high country is one of the more scenic around.

John Harvey (1850–1915) had his ranch on Rock Creek and, around 1900, entered into partnership with his brother-in-law, Tom Tregloan. They grazed cattle in summer pasture near this creek and imported and raised Clydesdale horses. As the post office was on the ranch with John as postmaster, the community that grew up became known as Clyde Park.

Sam Darroch (1864–1943) also had his ranch on this creek. (see Darroch Creek in the Absaroka-Beartooths section) Another who homesteaded on Rock Creek southwest of the national forest was Abraham Jackson Kenney and his wife, Margaret, who arrived in the late 1800s. Members of that family still remain in the area.

Rough Creek/Gulch

It is not an easy hike up this gulch just south of Upper Sweet Grass Creek.

Sawmill Creek

A fellow named Barrow, who also had the Ubet rail station, built the first sawmill on this creek in 1880. It is found at the very northern extent of the Crazy Mountains in the Lewis and Clark National Forest, so would have been well situated to serve the Musselshell country.

Scab Rock Mountain

Scab Rock Mountain is on the northwest border of the national forest and shares a ridge with Bear Mountain. It was sometimes mistakenly called Goat Mountain, but that is actually the next rise to the south.

Scab Rock gave its name to the USGS quad map, and comes from local usage. I believe that one can assume that the name does not come from its smooth, shiny surface.

Scofield Creek

According to a Forest Service ranger's notes, this creek to the west of Lebo Peak was named for "a distinguished pioneer who died in 1927." James Schofield (also spelled Scofield) was the popular roadmaster of the Montana division of the Northern Pacific Railroad, and in 1885 married Octavia Murphy, who was the sister-in-law of the Hamiltons of the Shields River Valley. (see Billie and Davey Buttes) He retired from the railroad in 1888 and bought land near her relatives, where he devoted the rest of his time to stock growing and ranch work.

Serrett Creek

William A. Serrett patented a homestead on Lodgepole Creek in 1916 on land that was close to where Serrett Creek joins the Shields River. The creek's name was certified in 1918.

Sheep Creek

Sheep Creek flows south out of the forest to join Rock Creek before going on to the Shields River south of Clyde Park. The name comes from the location of a domestic sheep grazing ground in the late nineteenth and early twentieth centuries. The herds were very numerous at that time, making Sweet Grass County one of the primary sheep raising areas in the U.S., and Big Timber one of the largest wool export points in the world.

Shields River

William Clark named this river on July 15, 1806, when his part of the Corps of Discovery passed it on the return journey. It honors expedition member John Shields (ca. 1769–1809) of Kentucky, who acted as gunsmith, blacksmith, hunter, and scout for the expedition. Shields was a second cousin to another Corps participant, the famous mountain man and explorer, John Colter. (see Colter Pass in the Absaroka-Beartooths chapter)

USGS surveyor Ferdinand Hayden called it the "Twenty-five Yard or Shields" River. That alternate name came from an Indian-militia skirmish that occurred 25 yards from the stream. The Crow Indians called it Deer Creek, but neither of these names persisted.

Jim Bridger had a wagon route from the Oregon Trail to the Montana goldfields that was supposed to be safer than the Bozeman Trail. It went north from the Yellowstone River up the Shields River and then west along Brackett Creek to Bridger Creek and the Gallatin Valley. After just two years, with the military defeats in Red Cloud's War, the route was closed. It wasn't until after 1876 and the Battle of the Little Bighorn, when most of the Indian conflicts ended, that the Shields River Valley was opened to settlement.

Sixteenmile Creek

Originating in the north Crazies on the slope of Bald Ridge, this historically significant creek flows east to the Missouri River.

Lewis and Clark gave it the name of Howards Creek for expedition member Thomas P. Howard. However, that disappeared and was replaced by Sixteenmile, which derives from the fact that the creek enters the Missouri River 16 miles downstream from the town of Three Forks. This river junction near the former town of Lombard is where Richard Harlow's Jawbone Railroad started and ran up the Sixteenmile Canyon to the silver mines at Castle. Unfortunately, by 1896 when the new track neared the mines, the price of silver had plummeted and the mines closed. Harlow continued the line through to Harlowton and on to Lewistown in 1903, where it hauled wool from the sheep ranches there. It was bought by the Milwaukee Road in 1908 and was abandoned in 1980.

Slippery Creek

This creek is a tributary of the eastern Cottonwood Creek and flows south of Ibex Mountain. One must assume that the name was given to the creek by some pioneer who got wet.

Smeller Lake/Creek

A name like Smeller conjures all sorts of strange images and weird stories. It can definitely be stated that this is not the sewer pond for the town of Big Timber, but two other theories on the name exist. It is possible that it was a misspelling of the name of a fellow called Schmelling, who drilled under the lake in order to pipe the water to the town of Clyde Park. More likely it refers to the policing of moonshine operations that were common in the Crazies. Some of those Revenue officers were called "high class smellers" by the *Big Timber Pioneer,* and the paper reported at one time that they used their noses to find 50 gallons of moonshine that was poured into the cesspool of the old Big Timber courthouse.

Smith Creek

Smith Creek comes from Goat Mountain to flow into Meadow Creek in the north Shields River Valley. The name of this creek comes from Foster Smith, who in 1883 filed for a "Ranch" deed in the Porcupine Basin immediately south of Smith Creek. The huge Smith Brothers' Ranch of the early 1900s had a sheep operation of several thousand head that ran from here along much of the east side of the Shields River. Current local Brad Wilson remembers that his grandfather's moonshine still on Goat Creek was near the junction of that stream and Smith Creek. (see Goat Creek) That gentleman also had legitimate employment, as he ran sheep for the Smith Brothers on their summer allotments in the Crazy Mountains.

As a sign of the changing times, the Adam Black homestead that was settled on this creek in 1925 has now been subdivided into the Smith Creek Cabin development with some 104 homesites.

Spring Creek

Water from the huge snowfall in the mountains sinks into the ground, and, when it hits a less permeable rock layer, flows laterally until it pops out of the ground as a spring.

There are many of these springs in the Crazies, so consequently there are several that begin a creek, and four of these are called Spring Creek. One is a short tributary of Cottonwood Creek. Another starts at a spring that is marked on the USGS Lebo quad and flows north to join Loco Creek. Of the other two, one joins the Middle Fork of American Creek and the other joins Lost Horse Creek on the northern edge of the national forest land.

Spruce Springs

The woods around this spring are part of a mature climax forest, which contains the Engelmann spruce, *Picea engelmannii*. This tree, along with the subalpine fir, *Abies lasiocarpa*, form one of the most common forest associations in the Rocky Mountains, where the pair are a major component of the interior high-elevation forests.

The spruce was named in 1863 to honor Georg Engelmann (1809–1884), a physician and botanist from St. Louis, Missouri. The spring named for it is found at the head of Honey Run Creek east of Woodchuck Ridge on the northeast border of the forest.

Stag Creek

Stag is another name for a buck, or male deer. This short creek is the northeastern fork of Smith Creek.

Station Creek

Station Creek is in the northeast part of the Crazies where it flows east onto the prairie to join Cinnamon Creek and then on to Two Dot where it meets the Mussellshell River.

The Milwaukee Railroad line, which ran from Chicago to Tacoma, passed through central Montana. The section from Harlowtown to Tacoma was all electric, because the engines powered by direct current (DC) gave greater torque for use on the mountain grades. However, DC current does not travel well on power lines, so about every 30 miles a station was built that took the local alternating current (AC) and converted it to the direct current (DC) that was put in the overhead lines. Electric Substation #1 was at Two Dot, and this is the station that gave the name to the creek that flowed nearby.

The Milwaukee Railroad went into bankruptcy in 1977, but the reorganization did not successfully improve its finances, and in the 1980s the Pacific Extension was abandoned and the track torn up. The remains of some of the concrete station buildings can still be seen as ghost structures.

Sugarloaf Mountain

Prior to the end of the nineteenth century when sugar cubes were introduced, refined sugar was sold as a molded loaf, a tall cone with a rounded top. This common shape is reflected in the name of many mountains, like this one at the head of the South Fork of the Shields River. (see Sugarloaf Mountain in the Absaroka-Beartooths chapter for an image of a sugarloaf)

Sunlight Peak/Lake/Creek

The names of these features all come from the mountain. Ranger notes from the late 1930s state, "The sun in setting reflects its rays on the peak... Its west slope is a flat surface upon which the setting sun plays."

Sunlight Creek flows north off the peak to join Deep Creek and the Upper Shields River.

Sunlight Lake is on the east slope of Sunlight Mountain and is headwaters to the North Fork of Sweet Grass Creek.

Swamp Lake/Creek

Swamp Creek flows out of the lake and gets its name because it passes through some marshy country before joining Big Timber Creek to the southeast of the Custer-Gallatin National Forest.

The **lake** is found at nearly 9,000 feet on the north slope of Fairview Peak, nestled in a cirque with surrounding talus rock and stunted conifers. Although the name does not make it sound like your favorite swimming hole, it is in fact a deep, cold mountain lake. It is certainly not "swampy" up here, but the name was applied in 1932 because the lake is at the head of the lower, swampy creek that it feeds.

Sweet Grass Creek/County

Sweet Grass Creek flows off Sunlight Mountain to the Yellowstone River near Greycliff. It was called the Otter River by William Clark when the Corps of Discovery passed by on the return to St. Louis in 1806. This was subsequently changed to Sweet Grass Creek as it was deemed not large enough to be a river, and there is an Otter Creek farther upstream. (see that citation) The current name for the creek is credited to Judge William G. Strong, and comes from the grass, *Heirochloe odorata,* which is common in the area. The smoke from this grass has a vanilla-like odor when burned and is used in Native American ceremonies. Wallace Black Elk in his book *Black Elk* wrote, "Sweetgrass is Mother Earth's hair. It is a perfume. When my grandma's spirit comes, she carries that smell, that perfume, and you can smell it. That's why we use the sweetgrass as a prayer at the alter."

The county was formed from Park, Meagher, and Yellowstone Counties in 1895 with Big Timber as the county seat. The new county's name was suggested by Mrs. Paul (Helen) Van Cleve, and also referred to that same native grass that was so abundant around her home near Melville.

Target Rock

Target Rock sits north of the upper Shields River between it and the Middle Fork of Cottonwood Creek. This 8,000-foot rocky promontory tends to collect the thunderstorms as they pass through the mountains, and the bald summit draws their lightning bolts—it is God's target.

Thunder Lake/Rapids

Druckmiller, Granite, Blue, and Thunder Lakes sit on the south slope of Granite Peak, and their outlet tumbles noisily down Thunder Rapids to join Big Timber Creek. The lake that is located just above these rapids is, naturally, Thunder Lake.

Trespass Creek

The Pacific Railway Acts were enacted between 1862 and 1871 to encourage the construction of the transcontinental railroads. In them, land grants were created as a subsidy to the railroads with the odd numbered sections given to the private railroads while the government kept the even numbered ones. Originally these extended 6 to 40 miles on either side of the tracks, but various exchanges moved some of the private railroad parcels up into the mountains. The result on a U.S. Forest Service map looks like a checkerboard with federal land usually in green and private white.

The trail across the Crazies from Big Timber Creek via Campfire Lake to the Ibex Ranger Station trailhead comes down Trespass Creek. Since it goes across checkerboarded land, the trail crosses some private sections and, although the Forest Service has negotiated an easement, any off-trail wandering will be trespassing.

Turkey Creek

Benjamin Franklin is said to have wanted the wild turkey, *Meleagris gallopavo*, to be our national bird. It was once quite common in the eastern woodlands, and the sub species, Merriam's turkey, *Meleagris gallopavo merriami*, is its western cousin. Merriam's prefers a mountainous and forested habitat like that along this creek, and it has a range through-out Wyoming, Montana, and South Dakota as well as the high mesas to the south. The name of the bird comes from Britain, where a similar

Wild turkey. NATIONAL PARK SERVICE.

domesticated fowl, named for the country of Turkey, had been imported years earlier from the eastern Mediterranean. Like buffalo and elk, the English colonists transferred that turkey's name to the similar North American bird.

In May of 1946 a C-45 plane was on a flight from Billings to Spokane when it ran into a severe snowstorm and crashed into the side of Lebo Peak on the saddle between Turkey and Fawn Creeks. Six airmen died, but the co-pilot, Frank Avery, bailed out just before the crash and survived. The remains of the plane can still be found there.

Twin Lakes

These two lakes on the north slope of Granite Peak at the head of Big Timber Creek are of similar size, and thus "twins."

The trail to them starts from the Half Moon Campground on Big Timber Creek and goes along a rough jeep road that was built to accommodate dredge mining for gold on private land near Twin Lakes. The road has since been closed to vehicles, but remains of the mining can still be seen.

The East Crazy Mountains and Inspiration Point proposal, which has been several years in the works, was finalized near the end of 2020. It was designed to eliminate some of the "checkerboarding" and to preserve some of the roadless/ wilderness quality of these mountains. With this swap, the Forest Service acquires some 5,000 acres that will consolidate public lands between Big Timber and Sweet Grass Creeks, and the ranchers get land that has been interspersed with their private acres. In addition, a new 22-mile-long public trail will be constructed to join current trails and create a nearly 40-mile loop through the entire Crazy range. The Half Moon to Twin Lakes trail will be part of this loop.

Virginia Creek/Peak

Ranger E.A. Schilling reported that this peak, and the creek that comes off it, was named for the girlfriend of a USGS employee. He did not share whether this "honor" resulted in the success of this relationship.

Willow Creek

There are many species of willow in the genus *Salix* that can be found in wetlands and along waterways throughout Montana where they are useful in preventing stream bank erosion. This creek near Cinnamon Mountain joins Big Elk Creek toward the Mussellshell River and has many willow patches along its route.

Willow Creek is also the site of some calcite mines that were active in the first half of the twentieth century. Calcite is a clear crystal of calcium carbonate that is deposited by hydrothermal water, and those of optical grade were used industrially from 1909 onward. During World War II, the Polaroid Company built them into anti-aircraft sights, but this use, and the mining, ended in 1945 when the calcite crystal was successfully replaced by plastic.

Wilsall Peak

Frank Magalsky, a resident of the town of Wilsall, Montana, suggested this name for the mountain in 2010. The 10,842-foot peak is just 15 miles from town and is the most prominent point that can be seen from that community.

The town of Wilsall is west of the Crazies along the Shields River. It was named by Walter B. Jordan, who platted the town in the late nineteenth century and named it for his son and daughter-in-law, Will and Sally Jordan. The Northern Pacific Railroad's Shields Branch arrived in 1909, and the town got its post office a year later. In the decade of the 1910s it became the center of the Shields River Valley as homesteaders, many of them Scandinavian emigrants, filled it. Their heritage continues with the annual December lutefisk dinner at the Lutheran church. Ja, Num!

Wolf Park

There is a broad, flat park on the eastern side of the national forest at the head of Basin Creek, which was named for the wolves that were once common, but then exterminated, and have now returned. (see Lebo Peak in the Crazies chapter and Wolf Mountain in the Absaroka-Beartooths chapter)

Woodchuck Ridge

The ridge, at the head of Honey Run Creek, was named for the yellow-bellied marmot, *Marmota flaviventris,* that is so common in Montana. Marmots are rodents, a type of ground squirrel, and are a close cousin to the prairie dog. They are very social, and their loud whistle is known to all who hike in the Rockies.

Yellow-bellied marmot. NATIONAL PARK SERVICE.

"Woodchuck" is an eastern name for a marmot that combines its woods habitat with a corruption of the American Indian word for the animal. "Rockchucks" are simply marmots that live in rocky habitat, and both "chucks" are the same animal as a groundhog. Marmot comes from the French *marmotte,* which was derived from the Romish word that means "mountain mouse." That is one heck of a big mouse!

Adding one important note to the last entry in this book—people who frequent the bumpy dirt roads in our mountains will appreciate the fact that the road that runs along the north side of Billie Creek and looks up at Woodchuck Ridge is listed on the U.S. Forest Service map as the Upchuck Ridge Road.

BIBLIOGRAPHY

INTERNET SITES

Beartooth Basin Summer Ski Area, www.allredlodge.com/ski_resorts/beartooth_pass.php. www.silverrunski.com.

British Columbia, Home Ministry, "Tree Book," https://www.for.gov.bc.ca.

Crazy Mountain Access Project, https://www.crazymountainproject.com/east-side-land-swap.

Custer-Gallatin National Forest, Incident Information System, www.inciweb.nwcg.gov/incident/7537.

Dome Mountain Ranch, https://domemountainranch.com.

Dornix Park, www.dornixpark.org.

Digital Public Library of America, www.dp.la. Billings Public Library

The Diggings, https://thediggings.com/mines.

Find A Grave, www.findagrave.com.

Gallatin County Emergency Managemant website, https://www.readygallatin.com.

Geology and Earth Science News and Information, www.geology.com.

Greater Yellowstone Resource Guide, www.greater-yellowstone.com.

The Gymnosperm Database, https://www.conifers.org.

History.com, www.history.com.

Legends of America, www.legendsofamerica.com.

Library of Congress, National Endowment for the Humanities, digitized newspapers 1789-1963, www.chroniclingamerica.loc.gov.

 Red Lodge Picket

 Livingston Enterprise

 New Idea, Red Lodge paper in 1893

 The Harlowton News

Mining History, www.thediggings.com.

Montana Department of Environmental Quality, www.deq.mt.gov.

 Abandoned Mine Project, history, 2020, http://deq.mt.gov/Land/AbandonedMines.

Montana Department of Tourism, www.visitmt.com.

Montana Fish, Wildlife and Parks website, www.fwp.mt.gov.

 FWP Field Guide and Gray Wolf History

 Mountain Lakes Guide

Montanahikes.com, Hiking, camping and Exploring Montana, www.montanahikes.com.

Montana Historical Society.

 Geographic Names card files.

 Montana Memory Project, mtmemory.org.

 Montana Place Names from Alzada to Zortman, http://mtplacenames.org.

Montana History: State History Guide, Bruce Gourley, http://www.montanahistory.net/statehistory.htm.

Montana Newspapers, http://www.montananewspapers.org.

 Big Timber Pioneer

 Montana Standard, Butte, Montana, October 9, 1935.

MTN Sports, www.montanasports.com.

Newspapers, Historic Archives, www.newspapers.com.

Rock Creek Resort, www.rockcreekresort.com.

Silver Run Ski Club, www.silverrunski.com.

***Toy Story* Quotes**, www.OhmyDisney.com.

U.S. Board on Geographic Names, Geographic Names information Service (GNIS), https://geonames.usgs.gov/domestic/index.html.

U.S. Department of Agriculture, Custer-Gallatin National Forest, www.usfs.usda.gov.

U.S. Department of the Interior, Bureau of Land Management, General Land Office Records, https://glorecords.blm.gov.htm.

U.S. Department of the Interior, National Park Service, Multimedia Collection, www.nps.gov.
Washington State Archives, Territorial Timeline, https://www.sos.wa.gov/archives.
Western Mining History, https://westernmininghistory.com.
Wikipedia, https://wikipedia.org.
Yellowstone-Bighorn Research Association, www.YBRA.org.
Yellowstone Up Close and Personal, www.yellowstone.co.

ARCHIVES, FILES, BOOKS, PHOTOGRAPHS, MAPS

Carbon County Museum
Files and obituaries

Gallatin County Clerk and Recorder
Deed and mining claim records

Gallatin History Museum
Files, obituaries, and oral history notes
Official claims notices

Gallatin National Forest Archives
Halcyon LaPointe, archaeologist
Roadside informational signs

Montana Historical Society—Archives, Helena, MT
"Elers Koch Reminisces" 1945-50. Manuscript
Contributions to the Historical Society of Montana, Vol. 8, 1917. "Bradley Manuscript– Book F"
p. 197-250, Helena
"Origin of Geographic Names, Montana National Forests Absaroka-Flathead,"
typewritten, recorded from ranger notes 1936-42.
Geographic Names Files

Montana State University, Special Collections Library
Merrill G. Burlingame papers, 1880-1990

Museum of the Beartooths, Columbus
Files

Museum of the Rockies
Archives and photographs

Park County Clerk and Recorder
Deed and mining claim records

Stillwater County Clerk and Recorder
Deed and miming claim records

Sweet Grass County Clerk and Recorder
Deed and miming claim records

United States Geological Survey, Washington, D.C.
Decision card file—not yet digitalized

Yellowstone Gateway Museum, Livingston, MT
Park County Family History Collection
Archives and photographs

Yellowstone Heritage and Research Center, Gardiner, MT
Letters Sent-Received 1887-1906

SPECIFIC REFERENCES

Aarstad, Rich; Arguimbau, Ellie; Baumler, Ellen; Porsild, Charlene; Shovers, Brian;
Montana Place Names from Alzada to Zortman, Montana Historical Society Press,
Helena, Montana 2009.
Alden, W.C., "Grasshoppers on Ice," *Nature Magazine,* vol 15, 1930, 379-382.
Alwin, John A., *Western Montana, A Portrait of the Land and Its People,* Montana Geographic Series,
Montana Magazine, 1983.

Anderson, Bob, *Beartooth Country, Montana's Absaroka and Beartooth Mountains*,
  Montana Geographic Series No. 7, Unicorn Publishing, 1994.
Andrews, Ralph, "He Knew the Red Man, Edward S. Curtis, Photographer,"
  Montana The Magazine of Western History, Vol 14, No 2, April 1964.
Annin, Jim, *They Gazed on the Beartooth*, Vol II and III, Reporter Printing, Billings, MT, 1964.
"Apsa'alooke Place Names In MT," Montana Historical Society, Pamphlet, January 14, 2004.
Axline, Jon, *The Beartooth Highway, A History of America's Most Beautiful Drive*,
  The History Press, Charleston, SC 2016.
Ballard, Jack, *Jack Ballard, Everything Outdoors*, www.jackballard.com, 2012.
Bergan, Joshua, *Flyfisher's Guide to Southwest Montana's Mountain Lakes*, Wilderness Adventures Press,
  Belgrade, MT, 2017.
"Big Draw," U.S. Geological Survey, Narative Field Report, November 21, 1985.
Birkby, Jeff, *Images of America, Montana's Hot Springs*, Arcadia Publishing, Charleston, SC, 2018.
Blevins, Bruce H., *Wyoming-Montana Border, They Followed the 45th, 1879-1880*, WIM Marketing,
  Powell, WY, 2001.
Blevins, Bruce, *Absaroka Mountains 1893 and 1897, Thomas Jagger's Diaries and Photographs*,
  WIM Marketing, 2002.
Bradley, Lieutenant James H., *The March of the Montana Column, Prelude to the Custer Disaster*,
  new edition, Univ of Oklahoma Press, Norman, OK, 1961.
Brown, Mark H., *The Plainsmen of the Yellowstone, A History of the Yellowstone Basin*,
  G.P. Putnam's Sons, New York, 1961.
Burlington, Joseph, "Development Sparks Concern…," *Montana Free Press*, September 19, 2019.
Carkeek Cheney, Roberta, *Names on the Face of Montana*, Mountain Press Publishing Co,
  Missoula, MT, 1983.
Chapple, Beth, "Yellowstone Treasures," Granite Peak Publications, Lake Forest, WA, 2019.
Clayton, John, "Camp Senia and Montana's Dude Ranching Heritage," *Stories from Montana's
  Enduring Frontier: Exploring an Untamed Legacy*, Montana Quarterly, 2008.
Clayton, John and the Carbon County Historical Society, *Images of America, Red Lodge*,
  Arcadia Publishing, Charleston, SC, 2008.
Cohen, Stan, *Montana's Grandest: Historic Hotels and Resorts of the Treasure State*,
  Pictoral Histories Publishing, Missoula, MT, no date.
Colenbrander, Andrew John, "Albert Charles Peale: Scientist-Explorer of the Hayden Survey 1871-79,"
  graduate student thesis, University of Montana, ScholarWorks at University of Montana, 1989.
Cunningham, Bill, *Montana Wildlands*, Montana Geographic Series, No. 16, *Montana Magazine*,
  1990.
Cunninghan, Bill, *Wild Montana: A Guide to 55 Roadless Recreation Areas*, Falcon Press,
  Helena, MT, 1995.
Daniel, Scott, "Montana Names," 1942. Monograph typewritten, Merrill Burlingame Collection,
  Montana State University Library.
Davis, Roger, "Features of the West Fork Canyon Region Named for Montana Residents,"
  Billings Gazette, September 30, 1956.
DePuy, David, *Paradise and Beyond*, self-published, 2012.
DePuy, David W., *Homesteads of the Shields River Valley*, self-published, 2018.
DeVoto, Bernard, editor, *The Journals of Lewis and Clark*, Riverside Press, Cambridge, MA, 1953.
Dore, Helena, "A Path Foreward," *Bozeman Daily Chronicle*, October 23, 2021.
Dwinelle, J.K., Historical Society of Montana, Vol. III.
Egolf, Jamie, and Kelley, Chavawn, "Hemingway in Wyoming," WyoHistory.org,
  October 1, 2018.
Emmons, Samuel Franklin, "Geological Guide Book for an Excursion to the Rocky
  Mountains," 1894.
Fagg, Harrison, "High Country Map Beartooth Area Absaroka Area N. Yellowstone Park,"
  KHP, Billings, MT, no date, prior to 1978.

Field, Richard M., "Yellowstone-Beartooth-Bighorn Region," International Geological Congress, XVI Session, U.S. Government Printing Office, Washington, DC, 1932.

Forest Park Nature Center, *Eagle Nest*, Facebook post, January 21, 2021.

Freedman, Lew, "Hemingway in Wyoming: Writer fished Clarks Fork, stayed in Cody," *Cody Enterprise*, January 28, 2019.

French, Brett, "Rustic Cabin north of Yellowstone Highlighted by Spectacular Views, Groomed Trails," *Billings Gazette*, January 24, 2019.

French, Brett, "Stories Behind Beartooth Mountain Monikers," *Billings Gazette*, July 25, 2013.

Fritz, William J., and Thomas, Robert C., *Roadside Geology of Yellowstone Country*, 2nd edition, Mountain Press Publishing, Missoula, MT, 2011.

Gallatin National Forest and Montana State University, *The Gallatin National Forest Companion, a Compliation of Fact and Legend*, MSU Press, Bozeman, MT, 1991.

Gemmell, Mel, and Fenlason, Edward, *Roberts, the Agricultural Metropolis of Carbon County*, E&M Books, Joliet, MT, 2000.

Glidden, Ralph, *Exploring the Yellowstone High Country, A History of the Cooke City Area*, 3rd edition, Cooke City Community Council, 1976, 2007.

Gooley, Lawrence P., "Chateaugay Olympian Karl Frederick: Literally A Shooting Star," *Adirondack Almanack*, August 2016.

Goss, Robert V., "Morphine Charlie, Prospector, Stagecoach Robber, Father of Margaret Reeb," *The Montana Pioneer*, 2011.

Graetz, Rick and Susie, *Lewis and Clark's Montana Trail*, Northern Rockies Publishing, Helena, MT, 2001.

Graetz, Rick and Susie, *Montana's Yellowstone River from the Teton Wilderness to the Missouri*, Northern Rockies Publishing, Helena, MT, 2003.

Graetz, Rick and Susie, *Montana's Missouri and Musselshell Rivers*, Northern Rockies Publishing, Helena, MT, 2004.

Greater Yellowstone Coalition, "Yellowstone Creek Finally Recovers from Toxic Mining Residue," Blog, July 26, 2019.

Hague, Arnold, *Geologic Atlas of the United States, Yellowstone National Park Folio*, U.S. Geological Survey, Washington, DC, 1896.

Hague, Arnold, *Geological History of Yellowstone National Park*, U.S. Government Printing Office, Washington, DC, 1921.

Haines, Aubrey L., *The Bannock Indian Trail*, Yellowstone Library and Museum and NPS, 1964.

Haines, Aubrey L., *Yellowstone Place Names, Mirrors of History*, University Press of Colorado, Niwot, CO, 1996.

Hamlin, Ken, "Did Gallatin County have a Medicine Tree?" *Gallatin History Quarterly*, Vol. 44, No. 1, 2021.

Hartman, Kelly Suzanne, *A Brief History of Cooke City*, The History Press, Charleston, SC, 2019.

Hayden, F.V., *Twelfth Annual report of the U.S. Geological and Geographical Survey of the Territories of Wyoming and Idaho 1878, Part II, Yellowstone National Park*, Washington, DC, U.S. Government Printing Office, 1883.

Hayden, Ferdinand Vandeveer, *Geological Report of the Exploration of the Yellowstone and Missouri Rivers*, Washington, DC, Government Printing Office, 1869.

Hayden, Ferdinand Vandeveer, *Preliminary report of the United States Geological Survey of Wyoming and Portions of the Contiguous Territories*, 1872, reproduction Eibron Classic Series, Adamant Media Corp., 2006

Henry and Geiger, *Tri-County Atlas, Meagher, Sweet Grass, and Carbon Counties*, Big Timber, MT, 2008, reprint of 1900 edition.

Holland, Linda L., *Images of America, Cooke City*, Arcadia Publishing, Charleston, SC, 2012.

Hooker, Patty, and the Museum of the Beartooths, *Images of America Columbus and Stillwater County*, Arcadia Publishing, Charleston, SC, 2011.

Hooker, Patty, *Images of America, Beartooth Mountains*, Arcadia Publishing, Charleston, SC, 2012.

Johnson, Joyce, "Hemingway's Yellowstone and notes along the Beartooth Highway," Park County Community Journal, undated web post.

Jones, Cedron, *Peakbagging Montana, A Guide to Montana's Major Peaks*, Riverbend Publishing, Helena, MT, 2011.

Kershaw, Linda, McKinnon, Andy, Poljar, Jim, *Plants of the Rocky Mountains*, Lone Pine Publishing, Edmonton, Alberta, Canada, 1998.

Kimball, James P., " The Granites of Carbon County, Montana," Bulletin of the American Geographical Society, Vol. 31, June 1899, 199-216.

King, Hobart M., "Sodalite," Geology.com.

Koch, Elers, *Forty Years a Forester, 1903-43*, Mountain Press, Missoula, MT, 1998.

Koch, Elers, "Geographic Names of Western Montana, Northern Idaho," *Oregon Historical Quarterly*, Vol. 49, No. 1, March 1948, 50-62.

Koch, Elers, "Elers Koch Reminisces" 1945-50, Manuscript, Montana Historical Society Archives.

Konizeski, Dick, *The Montanan's Fishing Guide*, Vol II, Mountain Press Publishing, Missoula, MT, 1970.

L bar T Ranch, promotional pamphlet, ca. 1938.

Lahren, Larry, "Crazies by Any Other Name," *Montana Quarterly*, September 2018, 50-55.

Lahren, Larry, *Homeland, an Archeologist's View of Yellowstone Country's Past*, Cayuse Press, Livingston, MT, 2006.

Lampi, Leona, *At the Foot of the Beartooth Mountains, A History of the Finnish Community of Red Lodge*, MT, Bookage Press, Coeur d'Alene, ID, 1998.

Leeson, *History of Montana, 1739-1885*, Warner, Beers and Co., Chicago, 1885.

Leforge, Thomas H., *Memoirs of a White Crow Indian, as told by Thomas B. Marquis*, The Century Co., 1928. Reprinted University of Nebraska Press, 1974.

Lehman, Tim, *Bloodshed at the Little Bighorn*, Johns Hopkins University Press, Baltimore, MD, 2010.

Lowe, James A., "The Bridger Trail: A Safer Route to Montana Gold," Wyoming History.org, Wyoming State Preservation Office, November 18, 2014.

MacLean, Vicky, *Home on the Range, Montana's Eastside Ranger Station*s, self-published, 2013.

Marcuson, Pat, *Fishing the Beartooths*, 2nd edition, The Lyons Press, Gilford, CT, 2008.

Marino, D.M., "Top of the World Map," revised ca. 1937, Red Lodge, MT.

McCune, Jenny C., "The Scenic Route to Yellowstone," *Distinctly Montana*, April 4, 2007.

McNeish, Jeff, with the Clark's Fork Valley Museum and Carbon County Historical Society, *Images of America, Clark's Fork Valley*, Arcadia Publishing, Charleston, SC, 2011.

Merrill, Marlene Deahl, *Yellowstone and the Great West, Journals, Letters and Pages from the 1871 Hayden Expedition*, University of Nebraska Press, Lincoln, NE, 1999.

Merrill G. Burlingame papers 1880-1990, Box 30-35, Montana State University Special Collections Library.

Miller, M. Mark, "Yankee Jim Tangles with Rudyard Kipling," *Distinctly Montana*, December 22, 2015.

Mouat, John C., *The Best Tales of the Beartooths and other Tales*, Author House, Bloomington, IN, 2005.

Murphy, Alicia, Yellowstone National Park historian, KBZK Television interview with Chet Layman, November 20, 2018.

National Geographic Maps, *Absaroka-Beartooth Wilderness West/Gardiner, Livingston*, Evergreen, CO, 2013.

National Geographic Maps, *Absaroka-Beartooth Wilderness East/Cooke City, Red Lodge*, Evergreen, CO, 2013

"Natural Bridge Falls and the Boulder River," MontanaHikes.com, 2020.

Nelson, Helen and Edwin, with Jack Wagner, *Growing up in Paradise*, Claremont Publishing, Glen Allen, VA, 1998.

New Oxford American Dictionary, Oxford, U.K., 1998.

Oldham, Forrest, *Honey Run Tribute*, Google Books, 2018.

"Pacific Flyway Management Plan for the Rocky Mountain Population of Canada Geese," Pacific Flyway Council, U.S. Fish and Wildlife Service, Canadian Wildlife Service, January 2001.

Parrie, Trout N., and Logan, Jesse A., editors, *Voices of Yellowstone's Capstone, A Narrative Atlas of the Absaroka-Beartooth Wilderness*, Absaroka-Beartooth Wilderness Foundation, Red Lodge, MT, 2019.

Patten, Leslie, *The Wild Excellence*, Far Cry Publishing, Cody, WY, 2018.

Peterson, Roger Tory, *A Field Guide to Western Birds*, 3rd edition, Houghton Mifflin Co., Boston, 1990.

Phillips, H. Wayne, *Northern Rocky Mountain Wildflowers*, 2nd edition, Falcon Guides, Guilford, CT, 2012.

Pioneer Memories II, by the Pioneer Society of Sweetgrass County Montana, Pioneer Publishing, 1981.

Porter, Ben and Athna May, *Expedition Magazine*, Vol. 50, No. 1, March 2008.

Progressive Men of Montana 1739-1885, 1900, typed and collated by Montana University students, Montana Historical Society Archives. Printed volumes and digital record at https://archive.org/details/progressivemenofo1bowe.

Randall, L.W. (Gay), *Footprints Along the Yellowstone*, Naylor Publishing, San Antonio, TX, 1961.

Reese, Rick, *Greater Yellowstone, The National Park and Adjacent Areas*, Montana Geographic Series, No. 6., American and World Publishing, 1991.

Reese, Rick, *Montana Mountain Ranges*, Montana Geographic Series, No. 1, *Montana Magazine*, 1985.

Reid, Roland R., McMannis, William J., Palmquist, John C., *Precambrian Geology of North Snowy Block, Beartooth Mountains, Montana*, Geological Society of America, Special Paper 157, Boulder, CO, 1975.

Rhoten, Jason, *2016 Mountain Lakes Guide, Absaroka-Beartooth & Crazy Mountains*, Montana Fish, Wildlife & Parks, www.fwp.mt.gov.

Richel, Mrs. Herbert, "Richel Lodge in the Beartooth Mountains" pamphlet, 1935.

Ricketts, Macy K., "Glacier: Poppies, Pika, and Lilies in a Climate Change," *Distinctly Montana*, March 21, 2021.

Robbins, Chuck, *Flyfishers Guide to Montana*, new edition, Google Books, 2017.

Robbins, Chuck, *Flyfisher's Guide to Montana*, Wilderness Adventures Press, Belgrade, MT, 2005.

Rowe, J.P., "Origin of Some Montana Place Names," Dept. of Geology, State University, Missoula, MT, 1933.

Rowe, J.P., "The Origin of Some Montana Place Names," Dept of Geology, State University, Missoula, MT. Typewritten, no date, ca. 1930.

Saunders, Ralph, "Mount Douglas-Mount Wood Topographic Map," Rocky Mountain Surveys, Billings, MT, 1984, revised 1994.

Saunders, Ralph, "Alpine- Mt Maurice Topographic Map," Rocky Mountain Surveys, Billings, MT, 1984, revised 1992.

Saunders, Ralph, "Cooke City-Cutoff Mountain Topographic Map," Rocky Mountain Surveys, Billings, MT, 1984, revised 1992.

Schneider, Bill and Russ, *Hiking Montana*, 3rd Edition, Falcon Guides, Guilford, CT, 2004.

Schneider, Bill, *Hiking the Absaroka-Beartooth Wilderness*, 2nd edition, Falcon Guides, Guilford, CT, 2003.

Sexton, Donnie, "Driving to Heaven on the Beartooth," *Distinctly Montana*, June 15, 2017.

Schiemann, Donald Anthony, *Wildflowers of Montana*, Mountain Press Publishing, Missoula, MT, 2005.

Schontzler, Gail, "Hunting for Hemingway in Yellowstone Country," *Bozeman Daily Chronicle*, August 9, 2015.

Sweetgrass Museum Society, Big Timber, MT, 2002.

Smith, Chrysti, "Wild West Words," *Distinctly Montana*, February 10, 2020.

Smith, Phyllis, *Montana Sweet Grass Country: from Melville to the Boulder River Valley*, Crazy Mountain Museum, Big Timber, MT, 2002.

Sobotka, Harry Hermann, and Reiner, Miriam, "Chemical Composition of a Lithia Spring near McLeod, Montana," *American Journal of Science*, Vol 235, May 1941, 383-385.

Sroka, Hayley, "See the Tallest Waterfall in Montana at Woodbine Falls," *Only in Your State*, May 6, 2021.

Staunton, Ruth, and Keur, Dorothy, "Jerkline to Jeep, a Brief History of the Upper Boulder," *The Times Clarion*, Harlowton, MT, 1975.

Stout, "Montana, Its Story and Biography," *Hardin Tribune*, July 30, 1953.

Strahan, Derek, "Where East Meets West, Historic Dude ranching in the Greater Yellowstone Area," *Heritage Magazine*, Summer 2007.

Stryker, Leslie Paulson and the Crazy Mountain Museum, *Images of America, Big Timber*, Arcadia Press, Charleston, SC, 2009.

Stuart, Douglas, family collective reminiscences, "A History (more or less) of the RDS, B-4, L-T, and Hancock Ranches in the Valley of the Upper Clarks Fork of the Yellowstone River, Park County, WY, 1995, typewritten.

Tilt, Whitney, *Flora of Montana's Gallatin Region, Greater Yellowstone's Northwest Corner*, Gallatin Valley Land Trust, Great Falls, MT, 2011.

Townshend, Debbie, "Up Our Way," pamphlet, no date.

Tri-County Atlas, Meagher, Sweet Grass, and Carbon Counties, Henry and Geiger, Big Timber, Montana 2008. Reprint of 1900 edition.

Turiano, Thomas, "Early Beartooth Survey Reveals Old Names," Thomas Turiano Forums, website, December 02, 2004.

Turiano, Thomas, *Select Peaks of the Greater Yellowstone, A Mountaineering History and Guide*, Indomitus Books, Jackson WY, 2003.

U.S. Civil War Pension Index: General Index to Pension Files, 1861-1934.

United States Department of Agriculture, "Annual Geographic Names Report," 1942.

United States Department of Agriculture, Gallatin National Forest Glengarry Mine Closure Construction Report, May 2007.

United States Forest Service, Beartooth Ranger District, "Area Name Origins," December 1961.

United States Forest Service, Custer-Gallatin National Forest, "Welcome to the Historic Main Boulder Ranger Station," ca. 2015.

United States Forest Service, Custer-Gallatin National Forest, Natural Bridges State Park, educational plaques.

United States Forest Service, "History of Red Lodge," pamphlet.

United States Forest Service, "Beartooth Mountains and National Forest," pamphlet, ca. 1975.

van Epps, Robert, "History of the Red Lodge-Cooke City Highway," Burlingame Papers, MSU Special Collections, August 14, 1967.

Wallace, Bob and the Carbon County Historical Society, *Images of America, Rock Creek Valley*, Arcadia Publishing, Charleston, SC, 2013.

Warren, Chris, *Ernest Hemingway in the Yellowstone High Country*, Riverbend Publishing, Helena, MT, 2019.

Watery, Elizabeth A., and Whittlesey, Lee H., *Images of America, Fort Yellowstone*, Arcadia Publishing, Charleston, SC, 2012.

Watery, Elizabeth A., and Gross, Robert V., *Images of America, Livingston*, Arcadia Publishing, Charleston, SC, 2009.

Weed, W.H.,"Geology of the southern end of the Snowy Range," U.S. Geological Survey Monograph 32, Vol. 2, 803.

Weir, Mitchell S., *Lippincott's Magazine*, July 1880.

Weiser-Alexander, Kathy, "Grasshopper Menace," Legends of America Newsletter, July 2020.

Whithorn, Bill and Doris, *Photo History of Aldridge, Coal Camp that Died A-bornin*, Acme Printing, MSP, 1965.

Whithorn, Bill and Doris, *Photo History of Gardiner, Jardine, Crevasse, Entrance to Yellowstone Park*, Wan-I-Gan Press, 2016.

Whithorn, Bill and Doris, *Photo History of Shields Valley*, Wan-I-Gan Press, Pray, MT, 1969.

Whithorn, Doris, *History of Park County, Montana*, Wan-I-Gan Press, Livingston, MT, 1984.

Whithorn, Doris, *Images of America, Paradise Valley on the Yellowstone*, Arcadia Press, Chicago, IL, 2001.

Whithorn, Doris, *Images of America, Emigrant Gulch—Searching for Gold in Park County, Montana*, Arcadia Publishing, Charleston, SC, 2002.

Whithorn, Doris, *Twice Told on the Upper Yellowstone*, Vol. 1, self-published, 1994.

Whithorn, Doris, *Twice Told on the Upper Yellowstone*, Vol. 2, self-published, 1994.

Whithorn, Doris, *Twice Told on the Upper Yellowstone*, Vol. 3, self-published, 2000.

Whittlesey, Lee H., *Death in Yellowstone, Accidents and Foolhardiness in the First National Park*, 2nd edition, Roberts Rinehart, Lanham, MD, 2014.

Whittlesey, Lee H., *Yellowstone Place Names*, Wonderland Publishing, 2006.

Whittlesey, Lee Hale, with the Geyser Observation and Study Assn, *Wonderland Nomenclature: A History of the Place Names of YNP*, Montana Historical Society Press, 1988.

Whittlesey, Lee H., "Abundance, Slaughter, and Resilance of the Greater Yellowstone Ecosystem's Mammal Population, A View of the Historical Record, 1871-1885," *Montana The Magazine of Western History*, Vol. 70, No. 1, Spring 2020.

Wuerthner, George, "Outdoor Recreation," *Distinctly Montana,* March 13, 2019.

Zupan, Shirley, and Owens, Harry J., *Red Lodge Saga of a Western Area—Revisited*, Frontier Press, Billings, MT, 2000.

PERSONAL INTERVIEWS

Carter, Alan (Shorthill), and Dodge, Dennis, interview, 5/14/2019.

Copeland, Emily, personal interview, photographs, maps, and family documents from Copeland family and L bar T Ranch.

Courtis, David, personal interview 7/17/2020, letter June 2021.

DePuy, David, personal communication, 7/10/2019.

Drivchal, John, Shields River Valley pioneer family, personal interview, 1/2/2020.

Earle, B.J., retired federal archaeologist, Livingston, Montana, personal interview, May 2018.

Fagg, Harrison, personal communication.

Graetz, Rick, personal conversation, Sept. 2020.

Hallestead, Elaine, pioneer ranching family, June 2021.

Hartman, Kelly, Cooke City resident, personal interview.

Holland, Linda, interview, 8/27/2020.

Kallenbach, David, executive director, Absaroka Beartooth Wilderness Foundation, personal interview, 8/16/2019.

McCleary, Dr. Tim, department head, General Studies, Little Bighorn College, personal communication.

Miller, Paul, retired ranger YNP, personal interview, 5/17/2019.

Moody, JV, Sweet Grass County commissioner, June 2021.

Rigler, David, pioneer family, personal communication, Nov. 2017.

Rigler, Paul, pioneer family, personal communication, Dec. 2017.

Roe, Melanie, Sweet Grass County commissioner, June 2021.

Ronneberg, Carol, retired forest ranger, June 2021.

Runyon, Jennifer, research staff, U.S. Board on Geographic Names, USGS, personal communication.

Sanders, Ralph, personal communication, Oct. 2021.

Jean Skillman, Marty and Virginia Swandal, and Tom Peterson, oral history session in Wilsall, Montana, 5/3/2018.

Teig, Ron, internet communication on his boyhood homestead at Lebo, MT, 4/12/2021.

Turiano, Thomas, personal communication, Feb. 8, 2020.

Whittlesey, Lee, personal interview.

Wilson, Brad, Crazy Mountain Foundation, personal interviews, 5/21/2019, 9/10/2020, 5/24/2021.

INDEX

ACKNOWLEDGMENTS

The contents of this book represent the work of four years gathering information that was as scattered as the names on the maps. It was an enjoyable search for me, and the results of this effort have left me indebted to many people and places.

The firsthand accounts from the various explorers and surveyors that I found in books and archives were fascinating, but the most interesting sources were the interviews that I had with local residents and some of the current descendants of the original pioneer families, who, in the typical open Montana way, shared their family stories. John Drivchal, Jean Skillman, Marty and Virginia Swandal, and Tom Peterson were full of information on the Shields River Valley, as were Bonnie Pinkerton, Alan Carter, and Dennis Dodge. The latter two, along with David and Paul Rigler, Brad Wilson, and Paul Miller, were particularly helpful on the Crazies and the Paradise Valley, and David DePuy's books and conversation on the Shields and Paradise Valleys were essential to understanding both of those areas. A special thanks goes to David Courtis, who summers in the Clarks Fork country, and Emily Copeland and Kelly Hartman from the L bar T and Cooke City, whom I met at the Gallatin History Museum. These latter two show that museums often hold more than books, archives, and old photographs. People with a special interest were also very open and helpful. A big thanks goes to Derek Lennon of Big Sky, who got me started by introducing me to Tom Turiano's book, *Select Peaks of the Greater Yellowstone, A Mountaineering History and Guide*, and to Tom himself, who was the source of much information. Ralph Sanders, whose maps of the Beartooths of the 1980s and 90s were the standard, was essential for lake names up the West Rosebud. Several individuals such as Lee Whittlesey, retired Yellowstone Park historian, Dr. Tim McCleary of Little Bighorn College, and Dr. Walter Fleming of MSU were very helpful. Harrison Fagg, a Billings architect and state legislator who has climbed all the 12,000-foot mountains in the Beartooths, was particularly open with his knowledge, as was David Kallenbach, the former director of the Absaroka-Beartooth Wilderness Foundation. To my good friend of 45 years, my hiking and backcountry skiing buddy, Rick Graetz, a special thanks. His photos grace the cover and the pages of this book, and his support and help have been invaluable.

The book could not have been completed without the resources found in the local museums. The towns and counties of Montana are filled with a fascinating collection of them, all dedicated to the preservation of the history of this place. Each museum was worth visiting for the displays alone, but each is also filled with books, archives and photographs unavailable anywhere else. Among these museums, a particular thanks to the Gallatin History Museum in

Bozeman with former executive director Cindy Schearer and research coordinator Rachael Phillips. It was the center of my research efforts and a constant source of support. All of the many local museums were very helpful as well, so thank you Paul Shea, Jay Kiefer, and Karen Reinhart and the Yellowstone Gateway Museum of Livingston; Mazey McClellen and Skye Rouwhorst at Big Timber's Crazy Mountain Museum; Penny Redli and the Museum of the Beartooths in Columbus; and the Carbon County Museum in Red Lodge. Among the larger institutions, the Museum of the Rockies in Bozeman where Michael D. Fox is curator of history and Steve Jackson does the historical photos is an unparalleled resource of information on southwest Montana. One could spend months mining the information at the Montana State Historical Society Archives in Helena where Zoe Ann Stoltz is reference historian supreme. Dr. Kim Scott and Heather Hultman at the Montana State University Special Collections in Bozeman, and Anne Foster, Chris Mather, and Miriam Watson at Yellowstone Park Heritage and Research Center in Gardiner were also very helpful. All were welcoming and held special treasures to share with you.

Among the government agencies, I must give special thanks to the Custer-Gallatin National Forest. Many of their rangers, both active and retired, shared what they knew, and Halcyon LaPoint, the Custer-Gallatin National Forest archaeologist, provided much information with archival notes, pictures, and her general knowledge. At the USGS, Jennifer Runyon and Matthew O'Donnell of the Board on Geographic Names had not only their Geographic Names Information Service website, but provided information from undigitized notes and maps as well.

Final thanks must go to my great friend, partner, and wife, Karen, who accompanied me on my many trips around the area and tolerated my hogging the computer, and who has provided lifelong love and support.

Dr. Jeff Strickler
December 2021

ABOUT THE AUTHOR

Dr. Jeff Strickler was born and raised in Minneapolis, Minnesota, but his family roots in Montana date back to the early years of the twentieth century. In 1975, after a pediatric residency at Stanford University and two years in the U.S. Air Force in Alaska, he and his wife Karen returned to those roots. They raised their children in Helena where he opened the Helena Pediatric Clinic and practiced for 30 years. Upon retirement in 2005, they moved to Big Sky to continue to enjoy the outdoor life with skiing, hiking, and wandering through the land and its stories.

Dr. Strickler has always had a love of history, and retirement has given him the time to write the books on local history that he always wanted to write. His previous efforts include *Big Sky Names, an Amble Through Western History and Ecology on the Roads, Streams, and Developments of Big Sky, Montana; A Skier's Guide to Big Sky Montana*; and, with Anne Marie Mistretta, *Images of America, Big Sky*. This book follows *Bozeman's Backyard, Names in the Bridger, Gallatin, and Madison Ranges* with a search through the mountains to the east. Where will he go next?